HISTORY OF SCITUATE, MASSACHUSETTS

Published by

Preservation

Of

Scituate's

Heritage,

Incorporated

2002

Preservation of Scituate's Heritage, Inc.

Directors
Barbara J. Maffucci, President
Phyllis J. Flynn, Treasurer
Charlotte K. Gillis, Secretary
Bernice Brown
Mary Kennedy Dean
Elizabeth Foster
Patricia Jones
Kathleen Meeker
Pam Mullin

Past Members and Directors
Ann Cusick
Susan A. Phippen
Nancy L. Thode

HISTORY

OF

SCITUATE,

MASSACHUSETTS,

FROM ITS FIRST SETTLEMENT TO 1831.

BY SAMUEL DEANE.

BOSTON:
JAMES LORING, 132 WASHINGTON STREET.

1831.

Entered according to Act of Congress, in the year 1831, by James Loring, in the Clerk's Office of the District Court of Massachusetts.

HISTORY OF SCITUATE, MASSACHUSETTS

By Samuel Deane

Trade Paperback ISBN: 1-58218-737-1

Cover Design by Digital Scanning Inc.

As Published in 1831

All rights reserved, which includes the right to reproduce this book or portions thereof in any form whatsoever except as provided by the U.S. Copyright Laws. For information address Digital Scanning, Inc.

Digital Scanning and Publishing is a leader in the electronic republication of historical books and documents. We publish many of our titles as eBooks, as well as hardcover and trade paper editions. DSI is committed to bringing many traditional little known books back to life, retaining the look and feel of the original work.

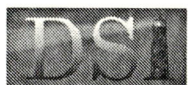

Published by DIGITAL SCANNING, INC. Scituate, MA 02066
781-545-2100 www.digitalscanning.com

©2002 DSI Digital Reproduction
First DSI Printing: 2002

Biography of
THE REV. SAMUEL DEANE

Rev. Samuel Deane, author of this book, to whom we owe so much, son of John and Abigail (White) Deane, and descended from John Deane, who came from Chard, England, in 1637, was born at Mansfield, Mass., March 31, 1784, and died at South Parish, Scituate, Mass., Aug. 9, 1834, aged only fifty years.

He is described as being an erect and handsome man, nearly six feet tall, with a beardless face full of character and thought. He loved a good horse dearly, as all great men do, and seldom travelled except on horseback.

A man of genius, a man of thought, a man of many noble qualities, a lover of truth and uprightness, he died in the Lord, a worthy soul for the kingdom.

He graduated at Brown University in 1805, and was ordained Feb. 14, 1810, as colleague of Rev. David Barnes, D. D., then in his 79th year, over the Second Church in Scituate, where he remained pastor for twenty-four years, resigning on account of ill health July, 1834. He died the next month and was laid at rest in the cemetery opposite the church, where most of his family are buried, and beside those of the senior pastor just mentioned.

His works are the "History of Scituate," published in Boston in 1831, "The Populous Village," a poem delivered before the Philermenian Society of Brown University, 1826, "Some Literary Errors of the Age," delivered before a literary society of Brown University, "Discourses on Christian Liberty," 1825, on "Human Nature," 1827, and many other poems never published. Several of his sermons were printed.

He married Stella Washburn, daughter of Hon. Seth, and had five children. She died Jan. 12, 1850, aged nearly sixty-three. Several of his descendants live in Chicago. His son, Charles Frederic, died in Chicago, 1860, leaving a family of nine children.

He will always be greatly remembered by the thousands of descendants of Scituate's early Puritan families, now scattered in all parts of the world for this Memorial which he erected to his name.

PREFACE.

THE value of Town histories if faithfully compiled, is readily acknowledged, since it is from such sources, that more general histories may acquire accuracy. The reasons for attempting a more perfect and copious history of Scituate, than has hitherto appeared, may be found in the facts, that it was one of the earliest settlements in New England, that it took the lead in population, and bore an important part in the civil and military affairs of Plymouth Colony, that it has produced eminent characters, and furnished colonists for peopling more recent settlements, in many of the States of the Union.

The first settlers came in by the way of Plymouth, and some of them were of the first ship's company. There was a large access to the settlement in 1633, which company came by the way of Boston, with Mr. Lothrop, their pastor, Previous to 1640, most of the population was from the County of Kent in England, but about the latter date, many came in from Hingham, Dorchester, Watertown, Weymouth and Nantasket, at which places they had resided a few years: many of these were from London, and more, perhaps, from Dorsetshire.

Though emigrations have been constantly making from this early settlement, yet we have noticed some remarkable periods of those emigrations: for example. In 1640, to Barnstable, when nearly half the population departed. In 1650, to York and its vicinity. In 1658, to Barbadoes. In 1670, to Rehoboth and Swansey. In 1690, to Norwich, Con. In 1710, to Newport and Scituate, Rhode Island. In 1760, to Chesterfield, Ver. and soon after to Turner, Harpswell and Topsham, Maine.

We make no apology for publishing even trifling incidents or barren genealogies, of those families which have opened a new world to civilization and religion.

It will be seen in the following pages, that we have diligently consulted the records of the Town and of the churches, as well as the records of both Plymouth and Massachusetts Colonies, and other works to which we have made occasional reference. We acknowledge the kindly facilities in consulting documents, &c. which we have received from Edward D. Bangs, Esq. Secretary, Rosseter Cotton, Esq. of Plymouth, Hon. John Davis, Hon. James Savage, Mr. Isaac P. Davis, of Boston, and other gentlemen, whose favours are noticed in the course of the work. We have attempted to correct some mistakes and inaccuracies in a former account of Scituate, published in the Historical Society's papers, A. D. 1816: for which mistakes we may have been, in part, responsible, having furnished to Samuel Davis, Esq. many of the notes from which that account was compiled: but we have been careful to quote authority, whenever we have adverted to the mistakes of any previous writer or compiler. We boast not of the accuracy of this work: we only venture to say, that we have endeavoured faithfully to use the materials that have fallen in our way, and that we shall esteem it a favour, for true history's sake, to have our mistakes, in turn, pointed out and corrected by future historians.

HISTORY

OF

SCITUATE.

SCITUATE,* a Post Town in the County of Plymouth. It has been ascertained by repeated observations at the Harbour, that it lies in North Lat. 42° 12´, and in West Long. from Greenwich, 70° 35´. The harbour is nearly 21 miles from Plymouth, and 28 miles from Boston, by the most direct roads.

BOUNDARIES.

The boundaries were not settled very early. It seemed to have been the intention of the Colony Court to grant lands from time to time to new planters as they requested it, until it should become a settlement of sufficient magnitude to require corporate powers within itself. March 7, 1642, we find this Court Order. "The bounds of Scituate Township, on the westerly side of said Town, shall be up the Indian Head River, to the Pond which is the head of said River, and from thence to Accord Pond, and from thence to the Sea, by the line that is the bound between Mass. & Plym." This settled the boundaries on the East, South and West the Indian Head River, with its continuation called North River, being understood to

---

* This name is derived from Satuit brook which falls into the harbour: it means "cold brook." The name of the Town was written Satuit and Seteat at first, and not until 1640 did the orthography become settled. The Town of Scituate, in R. I. probably derived its name from this town. A part of that township, called the "Westconnoid purchase" was owned by the family of Wanton (from Scituate) and others.

comprehend the whole easterly line – with one exception, however, which we will here notice. In 1636 we find the following entry in the Col. Rec. "Mr. Hatherly in behalf of the Church at Scituate, complained that the place was too straite for them, the landes adjacent being stoney, and not convenient to plant upon." The Court passed the following order "that they have liberty to seeke out a convenient place for their residing within the Colonie, or that some other lands be layed to them for more comfortable subsistence." This matter was in agitation nearly four years, for we find the settlers of Scituate were not satisfied until 1640, when a grant was made to them "of two miles in length and one mile in breadth on the easterly side of the N. River." We mention this here as an exception to the boundaries above; we shall notice the territory called "The Two Miles" hereafter. The boundaries continued as above until A. D. 1727, when that part of the town on the southerly side of the third Herring brook, was incorporated by the name of Hanover.* In this form it continued until 1788, when the "Two Miles" was ceded to Marshfield. The Town is now bounded N. W. by Hingham and Cohasset, N. E. by Massachusetts Bay, S. E. by N. River which separates it from Marshfield and Pembroke, and S. W. by Hanover and Abington.

The N. W. line of Scituate, being also the Colony line, was long a subject of tedious controversy. It may be proper here to subjoin a brief history of the transactions relative to that line. As early as 1636, there was found to be a want of a definitive settlement of the line. Hingham which then included Cohasset, claimed a part of the marshes on the East side of "Conihassett Gulph." The plea of Scituate was that the gulph was a good natural boundary, and therefore the proper boundary between the two patents. Hingham on the other hand pleaded, that

---

* The first Minister of Hanover was Mr. Benjamin Bass of Braintree, H. C. 1715 – ordained Dec. 1728. He has descendants in Hanover. The second Minister was Mr. Samuel Baldwin, H. C. 1752 – ord. 1757 – mar. Hannah, daughter of Chief Justice John Cushing, 1758. The wife of Mr. Robert Salmon of Hanover is his daughter. He was descended from Henry Baldwin, who came from Devonshire, Eng. and settled at Woburn, 1650. The son of Henry, was Henry, and the son of the latter was David, the father of Rev. Samuel, of Hanover. (Farmer.) The third Minister was Mr. John Mellen, H. C. 1740, Minister of Sterling, 1744 – installed at Hanover, 1782. His sons were Rev. John, H. C. 1770, and minister of Barnstable – Henry, Esq. of Dover, N. H., H. C. 1784, counsellor at law, and Hon. Prentiss Mellen, H. C. 1784, now Chief Justice of Maine. Rev. Samuel Mellen died at Reading 1807, aged 85. He was succeeded by Rev. Calvin Chadwick, Dart. Col. 1786. To whom succeeded Rev. Seth Chapin, 1816 – B. U. 1808. Rev. Ethan Smith is the present pastor.

the marshes were a natural accommodation to the highlands on both sides. Winthrop observes, (Vol. 1. 284), "We only desired so much of the marshes there as might accommodate Hingham," and adds, "We caused Charles River (patent) to be surveyed and found it to come so far southward as would fetch in Scituate and more — but this was referred to a meeting betweene us." In May, 1637, the Commissioners, Mr. Timothy Hatherly and Mr. Nathaniel Tilden, on the part of Plymouth, and Mr. William Aspinwall and Mr. Joseph Andrews on the part of Massachusetts were appointed to settle the line. Mass. Rec. I. 192: but we have not discovered that they came to any agreement. Again in 1640, Commissioners were appointed for the same purpose — viz. William Bradford, Gov. and Edward Winslow, gent. on the part of Plymouth, and John Endicott, Gov. and Israel Stoughton, gent. on the part of Mass. They met and settled the line as follows — "from the mouth of the brooke that runneth into Conihasset marshes, in a straight line to the middle of Accord Pond," P. C. Rec. I. Winthrop II. p. 18. adds that "60 acres of marsh on Scituate side" were adjudged to belong to Hingham. But this decision could not stand long, not giving satisfaction to the Plymouth government, because it was found, on review, that the marsh in question, at least a part of it, had already been pledged and appropriated by the Government to Scituate men. Again in 1656, another Commission was appointed, viz. "William Torrey and Capt. Brackett on the part of Mass. and Josiah Winslow and another on the part of Plym. who decided that "the Gulph shall stand as the boundary." Pl. Col. Rec. Again, June 1659, "Maj. Josiah Winslow, Lieut. Southworth, and Robert Stetson are appointed by the Court to join with such as the Bay Govt. may appoint, to run the line betwixt the Bay Govt. and us." Pl. Col. Rec. We are not sure that Mass. appointed Commissioners that year. There seems to have been some delay — and when in 1663, Maj. Ebenezer Lusher, Capt. Roger Clap and Lieut. Joseph Fisher were appointed for this purpose by Mass. Court, they speak of past "neglect grievous to our neighbours and hurtful to ourselves." In May 1664, a return of the above Commissioners was made, finally establishing the line as in 1656. We will here remark, that although the colony line was amicably adjusted, yet an uneasiness long continued between the towns of Scituate and Hingham. There were conflicting claims amongst individuals. The Mass. Government had made grants of certain lands which appeared to lie within the Plymouth Patent; and the Plymouth Court had done in like manner; and the grantees were not willing to recede on either hand. A. D. 1685, the town of Scituate voted "to block up the highway leading from Scituate Common lands to Hingham, to prevent the great trespasses by those of Hingham." They had several times recovered damages of individuals: the last which we notice on record was in 1692, when the Town recovered damages against Capt. John Jacob, Joseph Jacob, Joshua Lincoln, sen. Nathaniel Beal, jun. and Joseph Dunbar of Hingham and Joseph Green of Weymouth. Scit. Rec. Vol. 6.* As late as 1721 the Selectmen of Scituate were chosen agents to settle the line between their town and Hingham. We believe it was then adjusted so far as it has been or probably will be: for if the line were now run out according to the lines of the proprietors of the lands, it would vary somewhat from "a straight line from bound rock to Accord pond."

A. D. 1682, Agents were appointed to settle the line between Scituate and Marshfield. Thomas Turner and Samuel Clap on the part of Scituate, Nathaniel Thomas and Samuel Sprague on the part of Marshfield. Their report was as follows. "The main channel as it now runneth down the N. River, from the upper part of said Marshfield to the sea. And whereas, at a place in the said river called the Green islands, the channel doth divide and runneth on both sides, it is agreed that the said Green islands shall be equally divided into parts," &c. Scit. Rec. V. 6. As late as Oct. 1782, a Resolve of General Court established this line thus, "from the River's mouth following the channel to Thomas Little's bank – thence with the channel to the mouth of Bass hole channel – through the guzzle between the horse-shoe flat and great flat to a stake near Pincin's bank."

CONIHASSETT GRANT.†

Within the territory as above bounded, was included a large tract of land, which the Colony Court had granted to four gentlemen, usually called "merchant adventurers of London." The following Court Order, A. D. 1633, relates to this sub-

---

* The name of Edward Gillman (the first ancestor of that distinguished family) is perpetuated in Scituate, and "Gillman Plain" received its name from his trespass. Scit. Rec. V. 4. (old leaf.)

"Recovered of Edward Gyllman for damage done to the Town Swamps, 26£ 10S. 6d. Rec'd of Ed. Gyllman for damages, &c.
    Eleven ffirkins of sope at 18s. - - £ . 18 . o
    In Cassel sope and shoes - - - - 3 . o . o
    In Tobacco - - - - - - - 1 . 6

† Conihassett means a fishing promontory. Flint's century Sermon.

ject. "That the whole tract of land between the brook at Scituate, on the N. W. side, and Conahassett, be left undisposed of, till we know the resolution of Mr James Shirley, Mr. John Beauchamp, Mr Richard Andrews and Mr. Timothy Hatherly." Again in 1635, "The Gov. (Mr Prence,) Mr. Collier, Mr. Alden, Mr. Brown and Mr. Howland were directed to view that portion of ground on the north side of the North River (note – it is meant Satuit brook) and if they find it more beneficial for farms to Scituate than to these parts, then to allot it to them; if not, to reserve it." It was reserved. But in Oct. 1637, the above tract was granted to Messrs. Hatherly, Andrews, Beauchamp and Shirley, "extending three miles up into the woods from the high water mark in the brook," &c. This grant gave considerable uneasiness to the planters at Scituate. There were already several settlers upon the land. Adjustments were to be made with these. The line was not definite, and many controversies arose, of which we find traces in the Colony Records for many years. A review was ordered in 1652, but the Court decided "having seen and heard the Review, we cannot but allow and ratify the line done by our order." Still the controversy went on with as much spirit as before. It is difficult for us at this time to recount all the entanglements of this matter, and we will only remark, that, in addition to the trouble which the proprietors of the Conihasset grant had experienced in settling with the "squatters" upon their land, they had to encounter an opposition from the planters of Scituate, to their being admitted to common shares in the town lands. With reference to these controversies, the following Court order was passed in 1654. "In regard of sundry contentions and entanglements betwixt Mr. Hatherly and sundry inhabitants of Scituate, the Court doth grant unto Mr Hatherly, to satisfy the partners of Conihassett, a certain competency of land, out of the bounds of any particular township, on the westerly side of the town of Scituate aforesaid." Again, with reference to the above order, in 1656, it was ordered, "that the Town take some speedy course to run out their head or westerly line between the pond at Indian Head River and Accord Pond, otherwise, if they neglect it, and the Court grant land that may be found to prejudice them, they may blame themselves." In July, 1656, the Court granted to Mr Hatherly "a tract of three miles square, extending from Accord Pond three miles southerly." But the boundaries of the Conihassett grant were not yet settled. A review was had in 1671 by a committee of eight persons of

Scituate, four on each part, in conjunction with two magistrates. And finally, in 1682 agents were appointed by the Town, viz. John Cushing and Samuel Clap, to be joined by agents of the Court's appointing, and they agreed, "that the line should extend three miles from high water mark in Satuit Brook N. W. and by W. then three miles N. and by W. to Bound brook." Scit. Rec. V. 6.

We will now remark, that the Conihassett Grant was purchased by Mr Hatherly of the other Merchant Adventurers before 1646: and that in this year, he divided it into 30 shares (reserving one fourth part of the whole) and sold it for £180 to a certain company, since called the "Conihassett partners." Many of this company were such as had already located themselves upon these lands, and thus an amicable adjustment was made with those individuals.

The partners were Mr. Charles Chauncy, Thomas Chambers, John Williams, sen. James Cudworth, Joseph Tilden, Henry Merritt, Thomas Rawlins, Thomas Tarte, John Hoar, Richard Sealis, Thomas Ensign, Thomas Chittenden, John Stockbridge, John Allin, Thomas Hiland, John Whetcomb, John Woodfield, Edward Jenkins, John Hallett, Ann Vinall, William Holmes, John Whiston, Gowin White, John Daman, Rhodolphus Eellms and Richard Man. These partners appointed their clerks, surveyors, committees and agents, and conducted their affairs with all the efficiency of a corporate town. They laid out and maintained their own roads, until 1715; they made grants to their minister, &c. Their first clerk was Richard Garrett, he being a skilful penman, though not a partner; the second, James Torrey; their third, Stephen Vinall, and the fourth and last, Samuel Jenkins. Their records were kept of all transactions, conveyances, &c. in beautiful order, and fill a large volume. Their last meeting on record was 1767.

We have stated above, that in 1656, a tract of three miles square was granted to Mr. Hatherly as indemnity for his "entanglements" with the people of Scituate "and to satisfy the Conihassett partners" – and we will now add, that this tract was divided into 40 parts, and 27 of them assigned to the Conihassett partners. The boundary of this tract next to Scituate is called the "share line." Mr. Hatherly in 1663 having repurchased 10 shares, sold 23 shares to John Otis of Scituate, Matthew Cushing, John Thaxter, John Jacob, and Edward Wilder of Hingham, for £69. This tract of land now makes a part of Abington and Hanover.

THE "TWO MILES."

We have already mentioned that Mr. Hatherly had made complaint to the Court in 1636 "that the place was too straite for them." We now remark that a more pressing application was made in 1637, when Mr. Hatherly and Mr. Lothrop, accompanied by a committee of 15 of the principal planters, attended the Court and complained that "they had such small portion of landes allotted to them, that they could not subsist upon them." They obtained the following grant, viz: "all the lands between the north and south rivers, provided they make a township there, inhabit upon them, compose their differences with Mr. William Vassall and others before the next court, and establish and support a ferry at the North River (which Mr. Vassall is willing to do) that so the removal from Scituate may be without offence." These conditions, however, were not complied with, and the removal did not take place. The complaint of a want of room, at so early a period, seems singular to us, when now, about one half the original territory of Scituate supports a population of between three and four thousand. But we are to consider, that at that time, a peculiar value was placed upon the marshes, where forage was readily prepared for their cattle, and upon the lands near the river, the river being their highway. The complaints were appeased in 1640 by a grant of the "two miles" on the east side of the river. The bounds of this territory have been several times surveyed, as we see on record, (Scit. Rec. Vol. 2) but as no considerable controversies arose respecting them, we forbear to notice them further. The territory extended two miles on the river and one mile back. Its bounds might now be easily ascertained, Pembroke line being the southerly boundary and the "Ford farm" the northerly. A committee, appointed by the Court (Mr. Hatherly, Edward Foster and Humphrey Turner) laid out the lands. Among the earlier settlers there were Robert Sprout, Thomas Rose, Richard Sylvester, and some of the Hatch family. It was naturally provided with a good mill stream, and grist mills, saw mills and clothing mills were pretty early erected. The people of the "two mile" generally belonged to the south parish and attended worship there.

A. D. 1778, the people of this territory petitioned the General Court, to be annexed to Marshfield. The Town of Scituate being served with an order of notice, met and voted their consent "on condition that they resign their claim to common lands, and pay their proportion of all taxes hitherto assessed." This condition was not acceptable, because there were marsh lands in common, from which the Town at that time derived a considerable revenue, (letting them out yearly at vendue) though that income is now very small, owing to the reduced value of salt meadows, since the high lands are better cultivated. The petition did not then succeed. Again in 1786, the same was repeated on both parts, and the result was the same. Finally, in 1788, the annexation to Marshfield was accomplished, on the conditions proposed by the Town of Scituate.

SETTLEMENT AND PROGRESS.

We are without data as to the first persons who visited Scituate, or the first who took up their residence here. It is certain, however, that the Pilgrims of Plymouth explored the shores very early after their landing, and took notice of the eligible places for settlement. It is certain that William Gillson, Anthony Annable, Thomas Bird, Nathaniel Tilden, Edward Foster, Henry Rowley, and some others were here before 1628. The above named gentlemen and others, were called "men of Kent," having come from that County in England. The earliest notice of settlement at Scituate, which has record to verify it, bears date 1628. Henry Merritt sells to Nathaniel Tilden "all that land which I had of Goodman Byrd, lying within the fence at the North end of the third cliffe, unto the land of Nathaniel Tilden." Col. Rec. It is fair to infer from this, that settlements were made very early. On the 12th of April 1633, the "men of Kent" above named, with others who had joined them probably, proceeded to lay out lands, by order of Court. The first lots laid out were on the second cliff: which was divided between William Gillson, Anthony Annable, Edward Foster and Henry Rowley. The third cliff had already been appropriated, though we find no record of the laying out. Again, August 2d, 1633, the settlers proceeded to lay out a regular village, allowing to no one more than four acres for a house lot, in that place, proposing to build a compact street "for purpose of mutual defence." This street they called "Kent Street:" it led from the bridge as it now lies at the Harbour, easterly to the third cliff. The first lot was at the corner formed by "Kent Street" and the road which runs parallel with Satuit or Stony brook: bounded by the ways North and East, by William Gillson's lot South or South-east, and by the

SETTLEMENT AND PROGRESS.

common land West. The front line on Kent Street was eight rods in length, the side line "extending 80 rods up into the woodes." This lot was assigned to Edward Foster. The second lot on Kent street, of the same dimensions, was assigned to William Gillson; the third to Henry Rowley; the fourth to Humphrey Turner; the fifth to Henry Cobb; the sixth to Anthony Annable. These several gentlemen, we believe, erected houses on these lots; in fact some of them had already done it. Humphrey Turner, however, did not reside in this street, but on the East of the Colman's hills, and his son Thomas had a house on Kent street some years subsequent. Again, February 20, 1634, another assignment of house lots was made, Mr. Lothrop had arrived with thirty of his Church (by which we are to understand not 30 heads of families, but probably 30 souls.) These were chiefly from London. Many others joined them the same winter, some of whom were men of Kent. We proceed to mention the location of their house lots, as determined in February and April of the same year: or rather February 1634 and April 1635; the year then beginning in March. The lots before described on Kent Street reached to "Meeting-house Lane." We now begin on the South side of that lane. The first was allotted to Geo. Lewis; the 2d to John Hewes, (the Welchman); the 3d to Walter Woodworth; the 4th to Richard Foxwell; the 5th to Isaac Chittenden. These all abutted on Kent street, in like manner as those before described. We now come to "Greenfield," so called, we understand, because it had been an Indian planting ground, and was not covered with wood; as the cliffs and the glades were not covered with wood. The first lot on the greenfield (i. e. the northerly lot) was assigned to Samuel Fuller: the 2d to Barnard Lombard, and the 3d to Goodman Hoyt; these were of the same dimensions as the above, and abutting on Kent street. We now come to "Greenfield lane" running at right angles with the street and parallel with Meeting-house lane. The first lot was assigned to William Hatch; the 2d to Samuel Hinckley; the 3d to Nathaniel Tilden. These abutted on Kent street, and consisted of 5 acres each. We then come to a lane called at that time the "drift way." The first lot was appropriated to Isaac Stedman; the 2d to George Kendrick; the 3d to Daniel Standlake; the 4th to John Lewis, and the 5th to George Lewis, which seems to be a second lot assigned to him, or perhaps a choice. The above are all the house lots on Kent street, of which we find any record. This brings us to the East side of the "high hills" afterward called Colman's hills. Here Humphrey Turner had a house and farm (though as yet a Plymouth man) before 1633, and family tradition says in 1626: we have no means of determining the number of acres. Next to Humphrey Turner's farm was that of Mr. John Lothrop, the Minister, consisting of 20 acres, and assigned him, February 20, 1634. Next in order and south-westerly, consisting of eight acres, was that of William Hatch; but we believe his house was the lot assigned him at Greenfield lane. Next in order was a lot of twelve acres, assigned to Isaac Robinson. Here he built his house. And finally, John Hanmer's house lot, which brings us round the hills to the Herring brook. These lots extended from the hills to the "New Harbour Marshes."

We can form from the above statements a pretty distinct image of the village, as it appeared in 1633 and 34. Their houses were generally log houses, and covered with thatch cut from the sedges of the salt marshes. We now remark that, to complete this map of the settlement, we are to conceive of Isaac Stedman's house (notwithstanding he had a house lot on Kent street) standing twenty rods South-easterly of the Stockbridge mill dam, Mr. William Vassall's "belle house" on the neck (Cushing place), Mr. Thomas King's house near it on the South-west, and Resolved White's near it on the East. Then turning to the harbour, we are to conceive of a few "squatters" and principally fishermen. We find in Winthrop's History," February 22, 1633, Ship William, Mr. Travere, master, arrived at Plymouth with passengers and goods for the Bay. This ship came to set up a fishing stage at Scituate, and to trade." Then turning to the cliffs, we are to imagine them covered with corn, and William Gillson's windmill waving its arms upon the third cliff; and our image of the settlement is pretty complete, as it existed in the autumn of 1636.*

In tracing the progress of the settlement we shall now pursue the

DIVISION OF LANDS.

Until Oct. 1636, all lands had been laid out by a Committee of the Court's appointing. The Town was then incorporated, and the purchasers and freemen were commissioned to dispose of the lands. This was done (in open meetings) until 1647.

---

*The venerable Timothy Hatherly, although in Scituate in 1634, being unmarried, had no house here until 1637, when he erected one on "farm neck" within the Conihasset grant.

DIVISION OF LANDS.

A. D. 1647, Dec. 13th, those who were purchasers and freemen in 1636, voted to resign their power to the whole inhabitants of the Town. From this time it was found difficult to lay out lands on any plan or principle which would give general satisfaction. The principles generally followed were to grant lands to the freemen, and to such as had built or owned a house previously to 1647. This state of things continued many years, until on the 7th March, 1670, a petition was addressed to the Court "craving their counsell and advice and helpe and assistance herein." This was opposed by other inhabitants, and the matter was heard and reheard before the Court, when they decided (June 16, 1671) that "the resignation of the freemen and purchasers was unwarrantable and invalid: but if they would lay downe their power, it did return unto the Courte." The Court proceeded to appoint a commission of eight persons chosen from both parties, with instructions to agree on some principles of dividing the Common lands, and present it to the Court for their approbation. These Commissioners were Capt. James Cudworth, Cornet Robert Stetson, Lieut. Isaac Buck, and Isaac Chittenden, on one part; and John Turner, sen. John Turner, jr. John Bryant, sen. and John Damon on the other part. They agreed; that agreement was approved by the Court; but the Town met and refused to ratify the agreement. The Assistants then drew up proposals, and came in person to present them in Town meeting. But these were not accepted. A. D. 1673, the Court voted "to leave the Town to their liberties in the premises." Nov. 24th, 1673, the Town agreed, that a committee of eight appointed by the Court, with four appointed by the Town, should have the sole management of dividing lands, and that what they should agree upon should be binding. The Court appointed Capt. James Cudworth, Cornet Robert Stetson, Lieut. Isaac Buck, Michael Pierce, John Bryant, sen. John Turner, jun. John Damon and Isaac Chittenden. The Town added Charles Stockbridge, Michael Pierce, John Cushing and Thomas Turner. The principles agreed on by this Committee were, I. "That none shall have any interest in the undivided lands, that is not an allowed and approved inhabitant of the Town of Scituate by acte of this committee." II. "All that had an ancient grant of land from the freemen before the surrender." That is, between 1636 and 1647. III. "All the successors of such as had owned a house before 1647." IV. "The successors of such as had not received land from the freemen." By this, we understand, such as were inhabitants before 1647, who had not asked for a grant, while the freemen had the disposal of lands in town meeting. We find a list of 131 "allowed and approved inhabitants" by act of this committee, which henceforth had the sole management. (See List, hereafter.) We have already noticed the division of small lots by the Court, until 1636. We now remark that the last division made by the Court was in 1636, of "the greate lottes" so called. They consisted of 60 to 80 acres, and were laid out principally upon the N. River, from the "bell house necke" to the third Herring brook. From 1636 to 1647, no lands were laid out but by special act of the freemen. In 1647, the whole Town raised a committee and made divisions. In 1673, the joint committee of the Court and the Town, made large divisions of planting lands, and also of all the swamps, obliging each receiver to clear his part in a given time, or forfeit his grant. This was for the purpose of breaking up the haunts of wolves. In 1699 another considerable division was made. And in 1706 all the cedar swamps were divided by vote of the Town into 8 acre lots. Scit. Rec. Vol. 2.

ROADS.

We find no order of Court, and no record of any Jury to lay out the earliest roads. We conclude therefore that Kent street, and the road that runs parallel with Satuit or Stoney brook, and the road from the third cliff, running Westerly at the foot of Colman's hills, as also Meeting-house lane, Greenfield lane, and the drift way, were established by mutual consent of the proprietors, when they laid out their village in house lots. Mr. William Vassall was foreman of the first Jury for laying out roads. We have found no date of his appointment: but we can state for a certainty that it was as early as 1646. We find a record of the road laid out by that Jury, from Stockbridge's Mill-dam, to "belle-house necke" and turning to the South-west, as the cartway now leads. It is described as beginning at Isaac Stedman's house, and Isaac Stedman, we know, had sold his house to George Russell, and removed to Boston in 1646. In 1653, Cornet Robert Stetson was foreman of a Jury for laying out roads: and we find on record several ways laid out, viz. the road from the third Herring brook near Hanover Corners to Scituate Harbour; also the road from the "old mill" (so called at that time, and by which we understand Isaac Stedman's saw mill, at the place since called Stockbridge's mill) Northwesterly over Brushy hill towards Cohasset; also a way from Isaac

ROADS. 13

Buck's (near late Anthony Waterman's) Westward to the way last mentioned: also a road from Stedman's or rather George Russell's mill, or "the old mill," to George Moore's bridge and onward to the common lands: also a way from the road "a little above the second Herring brook" (now David Torrey's) down to the North River: and finally a way from the North River Bridge (then Barstow's bridge) to Hingham bounds. This was the Country road. In 1656, we find the following entry in the Colony records, "William Barstow of Scituate covenanted to make a good and sufficient bridge for horse and foot over the North River, a little above the third Herring brooke, at a place called 'stoney reache' and to lay out and cleare the way towards the bay as far as Hugh's cross brooke – to receive 12£ in current country pay." Previously, the crossing of the River had been at a ford a mile above, probably near where Curtis's Iron works now are. It was there that Gov. Winthrop was carried over upon a man's back, on his visit to Plymouth in 1632, (see land marks). A. D. 1658, the Colony Court deputed Mr. Hatherly and Capt. Cudworth, with a third man to be chosen by these two, "to lay out a foote way from the upper Meeting-house at the North River in Scituate, up the s^d River to the house of Robert Stetson." How it was rendered necessary to take such important steps to lay out a foot path we have not discovered: probably some proprietors of lands had objected to persons crossing their fields: and we know that Cornet Stetson was a valuable man in the town, and must be accommodated; and beside, several families in his neighbourhood could shorten the distance to meeting, and to the chief settlement in the Town, by a foot path nearer to the River than the road was laid out. The two gentlemen appointed by the Court, chose James Torrey, sen. as a third man. The path was laid out from the Westerly end of the Meeting-house to Cornet Setson's, as follows – (we omit the ancient names that we may be understood) viz. crossing the brook that falls into Stoney Cove, about fifty rods below the present road, to Thomas Oldham's house, which stood between the road and King's landing – thence in a pretty direct line to the place afterwards called the Block-house – thence to the second Herring brook, crossing it "where the old bridge did lye," that is, as we understand, near the mouth of the second Herring brook – and thence to Wanton's ship yard – then turning "over William Randall's cart bridge in William Curtis's land" and passing over Dwelley's creek, where we believe there has been a foot bridge ever since – and thence over Gowen White's farm (now Ruggles') and Humphrey Johnson's (contiguous on the S. E.) to Robert Stetson's, now the residence of Stephen and Charles Stetson.

January 16, 1694-5, we find the Selectmen proceeding to lay out roads, according to a "law of the Province." And they begin by renewing "several highways formerly laid out, but not found on the Town records." They renewed and established all the highways which we have described above, as having been used from 1633. They also established, by a new survey, the town landing at the mouth of the second Herring brook – viz. "4 rods upon the river and 8 rods up from the water side," and also the highway from thence "to the road that goeth up to John Palmer's." They also renewed the highway from the West end of "the new saw mill dam" (then Bryant's mill) Westward to Hooppole hill, and onward to Snappet. (Scit. Rec. Vol. 2 p, II.) Again in 1703-4 nearly all the roads that are now used, in addition to those above described, were laid out: we can except one only, viz. the road from Mount Blue to Hingham, which was not made a public road until a period more than a half century later. We will now notice a few variations in our principal roads, from their first location. We can name no important variations in the road that leads from Hanover Corners to the Harbour, save one near the South Meeting-house, where it formerly passed in nearly a direct line from Job Randall's (now David Torrey's) to the Parsonage house, crossing the second Herring brook, about fifty rods below the mill. This was altered in 1704 to accommodate the South Meeting-house when built where it now stands: and one other variation, viz. from the place where the first Meeting-house of the South Parish stood, the road went nearly parallel with the present road, but a few rods farther East, passing Easterly of Deacon James Torrey's house, which stood near Hobart's landing gate, in the Neal field, so called. A variation also has taken place near Hicks's swamp recently, (1829), passing across a corner of the Clap farm, instead of making an angle by the hills. The road from Bryant's bridge on the second Herring brook, to Spring brook (near late James Torrey's) passed on the North side of Meeting-house hill, until 1704.

The Conihassett Partners kept no record of their highways until 1694. They renewed and established all the principal roads about that time, viz. the main street at the Harbour, from Buck's corner to Bound brook, where it lay within their territory, from the bridge at the old Parsonage, to Farm neck and

Hooppole neck, &c. They surrendered their highways to the Town 1715. The highway over Mount Blue to Hingham was laid out 1801.

Bridges and Ferries.

The first bridge of which we have any notice, was a foot bridge over the creek at the Harbour, before 1633. The next was Mr. Vassall's over Rotten marsh creek, before 1636: and shortly after Isaac Stedman's at the mill. Near the mouth of the second Herring brook, was a bridge called the old bridge in 1658. Bryant's bridge, on the second Herring brook above the mill, was not a cart bridge, we believe, until 1704. In 1656 Barstow's bridge over the North River, on Plymouth road, was erected.* In 1660, John Palmer covenanted with John Bryant and Humphrey Johnson, town agents, to build a log way and bridge, and cover it with gravel "from firm upland to firm upland," over the third Herring brook, where the bridge now lies, near Hanover Corners. George Moore's bridge is mentioned in 1653. In 1670, the Town (having obtained permission of Charles Stockbridge) voted "that the common roade shall pass over his mill dam." In 1682, the Colony Court ordered a cart bridge to be built over the North River at Barstow's bridge, at the expense of three Towns; Scituate to pay £10, Duxbury £5, and Marshfield £5. In 1829, the Road Commissioners for the County, agreed to assess the County for one quarter of the expense of a Stone Bridge at this place. The bridge is now completed. The bridge at Bound brook was erected before 1656, probably by the Conihassett partners: and the bridge over Satuit brook, near the old Parsonage, was there in 1648. These we believe are all the bridges of any importance, named in our records before 1700.

In 1785, a subscription was raised to build a bridge across the North River, near John Stetson's (the ancient Wanton place). The Town chose a Committee to consult with the subscribers, and to learn what kind of bridge was proposed, and how to be kept in repair. The Town then voted their consent, on condition that a sufficient draw be kept. The project then failed. It was revived again in 1827; but is not yet accomplished.

---

* William Barstow received £12 of the Colony for erecting the bridge, and from 1662 to 1682, £20 for keeping it in repair.

In 1799, it was proposed by the Town, to build and maintain a bridge across North River at Oakman's ferry, jointly with Marshfield. A subscription of $370 was raised by way of encouraging the enterprise: but it was defeated by the refusal of Marshfield to accomplish its part. Subsequently, however, A. D. 1801, a Corporation erected Union Bridge with the privilege of taking toll. The income, we understand, has kept the bridge in repair, and paid an annual dividend of seven per cent. Little's Bridge, a toll bridge erected in 1825, crosses the North River three miles below Union Bridge, at a place called Doggett's ferry.

In 1637, two hundred acres of land were granted to Mr. William Vassall, "on condition that he keepe a ferry against his farme – toll 1*d* for a man and 4*d* for a beast." This was called Doggett's in later times, as noticed above.

In 1638, the Court ordered a ferry to be kept near the mouth of the river, below "New Harbour Marshes." This is now called White's ferry. Jonathan Brewster of Duxbury was the first ferryman. In 1641 he sold the ferry privilege to Messrs. Barker and Howell for £60. In 1645 it was kept by Ralph Chapman, who petitioned the Court to excuse him, "as it would bring him to extreme poverty." The Court excused him, "except on special occasions, as bringing over the magistrates who dwell there." Since that time we believe the ferrying there has been a private concern without any rates of toll established by law.

The "upper ferry" (now Union bridge) was first kept by Elisha Bisbe 1645: it was afterwards kept by Oakman: and the last ferryman before the bridge was built, was John Tolman.

MILLS.

The first mill in the Town, was a wind mill, on the third cliff. It was erected by William Gillson in 1636, on the North-east part of the cliff. After his decease in 1639, it became the property of John Daman, his nephew.

The next was a saw mill, erected by Isaac Stedman, where the well known Stockbridge mills have since stood. We are without data as to the year when it was erected: but we find it mentioned in 1640 – and in 1653 it is called "the old mill," (Scit. Rec. Vol. 2. p. 3.) It became the property of George Russell 1646. This was probably the first saw mill in the Colony.

MILLS.

In 1653, James Torrey erected a "clothing mill" on the same brook as above, a half mile or more higher up. A century afterward, Capt. John Clap had a grist mill and fulling mill in the same place: these had been Samuel Clap's (his father) in 1690.

In 1656, Cornet Robert Stetson, Mr Hatherly and Joseph Tilden erected a saw mill on the third Herring brook. Remains of the dam may now be seen, at the Bridge, near the house of the late Major Winslow. For this mill a very extensive tract was flowed, now called "the old Pond." We find the following act of the Town in 1673. "Whereas it is apprehended that the saw mill upon the 3d herring brooke will not stand longe, and when it is downe, the mill pond will be the occation of miring of many Cattell, for the preventing of which, and that improvement may be made thereof for meadow, it is agreed and concluded that when the saw mill is down, and seases to be a mill there, that then the mill pond shall be divided unto the now proprietors of the Towne, or their successors, and by them to whom division is made, to be well and sufficiently fenced." In 1676 this mill was burnt by the Indians; and soon after the pond was divided according to the above act.

In 1650, John Stockbridge erected a water grist mill on the first Herring brook. It became the property of his son Charles at his decease in 1657: and ever since has been in the possession of the family. In 1673, the Town's committee of lands offered a premium of "30 acres of land to any person who, within 6 months, should erect a grist mill on the 3d Herring brook, and engage to tend the mill for fourteen years." Charles Stockbridge accepted the proposals: but changing his mind in part, he agreed with the committee to accept of ten acres, on condition that he be allowed to erect his mill "on the Cornet's old dam: " but changing his mind again, he erected his mills in 1674 a half mile below, and received his thirty acres. This mill afterward became the property, in part, of Capt. Jonah Stetson: hence its present name "Jonah's Mill."

The family of Bryant built a saw mill on the second Herring brook, on or before the year of 1690; and soon after a grist mill. In 1688, Benjamin Curtis built a saw mill on the third Herring brook, above "the Cornet's old pond;" and afterward a grist mill: they were afterward the property in part, of Constant Clap and the Curtis family,

The family of Jacob, erected mills at Assinippi, vulgarly called Snappet, about 1730. They are now the property of the same family.

18   MILLS.

There was a wind mill on the South Meeting-house hill in 1720: and subsequently another, but it has not been used, save for a horse shed for many years: it was taken down 1830.

In 1702, the Town voted "to grant one acre of land to any man or men that shall see cause to sett up a good and sufficient windmill to grinde corne withall." (Scit. Rec. Vol. 3. p. 275). The mill was proposed for the North part of the town; but whether it was built we have not ascertained.

In 1746, the Town granted to John Stetson, his heirs and assigns, liberty to "flow any part of the landing place, near Mr. Ensign Otis's dwelling house, so long as he or they shall keep up the grist mill which he is about to build near the harbour."

In 1787, the Town granted leave to Amasa Bailey to erect a mill at the Gulph. In 1791, the Town granted leave to Elijah Turner to flow a part of the road, near John Hatch's, (South-east of White-oak plain), for the purpose of erecting a grist mill. It was afterwards built on Marget's brook, or Slab brook.

In 1792, the Town granted liberty of erecting a grist mill in the mouth of the Gulph, to Elisha Doane of Cohasset.

In 1802, Jesse Dunbar, Esq. petitioned the Legislature for liberty to erect a dam across mill creek and main creek at the harbour, for the purpose of erecting a tide mill. The Town consented, on condition that a sluice or draw should be maintained for the passage of vessels. This mill has proved a great public benefit in seasons of drought.

We will now state the whole number of mills in 1829. On Bound brook two grist mills and a carding mill: not to take into the account the large mill at the mouth of the gulph, which is owned in Cohasset. A tide mill at the Harbour. On the first Herring brook, a grist mill and a nail mill. On the second Herring brook; two grist mills, a saw mill and a shingle mill: and a saw mill on the East branch of the brook erected 1831, by S. A. Turner, Esq. On the third Herring brook, are three grist mills, three saw mills, and a shingle mill, (erected 1826.) On Groundsell brook two saw mills owned by the family of Stockbridge. On Marget's or Slab brook one grist mill.

Within the territory which is now Hanover, the "Drinkwater Iron works" were erected by Mighill in 1710. This is a place on the stream which forms the southern border of the Town.

On the Indian head river Mr. Bardin, an enterprising Scotsman, erected Iron works (now Curtis's Iron works) about 1730. A grist mill was early erected on Hugh's cross brook.

North River.

This stream received its name before 1633, and probably from the circumstance that its general course is from south to north, or that it was farther north from Plymouth than South River in Marshfield, which meets the North River at its mouth. The North River is a very winding stream, flowing through extensive marshes, sometimes, as it were, sporting in the broad meadows in the most fanciful meanders, and sometimes shooting away to the highlands which border the meadows. There is one reach which has long been called the "no gains" from the circumstance, that, after flowing from side to side, and almost turning backward for several times, it has in fact flowed several miles, and gained but a few rods in its direct progress to the sea. From the sea to the North River bridge on the Plymouth road, an air line would not exceed seven miles: while the line of the River amounts to eighteen miles.

The tide rises at the North River bridge from three to five feet: and there is a perceptible tide two miles higher up. It has three chief sources, the Namatakeese and Indian head, which flow from the Matakeeset Ponds in Pembroke, and the Drinkwater, which has its sources chiefly in Abington. The tributaries are the three Herring brooks on the Scituate side, and the Two Mile brook and the Rogers brook on the Marshfield side. Wherever the River in its windings, touches the highlands, there is a ship-yard, a landing or a fishing station. To name them in order, we observe, that just by the bridge on the Plymouth road, is a ship-yard, which has been improved as such since 1699, Daniel Turner having been the first builder there that has come to our knowledge. A few rods below, on the Scituate side (now Hanover) is a ship-yard, first improved by the Barstows in 1690. Just below the third Herring brook, and scarce a mile below the bridge, on the Scituate side, is a ship-yard, first improved by the Palmers and Churches, as early as 1690: now by Messrs. Copeland and Ford. Nearly opposite on the Pembroke side, at "the brickilns" so called, is a ship-yard, which has long been used by the Turners and Briggses. Nearly a mile below this on the Pembroke side is "Job's landing," so called from Job Randall jr., who we believe resided near the place. A little below on the Scituate side are "Cornet's rocks" in front of the ancient residence of Cornet Robert Stetson. A half mile below on the Marshfield side is "gravelly beach," a principal station for the herring fishery: and we believe vessels have formerly been built here. A little below, and at an air-line distance of two miles nearly from North River bridge above named, is the ancient Wanton ship-yard, used by that family in 1660, and subsequently by the Stetsons, Delanos and Fosters. Here the largest ships have been built, and more in number probably than at any other station on the River. A half mile (or something less) below on the Scituate side, is the ancient ship-yard of Job Randall, used by him about 1690; and subsequently by the Prouteys, the Chittendens and Torreys; and now by Messrs. Souther and Cudworth. A half mile lower on the Scituate side, is "the block house" where was a fort and a garrison in Philip's war. Here is a wharf and a ship-yard, which has been improved by the Jameses and Tildens for a century. Just above are "sunken rocks" on which vessels sometimes touch and are impeded. Just below, and at an airline distance of a little more than three miles from North River bridge, is Union bridge. A half mile lower on the Scituate side, is King's landing. And about another half mile, on the same side, is *Hobart's* landing. Here we believe the first vessels were built, by Samuel House, as early as 1650; and soon after by Thomas Nichols: then by Israel Hobart in 1677; by Jeremiah and Walter Hatch soon after. The family of Briggs also have built vessels here for near a century, and it is still improved by the latter family, Messrs. Cushing and Henry Briggs. Here the Ship Columbia, (Capt. Kendrick), was built by James Briggs, A. D. 1773. It was the first ship that visited the North West coast from this country. Capt. Kendrick explored the River Orregon, and named it from the name of his ship, which name will probably prevail henceforth. At the distance of another half mile below, is Little's bridge: at which point, we believe vessels have been built on the Marshfield side. The meadows above this station are of very various width, in few places exceeding a mile: but below, there is a wide expanse of marsh, anciently called the "New Harbour marshes." The scenery here is on a sublime scale, when viewed from Colman's hills, or from the fourth cliff. The broad marshes are surrounded by a distant theatre of hills, and the River expands and embraces many islands in its bosom. Here it approaches the sea, as if to burst through the beach, but turns almost at right angles to the East, and runs parallel with the sea shore, for nearly three miles before it finds its out-let, leaving a beach next the sea of twenty rods width, composed chiefly of round and polished pebbles, excepting only the fourth cliff, a half mile in length, which comprises many acres of excellent arable land. Nearly a mile above the river's mouth, is White's ferry, (see ferries), where is a wharf and a small village on the Marshfield side. Here vessels have been built, and many that have been built above, here receive their rigging. The river's width may be estimated as follows in ordinary tides: at Union bridge seven rods – at King's landing eight rods – at Little's bridge nine rods: it expands below to a half mile in width, where it is now called fourth cliff bay, and formerly "New harbour:" here the channel divides, and unites again a mile below: a half mile above its mouth it is fourteen rods in width. The channel at the mouth often shifts its place, owing to the nature of the sandy bottom, and to the violence of the stream and the tides. It seldom affords more than nine feet of water, even when there is but one channel: but it often happens that there are two channels when the water is something less. This fact accounts for the difficulty and expense of carrying out the vessels built upon this river: and yet only in part, for there are shoals above, over which vessels of 200 tons and upwards must be lifted with gondolas or heaved with kedges. The principal are Will's shoal at the upper part of the New harbour marshes, and the Horse shoe shoal.

Formerly, it is said, salmon were taken in this river. Bass had been abundant until within a few years: they are taken chiefly in winter. Shad and alewives are still taken, but they are gradually diminishing.

BROOKS.

Between Scituate and Hingham is a chain of hills, from which the brooks that rise, flow both easterly and westerly.

Bound brook, received its name, from being in part, a northern boundary of the Plymouth patent. Its principal tributaries are Merritt's brook and Groundsel brook in Scituate, and Hezekiah Tower's brook or pond in Cohasset. It falls into the Gulph between Scituate and Cohasset.

Musquashcut brook, rises in the great Musquashcut pond, in the Conihassett territory of Scituate, and unites with Bound brook, in the Gulph.

The first Herring brook has its rise in George Moore's pond or swamp, and Brushy hill swamp, and falls into North River at New harbour marshes. Its whole length is scarcely three miles. The second Herring brook rises in Ridge hill swamp,

Dead swamp and Black pond, and falls into the North River at a point about equally distant from the first and third Herring brooks. The third Herring brook falls into the North River about two and a half miles above. This is the line between Scituate and Hanover. It rises in Valley swamp, on the bounds of Hingham, where is a spring of extraordinary copiousness. It receives several tributaries, viz. "Assinippi or Rocky water," and Hugh's cross brook, from Hanover, and Marget's from Scituate. Its whole length may be five miles.

Satuit brook, or Stony brook from which the town received its name, is a small stream scarcely a mile in length, and falls into the harbour. These brooks are not sufficiently copious to afford an unfailing supply of water for the mills. The third Herring brook is the most abundant, and the second is the least so: but they all have failed in times of extraordinary drought. It was an object of the early planters, to seek the vicinity of these brooks, in locating their farms.

Harbour.

Scituate extends about eight miles on the sea shore, including the beach on the east, and the glades on the west. Nearly in the centre of this line, is the Harbour. It is small and difficult of access, on account of a bar at its mouth. It affords about ten feet water at the bar, in ordinary full tides, but at low tides cannot be passed with vessels of any considerable burden. Here are two wharves and a considerable village. The two points which form the harbour, are Crow point on the southeast, and Cedar point on the north-west. On this latter, is a Light-house, erected in 1811, showing two steady lights, white above and red below. "The four cliffs so well known to mariners, are all on the south of the Harbour, showing sandy fronts."

The harbour was within the Conihassett grant: but the town of Scituate enjoyed the privilege of landing: and two landings there, are still the Town's property. For an account of the early settlement here, see Conihassett Grant.

New Harbour.

The North River had obtained the name of New Harbour before 1636. Vessels undoubtedly early wintered in fourth cliff bay, and found good moorings at "Pincin's bank." We are unable to give much account of the foreign trade from the North River. "In 1681, the Bark Adventure of 40 tons, sailed from the North River for the West Indies. She was owned by Scituate and Marshfield people. (Hist. Soc. Col. vol. 4. 2d series.)

The fact that the River would form an excellent harbour, were it not for the shifting bar at its mouth, has given rise to various proposals for a remedy. It has often been in serious agitation, to cut a ship channel between the third and fourth cliffs: but the nature of the ground renders it probable that the same obstructions would there be met. At this present time, there is a petition before Congress, for a grant to improve the navigation by a canal from the River to the Old Harbour. It is estimated that $15,000 might cover the whole expense. Congress ordered the survey, and it was completed in July 1829. We are waiting the result with considerable interest, because it is confidently calculated by many, that it would improve the water both of the river and the harbour, and avoid every shoal that now impedes the navigation. The tides of extraordinary height flow through this proposed route, as has happened in October 1829, and several times before. Stetson's tide mill at the harbour was swept through this route and carried to Marshfield shore in the great snow storm Nov. 1786.

Brigg's Harbour

Received its name from Walter Briggs, an early settler in that vicinity: and was so called as early as 1650; and sometimes also called Strawberry cove. It is a small cove formed by the extreme north-east point of Scituate, called the glades. We believe that vessels of small burthen were anciently built there, and fishing and coasting craft used to winter there. The Indian name of this little harbour was *Mishquashtuck,* sometimes written in our Records Musquashcut.

Fisheries.

We first notice the fisheries of the streams. It is reasonable to conjecture that the first alewives were taken in the first Herring brook, as some of the earliest settlements were near that stream. These fish ascended this brook to George Moore's pond, and as the stream was narrow, they were easily taken in nets. They continued to ascend this brook until the mills prevented them in late years, by not being provided with suitable sluices. Recently, an attempt has been made to restore them, but without much success.

Mr. Hatherly had "a herring wear" on Musquashcut brook near his house in 1640. We believe that a few of these fish find their way through the gulph to the Musquashcut pond, at the present day.

On Bound brook was formerly an abundant alewive fishery. As late as 1794 an Act of General Court was procured by Scituate and Cohassett, for renewing the fishery, by providing sluices at the mills, regulating the time and manner of taking them and removing the obstructions to their ascending to Hezekiah Tower's pond, to which "they formerly ascended abundantly, to the great advantage of said Towns." We believe the act was repealed in 1800, and the fishery is extinct. In the second Herring brook these fish used to ascend to Black pond: but they have long since been repelled by the mill dams. Smelts continue to visit this brook. They are taken in the latter end of March. In the third Herring brook, these fish used to ascend to Valley swamp. But here they have been destroyed in like manner as above.

The shad and alewive fishery in the North River has long been a subject of controversy between Scituate and Pembroke, and is so at present. In their ascending to the Matakeeset Ponds, they used to be taken in great abundance. Since an Act of Court in 1761, permitting seines to be drawn in the North River, it is alleged that they have been fast diminishing. Whether this, or the mills at Pembroke, or some unknown cause has produced this effect, we know not, but certain it is that these fisheries were reduced to comparatively little value in 1825: but since that time the fish have increased.

In 1639, the Colony Court granted 'liberty to Mr. William Vassall to make an oyster bank in the North River sixty rods in length, near his farm there called the 'West New-land,' and appropriate it to his own use, &c." (Col. Rec.) This was near Little's bridge. We believe the project did not prove successful.

MACKEREL FISHERY.

We have shown before, that the ship William set up a fishing station at Scituate in 1633. This was doubtless the cod fishery: and mackerel were taken at that time, chiefly for bait. They were taken with the seine; and it is stated in Historical Collections, Vol. 4, p. 127. 1st series, that the settlers at Hull first taught the Plymouth Colonists, to take them at Cape Cod by moon light.

We find the following Court order, June, 1670: "Whereas we have formerly seen great inconvenience of taking mackerel at unseasonable times, whereby their increase is greatly diminished, and that it hath been proposed to the Court of the Mass. that some course might be taken for preventing the same, and that they have lately drawn up an order about the same, this Court doth enact, that henceforth no mackerel shall be caught, except for spending while fresh, before the first of July annually, on penalty of the loss of the same, the one half to the informer, and the other to the Colony."

In 1680, Cornet Robert Stetson, of Scituate, and Nathaniel Thomas of Marshfield hired the Cape fishery for bass and mackerel. In 1684, the Court enacted a law "prohibiting the seining of mackerel in any part of the Colony;" and the same year leased the Cape Fishery for bass and mackerel to Mr. William Clark for seven years, at £30 per annum.

Subsequently to 1700, it is certain that the mackerel were very abundant in the Massachusetts Bay. It was not uncommon for a vessel to take a thousand barrels in the season. The packing, as it is called, was chiefly done at Boston and Plymouth until late years. The vessels of Scituate now pack at our harbour. George Morton, who came from Plymouth in 1730, was the first cooper of whom we have heard, at Scituate harbour. Our vessels now find them less abundant, and farther from their former haunts. They used to set into the bay early in May, and again in autumn: but now they are found at Block Island channel in May – at George's Bank and Nantucket shoals in the summer, and at Mount Desert and along the shores of Maine in the autumn. Those first taken are lean, and favour the commonly received opinion, that they lie in the muddy bottom, in the winter: but towards the winter they are found well fed, fat and delicious. The full grown mackerel vary in weight from one to two and three pounds. The fattest, taken in the autumn, are not generally of the largest size.

In 1770 upward of thirty vessels were fitted out of Scituate, in this employment. We believe there are now about thirty-five annually fitted out, of various tonnage, from 50 to 150 tons: and carrying from six to fifteen hands. The number of barrels taken by our vessels in 1828 was something more than 15,000. A writer in the Historical Society's Collections gives the following description of these fish, and of those fisheries, Vol. 4, 2 series, p. 232. "The aboriginal name of this fish is *Wawunnekeseag,* a plural term signifying fatness – a very descriptive and appropriate name. The mode of taking these fish is, while the vessel is under quick way and the helm secured, when all are engaged at the long veered lines, of which it is said, that one man will attend three, and it may be more.*

They are a capricious and sportive fish. In cloudy and even wet weather, they take the hook with most avidity. They are very partial to the colour of red; hence a rag of that hue is sometimes a bait. A small strip of their own flesh taken from near the tail, is used with most success.

In early times, the shores of our bays were skirted with forest trees, quite to the water's edge. In the month of June, when all nature is in bloom, the volatile farina of the forest trees then floats in the air, and occasionally settles on the smooth surface of the seas. Then it is, that this playful fish, attracted by this phenomenon, leaps and bounds above the surface of the water. So again, at a later season, in July and August, winged insects, carried away by the south-west winds, settle and rest on the bosom of the ocean, a welcome herald, it is said, to the mackerel catcher. Such are the habits of many fishes: and hence the use of the fly as a bait, by the angler of the trout streams."

NAVIGATION.

The first account which we have gathered of enterprise in Navigation, was in 1663, when the ship William, Capt. Trevere, traded to Hudson's River, probably exchanging goods for furs. In 1646, there appear to have been several vessels at the Harbour, which carried on a coasting trade with the Natives,

---

* The first manner of taking Mackerel, was by seining by moon light. This perhaps was first practised by Mr. Isaac Allerton and his fishing company at Hull, as early as 1626. After a half century the mode of fishing was changed to that of sailing, with long lines, while the vessel was under easy way: and this mode has been changed, within these last twenty years. The mode of fishing generally practised now, is to invite the fish around the vessel, while lying to, by throwing out great quantities of fish cut in small pieces, and to take them with short lines, held in the hand, and drawn in with a single motion of the arm. By this method, it is thought that thrice as many fish may be taken, in a given time, as by any former method.

and to Europe and Jamaica. Mr. Hatherly, Isaac Chittenden, Thomas Ensign, John Woodfield, Edward Jenkins, and a great part of the substantial settlers had some interest in this trade. In the River, Capt. Collamore and the Wantons carried on a considerable trade before 1670. But we are not able to make any very accurate statement of the number of vessels engaged in fishing, coasting, and foreign trade in those early times.

We will briefly subjoin a statement of the business at this time. From the Harbour thirty-five vessels are fitted out for the mackerel fishery: some of them being of 100 tons burthen and upwards, and employed also in winter in the southern coasting, carrying lumber, fish, &c. and bringing grain and flour. Two regular packets from the Harbour carry on an almost daily intercourse with Boston. From the river, four regular coasters sail, principally to Boston, but making an occasional voyage to Maine. The persons who have the greatest interest in Navigation at present, are Messrs. Dunbar at the Harbour; Messrs. Jenkins and Mr John Beal: almost all the substantial citizens have some interest in the trade.

SHIP BUILDING.

The first ship-builder at the Harbour, who conducted the business with spirit, was Will James. He commenced about 1646. He dug a dock, into which his vessels were launched, which even now, bears his name. It was at the North town landing, and in front of the present dwelling of Jesse Dunbar, Esq. After him, Job Otis (though we are not sure that he was a shipwright) conducted the business of building and navigation on the same spot, and continued it since 1700. Few vessels have been built there for the last fifty years. We believe that vessels had been built first on the River, and at a place afterward called Hobart's landing, by Samuel House (see North River). And we have already named the principal ship-yards and shipwrights, in describing the River.

Many of the whale ships which have been employed for the last half century or more, by the people of New Bedford and Nantucket, have been built here. They generally rate from 300 to 350 tons. The largest, that we have known, was a merchantman, built by Mr William Delano, A. D. 1812, of near 500 tons. An average of the amount in twenty years may be nearly as follows: twelve vessels built per annum, rating from 70 to 350 tons: the average cost of carrying them out of the River, may be estimated at $1 per ton.

The timber is gradually diminishing in the vicinity, and yet has not become so scarce, but that ship building might still be a flourishing business, were the obstructions of the river removed. We are told, from good authority, that near a century ago, it was a general remark, that the building materials were so far exhausted, that the business must soon fail. The late aged and respectable Mr. Elisha Foster used to say, that about 1760, his friends earnestly dissuaded him from his design to become a shipwright, for the reasons above. But never, we believe, was the business conducted more successfully, than by him, until 1800 and later; and by his sons since.

The North River was celebrated for its ship-building in the early annals of the Colonies, and has held its ascendency until late years. It has been famous for the education of shipwrights, who have emigrated, and established their business along the whole coast, from New York to the farthest boundary of Maine. Scarce a ship-yard, or Navy-yard can be visited in this whole range of coast, without meeting many workmen, who themselves or their fathers, were educated at the North River.

The families, at present most actively engaged in the business, are Barstows, Ford, Copeland, Fosters, Souther, Cudworth, Torreys, James, Tildens, Briggses, Turners, Delano, Clap: the ancesters of whom, for many generations, have been employed in the same business.

Agriculture.

The cultivation of the soil was not an object of prime attention with many of the early settlers: being situated about the harbour and along the banks of the river, their first enterprises were those of navigation and the fisheries. The lands were cleared very slowly. Those lands upon the cliffs which had been improved, we believe, as Indian planting land, and the salt marshes, which were covered with a natural crop of grass, and the mellow intervales near the river, had all been laid out as early as 1636. The remaining part of the territory, it was thought, offered little encouragement to the planter. Hence it was, that in A. D. 1637, the settlers began to complain of "the straitenesse of their boundes," and the "want of lands proper for cultivation." The same circumstances, referred to above, have hardly ceased to exercise an unfavourable influence on agriculture. The soil in general is of a good quality, but rugged and stoney: a more ready subsistence can be gained from the seas, and the salt marshes produce an abundance of forage, though of indifferent quality. We can however state a favourable fact, viz. that salt meadow has fallen in value more than fifty per cent. within the last twenty years, owing principally to the better cultivation of the uplands. There are some farms at present, under a high state of cultivation; and skill and science begin to exhibit a respectable influence. The ancient Williams farm, north of the Harbour, enjoys peculiar facilities of sea manure, and in the hands of the present proprietor has become very productive. Capt. Samuel Barker obtained a premium from the Plymouth County Agricultural Society, for the best crop of rye in the County in A. D. 1830. Richmond Jacob and Nathaniel Cushing also obtained premiums the same year, for the general improvement of their farms. Col. James Curtis received a donation in 1829, for the general improvement of his farm: and Thatcher Tilden, a premium for the best crop of rye.

MANUFACTURES.

The want of permanent mill streams must forever forbid the people of this Town from engaging largely in those manufactures that are conducted by water power. Domestick manufactures were formerly carried on to some extent, but these have ceased, from causes that we need not name. The manufacture of Nails was commenced in 1825, by Lemuel and Samuel A. Turner, on the first Herring brook. The easy subsistence gained from the seas, operates against enterprise in domestick manufactures, as it has operated against the interests of agriculture. In 1720, the Town granted two acres of land on the Indian head River, between Pine Hill and Rocky run, to Joseph Barstow and Benjamin Stetson, "for the accommodation of a Forge or Finery." (see mills).

In 1692, the Town granted the privilege of Satuit Brook to set up a fulling mill. We believe it was never built.

Bricks were first made on the West side of Colman's hills. In 1643, near John Palmer's, South of the Church hill. In 1700, near Henchman's corner, one half mile west of the South Meeting-house. In 1770, on the south-west of Cordwood hill. Near the same time and also later, on the west side of Hooppole hill. For several years past there has been an extensive manufacture on the south side of Jacob's mill pond, by the families of Jacob and Collamore. Also on the west of Mount Blue, bricks have been made.

John Copp had a distillery in Scituate, "allowed to sell not less than 10 galls." (Col. Rec. 1666.) Deacon George King manufactured malt extensively from 1710 forwards.

PARISHES.

The north or first Parish in Scituate must be considered as originating in the first settlement of the Town. The earliest parish records having been lost, we are unable accurately to state when they first procured the services of a preacher, or levied taxes for the support of publick worship. Mr. Saxton had ministered there (though not ordained) sometime previous to 1634. But a church was not regularly formed, a minister settled, and a Society fully organized, until Jan. 18, 1634, O. S. The first house for publick worship had been erected some years earlier, but we are without data as to the year. In the laying out of lands in 1633, the Meeting-house is mentioned. It stood about one half mile south-east of the harbour on an eminence. The place is marked by the old burying ground, in "Meeting-house lane," and the foundation may still be traced. This house stood during the ministry of Messrs. Lathrop, Chauncey, Dunster and Baker. About the time of Mr. Baker's death, which happened 1678, the house had become ruinous, and the house of worship in the south or second Parish, (the origin of which will be noted in its proper place) was small and out of repair;* and the two Societies having become reconciled, after a dissension of thirty-two years, propositions were made for uniting the two Societies, and building one commodious house for worship. The propositions not having succeeded, as we shall show in our notes on the second parish, we may venture to assume the year 1682 for the date of the erection of the second house of worship in the first parish. This house was erected on the same spot where the former house had stood, and lasted during the ministries of Mr. Cushing and Mr. Pitcher.

October 1, 1707, "Voted to build a new meeting house upon some part of the meeting house hill, not to be farther west than where the ways meet below Lieut. Buck's shop." This

---

* They were covered with thatch, as were most of the first dwelling houses.

place "where the ways meet" was the four corners, in front of the old parsonage. It was also voted "that the cost should not exceed £300 with the old meeting house." The Agents chosen were Capt. Israel Chittenden, Capt. Benjamin Pierce, Mr. Samuel Clap, Mr. David Jacob and James Cushing. There arose a severe discussion on the subject of the situation of the house. The west section of the parish had become populous, and demanded it as their right to have the house nearer to the centre of the population; and in the mean time the building was delayed. In 1708, the people at the west end, made known their case to the General Court by a Memorial. The same year a Committee of the Court viewed the premises, and heard the pleas of both parties on the spot. Their report was against removing the house farther west: and it was erected on the site of their two former houses. August 1709, we find the following vote: "The Society impowered Mr. Joseph Otis to finish the meeting house by pewing of it, and also to appoint two and two to a pew (*where they do not agree to couple themselves*) each couple paying the cost of building the pew." We believe this house was not plastered, for the following item appears in the parish accounts that year: "Allowed Joseph Bates 12S for filling chinks in the meeting house."

March 17, 1729, "The Society in consideration of the great difficulty that the Society labour under, by reason of the meeting house standing so near to the easterly part of the precinct, and that the house wanteth repairing, the s^d Society agreed to take down the s^d house and remove it to a certain piece or gore of land betwixt two highways, which two highways open from that which goeth by Balch's towards Cohasset, the one by James Cudworth's house, the other by John Otis's which piece of land is the N. W. part of a 20 acre lot, and since exchanged with the Town; provided s^d gore of land can be obtained." February 9, 1730, "The Society voted to accept the piece of land where they want to set their meeting house, by way of gift from Mr. Nicholas Litchfield." Agents were appointed at the same time, to remove and rebuild the house. But the inhabitants of the easterly section, were now roused to opposition, and appealed in their turn to the General Court. In 1733, a Committee of the Court repaired to the place, and having admitted the parties to a hearing, reported against the removal. In the mean time the agents chosen to contract with workmen, had made a contract with James Stetson of Hingham: the undertaker had proceeded to purchase materials, brought an action of damages against the agents, and recovered £35, which the Society paid. There is no record of the dimensions of the house, nor of any alteration in its dimensions. We find that in 1737, so large a majority was obtained for removing it to "the gore of land" abovesaid, that it was harmoniously accomplished. In about thirty years, however, it became too small and was taken down.

March 13, 1769, "Voted to build a new meeting house, and chose a committee (of 24) to consult on a method, &c. and report to the next meeting." April 24 (same year) the committee reported their plan, and the society voted "that the dimensions of their house should be 67 feet by 50," (afterwards altered by vote to 66 by 48). At the same meeting "Voted that the house should be set on the top of the hill in Mr. Daniel Jenkins's pasture, if the land may be obtained." But now the old contest between the East and West-enders was revived. The subject was referred to a committee mutually agreed on, consisting of three gentlemen not of the Town, viz. Capt. Robert Bradford, of Kingston, Hon. James Humphries and Benjamin Lincoln, Esq. Their report was in favour of the spot selected by a majority of the parish, at their first meeting on the subject. The place was about forty rods farther west than the old house, and where it now stands. The contest delayed the building of the house for two years. It had been voted that the house "should be finished by the 1st of Nov. 1772," but it was not completed, so far as to be used for the purpose of worship, until November 1774. The undertakers were Capt. Joseph Tolman, Elisha Tolman, and Hawkes Cushing. It had a spire at the westerly and a portico at the easterly end. It is a building of just proportions and respectable appearance, and with proper attention to repairs, promises to last at least another half century, and exhibit its ancient model to posterity. In 1806, the spire had become so defective that it was thought proper to take it down; which was done, and its place supplied with a cupola. This house was thoroughly repaired in 1825; the cupola was removed and a spire erected; a portico built in front: the house new covered and painted, &c. and this at the cost of $1712.61. This house may with propriety be considered the fifth house of worship, which the Society has built, the former house having been removed from the ancient "Meeting-house hill" and rebuilt.

This Meeting-house is the first house of this Society which has been furnished with a bell. In 1811, the Society purchased their first bell. It weighed 1300 pounds. It was unfortunately

PARISHES.   33

broken in 1813, and in 1814 a new bell was purchased, weighing 1408 pounds. This also was broken in 1822, and a new one purchased of 972 pounds. It may be well to add; by way of noticing the progress of improvement, that Belknap's collection of Hymns was introduced in 1820: and stoves for warming the house in 1824. It is highly interesting to remark the commodious and comfortable state of things in our parish Churches at the present time, compared with the days, when our ancestors worshipped under a roof thatched with straw, by light admitted at an open shutter – without stoves in winter – and sung Sternhold and Hopkins, and the New England Psalms.

The law authorising the laying of taxes on the rateable inhabitants for the support of ministers, bears date 1677; previously it had been the chief burden of the freemen.

In November 29, 1679, the boundaries of the two parishes were fixed by order of Court, and from that time, each parish levied its own tax for religious uses. The taxes had previously been levied by the Town, and divided, probably according to the number of freemen in each society, or on some other principle agreed on. It does not appear that the money for religious uses, had been uniformly raised by taxing, until 1665: at which date we find the following vote: "The Town voted to mayntayne Mr. Baker and Mr. Wetherell, by way of rating yearly." (Scit. Rec. Vol. 6). The Town raised £105 that year – £60 for Mr. Baker, and £45 for Mr. Wetherell.

The first parish had a parsonage, on which their ministers resided from 1654 to 1806. It originated as follows. Mr. Chauncey having complained of poverty, and proposing to leave the country, Mr. Hatherly endeavoured to retain him by making his circumstances easier. He offered to give him a house and farm "bounded E. to Samuel Jackson's – W. to the way – N. to the undivided land – S. to the way, with 20 acres of marsh near the mouth of Satuit brook;" but Mr. Chauncey not being willing to stay with them, the farm was given to the Church. The same year the Church entered into a negociation with Mr. Chauncey, and as appears, had so much encouragement that they should prevail over his inclination to leave them, that a deed of the farm was made to Mr. Chauncey, and put upon record. He however left them at the close of 1654. We have seen no writings on record, by which the farm was then relinquished to the Church, and by the Church to the Society, but such relinquishments, we understand, were made. It appears, also, from the records of the Conihassett partners, that Mr. Hatherly and the Conihassett partners had given Mr. Chauncey a share in the undivided Conihassett lands: and that this share was relinquished to the Church and Society, (see Con. Rec.) These lands were, from time to time, sold in several lots; and in 1803, the Parish obtained an Act of Incorporation for their fund. The first trustees were Hayward Pierce, Esq. James Little, Augustus Clap, Calvin Pierce, and Seth Merritt, with the power of filling vacancies. In 1806, the parsonage was sold and the proceeds added to the fund. It now amounts to $5381.95.

The original parsonage house was built by Mr. Hatherly as early as 1640. January 1694, "The Society voted to build a new house on the Parsonage," which was accomplished. Again in 1742, it appears by the record that "a new Parsonage house was built." This last was the house now standing, and which was sold to Cummings Jenkins in 1806. The parish property had originated from so many sources that it would be tedious to trace out the whole. The parsonage we have sufficiently noticed above. In 1661, Mr. Hatherly gave his house and land at Farm neck "for the use of the ministry." The Town made several small grants: and the Society became successor to President Chauncey by purchase of Israel Chauncey in 1700. Some part of this parish property was sold and otherwise appropriated, many years before the Society raised their fund. For example, in 1701 they sold all the lands which they owned as successor to Mr Chauncey, and built a barn on the parsonage with the proceeds. And in 1707, they sold ten acres "in the beaches" and gave the proceeds to Mr. Pitcher for a settlement, (see Parish Rec.)

The South or Second Parish,

May be considered as having originated in a difference of opinion respecting the mode of baptism. Mr. Chauncey, who had been ordained in 1641, would baptize by immersion only. It was a point that was warmly discussed throughout the New England colonies about this time, and a difference of sentiment which occasioned divisions elsewhere, produced similar effects here. It appears that the minority in the Society and Church in Scituate, opposed to immersion, was relatively large and respectable, that they did not cordially receive Mr. Chauncey as their pastor, and – that Mr. Chauncey had been so far disturbed by the opposition, that he had requested those Church members in the opposition, to refrain from appearing at the communion, (see Notes on Ecclesiastical affairs). By the advice of the Elders in the Colony, this minority proceeded to renew their covenant, and to organize a second Church. This ceremony took place February 2, 1642.

We find no record of the building of their first house of worship. It was doubtless erected near the time of the settlement of Mr. Wetherell, in 1645. The house was small and covered with thatch. It stood on the south-east side of the road, on the top of an eminence, about fifty rods north-east of "Stoney cove brook." We have seen no record of the laying out of the Meeting-house lot; we believe it was not granted by the Town, because that land had been laid out to James Torrey and Thomas Robinson; it was therefore either a gift of the proprietors or a purchase of the Society. And we have met with no record to show the extent of the lot, or to show that it has ever been alienated from the Society, though it has been fenced in and improved by several persons who possessed the lands adjacent. This house lasted during the ministry of Mr. Wetherell.

A. D. 1679, attempts were made to unite both Societies, and to erect one large and commodious house of worship. There was however an opposition, and application was made to the General Court for advice and direction. A committee was appointed on the subject, and from the report of that committee we make a brief extract: "That by reason of distance of place and other considerations, it (the union) would not have the effect proposed. It being resolved by the Court that there is an inevitable necessity of mayntayninge two places of publicke worship in the Town, we judge it necessary that all due meanes be used for mayntayning the ordinances of Christ in each place, and therefore your mutual and joint concurrence hearein is vearie desirable for the strengthening and encouraging the good worke of God amongst you."

Signed
SAMUEL ARNOLD,   JOSIAH WINSLOW,
JOHN COTTON,   THOMAS HINCKLEY,
                    WILLIAM BRADFORD.

Plymouth Nov. 29, 1670.   (Col. Rec.)

The question of uniting the two Societies had been agitated in Town meeting. October 24, 1679, the Town by a majority had voted "That if our neighbours up River, above William Parker's house, will unite to us, that we may be one Societie in peace and love, that then the place for our publicke worship shall be at Walter Woodworth's hill, or the center of the present inhabitants of the Town." (Scit. Rec. Vol. 6). The hill mentioned was one quarter of a mile south of Stockbridge's mill. Again January 1, 1679-80, the Town (by a majority) voted "to unite and build a Meeting-house at the piece of land where Thomas Woodworth's shope stood." This place, we believe, was near the junction of the several roads a few rods south of Stockbridge's mill. The advice of the Court above quoted, strengthened the opposition, and the project failed.

There was also a dissension in the Town respecting the place most proper for the second Society's house of worship. In 1645, the first Society had complained that the second Society had placed their house too near to theirs, and now the subject was revived. An appeal to the Court was answered by the following advice, "That the new Meeting-house for the Society up River, be set betweene (or neare about) Timothy Foster's and John Turner, sen.'s lots, about half a mile higher than the old Meeting-house, and that payment thereof be made by all the inhabitants above the mill brooke, and up s^d River called the N. River on both sides."

Signed as above.

This did not give universal satisfaction: certain persons both above and below the brook feeling themselves pledged to support the respective Societies whose part they had maintained in the contest.

The next year, October 1680, the order of Court above was thus qualified: "That the s^d Order shall be observed with this proviso, viz. that the particular persons here named that live above the mill brook, viz. Jeremiah Hatch, Thomas Hatch, Mr. Thomas Palmer, and Samuel Clap, being of the lower Society, should be exempted out of s^d rate, and that these persons who live below the mill brook, viz. Mrs. Elizabeth Tilden, Richard Curtis, John Turner, jr. and Charles Stockbridge shall be put into s^d rate."

Attest, Nathaniel Morton, Secretary.

The above order was published at the new Meeting-house, October 31, 1680, (Parish Records). The Town did not easily resign their proposed plan of uniting, and in May 1681, instructed their deputies in the Court, to move a receding from their former order: but they did not meet with success. We may therefore (in the absence of exact record) venture to assume the year 1680, as the date of the erection of the second house of worship in the second parish. It stood on a small eminence on the easterly side of the road, about thirty rods north of the head of the road that leads to Union Bridge, and near the southerly line of Timothy Foster's lot, as the Court directed. An ancient burying ground marks the spot. We have met with no record of the purchase of this lot by the Society, nor of its alienation. It is now enclosed and improved by Timothy Foster, the great grandson of the Timothy Foster first named. This house stood only during the short ministries of Mr. Mighill and Mr. Lawson.

In 1706, it appears that the Society had become so numerous that a larger house was required. And henceforth we find fair records made and preserved, (commencing 1698).

"At a meeting of the Church and Society upon the North River, October 18, 1706. The sayd Church and Society agreed and provided to build a new Meeting-house, and set it upon the most convenient place of that parcell of land between the dwelling house belonging to Thomas Bryant and Joseph Bryant and the saw mill near the s^d house, if land may be obtained there to set it upon: and also agreed that the dimensions of the s^d house should be as followeth, viz. 46 feet in length and 44 feet in breadth, and 20 feet between joints, and a sloping roof with a turret upon it suitable to hang a bell on: and that it should be plaistered with white lime within side from top to bottom."

"Capt. Cushing, Dea. Thomas King, Job Randall and Ensign Stephen Clap were appointed to treat with the owners of s^d land, and to put out the s^d house to building at the charge of s^d Society."

An alteration in the proportions and form of the house was voted on the 25th of November following, viz. "50 feet in length and forty feet in breadth, and 20 feet between joints, and a flat roof of about ten feet rise." The turret for the bell, of course, was omitted. At the same meeting, it also appearing that the land of Mr. Bryant could not be obtained (note, the spot proposed was a few rods east of the mill) it was voted "to set the house upon John James's land near his gate, if it may be obtained." This place proposed was on the south side of the road, about thirty rods east of Bryant's Bridge at the second Herring brook. The land in this place not having been obtained, it appears from the Town Records Vol. 6. that the Society petitioned the Town for liberty to set it upon the common lands, and succeeded in their wishes; as appears by the following vote, May 28, 1707: "Voted liberty to the south Parish to set up their Meeting-house at or near the place where it is now framed, upon the Town Common, and to use of their common land, a conveniency for a burying place, and also for building a stable or stables. At the same meeting the Town ordered a highway to be laid out, for the accommodation of this Meeting-house, "from the way at Mr. Job Randalls, (now David Torrey's), along over at the westward of Benjamin Sylvester's house, and the westward of the saw mill pond, untill it comes unto the way near to Bryant's house." The Meeting-house was accordingly raised in June 1707, on the small hill at the junction of the ways, about thirty rods West of the mill. This house stood during the ministry of Mr. Eells, Mr. Dorby, and a part of that of Dr. Barnes.

It may be a proper place here to insert a vote of the Town February 28, 1706: "Voted to sell 200 ten acre lots of their common land at 3£ per lot, and divide the money to the two Churches and Societies for the purpose of building a Meeting-house for each." This vote was carried into effect: and as the expense had not been defrayed by the Society, it explains the following vote of the South Parish, July 13, 1708: "Chose Mr. Eells, Dea. Thomas King, Dea. James Torrey, Capt. John Cushing, Lieut. Stephen Clap, and Job Randall to be a committee of Seaters, to appoint persons in which seat he or they shall sit in at the s^d Meeting-house; and the Church and Society agreed that their Meeting-house should be made up of wainscot work, as conveniently as the space of room will afford, at the discretion of the above s^d seaters; and the above s^d seaters are to admit of suitable persons that will be at the charge of building said pews upon the terms hereafter expressed, viz. the Church and Society reserving that privilege in and to s^d pews, that no person shall have liberty to give or sell or dispose of their pew to any person, without the consent of the Society; and that the above s^d seaters and their successors in s^d office, shall have liberty to appoint suitable persons to sit with the owners of s^d pews, in case they be not conveniently filled up from time to time, by the owners thereof." Such an office would be highly perilous at the present day.

At a meeting of the Society, October 1738, a committee was appointed to consider and report on the propriety of enlarging the Meeting-house or repairing it. Their report was in favour of repairing without enlarging it. But the Society being nearly equally divided in opinion on the question, the repairs were not effected. In November 1740, a vote was carried to enlarge it: but before any progress in the work had been made, another meeting was called and the vote reversed; but the repairs were not made. In 1743, October 10, the vote to enlarge prevailed again: but on the first of November following, it was again reversed. In April 1744 and 1745, the same alternation of votes took place: but in July 1745, a petition of John Cushing and fifteen others, for leave to add thirteen feet to the length of the house, and make the same into pews, and to take the hazard of profit and loss upon themselves prevailed, and the work, we believe, was accomplished. The Society moreover voted to lay aside the diamond windows, and procure "window sashes and square glass," and to build another seat "forward of the galleries." Again in March 1764, sundry persons petitioned for leave to add ten feet to the back side of the house, and were denied. The same was repeated in 1768, and granted: but on reflection it was judged "to be much better to build a new house."

We come now to the fourth house of worship erected by the second Society. At a meeting April 24, 1769, "Voted that Mr. Joseph Tolman be desired to draw a plan of a new Meeting-house, to be laid before the precinct at their next meeting."

May 30, 1769, "Voted to build a new Meeting-house agreeable to s^d plan, using what of the old house may be convenient, and that the old pews be set up in the new house, as near as may be where they are in the old house, and that each proprietor enjoy his pew in the new house, saving those who have not agreed to give anything to encourage s^d work, or for taking down and setting up their pews. Their pews shall remain for further consideration by s^d precinct. But it is to be understood that this vote is upon condition that s^d house be built without any cost or charge to s^d precinct as such. The Hon. John Cushing, Nathaniel Clap, Esq. Joseph Tolman, Galen Clap, and Nathaniel Turner were appointed agents to agree with some suitable person or persons to complete s^d work as soon as may be, not to exceed the first of November 1770."

The undertakers were Joseph Tolmarr, Elisha Tolman, and Hawkes Cushing. The house was erected on the same scite where the former house had stood. It was seventy-two feet in length and forty-eight in breadth, with a portico at the east end and a belfry and spire at the west end. It was decent in external appearance, though without pretensions to elegance of architecture. But it was slightly built, and uncouth in the interior, as we might presume it would be, from reading the above vote. The undertakers took on themselves the hazard of profit or loss, and it is well known, were richly repaid. This house stood without alterations, until March 9, 1830, when it was taken down. It was then apparent that the house had not been substantially built; and indeed, it was so considered at the time of its erection; for in looking into the precinct records, we find that the undertakers were allowed to use the materials of the old house at their own discretion. The object of obtaining a large house at small cost was gained: but it was bad economy, for in sixty years it became ruinous.

January 4, 1830, at a meeting called "to know if the parish would build a Meeting-house the ensuing year," a preliminary step was taken, by appointing a committee "to appraise the pews" in the old Meeting-house, viz. Melzar Curtis, Esq. Elisha Bass, and Horatio Cushing, all of Hanover. At an adjourned meeting, January 12, 1830, "it was voted to build a new Meeting-house," forty-seven affirmative, twenty-eight negative. Also another committee was chosen "to appraise the interest of the pew holders in the old house, viz. Jotham Tilden, Charles Jones, and Daniel Philips." It was thought to be a more regular and legal proceeding, to appraise the old house, after the vote to build a new one. The committee appraised the interest of the pew holders separately, and reported a sum total of $806.

At an adjourned meeting, January 27, 1830, "Voted to choose a committee of twenty-one to have the management of the building of the new Meetinghouse," viz. Hon. Cushing Otis and others. At the same meeting "Voted that the new house be placed on the scite of the old one, and fronting south."

At an annual meeting, March 10, 1830, "the vote of the last meeting in regard to the location of the new Meeting-house was reconsidered, and that it be placed near the wind mill, so that a part of it stand on the scite of the wind mill, provided land can be purchased of the heirs of Warren Sylvester at a reasonable price."

At a meeting, April 26, 1830, the above vote was reconsidered, "and it was voted that the new Meeting-house be placed on the common, about half way between the pound and the wind mill, that it front the east, and that the west end be placed in a line with the field of the heirs of Warren Sylvester deceased."

The building committee made a contract with Messrs. Whittemore Peterson, and Christopher Oakman, to supply the materials and do the work, excepting the painting, the window blinds, and the frame. This latter exception was, we believe, made chiefly with the expectation that the old frame would serve for the new house; but the expectation was disappointed, and a new frame procured by the committee.

The dimensions of the house had been ordered by the committee to be the same as the former house, (viz. 70 feet by 48), but afterwards reduced to 69 by 48. The house was completed about the first of October, and on the thirteenth of the same month it was dedicated in presence of a very large assembly. On the following day, the pews were exposed to sale, and in less than three hours, they were all taken up, at an advance of $773, above the cost of the house. The whole cost of the house was $4,650. It is a beautiful and commodious house, adorned with a handsome spire, accommodated with a portico of nine feet depth, containing seventy large and convenient pews, and a circular gallery in front sufficiently deep to accommodate one hundred persons, exclusive of the organ loft and seats for the choir. The model does honor to the gentleman who drafted it, Mr. William Sparrell of Boston. It was raised May 10, 1830,

Parsonage.

The south or second Society had no parsonage during the ministry of Mr Witherell. In 1684, on the settlement of Mr. Mighill, the Society voted at first £60 for his annual compensation; which he declining, it was afterwards voted to add "fire wood and house rent." The house was doubtless purchased or built at the Society's charge, for we find no grant of the Town to that effect. The house stood a few rods east of Bryant's bridge, on the north side of the way.

A tract of land had been appropriated for ministerial uses before the separation of the parishes, as follows: February 26, 1673, "It is agreed that the parcell of land ajoining the second Herringe brooke and Edward Wanton's land, from the way down to the marish, is reserved for the use of the ministry as occation may requier, and a common privilege belonging to it." (Town Rec). That this land was assigned to the second Society on a division of parishes, appears from the Society's Records, Jan. 1702-3, "Voted to sell the land granted by the Town's committee, between the second Herring brook and Edward Wanton's land." In 1694, the Town made another grant as follows: "The Town ordered five acres of swamp to be laid out to the Tenement belonging to the upper Society on the North River." This was on the second Herring brook just above the parsonage house. Again in 1703, the Society chose a committee "to purchase some salt meadow for the use of the parsonage – also the same committee to settle with Israel

Sylvester, who had hired the parsonage, and to put the building in good repair for the accommodation of Mr. Eells," who was about to be settled. Lastly, in 1711 "The Town granted to the Society up River 20 acres on Cordwood hill, for the use of their parsonage."

From such sources originated the parish property.

January 6 1737, "The Society voted to make sale of the parsonage house and land adjoining it, belonging to the Society, to the highest bidder." This was at the juncture when Mr. Eells had furnished himself with a house, by purchase of Joseph Henchman. But the parsonage was not then sold. Dr. Barnes lived at the parsonage from 1754 to 1770, when he purchased a farm and built a house, and continued to improve and receive the rents until 1784. April 6, 1784, "the Society chose a committee to confer with Mr. Barnes in relation to selling the parsonage house and lands, salt marsh, &c." At an adjourned meeting, on the 12th of the same month, "agents were appointed to sell the parsonage and lands;" and at an adjourned meeting on the 17th of the same month, "The agents reported that they had made sales as follows: the Homestead to Israel Turner for 230£ – the lands on Cordwood hill to George Torrey for 96£ 12S – a part of the salt marsh to Benjamin Delano for 49£ 8s – and the remainder of the marsh to Seth Ewell for 47£ 10S." Dr. Barnes at the same time was allowed £20 per annum in addition to his salary, instead of the use of a parsonage. The monies raised by these sales, were from time to time invested "in State securities, Continental notes, and final settlement certificates," as opportunity presented, and in 1799, an act of incorporation was obtained – the first trustees being Elijah Turner, Elisha James, Charles Turner, jr. Samuel Tolman, and Joshua Jacobs, having the power to fill vacancies, when the parish shall neglect to do it within three months. The amount of the fund in 1799, was $7347.33, which has since been increased to a small amount.

In 1727, a committee had been authorized to view the parsonage house, and to report what repairs were necessary. That committee reported that the house was so defective "that it was not worth repairing." In June, 1728, "a new parsonage house was ordered to be built, 40 feet in length, 17 feet in breadth, and 17 feet between joints, with an L on the back side 16 feet in length, 16 feet in breadth, and 17 feet between joints." This is the house bought by Israel Turner in 1784: it is now in the possession of his children, and is in good repair.

An attempt was made as early as 1753, to procure a church bell for the second Society. "It was put to vote whether the precinct would be at the charge of ringing a bell, provided particular persons would be at the charge and trouble of procuring it, and passed in the affirmative." Again in 1764, "It was put to vote whether the precinct would raise money to purchase a suitable bell for the Meeting-house, and passed in the negative." The same was repeated in 1767.

March 25, 1771, "It was put to vote whether the precinct would accept of a bell, (as the gift of individuals), cast in this country, and passed in the affirmative." At the same meeting a committee was chosen (Elisha Jacob and others) to go to Abington and see a bell cast by Aaron Hobart, weighing 658 pounds, and report whether they think it will answer, provided it be purchased." There is no further record of the transaction; but we notice that at a meeting in October following, John Jordan was chosen to ring the bell. This bell was broken in 1810, and another purchased of Col. Revere at Boston, weighing 1018 pounds. This bell was transferred to the new Meeting-house in 1830.

By way of noting the progress of improvement, we will add that this Society by vote, introduced the singing of Tate and Brady's hymns in 1764. Belknap's was introduced without any formality, we believe, (as no record appears), in the year 1799. Greenwood's was adopted by parish vote, March 21, 1831.

In October 1830, a handsome church organ was received as a present from Mr. Thomas Otis; an act of the greatest individual munificence, since the days of Mr. Hatherly.

A handsome clock was also placed in the front of the gallery, January 15, 1831, by the generosity of Hon. Cushing Otis. Church stoves were first used in December 1821, and pocured by subscription. A hearse was procured at the Society's expense in 1825.

ASSINIPPI.*

The people in the westerly section of the south parish began to be desirous of forming a Society within their own vicinity, as early as 1766; and in that year petitioned to the south parish to be set off by mutual consent.

---

* Assinippi was the Indian name for a branch of the third Herring brook, and means "rocky water:" this name in modern times, has been corrupted to *Snappet*.

March 3, 1767, we find the following record in the south parish: "It was put to vote whether the precinct would grant the request of a number of inhabitants in the westerly part of s^d precinct, in order for their being a precinct by themselves, viz. all the land to the westward of the following bounds, beginning at the brook by Margaret Prouty's, southward with the brook to Hanover line – northward with the brook to Joseph Benson's land – then north by west between Lazarus Bowker's and John Bowker's, to Taunton Dean brook or bridge, and so northward with s^d brook to the patent line: and passed in the negative." The same was repeated in 1770, and negatived: at the same meeting "it was put to vote whether the Rev. Mr. Barnes should preach in the Meeting-house near Joshua Jacob's, while our new house is building, and passed in the negative."

October 1771, Joshua Jacob and others petitioned to General Court that they might be set off by their act. The south precinct appointed Nathaniel Clap, Esq. Nathan Cushing, Esq. and John Palmer, to meet the Court's committee on the premises, and make a representation of the case. The committee reported against the separation.

March 1792, "The south precinct voted that Charles Turner, jr., Esq. and Capt. Enoch Collamore be a committee to wait on the Rev. Mr. Barnes, and enquire whether he is willing to preach in the west Meeting-house a part of the year." The committee reported that Mr. Barnes replied, "he should wish to gratify the precinct." It was then voted "that he should preach in the west Meeting-house" the second Sabbath in each month, from the first of April to the first of December. The next year, 1793, the same question was taken in the precinct and passed in the negative. Some attempts, subsequently, were made to raise money to assist the people in the westerly section in defraying the expense of worship by themselves, but always negatived.

In 1797, David Jacob and others petitioned to the General Court to be set off as a separate Society, and to be allowed to receive their ratable proportion of the south parish funds. This was opposed successfully by the agents of the second or south parish, viz. Elijah Turner, and Charles Turner, jr. Esquires, The parish had given them instructions to urge several reasons, the most weighty of which seem to be the following, viz. "that the limits proposed for their new parish would include many families which desired still to belong to the south parish; and as to the fund, it was given by the Town for the special purpose of supporting the ministry in the second

Congregational Society in Scituate; and therefore no part of it could be legally alienated to a third Society."

In 1812, several inhabitants of the same district petitioned to the General Court for an Act of Incorporation as "a Universalist Society." The south precinct voted not to oppose, and they were accordingly incorporated. The above records, we believe, as we have extracted, contain the essential parts of the history of this Society. We may add, that since their incorporation, they have uniformly procured the service of a minister, and hired him from year to year. The ministers who have officiated for the longest terms have been Rev. Joshua Flagg, Rev. Benjamin Whittemore, and Rev. Mr. Kilham. Their Meeting-house that was erected in 1769, was repaired and plaistered in 1814.

St. Andrew's Church.

The earliest notice with which we have met, of Episcopalians in Scituate, bears the date of 1725, (see Nichols's recollections, or literary anecdotes). It is related in Nichols's collection of anecdotes, that the Rev. Dr. Timothy Cutler, of Christ Church in Boston, with several attendants, came to Scituate, during an absence of Rev, Mr. Bourn, minister of the north parish; "by the invitation of Lieut. Daman (then at variance with Mr. Bourn,) and another gentleman of large estate," and performed divine service in the Church form, in the north Meeting-house. After returning to Boston, Dr. Cutler or some one of his attendants published an account of their excursion in the Boston Gazette, setting forth the respectability of the gentlemen who had invited him, the numbers who attended the service, and the happy prospects of Episcopacy in Scituate. A counter statement of facts from a Scituate gentleman, soon after appeared in the Boston News Letter, contradicting in some measure, the statement of Dr. Cutler; denying that any principal inhabitants of the Town had invited the Doctor hither, and stating for a fact, "that only three men of Scituate, a number of disaffected men from neighbouring towns, and about forty school boys," were present at the services. This counter statement in the News Letter was thus endorsed: "By authority." Dr. Cutler complained to the Governor and Council, demanding justice and protection. The only notice, however, that was taken of the complaint, appears in the following order in Council.

"September 2, 1725, Whereas inconveniences have once

and again arisen to the Government, by several matters being printed in the news papers, and said to be published by authority, which have never been known to the Government, nor offered for their approbation, therefore advised – that the Lieutenant Governor give his orders to the several publishers of the several news papers, not to insert in their papers those words, 'by authority,' or words of the like import, for the future."

J. WILLARD, Secretary.

We have not had access to any records of the Church of St. Andrew's, and have not been able to learn that any regular records of its early annals have been preserved: we therefore can give but a very imperfect sketch of its history.

We observe in the records of the south parish, that the churchmen's rates began to be remitted under the item of "Contingent Charges," in 1741, and varying in amount from £5 to £15 per annum. In 1699, the Town had ordered a piece of land to be appropriated for a common, "surrounded with ways, &c." (see notes on commons). This was on the south side of the hill, where St. Andrew's church was first erected. In 1725, ten acres more were ordered to be laid out for a burying place and training field. This was an enlargement of the same common. But in what year the church was erected, we are not able to state; probably 1730. It was enlarged 1753.

Their first clergyman who officiated for any time, was Mr. Brockwell, born in England, and a graduate of Cambridge in England: but we are without dates with respect to the term of his services. Their second clergyman and the first official rector, was Rev. Addington Davenport, who graduated at Harvard University in 1719, and also received a degree at Oxford. We can only state that his ministry was of short continuance. and must have been between 1730 and 1740. He removed to Boston as early as 1740, where he became assistant at King's Chapel, and afterward rector of Trinity Church. In 1743, he gave his house and land in Scituate to the Society for propagating the gospel in foreign parts, in trust, toward the support of the ministers of St. Andrew's Church in Scituate, in perpetuity. In this conveyance he adverts to the fact of his having been their first rector, (Hist. Soc. pap. year 1816). The second rector was Rev. Ebenezer Thompson from Connecticut. He died November 28, 1775. His descendants are in Scituate and Providence. The third rector, Rev. William Willard Wheeler of Concord, officiated most of the time, from the decease of Mr. Thompson to 1810. He died January 14th the same year. He married the daughter of Mr. Thompson, whom he succeeded in the rectorship. She died 1827.

The fourth rector, Joab Goldsmith Cooper, officiated from 1812 to 1816, when he retired. He was from Long Island.

The fifth rector, Rev. Calvin Woolcot of Gloucester, was instituted in 1818, and officiates in 1831.

St. Andrew's church was taken down in 1811, and a new one erected within the town of Hanover, and near the four corners.

Another small church in Marshfield, established as early as 1745, has always been connected with St. Andrew's, the rector officiating there one Sabbath in four. A new church edifice has been erected there in 1826, near "three Pine hill," and two miles to the northward of the former edifice.

Another Episcopal church situated in Taunton, was for many years connected with St. Andrew's, the rector officiating there one Sabbath in four. That church edifice was situated two miles from "the green," on the Providence road. It was taken down many years since, and it was not until 1828, that a neat little Gothic church was erected, a few rods south of "the green."

St. Andrew's church obtained an act of incorporation in 1797. The wardens then were Charles Bailey and Thomas Barstow, jr.

Society of Friends.

We begin by remarking, for the benefit of those readers who may not have at hand Gouth's or any other general history of this sect, that George Fox, one of its principal founders, began to preach in England in 1647. None of his followers found their way to this country until 1656, when Mary Fisher and Ann Austin arrived at Boston from Barbadoes. In 1657, eight more came to Boston through Rhode Island. They immediately spread throughout Plymouth Colony. It is uncertain what notice would have been taken of them here; but this is certain, that the General Court of Massachusetts communicated to Plymouth Colony the first impulse of opposition to this sect. In 1656, the General Court of Massachusetts addressed a memorial to the Commissioners of the United Colonies, who met at Plymouth in September of that year: a brief extract from which will serve to show its spirit and its design, viz.

"Here hath arrived amongst us several persons professing themselves Quakers, fit instruments to propagate the kingdom of Sathan. For the securing of ourselves and our neighbours from such pests, we have imprisoned them, until they be despatched away to the place from whence they came," &c. They then request that certain laws may be propounded by the Commissioners to the General Court of each of the United Colonies. In pursuance of this impulse, and "acknowledging the Godly care and zeal of the gentlemen of Massachusetts," the Commissioners at their meeting in Boston 1657, began with recommending to the Government of Rhode Island, "that means be taken to banish the Quakers, &c." Capt. James Cudworth of Scituate, one of the Commissioners, refused to subscribe to this instrument, and from this time suffered much persecution himself, (see life of Cudworth in Family Sketches). The reply of the Government of Rhode Island is to be admired for its moderation and discretion. We give a brief extract, viz.

"We have no law amongst us, whereby to punish any for only declaring their minds concerning the things and ways of God. We are informed that they begin to loathe this place, for that they are not opposed by the civil authority, but with all patience and meekness are suffered to say over their pretended revelations," &c. At their meeting in Boston 1658, the Commissioners addressed a circular to the Government of all the United Colonies, propounding laws against the Quakers, &c. e. g. "that after due conviction that either he or she is of that cursed sect of hereticks, they be banished under pain of severe corporal punishment, and if they return again, then to be punished accordingly, and banished under pain of death: and if afterwards they shall yet presume to come again, then to be put to death as aforesaid, except they do then and there plainly and publickly renounce their said cursed opinions and develish tenets." The General Court of Massachusetts followed out this recommendation to its greatest extent:* but Plymouth

---

* The preamble of the law of Massachusetts, in 1658, is as follows: "Whereas there is a pernicious sect commonly called Quakers lately risen, who by word and writing have published and maintained many dangerous and horrid tenets, and do take upon themselves to change and alter the received laudable customs of our Nation, in giving civil respect to equals or reverence to superiors, whose actions tend to undermine the authority of civil government, and also to destroy the order of the churches, by denying all established forms of worship, and by withdrawing from the orderly assemblies allowed and approved by all orthodox professors of the truth, &c. therefore ordered, that if any person or persons of the cursed sect of the Quakers shall be apprehended, &c. upon trial and conviction they shall be banished on pain of death."

Colony at first met with opposition within her own counsels. The venerable Timothy Hatherly of Scituate, one of the magistrates, was firmly opposed to the cruelty of the laws propounded, and to their whole policy in such proceedings. It was necessary to get rid of such opposition, and accordingly in 1658 he was left out of the magistracy. Capt. Cudworth, who had been left out of the board of United Commissioners, was returned a deputy from Scituate in 1659, and set aside by the Court, (see Town proceedings).

Isaac Robinson, son of the venerable pastor of the Pilgrim Church at Leyden, and some others, were removed from their places in the government and disfranchised. It is probable that the influence of this highly respectable opposition was felt notwithstanding, and prevented the Colony from following the bloody steps of Massachusetts.

The Court of Plymouth Colony passed many laws of great severity: and it may be enough to give brief extracts from the records, e.g. In 1657 a law was enacted providing the penalty of "whipping and 5£ fine for entertaining a Quakuer: also 40S fine for being at a Quaker meeting." In 1658, it was

---

In 1659, Samuel Shattuck, Lawrence Southwick and Cassandra his wife, Nicholas Phelps, Joshua Buffum and Josiah Southwick were banished. The same year was Edward Wharton sentenced to be whipped "for piloting the Quakers from place to place."

In 1659, "It is ordered that William Robinson, Marmaduke Stevenson and Mary Dyer, now in prison for their rebellion, sedition and presumptuous obtruding themselves upon us, notwithstanding their being sentenced to banishment on pain of death, &c. shall be brought to tryall to-morrow morning. Next day the above s^d were sent for, acknowledged themselves to be the persons so banished, and were sentenced to be hanged." Edward Michaelson the marshall was to see them executed. James Oliver with one hundred soldiers to guard. Rev. Zechariah Symmes (of Charlestown), and Mr. Norton (of Boston) "to make the prisoners sensible of their danger." Robinson and Stevenson were executed; Mary Dyer, on the petition of her son William, was dismissed on condition that she depart the colony, but to be present and stand with a rope round her neck when the others should be executed. The next year she returned and offered herself to the government with the zeal of a martyr, and she was hanged June 1660. Her husband petitioned in vain for her life. We add on the authority of Dr. Snow's History of Boston, that William Leddra was also executed: but it escaped our notice in consulting the Colony Records. June 13, 1661, was appointed for the execution of Wenlock Christopherson: but we believe he was reprieved.

In 1661, John Brown and Peter Pierson "having been indicted for Quakers, and standing mute, were sentenced to be stripped from the girdle upwards, tied to a cart tail and whipped through the streets of Boston, Roxbury, Dedham, &c. out of the jurisdiction." At the close of this year the mandamus of the King put an end to these proceedings. We notice in the Plymouth Colony Records, that William Leddra was apprehended at Plymouth in 1659, and imprisoned "as a foreign Quaker:" also that Mary Dyer having been conducted to Sandwich from Rhode Island by Thomas Greenfield, they were both arrested, and Greenfield was adjudged by the Court, "to pay 16S. to defray the expence of sending her back to Rhode Island."

enacted "that no Quaker or ranter be allowed the freedom of the Colonie, or an oath in any case." In 1658, "Ordered that all Quakers shall depart the Jurisdiction on pain of 20S fine per week — their books to be seized: also 10£ fine for guiding a Quaker into the Colonie: Constant Southworth with the marshall to execute the above orders."

The general allegations against the Quakers may be found in the preambles of these laws, and in the communications of the board of Commissioners that recommended them. Such as that "they take upon them to be immediately sent of God and infallibly assisted — they speak and write blasphemous things; despising government, reviling magistrates and ministers of the gospel — wander up and down and follow no lawful calling to earn their own bread, &c."

We select a few of those who suffered under these laws, as belonging to Scituate, (see Colony Records).

In 1660, Rhodolphus Ellmes of Scituate, was fined 10S for being at a Quaker meeting. Same year, William Parker was fined 40S for permitting a Quaker meeting in his house. Same year, Capt. Cudworth was tried before the Court for "a scandalous letter," sent to England. Major Josiah Winslow and Mr. Thomas Southworth were appointed to implead him. John Browne testified "that he had heard a printed letter read, which was supposed to be sent to England from Capt. Cudworth," (see Cudworth). (Released for the present). At the next court, same year, "Capt. Cudworth being found a manifest opposer of the laws of this Government, as appears by sundry expressions in a letter to the Governor, is sentenced accordingly to be disfranchised of the freedom of this Commonwealth."

In 1660, "Robert Whetcombe and Mary Cudworth, for disorderly coming together without consent of parents and lawful marriage, were sentenced to pay 10£ fine, and be imprisoned during the pleasure of the Court: but being desirous to be orderly married, they were so, March 9, 1660." Henry Hobson of Rhode Island was summoned for solemnizing the above marriage. That this was a Quaker marriage, we judge from the fact that the parties were Quakers.

In 1670, "William Randall, sen. John Palmer and Henry Ewell, refusing to pay the minister's tax, the Court ordered the constables to take their goods."

In 1675, Lieut. Robert Barker "broke away from the army, when they were on their march, in a mutinous way, and by his example allured others to come away." Barker was deprived of his commission – he was of Duxbury. That this meeting was the result of Quaker principle, we judge from the other circumstance, that of the fifteen others whom he allured away, five were Scituate men, and Quakers, viz. Zechariah Colman, Joseph Colman, Thomas Colman, John Rance, and John Northey: who were fined from 1£ to 8£, according to their respective offences.

In 1661, "Josiah Palmer (of Scituate) was fined 10S for saying that 'Mr. Witherel's Church was a Church of the Devil.'" In 1677, "John Rance (of Scituate) for railing on Mr. Baker, in saying he is a false prophet, and saying Major Cudworth is a false, hypocritical man, (note: Cudworth was now restored to a place in the government), and saying that Mr. Baker had received stolen goods; (note: alluding probably to taxes exacted from some of the Quakers); also for going up and down to entice young persons to come and hear their false teachers, was sentenced to be publickly whipped." (performed), In 1678, "Edward Wanton (of Scituate) for disorderly joining himself to his now wife in marriage, in a way contrary to the order of Government is fined 10£."

To illustrate the history of those times, we subjoin a notice of the proceedings of the Colony Government, against two or three others who were not of Scituate.

In 1663, "Robert Harper was sentenced to be publickly whipt for his intolerable insolent disturbance, both of the Congregation of Barnstable and Sandwich," Again the same sentence was passed upon Robert Harper in 1670, "for reviling Mr. Walley," minister of Barnstable.

In 1657, "Humphry Norton was sentenced to depart the colony." In 1658, Norton came back, (with John Rowse), and being taken before the Court for examination, Norton repeatedly used such insolent language to Gov. Prence, as "thou lyest." Christopher Winter of Scituate appeared as an accuser, and "deposed to a paper containing sundry notorious errors expressed by said Norton." The oath of fidelity to the Government being tendered to them, and they refusing to take it, they were publickly whipped; and on refusing to pay the fee to the under marshal for whipping them, they were remanded to prison: but having satisfied the marshal, they were soon after liberated on condition of leaving the Jurisdiction. After retiring, Norton addressed letters to Gov. Prence and John Alden one of the assistants, which surpass the ravings of madmen. They are dated Rhode Island, 16, 4th m. 1658; and filled with such railings as the following: "Thomas Prence, thou hast perverted justice and true judgment, and has defrauded the poor and needy. John Alden is to thee like unto a pack horse, whereupon thou layest thy beastly bag: cursed are all they that have a hand therein. The cry of vengence will pursue thee – the anguish and pain that will enter thy reins will be like gnawing worms lodging betwixt thy heart and liver. When these things come upon thee, in that day and hour thou shalt know to thy grief, that prophets of the Lord God we are, and the God of vengeance is our God." (see Hazard's Collections). (See Rowse in Family Sketches).

His letter to Alden was alike furious, e.g. "John Alden, if there be in thee any expectation of mercy, do thou follow the example of Timothy Hatherly, and withdraw thy body forever appearing at that beastly bench where the law of God is cast behind your backs: let the cursed purse be cast out of thy house, wherein is held the goods of other men, lest through it, a moth enter thy house, and a mildew upon thy estate, for in keeping it, thou art no other than a pack horse to Thomas Prence – thou art set in the midst of a company that's like a hedge of vipers; the best of them is not worthy to hew wood in the house of our God, &c."

These severities against the Quakers were happily checked soon after the restoration of Charles II. The government of Plymouth Colony, in June 1661, despatched a declaration of adherence, as did the other Colonies. The King's mandamus which followed, was addressed to Gov. Endicott and all the other Governors of New England. It is worthy of a place in the history of these times.

"Charles   R.

"Trusty and well beloved, we greet you well. Having been informed that several of our subjects amongst you called Quakers, have been, and are imprisoned by you, whereof some of them have been executed, and others (as hath been represented to us) are in danger to undergo the like: we have thought fit to signify our pleasure in that behalf, for the future; and do hereby require that if there be any of those people called Quakers amongst you now, already condemned to suffer death, or other corporal punishment, or that are imprisoned, and obnoxious to the like condemnation, you are to forbear to proceed any farther therein: but that you forthwith send the same persons (whether condemned or imprisoned) over to this our kingdom of England, together with the respective crimes or offences laid to their charge, to the end that such course may be taken with them here, as shall be agreeable to our laws and their demerits; and for so doing, these our letters shall be sufficient warrant and discharge. Given at our Court at White Hall the 9th day of September, 1661, in the 13th year of our reign.

By his Majesty's command,
WILLIAM MORRIS."

Such severities against the Quakers were both cruel and impolitic. No one is found to justify them now: and on reviewing the language of the government and that of the Quakers, we can scarcely decide which had the advantage in "railing accusations." After the government of Massachusetts had proceeded to extremities with the Quakers, they seem to have felt some anxiety, how the story would tell in history, and therefore they entered upon their journals a kind of justification of their proceedings, October 8, 1659. We will let them speak for themselves. (The following is an extract).

"A law was made and published, prohibiting all masters of ships to bring any Quakers into this Jurisdiction, and themselves from coming in, on penalty of the house of correction, till they could be sent away. Notwithstanding which, by a back door, they found entrance; and the penalty inflicted on them (proving insufficient to restrain their impudent and insolent obtrusions) was increased: which also being too weak a defence against their impetuous and fanatic fury, necessitated us to endeavor our security; and upon serious consideration, a law was made that such persons should be banished on pain of death, according to the example of England in their provision against Jesuits; which sentence being regularly pronounced at the last court of Assistants against these parties, and they either returning or continuing presumptuously in this Jurisdiction after the time limited, were apprehended, and owning themselves to be the persons banished, were sentenced by the Court to death, which hath been executed upon two of them. Mary Dyer, upon the intercession of a son, had liberty to depart, and accepted of it. The consideration of our gradual proceedings, will vindicate us from the clamorous accusations of severity. Our own just and necessary defence calling upon us (other means failing) to offer the point, which these persons have violently and wilfully rushed upon, and thereby become *felones de se* as well as the sparing of one, upon an inconsiderable intercession, will manifestly evince we wish their lives absent, rather than their deaths present," It would seem that this justification was necessary to be made publick at the time, in order to subdue the clamours of the people.

This is the only apology that can have any weight, for those proceedings, viz. the fact that it was not so much for their religious principles, as for their disturbance of the peace by their disorderly conduct, that they were punished: nor can this bear out the government in their severities. Cotton Mather collects a variety of their sayings, both from their books and their preachers, such as "we deny *thy* Christ – we deny thy God, which thou callest Father, Son and Spirit, &c." They held that no respect was to be paid "to the outward Christ now, he having ascended to heaven, but to the Christ formed in them." They held "that the Scriptures do not tell people of a Trinity, nor three persons in God, but that those three persons are brought in by the Pope – that justification by that righteousness which Christ fulfilled in his own person without us, is a doctrine of devils – that all governments and courts of justice are a tree that must be cut down." The same historian, after naming some of their wildest and most frantic disorders, and relating for a fact that two women were "adjudged to the whipping post for coming into our assemblies," entirely divested of their clothes; still does not venture to justify the government in capitally punishing the Quakers. He commends "the wise and prudent counsellor in Plymouth Colony who propounded 'that a law might be made for the Quakers to have their heads shaved,' " for which we thank him, and, could have thanked him more, had he informed us who that facetious counsellor was. On the whole, it is now pretty well understood that the true spirit of religion, as well as the true policy of government, is, to tolerate. Nothing will soften the fury of fanaticism like this: and the government of Rhode Island fairly outwent the age, and stepped forward nearly a whole century, when they were meek and politic enough "to let them say over their revelations" without molesting them.

This sect may be said to have been established in Scituate by Edward Wanton, who, after having assisted in Boston in the execution of the Quakers in 1659, became at first won to pity, then convinced of injustice on the part of government, and then converted to their principles. He retired from Boston to Scituate, about the time that the corporal punishment was ended by king Charles, (see life of Edward Wanton in family sketches). He soon gathered a considerable audience, and may be said to have been a successful propagator of his sect. He now stood in danger of no fine for holding meetings, for no punishments after 1661 were inflicted, save such as were proper to be inflicted on breaches of the peace in a civil sense. He had free access to many houses in Scituate, and won some respectable followers, particularly several of the family of the distinguished Cudworth. But it was not until 1678, that the society became so numerous as to require a house of publick worship.

In 1678, Henry Ewell sold a small piece of land to Edward Wanton, John Rance* and others, for the scite of a Meetinghouse. This scite is now enclosed in the garden of the late judge William Cushing, at the north-east end. The house was sold to the Cushing family, many years after, as tradition tells, and converted to a stable. Another was built, which is now standing in Pembroke, a half mile south of Barstow's bridge, in 1706. This place was selected because the society in Scituate had diminished. It is a curious fact, that this sect in Scituate, which had been shielded rather than persecuted, and which was numerous in Wanton's time, had become almost extinct in one century, and that now, it is reduced to two families.† Previous to 1700, the principal families of this sect in the Town, were Wanton, Colman, Ewell, Booth, Chamberlain, Cudworth, Rogers, &c.

Several marriages in the Quaker form are recorded in the town records of Scituate: they are all nearly in the same form; one of which we will copy, for the purpose of showing that the name of Quaker, if it were an appellation of reproach given them by their enemies at first, as has often been suggested, it was afterward a name that they recognized in their solemn acts.

"This is to certify the truth to all people whom it may concern, that Richard New of Newport on Rhode Island, and in the Colony of Rhode Island and Providence Plantations in New England, and Sarah Colman of Scituate in the county of Plymouth, in the province of Massachusetts Bay in New England, daughter to Thomas Colman of s^d Scituate, having intentions of marriage, according to the ordinance of God, and his joinings declared of in the Scriptures of truth, with their parents' consent, did lay or declare their intentions before the men and women's meeting, at the house of Robert Barker in the township of Duxbury, in the province aforesaid, the 2d day of the 7th month called September 1702: which said meeting

---

* John Rance removed to Barbadoes, (Scituate Records).
† The respectable families of Daniel Otis and Adam Brooks.

ordered them to wait till the next men and women's meeting for answer; which s^d meeting, appointed two men and two women to enquire whether the woman was clear from all other men: and so the next month the said Richard and Sarah appeared the second time before the men and women's meeting at the house of s^d Robert Barker, the seventh day of the eighth month 1702, and the persons appointed to inquire made answer, they had enquired and no opposition appeared, having also a certificate of the man's clearness, and satisfactory account of the woman from the friends of Rhode Island, the place of his outward abode, she also having sometimes inhabited there, having a publication set up in each town of Newport and Scituate, according to law; and all things in pursuance of the same being clear, the meeting acquainted s^d Richard and Sarah that they were left to their freedom, to consummate their marriage in the counsel of God, and to have not less than a dozen witnesses of relations and people: and all things being clear as abovesaid, a meeting of the people called Quakers, with others was appointed at the house of Thomas Colman in the afores^d Scituate, the 8th day of the 8th month called October 1702, where after some time in waiting upon the Lord, the s^d Richard New and Sarah Colman did stand up together, and first the man and then the woman in a solemn manner did declare, in the face of the Lord and before that assembly and meeting, they took each other to be man and wife, then and there both promising to live faithfully together man and wife, till death should separate them, according to the law of God, and the practise of holy men and women of God mentioned in the Scriptures of truth, they both then setting their hands unto it."

We also are witnesses to what you say
RICHARD NEW.
SARAH NEW.

JOHN CUSHING, JR., Jus. Peace.
THOMAS COLMAN (and 26 others)."

The marriage of Daniel Coggeshall, son of Daniel Coggeshall, late of Portsmouth, and Mary Wanton, daughter of Michael Wanton of Scituate in 1726, is recorded at large in Scituate records: also that of Thomas Colman of Scituate and Mary New of Newport in 1702.

The most distinguished preachers of this society in Scituate have been Edward Wanton, who was its founder, and who continued his services unto old age, from 1660 to 1710, or later. Michael Wanton his son, succeeded his father as a preacher, and with nearly as much success, from 1710 to 1740, or later.

It now gives us much pleasure to acknowledge, that this sect, having softened into a distinguished mildness, and having manifested a peculiar generosity in maintaining and assisting the poor and unfortunate of their own society, besides bearing a part in the common burden of supporting the poor, have well earned the name of Friends, by which they have lately chosen to be known.

Baptist Society.

A Society of Baptists was formed in 1825. Meetings had been held and religious worship performed occasionally for several years; but not until the above date, did they find themselves sufficiently numerous to encourage their attempts to enjoy the regular services of a religious teacher. A small, but convenient house of publick worship was erected in 1825, and dedicated on the 17th day of August.

Their first minister was Rev. Mr. LeFavor, who officiated during the year 1825. Rev. Mr. Niles officiated something more than two years, having commenced some time in the year 1826, and retired in 1829. Rev. Edward Seagrave, a graduate of Brown University in 1822, was ordained in March 1830.

Between the terms of services of Mr. LeFavor and Mr. Niles, we may add, that the Rev. Mr. Judson officiated about nine months, and deceased at Scituate, November 26, 1826. It is worthy of remark that Mr. Judson had preached as a candidate in the first Congregational Society in 1783, and received an invitation to settle with them. He was afterward settled at Taunton over the first Congregational Society – and subsequently over the second Congregational Society in Plymouth. He became a Baptist in 1815, and left the latter Society. It is due to his memory to record his catholic and candid temper and demeanor. He remembered the former kindness of the Congregational Society, within whose precincts he had become associated with a small society of Baptists; and it was one of his last acts, to request that his remains might be buried from the Congregational church, and that the Congregational clergymen in the vicinity, as well as the Baptist, should be invited to his funeral. He was the father of the Rev. Dr. Judson, a missionary to India, well known for his zeal and perseverance in that enterprise.

The Baptist Meeting-house stands on the Cohasset road,

about sixty rods in a southerly direction from the Meeting-house of the first Congregational Society, and about ten rods easterly from the intersection of the road above said Meeting-house, and the road that leads westerly from the harbour. It is small and without a turret, but neat and commodious.

First Trinitarian Society.

In A. D. 1824, a number of persons in the first Church and Society became desirous to introduce a church covenant, which recognized the doctrine of the Trinity: but not having a majority of the church, and having less than one fourth of the parish which were ready to favour their views at that time, they seceded, and formed a new Society. Their first meeting was held by virtue of a legal warrant from John B. Turner, Esq. April 15, 1825. The next year they proceeded to build a house of publick worship; and it was dedicated November 16, 1826. It stands on the Cohasset road about sixty rods westerly from the house of the first Society, and thirty rods northerly from that of the Baptist. It is a handsome church, furnished with a spire, with one row of windows, a gallery in front, and containing fifty-six pews.

The Rev. Paul Jewett, a graduate of Brown University in 1802, and who had previously been settled at Lebanon, Me. and Fairhaven, Mass., was installed in this Church and Society, November 16, 1826.

We may mention amongst the principal founders of this Society, Messrs. Ward Litchfield, Rowland Litchfield, Deacon Israel Litchfield, Calvin Jenkins, sen. and jr. Levi Vinal and Charles Curtis.

Methodist Society.

Occasional meetings had been held by the Methodists in the vicinity of Scituate harbour, previously to 1820. In 1825, we believe, a Society was organized so far as to be legally exempted from the ministerial taxes of the first Congregational Society. In 1826, a small but neat Chapel was erected near the harbour. It stands on the lane which leads from the old parsonage to the harbour, about thirty rods north-easterly from the parsonage, and on the ancient farm of Samuel Jackson. Mr. Tailor, of the Methodist connexion, was one of the earliest preachers to this people, and instrumental in promoting the Society. Since the erection of their Chapel, Mr. Avery, Mr. Barker, Mr. Keith, and Mr. Holaway, have officiated each their year, according to the practice of rotation in the government of the Methodist Church.

ECCLESIASTICAL HISTORY.

A Church was regularly gathered in Scituate, January 18, 1634, O. S. On the arrival of Mr. Lothrop and his company, he found a considerable settlement here, a Meeting-house already erected; where divine service had been performed several years, but we are not able to ascertain precisely how long. By the arrival of Mr. Lothrop and his company in 1634, a congregation respectable for numbers, was made up, and Christian worship and ordinances established in due order. There was a ready and cheerful union between the earlier settlers and the later: it may therefore be safely concluded that they entertained nearly the same religious sentiments, and agreed in the main, in practice. For the peculiar views, sentiments and practices of the first Church in Scituate, we refer the reader to Neal's history of the Puritans; from whence it can be learned that their sentiments in general were those of Mr. Robinson of Leyden, who was properly the founder of the Independents or Congregationalists. They differed from the Brownists, (a peculiarity of which sect was, that the laity might ordain their pastors), for they held to the practice of ordaining their pastors by the laying on of the hands of the ordained elders of their own churches. Mr. Lothrop was "called to office," as it was termed, in this manner by the elders of his own church, so also Mr. Chauncy his successor, and Mr. Witherell the first pastor of the second Church, neighboring churches being invited only as witnesses of the proceedings. The first Church at Scituate, however, was not perfectly united. The controversy respecting the mode of baptism had been agitated in Mr. Lothrop's Church before they left England, and a part had separated from him and established the first Baptist Church in England in 1633.* Those that came with him seem not all to be fully settled on this point, and they found others in Scituate ready to sympathise with them. Mr. Lothrop with the greater part of his Church, removed to Barnstable in 1639,

---

* See Neal.

ostensibly for the benefit of the "hay grounds," that is, the salt marshes, but probably with a view also to avoid the agitations which began to trouble his church and people, on two subjects, viz. that of the mode of baptism, and that of removing their Meeting-house farther to the south part of the plantation. On the settlement of Mr. Chauncy in 1641, the question of the mode of baptism occasioned a separation of the Church. Mr. Chauncy would baptize by immersion only, and nearly half the Church were resolute in not submitting to that mode. This was the principal cause of the division: but we must also add that Mr. Vassall who was at the head of his opposers, entertained more liberal views of Church communion, and was willing to admit to that ordinance the members of the Church of England. The same may be said of his friend Thomas King, and Mr. Chauncy and his adherents were jealous that they "inclined to the Bishops." Some writers on the early history of Plymouth Colony, do not hesitate to pronounce him an Episcopalian; and think they find in this assumed fact, the reason why so eminent a man was not employed in some high office in the government. Whatever he may have been after he retired from this country, he seems while in Scituate to have been as well informed in, and as zealous in supporting the principles of Congregationalism as any other man in the country, (see Vassall in Family Sketches).

The Ecclesiastical history of Scituate from 1634 to 1675, cannot be related more accurately perhaps, than it may be found in certain documents hitherto unpublished, which have been carefully preserved in the second Church, in the hand writing of Mr. Vassall and Mr. Witherell. They are as follows.

Renewal of Covenant by the Church of Christ in Scituate, "distinct from that of which Mr. Chauncy is Pastor."

"February 2d, 1642,

"Wheras in former tyme, whilst Mr. Lothrop was at Scituate Mr. William Vassall, Thomas King, Thomas Lapham, Judith Vassall, Suza King, Anna Stockbridge, together with many more, were together in Covenant in one Church, and that many of them, with Mr. Lothrop our Pastor, departed and went to live at Barnstable, and did leave one part of the Church at Scituate, who by consent of all the Church, became a Church, remaining at Scituate, and admitted into their fellowship John Twisden and many more, and so continued in one Church some tyme till part of this Church called Mr. Chauncy to be their Pastor, which William Vassall, Thomas King, John Twisden, Thomas Lapham, Suza King, Judith White* and Anna Stockbridge refused to do: and that since Mr. Chauncy was called to be their Pastor, the s^d Mr. Chauncy and that parte of the Church that called him, have renounced their Church standing whereon we stood a Church together, and will be a Church together by some other standing, and so refuse us to be parte of their Church, except we will enter into a new Covenant with them, which for diverse reasons we find we may not do, but remaining still together in a Church state, and knowing that being forsaken by them, we remain a Church, yet forasmuch as some are not clearly satisfied that we are a Church — therefore —

We do here now further Covenant, and renew that Covenant that we were formerly in together as a Church, that as a Church of Christ, we, by the gracious assistance of Christ, will walke in all the ways of God that are and shall be revealed to us out of his word, to be his ways, so farre as God shall enable us. And to this end, we will do our best to procure and maintain all such officers as are needful, whereby we may enjoy all his ordinances, for the good of the souls of us and ours: and we shall not refuse into our society such of God's people, whose hearts God shall incline to joyne themselves unto us, for the furtherance of the worship of God amongst us, and the good of their souls."

A declaration entered on the Church Records, 1643.

"Whereas, since the Covenant above written was made, we have met with many oppositions from Mr. Chauncy and the rest of the Church with him, and that at the last meeting of the Elders in the Bay, and this present, it was their judgments, and that from the tyme that they denied comunion with us we were free from them, that their advice to us was, to renew our former Covenant in a publicke manner, which we are contented to do in convenient tyme: yet nevertheless we hope that all the Churches of Christ that shall take notice of our Covenant, will acknowledge us to be a true Church of Christ, and hold communion with us in the mean tyme: and whereas there was great desire of the Elders manifested that we should divide the Town and become two, Towns, as well as two Churches, some alleging that we must give way to let the other Church have

---

* Judith Vassall married Resolved White.

the larger boundes, because they were the ancient Church. We answer – that neither in respect of inhabitants in the Town, nor yet in respect of Church state in this place, is there much difference, not above two or three men: for when Mr. Lothrop the first Pastor left us, most of the inhabitants and church members went with him, in so much that of seven male church members left by the Church that went, we were three.

"2. In regard that they cast us off wrongfully, they ought to be contented that they should be at least equal with them, in the division of lands and commons: although, indeed, the lands are mostly divided already.*

"3d. Whereas some have thought fitting that their towne should come three miles from their Meeting-house toward us, we say, that such a division would take in all our houses into their town (nearly) or if they leave us that little necke of land that some of us dwell upon, that is but one hundred rods broad of planting land, and their towne would goe behind our houses and cut us off from fire wood and commons for cattle, for a mile and an half beyond our houses: and therefore the Governor's motion was most equal 'that we should set our Meeting-house three miles from theirs, and so the members of each Church would draw themselves to dwell as neare to each Meeting-house as they can, and the Town need not be divided.'

"Lastly. If that it were needful to divide the town, it were most fitting for them to set their Meeting-house a mile further from us, towards their farms and hay grounds, and then they may use those lands that now they cannot conveniently doe, and so have convenient room to receive more inhabitants and members, and that is the only way to give maintenance to their officers and enlarge themselves."

A Letter from Mr. Chauncy to the Elders and Church of Roxbury.

"Scituate 22d. 12 mo. 1642.
"Rev. and well beloved in Christ Jesus our Saviour.
"It is an argument of greate weight with us that (feeling as we are persuaded you do) is urged by the Apostle 'that the name of God and his doctrine be not blasphemed.' Therefore, in regard that it hath been credibly reported unto us, that our Church hath been grievously tra-

---

* The marshes on the river and lands adjacent to the harbour are here referred to.

duced to some of you and of other Churches in the Bay, as also in respect that some of the church members do live amongst us, whose welfare we believe you do tenderly desire to further, we have thought it our duty to wipe away this dishonor of God's name, (at least to endeavor so to do) that might any way be occasioned by us. Now for any imputations that are laid to our charge, because we are uncertain in parte, we have sent two of our brethren to give satisfaction to yourselves and others as farre as may be, withal persuaded that you walk so far by rule, as not to receive, any accusation against us, without sufficient witness and hearing of our just defence."

"Now because that other things have fallen out amongst us, that do serve to lay some blemish upon us, we have thought fit to acquaint you and other Churches with them: and they are these. That there are four persons in our plantation (by name Mr. William Vassall, Thomas Lapham, Thomas King, and John Twisden) that have challenged of late, the name of a true Church of Christ distinct from us, the beginning and foundation of which pretended Church, we have found to be this. Upon Mr. Lothrop and his brethren's resolution to depart from this to Barnstable, there was a day of humiliation kept at Mr. Hatherly's house, by the rest of the brethren that purposed to stay at Scituate, and as some of them do constantly affirm they entered into Covenant with God and Christ and with one another, to walke together in the whole revealed will of God and Christ.

"This meeting, the four above named persons account to be the beginning of their Church, and yet two of them (by name Mr. William Vassall and John Twisden) were absent from it, and the other two (Thomas Lapham and Thomas King,) tho' they were present, yet since, before many witnesses, have resolutely denied that themselves expressed. any covenant by word of mouth: but however, they say that they made an implicit Covenant, which they judge sufficient to constitute a true Church, whilst we do not, and therefore could not hold communion with them upon any such ground.

"Besides, though they have of late renewed Covenant together, yet we judge that it was done surreptitiously, without any notice given to our Church beforehand, who had just exception against some of their members that renewed it.

"And that it was done suddenly, in that extremity of the greate snow on the 26 of the 11 mo. when few could come at them without apparent danger. and

"Also (we hear) it was done irreligiously without fasting or prayer needful for so greate a business.

"Besides, we cannot excuse the meeting from being factious, there being already a Church gathered: and we have offered them several tymes, that in case we saw cause, they might joyne with us, which they still refused.

"Lastly. They have since great multitudes added to them, (as we hear) nine or ten in a day, concerning diverse of whom we have just cause to doubt, that they are not lively stones for such a spiritual house.

"And these things we desire you, as you have opportunity, to acquaint at least the elders of other neighbor Churches withal, that neither yourselves nor they may have communion defiled by any of them offering to communicate with you.

"Now our Lord J. C. and God even our Father give you to hold fast your integrity and increase all heavenly graces in you.
"In our Common Saviour
"Your loving brother

"CH. CHAUNCY { in the name and with the consent of the rest."

The following answer was addressed to Mr. Chauncy, March 1643, and entered on the Church records.

"Sir. Since we must answer your letter of complaints against us, we will let pass your preamble, and rank your discourse of causes and complaints and much untruth under ten heads, for order and brevity's sake, as you will find them signed in the margin.

"1. It is well that you have found a beginning and foundation for our Church (though you intend to rase it, as you have done your own) and we assure ourselves that you can find no better for yourself; for if you found us a Church, you were received a member and ordained a Pastor of that Church.

"2. 3. We count not the meeting at Mr. Hatherly's house, the beginning of our Church, and you did not well so peremptorily to affirm what you knew not: neither do we hold, much less say (as you subtly insinuate) that we have no express Covenant, much less slight it, but have our Church grounded on express Covenant.

"4. We did not renew our Covenant surreptitiously: we secreted nothing by fraud from you: for you had before sent messengers to tell us that we were not of your Church: and if you have any just exceptions against some of our persons you have broken Christ's rule which requires 'If thou hast aught against thy brother, to tell him between thee and him, &c.' but thy brother intreats thee to shew him his offence and offers satisfaction, and yet you will cast evil reports abroad of him, who may not know the fault committed. Can you clear this your passage from slander?

"5. You have untruly reported the suddenness of our meeting, the extremity of the greate snowe, the month, the day of the month in which it was: and also the apparent danger of the meeting, and all to the intent to defame us, as if it has been appointed to avoid others coming to us: whereas, some of your members were invited to be with us, and members of Roxbury and Barnstable, and both men and women were present, without any appearance of danger.

"6. You would have it understood that our meeting was so irreligious as that we did not call upon God by prayer for his blessing upon us and others: you subtly insinuate when you say it was done without fasting and prayer: and having written fasting *or* prayer, lest that would be too greate to affirm you dashed out or and put in and, so that you might have some color of excuse: but if you had meant plainly, you would have also have put out prayer from your exception; so that we cannot but observe that you would write what you could devise in the subtlest manner that you could, against us: and yet, for that we had not a fast, we had the precedent of our first division when Mr. Lothrop was here, before us.

"7. Your charge of faction is (on the ground) that there were a Church here; and yet you were no more a Church without us than we were without you: and indeed you had cast us off and we were not of you. Nor doth the Township make a Church. And as for your offering us to joyne you, 'if you see cause,' you might have mocked a Papist with such a delusion, for they may join with you 'if you see cause.' And what cause did we see more to take you to be our Pastor, than the Church of Plymouth did of which you were a member? And yet you would insinuate that we wilfully and without cause refuse communion with you.

"8. And for the exception which you have against some of those that we have added to us, you ought to tell us the persons and the grounds of your exceptions. And then it may so appear that there may be to us as many exceptions and as much ground of rash censures of some of yours, as you can have against ours, if we should give ourselves to be. 'busybodies in other men's matters,'

"9. For your greate care that you had to write to other

Churches, that they should be kept from defiling themselves by any of ours offering to communicate with any of them; it is a new doctrine to us, that if any of those that communicate together be in sin, and the church be ignorant of it, the Church's communion is defiled, and yet your words import no less.

"In the former parte of your letter, you seem as if you had often offered us holy communion with you, and seem to blame us for refusing thereof, and here you deem us so filthy, every one of us, that our holding communion with others would defile the communion of other Churches: a sudden change, too sudden to be well grounded.

"Lastly. For your subscription 'in the name and with the consent of the rest,' you might well leave out the word add, as you have done. For any thing that we can yet learn, but few ever did hear your letter read: and we have no cause to believe that all your Church would ever have been willing that you should have scandalized us in their names; and therefore blame us not because we do not answer your letter with reference to *all* the members of your Church, seeing we find such subtilty in the subscription, that three fourths of your Church may be excused, if you please.

"Blame us not for want of styles and compliments, seeing we are only to make our bare answer to an accusation."

To Rev. John Wilson, Boston.

"Scituate June 7, 1643.

"Rev. Sir. We give you hearty thanks for your courteous entertainment at our last being with you, when you were pleased to give us notice of a letter that Mr. Chauncy sent to Mr. Elliot, with the intent to be showed to the Elders, wherin he intimated some complaints of us: which letter the Church is desirous that I should answer, because Mr. Elliot hath told me the effect thereof, but not delivered us the letter or a copy. The effect I take to be this. 1. He blames us for calling ourselves the old body or Church. 2. for schisme. 3. for close combining ourselves. 4. for not calling the Church to see our proceedings, which he is pleased to call faction. 5. suspicion of some ungodliness in the meeting. 6. for injury to their Church. 7. with wrong to God's ordinances, opposing them. 8. that many poor souls may be snared by our example. 9. that his ministry is opposed by our practise. All men may perceive that the accusation is very sharp, and we conceive without cause.

"1. To the first we answer, that we and they were one Church together, and they disclaimed their Church state wherin we stood; reason and religion will show that we must needs remain the old Church, themselves being become a new one. I will not find faulte with him for unorderly proceeding, desiring only to clear ourselves. But that we were a Church, the Church at Barnstable can and doth witness, and nothing to the contrary can (I think) be said from God's word: and to this Church was Mr. Chauncy dismissed by the Church at Plymouth, and by this Church, as it then stood, was he called and ordained a Pastor, and with us the Churches here have rightly held communion. And that he hath rejected the church state in which he stood, when he was ordained a Pastor, is clear; for in the publick assembly on the Lord's day he declared it, and then admitted members anew, who were members with us before, and refuseth communion with us because we will not do the like, sending messengers to us for that purpose. So we take it to be no offence to term ourselves the old Church, that was left here at Scituate, when Mr. Lothrop our Pastor and the rest departed from us.

"2. Neither can we be charged with schism, seeing that we neither rend from them nor any other Church, but desire communion with all the Churches. 3. Nor with close combination, who were combined formerly in publick, in the presence of the whole Church before they departed, and now have renewed our Covenant, before more than twenty witnesses, some of whom were members of other churches, and some of their members were invited to be with us; so that we cannot be charged with close combination, who did only renew our Covenant and that so publickly: neither do we find either precept or practise in the Scriptures against us, nor the practise of any Church in New England or elsewhere, but the contrary in some Churches who have divided and changed their Church state, and did not call other Churches to see their proceedings (as Mr. Lothrop and Mr. Chauncy and the Churches of which they are Pastors). 4. Nor can we be blamed for not calling their Church to see our proceedings, seeing Mr. Chauncy was offended because we refused to call him into office, and it is likely he might have disturbed our peaceable proceedings. 'Nor can there be any faction in our proceedings, for faction is for some parte of a body to rise against that body, but we were, before this time, declared by them to be no parte of their body. 5. Suspicion of ungodliness upon little, and indeed no grounds, argueth greate want of charity. 6. We cannot perceive how we can do their Church any injury, by seeking the ordinances of God for the good of our souls; but it is our duty, and we sin if we neglect it. Now with them we cannot enjoy them, except we will receive Mr. Chauncy to be our Pastor, upon his terms, in his difference with us and with other Churches, in the administration of the seals,* and some other things which in conscience we cannot do. Nor can we hurt their outward estates, by leaving them to bear a greater burden than they can bear, to maintain their officers; (for which, if it were so, they should blame themselves and not us, who in all their agitations concerning the bringing in of Mr. Chauncy, neglected to call us to advise with them); but the truth is, that before we came hither, which is more than seven years since, the old Church were at difference about removing the Meeting-house toward that end of the Town, where our hay grounds and most of our lands lie, it being set, for Mr. Hatherly's ease, at the very outside of our plantation: Mr. Hatherly and some of London, having by estimation eight if not ten thousand acres of land,† beginning very near our Meeting-house, on which Mr. Hatherly makes farms, one of which is three miles northward from the Meeting-house, and our lands reach ten miles or more to the south-westward, by which runneth a faire River, navigable for boats ten miles, and hay grounds on both sides, and hath an outlet into the sea about four miles from the Meeting-house, with lands sufficient for a Township to settle upon: by that River lieth the most of our land, and there is little hay ground near the Meeting-house, but east and west remote from it, lieth good store; so that if all other differences were reconciled, yet it were the undoing of us and them both, if we do not become two Congregations, and take in more to them and us. And God, by his providence, hath so ordered things lately, that most of the lands eastward, are come into Mr. Hatherly's hands, and by wise ordering of things, a convenient Congregation may be settled with Mr. Chauncy, and another with us, and tho' we cannot live to be one Congregation, yet if we be two, we may live comfortably both. I might be longer on this point, did I not see that I shall be tedious.

" 7. He seemeth to imply that we, in our way, do oppose the ways or ordinances of God. Supposing some difference between ourselves and other Churches, or at least between

---

* This refers principally to baptism.
† See Conihassett grant described in this history.

him and us, either in judgment or practise: (an unfitting objection for him to make, who is himself differing from most of the Churches in this land, and most of the reformed Churches in the world, both in judgment and practise, in so weighty matters as the *seals*), yet we do not believe that we differ from most of the Churches, or yet from any here, in any fundamental thing, not in point of grounds of religion, for none of us ever inclined to any of those things that by the Churches here are called errors or schism, which have been or now are in question: and as for particular orders in Churches, we know that their states have in all places and ages something differed and are likely to differ, and yet without refusing holy communion; that sweet communion of souls, the love of brethren, so highly commended to us by the Holy Ghost is not broken but for great failings, unless where the adversary do get to great advantage, by the infirmities of the part refusing: from which fault we pray the Lord to keep us.

"Mr. Chauncy needs not to tell others of our differences (which many Elders both in the Bay and with us, knew before him, and it may be, more fully than himself), and yet hold it to be no such matter to refuse to hold communion with us, Neither can our own grounds breed offence in practise; for (to give you a touch in brief) we hold the practise that particular church fellowship is an Apostolic ordinance, which should be entered into by all than can attain unto it, and that the best entrance thereinto, is to manifest our graces by covenanting one with another; but in case that God denies any the means of particular Church fellowship, then the Churches, upon the manifestation of their grace, should receive them to communion: but if it be objected that such a case cannot be; I answer that it might have been my case, who, in tenderness of conscience, could not have enjoyed it with Mr. Chauncy, in respect of his judgment and practise in the governments, (and many other cases I could instance), for had not the Lord provided that we were in fellowship before, and we had wanted matter for a Church, I had been debarred Church fellowship, except I should have undone myself and family by removing, as some have done. And as for that some may think that we incline toward the Scottish discipline, I conceive the difference in that, to be more in words than in substance, and not that we differ much in the main, and this is the great matter that causes reports to grow like snow-balls bigger and bigger by rolling. But those that know us fear not our inclining to the bishops, or to receiving profane persons to the sacraments: our only wish is that some more care were taken to instruct all in religion by catechising, that we might win more to God and fit them for the ordinances: and whatever many may think, I cannot see how we are likely to practise contrary to the general practise of the Churches here: and moreover if at any tyme there be any other question that may breed suspicion of us, we are, and hope ever by God's grace shall be, not only willing but very desirous, to crave the help and counsel of the Churches of Christ, not presuming on our own conceivings: we desire to be open and free, and to come to the clearest light. 8. 'Many poor souls may be snared by our examples.' If he mean by our example, our not closing with him wherin he differeth from other Churches, we are not in fault for that: but other ensnaring I cannot perceive. 9. 'For opposing his ministry by our practise.' Be it far from us, if we take his ministry for the pure preaching of the gospel of Christ: but we must give him his due, that God hath blessed him with many excellent gifts in that kind that we oppose not: yet he is a man, and Paul had something to keep him down after his great revelations, and for aught we know, the Lord in mercy, may let him discover some weakness, lest too much should be given to man. But we do as little as oppose his doctrine, as any Pastor's doctrine in the land is opposed: but if he mean, that to practise contrary to him in some things, is to oppose his ministry, it is unfitly alledged by him that practiseth contrary to all the Churches, for by that rule he would be found to oppose all the ministry of all the pastors. Nor do we pretend to build up our Church because he is not an able teacher, but for other weighty reasons; wheras we are necessitated so to do in respect to spiritual and temporal wants that urgeth us.

"Thus having a little imparted our condition to you, hoping that you will be pleased to acquaint other elders with our just defence against former accusations or intimations of jealousy that may have come to any of your ears, I humbly crave pardon for my long letter, being very sorry that I am forced to be so large: and yet I could not avoid that particularity, for I have been much briefer than the nature of the thing requires, yet I doubt not but you in your wisdom will conceive the truth by this brief relation. Intreating your favorable construction of our candid intentions – I commend you to the grace of our Lord Jesus Christ and remain

"Your obliged in all Christian service

"WILLIAM VASSALL."

To Rev. JOHN COTTON, Boston.

"Scituate, March 9, 1643.

"Rev. and beloved in the Lord Jesus, and his grace be multiplied on you and yours. After our thankfulness to you for your great love and pains manifested to clear up our differences between us and Mr. Chauncy, and your Christian charity in holding communion with myself, notwithstanding the rumours spread of us; (tho' nothing proved); and I hear that Mr. Chauncy by his letter hath blamed you therefor.* Now further for your own and the rest of your worthy elders and brethren of your Church, as also for satisfaction of other elders and Churches of Christ living in the Bay, I have herewith by the appointment of our Church, sent you an answer to Mr. Chauncy's letter, and also a relation of our church state, beseeching you to acquaint the elders amongst you with our condition, and give us your counsel and acceptance, as you shall in godly wisdom see cause. You know that all men are subject to failings by prejudice, for they are men and not gods; and we fear that Mr. Chauncy hath conceived too much prejudice against us without grounds. And wheras he would have his letter answered, and seems to be willing to have a hearing before some elders, yet he is not contented to show us before hand who are the persons nor what are the faults he will charge our members withall, which he in general terms doth complain of in his letter, but would have us hear his accusations at the meeting without preparation to answer, which is not reasonable, and according to the rule of Christ which requires private satisfaction; and we care not to bring forth any member to publick reproof, till he refuse to give private satisfaction, much less come to the hearing of strangers before the Church have heard the same: and although we have cause to believe that he hath little against our members, yet we must walk by rule, and desire first to clear our Church state, and then let him come and see if the Church will not deal with her members according to rule. And having little hope of a fair hearing upon equal terms, we answer his accusations by writing, and have sent you two copies, to the intent that you may, if you think meet, send him one, and keep the other, to make use thereof as you see fitting opportunity, hoping that you will be pleased deliberately to weigh our condition, and commend our cause to the Lord, and also to the elders; and we shall rest at present,

---

* This has reference to a letter which we have not been able to recover.

waiting God's providence which we pray may be for his glory and our good, and commend you to the grace of Christ.

"Yours in all Christian service

"WILLIAM VASSALL."

"Sir, I entreat you to excuse me to your worthy pastor* and Mr. Elliot, that I did not write in particular to them, for paper is so scanty, that this is all that I have for the present."

To Mr. COTTON.

"Scituate, April 6, 1644.

"Rev. Sir. All due respects to yourself and your worthy pastor. I have herewith sent you, by the appointment of the Church, an answer to the letter of Mr. Chauncy to Mr. Elliot's Church. You may also be pleased to understand, that since I last spake with you, there hath been a day appointed for the meeting of the Elders in Plymouth Patent, at Mr. Partridge's house in Duckesbury, which is lately past; at which meeting some of us did attend to present to the Elders the relation of our Church state, and desire their counsel: but it so fell out that no Elders came thither but Mr. Chauncy and Mr. Bulkley: and when we saw that there came no more, we sent it to Mr. Partridge and Mr. Bulkley, and did intreat them to show it to Mr. Chauncy and desire him to make his objections against it, if he had any: and also to consider it well themselves, and be pleased to shew us their minds therin: and they shewed it to Mr. Chauncy, and they tell us that Mr. Chauncy did not deny or except against the truth of the relation, nor yet greatly against the manner of our Church state, but seemed to have some personal offence. To which we answer, that we are ready to give due satisfaction, according to the rule of Christ. And for themselves, they say, they do not deny that we are a true Church, but yet they desire to hear the minds of other Churches.

"Now Sir, the case so stands with us, that we are about to procure a member of the Church of Duckesbury to be a pastor to us: his name is Mr. Witherell, who sometime lived at Charlestown and Cambridge: he is a teacher of Grammar by profession, a man of good report here and elsewhere, and it may be he is known to yourselves, (whose advice herin we

---

* Mr. Wilson was Pastor and Mr. Cotton Teacher in the first Church in Boston.

also do entreat): but for want of approbation, it may be that their Church may refuse to part with him; and he is for the present unsettled, and he must presently be settled in some way, as God shall direct him. If therefore you shall be pleased to lend your helping hand in advising them and us, we shall remain ever thankful to you: and saving further troubling you at this tyme, I commend you and our business to Christ the Lord, the head and director of the Church, and remain
"Yours in all Christian service
"WILLIAM VASSALL."

A RELATION, &c.

"To the Elders and Churches of Christ both in Plymouth Patent and the Bay.

"The Church of Christ in Scituate, distinct from that of which Mr. Chauncy is Pastor, sendeth greeting in our Lord Jesus Christ.

"Rev. and beloved, &c.

"It is an argument of great weight with us, that in all things we should 'approve our ways before the Lord;' and knowing that there have been some doubts and scruples raised concerning our Church state amongst some of the Churches, we are desirous to present unto your view a brief recital of the same, in humility and sincerity, craving your judgments concerning our Church state, whether you judge it to be according to the rules of Christ or not, that you may consent to give us the right hand of fellowship as we now stand, if we be in the right way, or otherwise that you would be pleased by the direction of God's word, to help us to be settled in the right order of the Churches of Christ.

"In former tymes, many of us, with Mr. Lothrop our Pastor were in Covenant together; and that state is not questioned. The greater parte, with the Pastor, departed and live at Barnstable. Before their departure, the Church assembled of purpose that they might provide to leave the remaining parte in a Church state. The Pastor propounded to those that stood up, whether they resolve to become a Church or not. Certain of the brethren answer that they desire so to do. The Pastor then desires them to show themselves, who they be that desire it, who declare themselves, and they were about eight men. Then he propounds to the Church whether they judge these brethren meet to be left as a Church by themselves, and the

Church answers in the affirmative. Then the Pastor replies to the brethren that desire to be a Church, that they must covenant to walk together in the ways of God, according to his revealed will; to this they answered that they would so do; and one of them answered, 'for aught I know in the same ways that we now do.' So that the Church was well satisfied, and agreed to declare in publick on the Lord's day 'that these were separated and become a Church.' And so when the day came, the Pastor began to declare the same, and then one of the brethren that had before agreed, upon his own mind, and without consent of the rest, desired to have the Pastor forbear for the present. It seems that he had taken some conceit, that those that were to remove would not remove: so that after this it was thought fitting to set a day apart to seek God, partly to clear up his doubts, and partly to know God's mind concerning Mr. Blackwood, whom we had some thoughts to procure to be an officer for us. So we sent for him and he came to us and kept the day; and after the exercises performed, then every one being asked about his mind to proceed, there was a full consent manifested by all that were present: and this was soon after published on the Lord's day by the Pastor, who required those brethren 'to walk together in all the ways of God,' and they all consented. After this, both the Church that departed, and all other Churches that knew us, held communion with us as they had occasion, and to us as a Church was Mr. Chauncy dismissed by the Church at Plymouth, and by this Church was he ordained a Pastor. And this is that Church state that Mr. Chauncy now questions, and hath publickly disclaimed (having said in publick that the Church could not stand thereby) and finds another, that is to say, from the time that he was admitted a member to us, being a day set apart for a fast upon other occasions. But it seems, that on that day, they did also renew our Church Covenant as we then stood a Church: and himself confessed, when he disclaimed our Church state, 'that they did not intend to make a Church by renewing Covenant;' for said he 'we thought ourselves to be a Church:' and he said, however there was a Covenant and that was sufficient, and to that Church state we will stand, and presently admitted diverse of our members over again, because they were not present at their renewing Covenant that he speaks of when he was received a member of our Church. Till this tyme we stood together as a Church. But after this they sent us word that we were not parte of their Church, and except we would renew our Covenant with them again, they would not accept us to the seals with them. And this is the ground of their Church without us.

"Then we, seeing that they had cast off their Church state that we stood in together, conclude that we remain the Church which we were but a part of before the other part had fallen off from us. We resolved not to wrong ourselves, nor yet the Church of Barnstable that left us here a Church, so much as to disclaim our true Church state, for so uncertain a Church state as they that had forsaken us had, and desired us to stand by with them. And therefore we met together and called many witnesses unto us, both members of other Churches and others, and renewed our Covenant, and did 'further covenant (for avoiding all doubts and scruples that have arisen or might arise) that we, as a Church of Christ would walk in all the ways of God that are or shall be revealed to us by his word to be his ways, so farre as the Lord should be pleased to enable us.' And this is the Church state that we stand by without them. And if you shall find it to be according to the rules of Christ, we entreat you to manifest the same to us, and give us the right hand of fellowship, but if otherwise, we entreat you to shew us our mistake, and to direct us by God's word what we ought to do, to be settled in the right order of the Churches of Christ: and we shall bless God for your help, and be thankful to you for your brotherly love and pains for us, desiring the Lord to manifest his mind to us, that we may do his will."

The above relation having been sent to the elders in both Colonies, received formal answers, near the close of 1643. The answer of the elders in the Bay we have not been able to recover; we learn however from Mr. Vassall's letters, and from the proceedings of the Church afterward, that it was of a different tenor from that of the elders of Plymouth Patent, in some respects.

Answer of the Elders of Plymouth Patent to a Relation, &c.

"From what we have heard alledged and proved, we consent —

"1. That the brethren that were left at Scituate by the Church that went to Barnstable, were left in a Church state.

"2. That Mr. Vassall was really dismissed by the Church that went to Barnstable, to the Church that was left at Scituate.

"3. Therefore we judge that the message sent to Mr. Vassall and the rest, to signify the denial of them from communion with them, cannot be excused.

"4. We do further judge, that the afores^d members, who, upon the message sent to them, did gather themselves into a new body, was irregular, 1, because done without seeking consent of the Church whereof they were members: 2, because done without consulting with other Churches: 3, because done without solemn humiliation.

"5. We do desire that both parties would seek mutual reconciliation and reunion, by all due means: but if reunion cannot be obtained, we see not how the aforesaid members can proceed to be a distinct body, without the consent of the Church whereof they are members. And we also earnestly desire, that after their mutual conviction of miscarriage, the Church should grant them, upon their request, an orderly dismission."

To Rev. JOHN ELLIOT,* Roxbury.

"Scituate, April 6, 1644.
"Worthy Sir.

"All due respects to you premised, &c. Be pleased, I pray, to take notice of our condition, and lend us your helping hand to advise us in our business. You may be pleased to remember that at my last being with you, we had some little speech about Mr. Witherell's being invited to us to be an officer, either Pastor or Teacher, and you did give a good report of him: and that I informed you, that he made such doubts of his fitness for the place, that I feared he would not embrace our offer. But since which time, we perceive that God has given him more freedome of spirit for the work; our desire therefore is, that you would be pleased to advise with the Elders of Boston, and some others, as you shall see fitting, and help us by your godly counsel, that both he and we, and the Church of Duckesbury, of which he is a member, may receive such light from God's word by your means, that in our progress, God may have the glory, and his people satisfaction and comfort. As for our Church state, Mr. Cotton hath the relation therof, and also an answer to Mr. Chauncy his letter, and further relation of what hath since been done at Duckesbury: and if I thought that you did desire the relation of our Church state, and the answer to Mr. Chauncy his letter, for your own particular use, or the satisfaction of the Church, I should send them to you: but I desire the rather to forbear awhile, till I

---

* This was the famous "Apostle Elliot," so called, on account of his success in establishing a Church amongst the Indians at Nonantum, now Natick, about 1646. He was pastor of Roxbury from 1632 to 1690.

see whether Mr. Chauncy will reply or not: though I think he will not, for I cannot see to what purpose it should be, seeing we have written nothing but what is evidently to be proved: and our case so stands with Mr. Witherell, that he must suddenly resolve on his course, having no means to live upon at Duxbury. Now that I be not tedious to you, I shall cease to trouble you any farther at present, commending you to the Lord, beseeching him to direct you and us, so to order our counsel and proceedings, that himself may have the glory, and his people comfort, and ourselves peace and increase of grace.

"I remain yours in all Christian service

"WILLIAM VASSALL."

To the Rev. RALPHE PARTRIDGE, Duxbury.

"Scituate, May 1, 1644

"Worthy and Rev. Sir.

"After many thanks for your love and desire to clear up the differences with Mr. Chauncy and ourselves, you may be pleased to remember, that at our last being with you, you returned us answer from Mr. Chauncy (after a sight of our Church state) that he was desirous to refer the differences amongst us to the Elders of Plymouth; with which we have acquainted the Church, and their answer is this.

"That they desire to refer the Church state to the Elders and others, and to give satisfaction to all Churches: and also will not refuse any hearing at Plymouth as he desired: but for personal offences, they must proceed according to rule, first in private, and if we cannot satisfie him, to require the Church to deal with the offender, and if the Church do not see him satisfied, then the Church will be ready and willing to show their proceedings before the Elders, and the reasons of their not being satisfactory to him; and this they desire that you would be pleased to return him for our answer.

"Now wheras you know that we desire to enjoy Mr. Witherell to be an officer unto us, if God shall be so pleased, we desire that the Church of Duckesbury would be freely willing to consent to us, and for that purpose that you would shew them the Relation of our Church state, and we shall be ready to approve the same for truth; but we intreat them not to hinder our proceedings, without shewing us the cause of offence, that it may be removed by us.

"I commend you to the grace of God in Christ Jesus, and remain   Yours in all Christian love and service

"WILLIAM VASSALL."

A Reply to "the Answer of the Elders of Plymouth Patent to a Relation, &c."

"N.B. Entered on the Church Records without the preamble.

"At your meeting at Plymouth you judged our act irregular in gathering our Church: 1, for want of the consent of the Church of which we were: 2, for want of consulting with others: 3, for want of a day of solemn humiliation.

"We further wish that you would shew us what rule of God's word we have broken, for want of asking their consent, that denied us to be of their Church, and denied the Church state that we stood in together with them: or to shew us how we were bound to them during their pleasure: or that we nay not leave the Church for their bringing in a Pastor that in conscience we think not fitting. And is it not a sufficient discharge to consent that we should not have their Pastor to be our Pastor, and that we may join any other Church, and they will hold communion with us? We entreat you to prove by the word of God our irregularity. 2. We do not see that it is essential for members of a Church to consult with other Churches, when they renew their covenant, to establish them a Church, when they had been fitting church members before: we desire you to prove by God's word, our irregularity. 3. We see not that solemn fasting is essential to renewing a covenant; therefore we desire you to prove from God's word, our irregularity in that point. We desire, in point of irregularity, whether you mean the irregularity to be such that it annihilates our Church state; if so, we pray you prove that by God's word: or whether you mean some rule amongst you that we know not of: if so we are willing to give you such reasonable satisfaction as is meet."

Letter to Rev. JOHN RAYNER,* Plymouth.

"Scituate, August 28, 1644.
  "Worthy Sir,
"You know what trouble hath arisen amongst us, about your expression of your opinions at Plymouth, about our remaining members of Mr, Chauncy's Church. You gave three reasons for what you said, all which did not give satisfaction either to ourselves or to others. Neither did that letter of

---

* Mr Rayner was pastor of Plymouth from 1635 to 1655, when he removed to Dover.

yours give Mr. Chauncy any cause to do as he hath done, but his prejudice is since more manifest, by his complaint to government that he is in fear of his life for me: this you all and all that know me, will conceive to arise from passion and not from any just cause for fear. Because we deny his authority over us, and justify ourselves in forming a Church after we were cast off, he breaks forth into passion against me, and accuseth me that he is in fear of his life. We have offered them to confer in private, or to dispute it before the Governor, Mr. Hubart* on our part and any two that they will bring on their part, but nothing will be accepted. Consider now I pray if it is meet for us to come into Mr. Chauncy's company, or to have any dispute with him in any way, or to be under his authority. Passion and prejudice are no fit Governors. Messengers from Mr. Chauncy's Church inform me, that there is a meeting at Marshfield, and that their Church would meet us there, and reason on our business. If they will appoint a man to dispute before you, I will lay all aside to attend the business, provided that their Pastor be absent, for it is not reasonable that I should meet where he is, seeing he complains that he is in fear of his life for me.

"Thus commending you to the grace of Christ, I rest

"Yours in all Christian love

"WILLIAM VASSALL."

To the Rev. RALPHE PARTRIDGE, Duxbury.

"Scituate, April 9, 1645.

"Worthy Sir. My love and my wife's to you and yours. I read your letter dated 8th Apr. 1645, wherein you intimate that some advise us to forbear our work in hand, and that they say that they have many weighty reasons for it. And do you think us such dupes that we cannot discern thereby, that there is a plot of Mr. Chauncy in it, and of those that adhere to him? Shall we never be at rest, nor suffered to worship God according to our consciences? Is it a small persecution to keep us and ours in a state of heathen? And how is it that the persecuted have become persecutors? The Lord judge between them and us. For my part, I hope I shall never give over all lawful means to enjoy God's ordinances: and if through persecution, we be debarred in New England, we must wait till the Lord remedy it here, or we can return to the land of our

---

* Without doubt, Rev. Peter Hobart, first pastor of Hingham.

nativity again. But I admire that you are so soon taken in this plot, as to advise us to forbear God's worship. What evil are we about, that we should be advised to forbear? Is it not lawful and commendable to seek God's favour by fasting and prayer? And is it not lawful for God's people to renew a covenant of obedience to him in his ways? Sure I am that our greatest enemies cannot charge us that we are going about any evil. The Lord direct us, that we sin not against him, nor fear the faces of our persecutors. As for their weighty reasons, when we shall see them, we shall desire the Lord to show us the weight of them, and if there be none, I desire that we may not be troubled with them. In the mean tyme we must not mock God; seeing we have appointed a day for his worship we must perform it, and we conceive it is sinful to dissuade us from it. Thus commending you to the grace of Christ, I remain

"Yours heartily in all good service

"WILLIAM VASSALL."

Before finishing this letter I read the Elders letter, wherein the plot of Mr. Chauncy is discovered. I have answered their letter to Mr. Bulkley, which you may see.

To the Rev. EDWARD BULKLEY,* Marshfield.

"Scituate, April 9, 1645.

"Rev. and worthy Sir.

"I have received your letter of April 8, 1645, and take notice that you would have us defer our meeting till the Elders in the Bay may come hither, and that our members (as I understand it) may be catechised concerning their work of grace; and that myself may give you satisfaction concerning my judgment in Church matters. I answer, that we were not advised to any such thing by the Elders at their meeting: — further, that the Elders in the Bay did not wish to be present at our renewing Covenant, and agree that we are in a Church state. The scruple at the meeting was not what we were nor what we held in judgment. At Mr. Hatherley's house, I gave them for myself as much satisfaction as they desired.

"If I differ from you in judgment, I shall be thankful to any of you to show me the light; and if any of our members be

---

* Mr. Bulkley was a minister at Marshfield from 1642 to 1658, at which date he removed to Concord, and was successor to his father in 1659. John Bulkley, a son of Mr. Edward, died in Marshfield 1658.

accused by any as not fitting matter for a Church, we are ready to hear any complaint in a Church way according to godliness. But our work is to manifest our Church Covenant, and to renew our Covenant according to advice and counsel. The day is appointed, and I conceive the Church is not likely to alter it; if therefore any be pleased to take notice thereof, they may be satisfied that we are in a Church state; and then if any officers can reprove us of unsoundness, we shall be ready to hear them according to God's word. But sure I am that it cannot be an offence to any, that we seek God's favour by fasting and prayer and to declare and renew our covenant: and therefore I intreat you to rest satisfied in what we are about: and I intreat you to signify to Mr. Partridge and Mr. Rayner what my answer is, as soon as you can.

"Thus commending you to the grace of Christ I remain
"Yours in all Christian service.

FACSIMILE.

"To the Churches of Christ in Duckesbury and Marshfield.*

"Scituate, August 19, 1645.
"Grace mercy and peace be multiplied, &c.
"Beloved Brethren.

"You may be pleased to understand, that by the gracious assistance of God, we purpose on this day fortnight, being tuesday the 2d day of Sept. to hold a solemn fast: and then we purpose to call our beloved brother Mr. Witherell to the office of Pastor of our Church. If it please you to send any of your brethren to us to be witnesses of our proceedings, and help us by their prayers in that work, their presence shall be acceptable to us.

"Our meeting is intended at the house of our brother William Hatch.

"WILLIAM VASSALL,
WILLIAM HATCH,
} in the name and by the appointment of the Church."

---

* Mr. Richard Blinman from Wales arrived at Boston 1642, (says Winthrop II. 64), and went to Green's Harbour. He was the first officiating minister at that place – called Rexham by Mr. Blinman and his people: but when it

Mr. Vassar and his friends went steadily but deliberately forward in their objects and designs, following the advice of the Elders in the Bay, over whom Mr. Chauncy seemed to have much less influence than over the elders of Plymouth patent. Early in 1645, it began to be foreseen that Mr. Witherell had resolved to yield to the importunities of the Church at Scituate, and to a sense of his own duty, even in the face of the opposition of the Elders of Plymouth, and the resolution of the Church of Duxbury not to dismiss him and recommend him to the Church which desired him for a pastor, and as a last effort to defeat these proceedings, several Churches were induced to interpose their advice, as it would seem unasked by Mr. Witherell and his friends. We copy one or two messages of this kind from our records.

"A message to Mr. VASSALL from the Church of Plymouth. By JOHN COOK.

"Plymouth, April 14, 1645.
"The Church of Plymouth is of the same mind together with the Elders which sent unto you, hoping in charity that you will desist upon it, from your present and intended proceedings; but in case you should go on notwithstanding the advice given, the Church of Plymouth shall question communion with you."

The "calling to office," that is, the ordination of Mr. Witherell, took place September 2, 1645. It was unquestionably performed by the laying on of the hands of the ruling elders of his own Church, and perhaps other church members. Mr. Witherell had been received by the Church as a member, without any doubt, notwithstanding the Church of Duxbury, as it would seem by Mr. Chauncy's influence, refused to dismiss him. This was a case which was not provided for, we believe, in any of the practical rules of Church order, previous to that time, but a case which might happen often again. A member of a Church being oppressed in that manner, certainly ought to find some remedy for his case: And it is more than probable that this very case was one principal cause of that clause in the platform providing for such cases. The synod that formed

---

was incorporated, called Marshfield. Mr. Blinman left Rexham after a few months, officiated a short time at Gloucester – then at New London – afterward at New Haven – and at Newfoundland 1659, where he was invited to settle – but he proceeded to England, and died in the ministry at Bristol.

the platform met the next year, (1646), and the controversy here, had agitated both colonies.

At Mr. Witherell's ordination there seem to have been present some messengers of neighboring Churches, but we believe they were present rather to remonstrate against than to assist in the ordination. For example, Josiah Winslow, Esq., afterward the Governor, was present as a messenger from the Church of Marshfield, and delivered in writing the following message, which we find on record.

"Marshfield, September 2, 1645.

"The Church at Marshfield advise Mr. Vassall and the rest to forbear for a time the ordination, till Mr. Witherell shall have tendered satisfaction to the Church of Duxbury for his sudden departure." Whether Mr. Winslow, who was a magistrate, approved of the message which he brought, or otherwise, we know not: but this is certain, that he soon after began to attend on Mr. Witherell's ministry, though living ten miles distant, and brought his children hither to be baptized by his hand.

An answer to the Message of the Church of Marshfield.

"Scituate, September 2, 1645.
"Rev. and dearly beloved in our Lord.

"We cannot but with thankfulness acknowledge our engagements to you all, jointly and severally, for your advice, counsel and countenance heretofore, so now in particular, for your assisting us a second tyme, in a further work by our well beloved brother your Church's messenger, to whose message unto us concerning our brother Mr. Witherell's not *walking blamelessly* and therefore forbidden by the Apostle to be admitted into office for the present, we answer: that wherein he can be convinced by any present practise, or undeniable precept from the word of God, (the only rule of faith and worship), that what he hath done hath been done repugnant thereunto, he is willing with all readiness to submit, and he hath tendered any satisfaction to the Church of Duckesbury, by the messenger sent unto him, so that he may but hear the call of the great Shepherd. Our honoured and well beloved brother Mr. Thomas your fellow member, can confirme you, how submissively he gave them satisfaction to the full, when he was last at Duckesbury, how he desired a dismission from them, waited for it longer than was by some intimated, and after this, again humbly petitioned, and was yet deferred, without any warrant from sacred Scripture, to make him hover in uncertainty. We leave to your judgments to consider of the premises. Though we could say much more, yet if any further light could be reached to our brother from the word of life, we persuade ourselves he will not dare to close his eyes against it. Let it be evidently made manifest by the word, that our brother is still a member of them, and then both they and you, and all Churches in the Country, to whom he hath by this act given offence, grieved their consciences, and scandalized the gospel, shall have Christian satisfaction. Thus, dearly beloved and affected in the Lord, returning you hearty thanks for your Christian, godly and grave advice to us, and carefulness for us, we take our leave, and commend you to the grace of God in Christ.

"WILLIAM WITHERELL,
WILLIAM VASSALL,
WILLIAM HATCH,
THOMAS ROBINSON, } by the appointment of the Church."

There was a mutual attempt to become reconciled without the interference of elders or magistrates in 1649. A conference was held December 25th, at the house of Mr. Thomas Robinson. The agitators on the part of the old Church were Mr. Timothy Hatherly, Mr. Charles Chauncy, Deacon Richard Sealis, Humphrey Turner and John Woodfield. On the part of the new Church, Mr. William Witherell, elder William Hatch, Mr. Thomas Robinson, deacon Joseph Tilden and John Stockbridge. We find no trace of Mr. Vassall in this conference, nor subsequently. We know that he had gone in 1648 to England. The same accusations were brought forward by Mr. Chauncy in this conference, that appear in his letter of 22, 12 m. 1642, and nearly the same replies made that appear in Mr. Vassall's letters above. The minutes of that conference are on record, but nothing appears in them to throw any further light upon the subject in dispute, and nothing worth extracting, unless it be an answer of the venerable Mr. Hatherly to his own pastor, Mr. Chauncy, when he brought forward his accusation of schism, viz. "it could be no schism, because we had promised them a dismission whenever they should require it, and sent it to them before they did demand it."

We have many proofs that Mr. Hatherly, though he adhered to Mr. Chauncy, admired his talents, and was his principal supporter, was yet often grieved at his hasty and ardent temper.

In 1652, another motion towards reconciliation was made as follows:

"Scituate, March 5, 1652.

"To the Church of Christ in Scituate, whereof the Rev. and well beloved Mr. Chauncy is Pastor. Grace, mercy and peace be multiplied, &c. Dearly beloved in our blessed Saviour.

"Wheras for a long tyme you have stood at a distance from us, in the point of Communion in the holy things of God, we the Church of Christ in Scituate wherof Mr. Witherell is Pastor, as yet not knowing what the evil in us is that occasions the same, do earnestly entreat you as brethren, in charity you would deal faithfully and plainly with us, in discovering to us what that evil is that you see in us, which yet unto this day occasioneth the distance, so that we may be brought to the right way towards God, and give satisfaction to his people – we, not doubting that you will deal ingenuously with us, commend you to God and the word of his grace.

"WILLIAM WITHERELL,
THOMAS KING,
THOMAS ROBINSON.
JAMES TORREY,
} in the name and with the consent of the Church."

ANSWER.

"Scituate, Jan. 30, 1652.

"To the Rev. and well esteemed Mr. William Witherell, with the rest of the Society give these.

"Grace, mercy and peace be multiplied, &c.

"Rev. and Beloved in the Lord.

"It hath been no small grievance of spirit unto us, that there hath been so great and so long a distance between you and us in Communion: and there is much cause for humiliation before the Lord for it: and we do earnestly desire that the Lord would show both you and us a clear way to put an end unto it. But we are, many of us, very much in the dark about it at present: and all that we answer to your letter is this.

"That your motion that we should deal faithfully and plainly with you, in discovering unto you what that evil is that we see in you that occasions the distance, were very equal, if nothing to the purpose had been done by us before: but now seeing after three meetings of the Elders of the Churches, and one of them having the presence of the magistrates, and also another meeting of five messengers chosen by each of our Societies, you do still write unto us that you do not yet know what that evil is that is in you that occasions the distance, we cannot hope to do more nor yet so much as so many Honored & Reverend persons and such as were thought meet for the purpose, have endeavored to do already, (as it seems) to little effect. Thus desiring you to take in good part this answer of the greater company of our assembly, we commend you to him who is the Author of peace in all the Churches of the Saints.

"Yours in the Lord

"CHARLES CHAUNCY, { in the name and with the consent of the greater part."

REPLY.

"Scituate, July 8, 1653.

"Grace, mercy and peace be multiplied, &c.

"Rev. and well beloved in our blessed Saviour.

"You may be pleased to remember that some four months agone, we presented you with a request, which we conceived to be both Christian and pious in the sight of God and man, viz. 'that you would deal faithfully and plainly with us, in discovering to us what that evil is that you see in us, which yet unto this day, occasions that distance in point of communion.' Since which tyme, we received a letter from your Rev. Pastor, subscribed 'in the name and with the consent of the greater part,' wherein you intimate your grievance of spirit, cause of humiliation, and earnest desire, that the Lord would show both us and you, a clear way to put an end unto it: for, say you, (many of us are very much in the dark about it.'

"As for your grievance of spirit, it hath been the like grievance of spirit unto us, though we are not conscious of any cause of that distance between us, and therefore for our part, we do not find any cause of humiliation for it.

"We cannot but admire at your intimation of the unequalness of our motion, in desiring to see our sin which occasions the distance, for if there had been means used, as you say, to convince us of our sin, and we would not be brought to the sight of it, yet notwithstanding, when we do manifest our willingness to be brought to the sight of it, we judge it an *equal* motion.

"As concerning those meetings of Elders, whereof one had the presence of the Magistrates, which you bring as an argument to prove that there hath been means used to convince us of our sin, we acknowledge one of them, viz. that which had the presence of magistrates, altho' we had no hand in procuring them, neither did they show us any sin; but as for the other two, we are ignorant of what they met about, or of any sin they charged our Church withal. And for the other meeting of five messengers of each Society, which you bring as another argument to prove that there hath been means used, and the unequalness of our motion, you seem hereby to lay a charge of unfaithfulness upon our messengers who brought us intelligence, that we were cleared of those things which were laid to our charge, and that your messengers also seemed well satisfied; and therefore we desire you to make good that charge against them, that we may so deal with them, that neither you nor we may be guilty of the sin of not reproving our brother. Lev. 19. 19.

"And as for that you say in your letter that 'many of you are very much in the dark' concerning the distance between us, we much marvel that you should so long debar us from communion and yet many of you not know wherefore, especially considering that your Rev. Pastor himself hath declared 'that he could freely hold communion with as many of our Church as he knew,' (at our brother Robinson's wedding).

"And whereas you manifest an earnest desire that the Lord would show both us and you a clear way to put an end to the distance, our hearty and earnest desires concur with you; and therefore we do once again, in the bowels of Christ, entreat you to answer our former request, or else to refer the difference betwixt us to some Elders of other Churches mutually chosen. Thus desiring that you will now deal ingenuously and Christianly with us, we commend you to the Lord and rest

"Your brethren in Christ.

"WILLIAM WITHERELL,
THOMAS KING,
EPH^M KEMPTON,
ROBERT STETSON, } by order of the Church."

Note in the margin in Mr. Witherell's hand writing.

"This letter was read in Mr. Chauncy's Church July 16, 1653, and the Wednesday following we had lightning and thunder and storms and hail-stones flung on our innocent heads, viz. Acts 19, 20 in the application of the doctrine."

In the autumn of 1654, Mr. Chauncy retired from Scituate, and we find no further traces of these ecclesiastical troubles, until 1674, when we find on record a formal reconciliation, as follows:

"To the Rev. Elders and brethren of our neighbour Church of Christ in Scituate, grace, mercy and peace be multiplied, &c.
    "Scituate, April 1, 1675.
"Rev. and beloved in our Lord and Saviour.
        "We received a letter from you dated Feb. 18, 1674: a very Christian and loving expression of your minds, inclined to remove any just grounds of offense given in a former letter, and to desire love and fellowship with us in the holy things of God, according to the mind and will of Christ, which we have perused and considered with thankfulness to God and due respect unto yourselves, and accept it as a pledge of future mercy from God, both to yourself and to us: and we do hereby certify you that we are thereby fully satisfied, and do willingly and gladly lay aside all former offences taken up, or ancient disagreements and differences betwixt us; we desire God to forgive you and us whatsoever may have been displeasing to him. And in that you desire fellowship with us in the gospel that we may have communion one with another as the Churches of Christ, we do cordially embrace your motion, &c.

"NICHOLAS BAKER, ⎫ in the name and
THOMAS CLAP,   ⎬ with consent
JOHN DAMAN,   ⎭ of the Church."

Thus happily terminated an ecclesiastical controversy of thirty-three years. We have made large extracts from the documents, because the reader may find in them illustrations of the principles of the early settlers, and other useful lessons. It is certain that Mr. Chauncy held fast his integrity, as he called it, and never recognised any other Church in Scituate than his own. His letters were addressed to the Society, not the Church. The question which was the first Church was never settled in form. The last letter of reconciliation which we have inserted above, was directed, "to our neighbor Church," not to the first or second Church in Scituate. There was certainly much plausibility in Mr. Vassall's argument that the Church of Mr. Chauncy were the seceders, and therefore the second Church. But principles much more recently settled, decide the question otherwise, and very properly; because it was conceded that Mr. Chauncy's Church and Society together, were a majority of "two or three men," and retained the Meeting-house.

A reconciliation was easily accomplished after Mr. Vassall and President Chauncy had left the ground. The causes of the opposition between these two eminent men may partly be gathered from the above documents. Mr. Vassall often alludes to the uncertainty of the Church state which Mr. Chauncy had established for himself. He probably held him in less respect on account of the well known fact that he had been a Puritan, and had made a publick recantation, and again repented of that recantation, and fled to this country. Then his practice in the *seals,* in the phraseology of that day, was offensive to Mr. Vassall's conscience. Mr. Chauncy would baptize by immersion only, and administer the Lord's supper in the evening, and on every Lord's day. Mr. Vassall very early engaged in controversy with him on these points, as credible tradition inform us: but the substance of that controversy will probably never be recovered. On the other hand, Mr. Chauncy took offence at Mr. Vassall's liberality in admitting members to the ordinances, and suspected him of being an Episcopalian. We will not attempt to decide this question at this late period: we will only remark that the facts of his having been an approved member of Mr. Lothrop's Church, having held a familiar intercourse with such men as Wilson and Elliot and Cotton, having also recognized the validity of Congregational ordination in case of Mr. Witherell, show at least that he was no rigid Episcopalian: and we may add, that the Church in Scituate, which he laboured nearly twenty years to build up, bore no marks of Episcopacy. An exposition of his principles in his letter to Mr. Wilson quoted above, confirms also these remarks. The reader will not fail to remark in the above controversy, that the hasty and ardent temper of Mr. Chauncy often exposed him to his cooler adversary: nor can he fail to remark that the whole might have been saved, could they have appealed to any settled principles of order in the independent Churches, at that time.

The practice of immersion in the first Church in Scituate was unanimously yielded up, after Mr. Chauncy retired in 1654, and he himself was thenceforth silent on the subject.

The early Independent or Congregational Churches made a distinction in the offices of pastor and teacher: thus we account for a debate which seems to have been carried on in Scituate in 1644, whether Mr. Witherell should be called to the office of pastor or teacher. Some Churches, who were able to support both, enjoyed the services of both officers: for example, the first Church in Boston, in which Wilson was pastor, and Cotton teacher for many years. The Cambridge platform in 1648, recognizes this distinction, and describes the duty of the pastor to attend to "exhortation," and the duty of the teacher to attend to "doctrine," &c. But this distinction was soon found to be without difference enough to be preserved.

The office of Ruling Elder was also held for a time to be authorized by Scripture, as distinct from pastor or teacher or deacon. They sometimes officiated as teachers, as the learned and devout elder Brewster taught often in the Church of Plymouth, when they were destitute of an official teacher. The Cambridge platform recognizes this office, and describes its duties: "To attend to admission of members, to ordain officers chosen by the Church, to excommunicate obstinate offenders renounced by the Church, and to restore penitents forgiven by the Church, &c." The office of Deacon, according to the platform, was "limited to the care of the temporal things of the Church, the contribution of the saints, &c." But the distinction in these offices was soon yielded. The first ruling elders in the first church in Scituate were Nathaniel Tilden and Henry Cobb. Elder Cobb removed to Barnstable in 1639 or 40, and elder Tilden deceased in 1641, and no successors were chosen. The first deacons in the first Church were Richard Sealis, William Gilson and Thomas Besbedge. At the establishment of the second Church, Thomas King and William Hatch were chosen ruling elders. Elder Hatch deceased in 1651, and no successor was chosen. Elder King lived to 1691. The first deacons in the second Church were Thomas Robinson and James Torrey.

It was the practice of the early Congregational Churches to elect and ordain all officers, without any reference to the Society, and this practice continued so long as the law was in force which required church-membership as a qualification for the freedom of the Colony, or the right of franchise. Thus in all the transactions of electing and ordaining Mr. Lothrop in 1634, or Mr. Chauncy in 1642, or Mr. Witherell in 1645, there is no mention of any part which the Society bore. But Mr. Witherell's successor in 1681, was invited to become their pastor, first by vote of the Church, then by a concurrent vote of the Society: and then his support was provided for by vote of Church and Society in one body. This order of things has prevailed in this Town to the present day. Some Churches and Societies have lately begun to lay aside this distinction, and it may eventually be abolished in all transactions in which Church and Society have a common interest and responsibility.

The custom prevailed in many Churches, we believe, in all the New England Colonies, of permitting grand-parents to bring their grand-children to baptism, when the parents were deceased or were not visible members of the Church. Thus we see in the records of the second Church in Scituate, that in 1655, Humphrey Turner brought to baptism a child of his son John Turner, jr. The same year also Richard Sylvester brought two children of Nathaniel Rawlins, whose wife was Sylvester's daughter. In 1656, was baptized "Daniel the son of Daniel Pryor, and grandchild to our sister Spring." The same year also, "Mary the daughter of John Adams of Marshfield, and great grandchild to widow James." But after the above date, the custom seems to have been dropped. In Massachusetts the elders assembled by order of General Court in 1662, discountenanced this practice in that Colony, (see their answer to questions propounded to them by the Honorable General Court, proposition second).

We believe no ecclesiastical transactions have taken place in this Town in more modern times, to which we have not paid sufficient attention in our notes on Parishes, and in other parts of this work. A history of the gradual changes of religious sentiments would be both difficult and uninteresting, intermingled and often undefined as those sentiments must have been in every generation. We may say in general terms, that the doctrines preached and held were on the ground of moderate Calvinism until about 1750.* Mr. Eells in the second Church and Society, from 1704 to 1710, often preached the doctrine of election, but accompanied it with explanations closely bordering on the free will of Arminianism. He was a stout opponent of Whitefield, and induced the association in which he was a leader, to vote not to admit him into their pulpits, and to publish that vote. Since 1750, a majority of the people may have been denominated Arminian in their sentiments: and at the present time, as names are now used, a considerable majority may be termed Unitarian.

The records of the first Congregational Church are entire since the year 1707. All records previously are lost. The records of the second Church are entire from 1645 to 1690. From that time to 1704, there is a deficiency, Mr. Lawson having retired somewhat irregularly, and probably carried the records with him. From that time, the records are entire to

---

* For a representation of the liberal principles of the early pilgrims of Plymouth Colony, see Magnalia Vol. 1. p. 58.

the present, with the exception of several years during Dr. Barnes's ministry, the records of which are unfortunately lost. The records of the first Church during Mr. Lothrop's ministry were carried with him on his removal to Barnstable: and these records with those of Barnstable, were carried away by some of his descendants to Connecticut. President Stiles found them in the hands of a Rev. Elijah Lothrop of Gilead, Conn. in 1767. Holmes's Annals.

EDUCATION.

It is well known that many of the early settlers in these plantations were men of intelligence and education. It was an object of high emulation as well as of religious principle with the early Congregational Churches, to be supplied with a thoroughly educated ministry: and such, without exception, were those pastors who, having been silenced in England, came hither to minister to the little flocks in the wilderness: nay, men of education and talents were selected for the subordinate offices in the Churches. Amongst the first settlers of Scituate, (not to mention here their learned pastors), we may name Mr. Vassall, Mr. Cudworth, Mr. Hatherly, Mr. Gilson, Samuel Hinckley, (father of the Governor), Isaac Robinson, (son of Rev. John, of Leyden), Anthony Annable, Thomas King, Thomas Clap, and others, as men eminently qualified for transacting not only the municipal concerns of the settlement, but for taking part in the government of the Colony. We may add Edward Foster, John Hoar and John Saffin, who were well educated lawyers. The next generation suffered, as we may easily conceive, a considerable privation in the want of the means of education, and perhaps the third generation still more. But we are happy to find, that though the exigencies of the times forbade much attention to education, yet the secondand third generations were far from being an illiterate race of men: and that the sons of the first settlers supplied respectably the places of their fathers. As much attention, or more perhaps, than has ever since been paid to private education must have been given by that exalted race of men. Professional school-masters were few, and there was no publick provision for their remuneration. Not only the pastors, but other men of learning must have given instructions, and almost gratuitously, in their own houses. It is known that Mr. Chauncy prepared his own sons, and others, for college, and also several young men for the ministry, between 1640 and 1650. Mr.

Witherell had been a Grammar school-master by profession, before leaving England, and many proofs are left of his skill in the languages. But we are without data as it respects the schools in Scituate previous to 1677. At that date the Colony passed a law, which we believe may be fairly considered as the foundation of the present beautiful system of Free Schools in this country. The subject was commenced in 1663, in the Colony Court, by the following proposition. "It is proposed by the Court unto the several townships in this jurisdiction, as a thing that they ought to take into serious consideration, that some course may be taken in every town, that there may be a school-master set up to train up children to reading and writing." In 1670, "The Court did freely give and grant all such profits as might or should, accrue annually to the Colony, for fishing with nets or seines at Cape Cod, for mackerel, bass or herrings, to be improved for and toward a *free school* in some town of this jurisdiction, for the training up of youth in literature for the good and benefit of Posterity, provided a beginning be made within one year after s^d grant, &c." This school was immediately established at Plymouth, and was supported by the proceeds of the Cape fishery until 1677, when the following change was ordered, viz. "In whatever Township in this Government, consisting of fifty families or upwards, any meet man shall be obtained to teach a grammar school, such township shall allow at least twelve pounds, to be raised by rate on all the inhabitants of s^d Town: and those that have the more immediate benefit thereof, with what others shall voluntarily give, shall make up the residue necessary to maintain the same, and that the profits arising from the Cape Fishing, heretofore ordered to maintain a grammar school in this Colony, be distributed to such towns as have such grammar schools not exceeding five pounds per ann. to any town, unless the Court Treasurer or others appointed to manage that affair, see good cause to add thereunto. And further this Court orders, that every such town as consists of seventy families and upwards, and hath not a grammar school therein, shall allow and pay unto the next town that hath a grammar school, the sum of five pounds to be levied on the inhabitants by rate, and gathered by the constables of such towns, by warrant from any magistrate of this jurisdiction," &c.

The Cape fishery was rented annually for from thirty to forty pounds. We observe that in 1680, Robert Stetson of Scituate and Nathaniel Thomas (probably of Marshfield) hired the fishery. We cannot discover that the Town of Scituate availed itself of this bounty of the Court. It continued but eleven years: for we observe that in 1689, the rent was appropriated towards the salary of the magistrates; and after the union of Plymouth and Massachusetts in 1692, the fishery was free, as we believe. The towns of Duxbury, Rehoboth and Taunton received the five pounds, a part of the term when this court order was in force.

The first money raised towards supporting a free school in Scituate, (at least that appears on record), was a very small appropriation in 1700, viz. "The Town desired James Torrey to teach children and youth to read and write as the Law requireth, and said Torrey consented to make tryall thereof awhile, on these conditions, that he be paid 20s in money for each and every person sent to school, the parent or master engaging to pay fifteen shillings of the s^d twenty, the Town having agreed to pay the other five shillings for each, and that those that send any children or youth to the school, shall provide books, pen, ink and paper suitable for their learning as aforesayd."

In 1701, "The Town agreed with Dea. David Jacob to keep a reading, writing and grammar school for one year, in consideration of the sum of 20£; also agreed with the same person to build a school house for 20£." It was situated near Stockbridge's mill.

In 1704, "The Town directed the school to be kept one third of the year at each end of the Town, and one third in the middle."

In 1711, "The Town voted that the Select men should provide but one grammar school, and that to be kept in the middle of the Town and not be removed."

In 1712, "The Town ordered three schools, one in the middle and one at each end, appropriating 32£ for that in the centre and 16£ each for the other two."

In 1725, Mr. Timothy Symmes was employed as a grammar school master.

In 1733, "The Town voted to allow that part of the Town called the Two Miles, 6£ for keeping a school that year."

In 1765, "The Town voted to raise 10£ toward the support of a 'Latin School.' "

We need only remark, that the Town proceeded gradually to increase the expenditures for the free schools, without any remarkable change until the law of 1790. The Town had a sufficient number of families to be liable under that law to support a grammar school during the year, in which school the

EDUCATION.

Greek and Latin languages should be taught. But that law, we believe, was never complied with, according to the intent of its framers. An additional sum was raised, which was presumed to be sufficient,* and divided into five parts, and added to the money of five school districts,† requiring said districts to be furnished with a teacher qualified according to law, for teaching the grammar school. Thus the law which, doubtless contemplated one continuous grammar school through the year, was evaded by keeping five grammar schools two months each, and at the same time. This order of things continued until 1827. The law of that year has been fully complied with, save in point of the high school. This has been evaded in a similar manner to that named above. The sum appropriated for free schools has been generously raised from $1400 to $2000, but is divided to the several school districts, and no high school has yet been established. The number of school districts since 1816, has been eighteen. The number of persons over four years of age and under twenty-one, which compose the school list, amounted in 1830, to 1342. In 1827, the school district near the second Congregational Meeting-house, commenced the custom of dividing their school into two, and placing those pupils who were over eight years of age under the care of an instructer, and the younger division under the care of an instructress. In 1828, the first school district, near the harbour, with two adjoining districts, united in building a large and commodious school-house, in which all the pupils over fourteen years of age are placed under the care of a well qualified instructer.

We believe that instruction in the languages was given principally by the ministers of this Town previously to 1750. We can however name Mr. Timothy Symmes and a Mr. Fitzgerald who taught several years before that date in Scituate and its vicinity. We might name Thomas Clap and Joseph Cushing. Col. William Turner also, who graduated at Harvard College 1767, was a teacher by profession, and spent his life in that employment, chiefly in this Town.

It may be a proper appendage to these notes, to subjoin a list of such persons as have received degrees at Harvard University, and who were born in the Town, or resided here, at least in their youth.

---

* The sum raised previously had been for grammar school $133.33, in 1809, $200.

† The Town was first divided into sixteen school districts in 1790.

EDUCATION.

Isaac Chauncy, 1651, minister in Berry street, London.
Ichabod Chauncy, 1651, physician in Bristol, England.
Barnabas Chauncy, 1657, a preacher, and died early.
Nathaniel Chauncy, 1661, minister of Hatfield, Connecticut.
Elnathan Chauncy, " physician in Boston.
Israel Chauncy, " minister of Stratford, Connecticut.
Caleb Cushing, 1692, minister of Salisbury.
Samuel Mighill, 1704, died early.
David Turner, 1718, minister of Rehoboth 1721.
Joseph Bailey, 1719, minister of Weymouth.
Thomas Clap, 1722, president of Yale College.
Thomas Clap, 1725, minister of Taunton, and afterward Judge Common Pleas in Plymouth County.
Nathaniel Eells, 1728, minister of Stonington, Conn. 1733.
Nathaniel Cushing, 1728, reading law in Boston, died 1729.
Ephraim Little, 1728, minister of Lebanon, Conn.
Joseph Cushing 1731, latin school master Scituate.
Edward Eells, 1733, minister of Middletown, Conn.
Timothy Symmes, 1733, minister Millington village, Conn. 1737.
Samuel Holbrook, 1734, died early, we believe.
Isaac Otis, 1738, physician in Bridgewater.
Lemuel Bryant, 1739, minister of Quincy.
William Cushing, 1751, Judge United States' Court.
Jonathan Vinal, 1751, a preacher but not settled.
Joseph Cushing, 1752, died early.
Charles Turner, 1752, minister of Duxbury, afterward senator in Massachusetts.
Charles Stockbridge, 1754, physician in Scituate.
Charles Cushing, 1755, clerk of the Courts in Suffolk County.
Ephraim Otis, 1756, physician in Scituate and Taunton.
Nathan Cushing, 1763, Judge Supreme Court, Mass.
Joseph Bailey, 1765, died early, at Chesterfield.
Charles Curtis, 1765, deceased in New York.
Lemuel Cushing, 1767, physician, deceased in the Revol. Army.
William Turner, 1767, colonel of Militia, and latin schoolmaster, Scituate.
Rowland Cushing, 1768, a lawyer in Maine, Pawnalboro.
Paul Litchfield, 1775, minister of Carlisle.
Isaiah Man, 1775, minister of Falmouth.
David L. Barnes, 1780, U. S. District Judge in Rhode Island.
Gushing Otis, 1789, physician in Scituate.
Foster Waterman, 1789, lawyer in Maine.
Christopher Cushing, 1794, deceased in Scituate 1819.

AFFAIRS OF GOVERNMENT.

Freeman Foster, 1799, physician in Scituate.
Jotham Waterman, 1799, minister of Barnstable.
Anthony Collamore, 1806, physician in Pembroke.
William T. Torrey, 1806, minister at Canandagua and Plym.
Benjamin Hatch Tower, 1806, died early.
Henry S. Wade, 1822, physician in Hanover, died 1829.
Francis Thomas, 1828, preparing as a physician.

The above list is probably imperfect, especially in the earlier part. We think it highly probable that several persons, born in this Town, may have been educated at other Colleges, but we pursue the inquiry no further. We will only add, that Joseph J. L. Whittemore is now a member at Harvard University, and Charles Torrey at Yale. Rev. Wm. Collier graduated at Brown University 1797, and Joseph Litchtield 1773.

A list of the gentlemen who have practised Law in the Town.

Edward Foster, one of the first settlers. } had been lawyers
John Hoar, who removed to Concord 1659. } in England.
John Barker practised subsequent to 1676, a native of Duxbury.
John Saffin, 1649, and a few years later.
Thomas Turner, commenced about 1690.
John Cushing, commenced about 1680.
John Cushing, jr., commenced about 1725.
David Little, from Marshfield, 1708.
William Cushing, about 1754, died 1810.
Nathan Cushing, about 1768, died 1812.
George Little, about 1807, a native of Marshfield, died 1811.
John Thaxter, 1817, of Hingham, died 1825.
Ebenezer T. Fogg, 1821, of Braintree.

AFFAIRS OF GOVERNMENT AS CONNECTED WITH THOSE OF THE TOWN.

The laws of Plymouth Colony until 1639, had been made and executed by the Governor and assistants, the usual number of which was seven. These were elected by the whole body of freemen assembled at Plymouth annually, in the month of March. In 1642, however, the election was changed to the first Tuesday in June. The settlers had gone out into so many and so distant places, that it was found difficult for a sufficient number to attend in the inclement month of March, to give a just expression of the public mind at the polls. The Governmeat having originated in a Pilgrim Church, it was very natural that church membership should be made an indispensable qualification for a freeman or elector.* In 1636, a fine of three shillings was ordered for not appearing at the polls in the annual election. The same year it was ordered that eight additional assistants should be chosen, "to acte for the whole bodie of the Commonweale." James Cudworth and Anthony Annable of Scituate were two of these additional assistants. The fine imposed in 1636, was soon found insufficient to secure the object, and perhaps inequitable; for in 1638, it was ordered and enacted: "Wheras it is inconvenient for the freemen to attend the Courts, each Town shall choose two Deputies and Plymouth four." This was the origin of the General Court.

The following is a list of the Assistants, Deputies, &c. from Scituate, from 1632 to 1692, when the Colony was united to Massachusetts.

Assistants.

William Gillson, 1632 to 1634, inclusively.
Timothy Hatherly, from 1634 to 1655, with the exception of 1638.†
William Gillson and James Cudworth, extra assistants in 1636.
William Gillson and Edward Foster, extra assistants in 1637.‡
Timothy Hatherly and James Cudworth, assistants from 1656 to 1658.§
James Cudworth (having been restored to his proper place by Gov. Josiah Winslow, from which Gov. Prince's bigotry had for sixteen years excluded him,) was assistant again from 1674 to 1680, inclusively, when he was appointed agent for the Colony in England.

After Sir Edmund Andros, whose General Government of the New England Colonies commenced in 1686 and terminated in 1689, was seized by the people and confined to Castle William, the government of Plymouth proceeded again as usual until 1692, and John Cushing was assistant from 1689 to 1691, inclusively.

We will here add that Timothy Hatherly was Treasurer of the Colony in 1640: also a Commissioner of the United Colonies in 1645, 1646 and 1650. And James Cudworth was Deputy Governor 1680: also Commissioner one year, viz. 1657.

---

* It was yielded up also in proper time.
† He was elected that year and declined.
‡ On account of Pequot War, (see Josiah Winslow).
§ They were then left out for their lenity towards the Quakers.

AFFAIRS OF GOVERNMENT.

DEPUTIES,

Anthony Annable Edward Foster	1639-40.	James Torrey Robert Stetson	1661-62.
Edward Foster Humphry Turner	1641.	James Torrey Isaac Buck	1663-4-5.
Richard Sealis John Williams	at the adjournment.	Robert Stetson Isaac Chittenden	1666-67.
Thomas Chambers Edmund Edenden	1642.	Thomas King	1668.
Humphry Turner George Kenrick	in Oct.	Robert Stetson Isaac Chittenden	1669 to '73.
Thomas Chambers John Williams	1643.	Robert Stetson John Cushing Isaac Chittenden	1674.] additional deputy on account of a prospect of war
John Williams George Kenrick	in Oct.	John Daman Jeremiah Hatch	1675.
John Williams Humnhry Turner	1644.	John Cushing John Daman	1676.
Humphry Turner Tohn Lewis	1645-46.	Capt. John Williams Jeremiah Hatch	in Oct.
Humphry Turner John Williams	1647.	Robert Stetson John Bryant, sen.	1677-78.
Thomas Chambers John Williams	1648.	John Cushing Jeremiah Hatch	1679.
James Cudworth Thomas Clap	1649.	Jeremiah Hatch Samuel Clap	1680.
James Cudworth Humphry Turner	1650-1-2.	Capt. John Williams Samuel Clap	1681.
James Cudworth Robert Stetson	1653 to 56.	John Cushing Samuel Clap	1682 to 1686.
Edward Jenkins John Bryant	1657.	Vacancy under Andros, G. Gov.	
Robert Stetson Isaac Chittenden	1658.	Capt. Joseph Sylvester Jeremiah Hatch	1689.
Robert Stetson James Cudworth	1659*	Capt. Joseph Sylvester Samuel Clap	1690.
Robert Stetson Lieut. James Torrey	1660.	Samuel Clap Benjamin Stetson	1691.

We add a few miscellaneous matters which relate both to this Town and the Government of the Colony previous to 1692.

---

* Capt. Cudworth was rejected by the Court for his lenity to the Quakers, and not allowed to sit.

AFFAIRS OF GOVERNMENT.

The government of Plymouth Colony transacted all their business of legislation in one body, deputies and magistrates forming but one board, throughout the whole term of the separate existence of the Colony; and we believe no serious embarrassments ever occurred.* The question was agitated in 1650.

In 1636, a committee was appointed by the Court to revise the ordinances of the Colony: the committee consisted of four of Plymouth, two of Scituate, and two of Duxbury: those of Scituate were Anthony Annable and James Cudworth.

In 1654, Plymouth Colony set up the form of a government at Kennebec: two of the commissioners for this purpose were Timothy Hatherly and James Cudworth of Scituate.

In 1658, Mr. Hatherly was authorized to solemnize marriages. This was done for the accommodation of Scituate, Mr. Hatherly having declined, or rather having been left out of the magistracy. We believe it was a license for that year only, because we observe that the people of Scituate for several succeeding years were obliged to resort to magistrates in Duxbury and Plymouth, there being no magistrate in Scituate after 1658, until 1674.†

In 1665, the Town instructed their deputies "that they should move the Court to appoint some man in our Town to administer oaths, grant warrants and subpœnas, and to marry persons, &c." but we believe the Court passed no order to that effect, being determined to punish Scituate for their want of assent to the persecution of the Quakers.

In 1665, though the Town was excluded from any part in the magistracy, yet they seemed fully attentive to the common weal, as appears by the following instructions to their deputies.

---

* In Massachusetts, frequent collisions happened between the deputies and magistrates, the magistrates claiming a negative on the doings of the deputies, though sitting in the same body: therefore in 1643, it was enacted "That the Deputies and Magistrates should sit in separate bodies and send each other their acts, which should not become law without a concurrence." Thus each had a negative on the other. Hence our present Senate and House of Representatives.

† Ministers were never licensed to solemnize marriages in Plymouth Colony: and in Massachusetts, previous to the union in 1692, the magistrates retained this office in their own hands with peculiar jealousy. In 1647, the Rev. Peter Hobart of Hingham, was invited by one of his own Church, who was about to be married in Boston, to accompany him and preach on the occasion. But the magistrates being informed of the circumstance, forbade it. In their veto, one reason assigned was, "We are not willing to bring in the English custom of Ministers performing the solemnity of marriage, which Sermons at such times might induce." (Winthrop, 2d. Vol. 314).

"The Towne instructed their Deputyes to move the Corte that the Corte would be pleased to provide that law may bear its own charges; that the plaintiff suing for a just debte may not lose his labour and charges in recovering his own: and that likewise the Court would be pleased to consider a greate abuse that is amongst us, by paying of juste verdicts with old rusty barrels of guns, that are serviceable for no man, unless for to work up as old Iron." (Scituate Rec. Vol. 6.) This is the first motion that we have noticed, towards our present equitable rules of levying costs of Court, and of legal tender. Probably Mr. Cudworth was the author of it.

In 1658, the Colony Court for the second time ordered the laws to be revised, and for the first time to be published. Scituate bore no particular part in this revision, that we can learn. Indeed it was done by secretary Morton, by writing out a copy for each Town. The copy for Scituate is now extant in the Clerk's office.*

Again in 1671, a committee was raised "to peruse the laws and gather up from them or any helps they can get, and compose there from a body of lawes, and present them at the next Court for further settlement." This committee consisted of Gov. Prence, Major Winslow, Mr. Thomas as Hinkley, and Mr. Walley. The volume was printed in 1672, by Samuel Green, of Cambridge. But this volume of laws met with objections, and in 1673 another committee was raised to make a revision and collect further from the written book of laws. The following transactions of the town of Scituate seem to relate in part to the new book of laws, and in part to apprehensions of some evil to arise to the Colony, from the accession of the capricious and tyrannical James the second.

Scituate, March 11, 1684-5, "The Town being met together and being sensible that some changes and alterations may fall upon our Colony, and being willing to contribute something to the general good, by way of instructions to our Deputies, do choose seven men to consider seriously of the premises, and to impart their apprehensions to the town before the next General Court. The men chosen are Capt. John Williams, Mr. John Cushing, Jeremiah Hatch, Capt. John Briggs, Samuel Clap, Thomas Turner, Isaac Buck, sen." The committee on May 28th following, reported these instructions to their deputies.

---

*It is in secretary Morton's hand. The continuation from 1658 to 1665, is in Lieut. James Torrey's hand, and from 1665 to 1692, in the hand writing of Lieut. Isaac Buck.

"Wheras it hath been the Endeavor of this Government for the faithful and impartial administration of Justice, to have recourse to the good and wholesome laws of England, and that no laws or orders of our own should infringe upon or be repugnant thereto; yet notwithstanding our wilderness condition being so unparallelled with the state and condition of our Native Country, and ourselves unacquainted with the laws of England, may occasion some orders to be made wherin there may not appear so clear a precedent for them in the laws of England, as might otherwise have been, we do therefore commit it in trust to our Deputies, that the like care be still continued; and that in respect of making any further orders, that they be diligently compared and revised with the laws of England, in all such cases provided; and that in all civil actions commenced in any Court of this Government, if either party produce a known Law of England, in defence of his case or his person, it may be made publickly to appear that it is the law allowed of in this Government as the rule of Justice in all known Cases. And whereas there are divers acts and Court Orders yet extant, refering penalties to the judgment of the Court, without any penalty therunto annexed, that as circumstances may concur, it remains in the breast of the Judge to determine after the offence is committed, and thus give much ground to disaffected persons to entertain jealousy of partiality in Justice, being swayed according to affection or disaffection in the breast of the Judge towards the party offending, the which particular seemeth more than any other to differ from the privilege granted to us by the laws of our Nation, the which we leave with our deputies to alter, or perfect in that kind what may be already begun, hoping through God's goodness, that we may still enjoy our precious liberties, granted to us by our Gracious Sovereigns King James the first and King Charles the first and second, and by charitable constructions hoping to enjoy the like from King James the second. We also give in charge to our Deputies, that due care be taken that we have annually an able Secretary in place, and that all Justices in our Colony at each Court or Session give to the said Secretary a list of all fines, that the Secretary may record them in a Book, that the Deputies thereby may be able to call the Treasurers to a fair account, to the satisfaction of the Colony: and that Justices and all inferior officers in the Colony capable by law to receive fines by virtue of a known law, be required to give in the fines: and this to be annexed to their oaths. And that a clear and fair account be annually taken of the Treasurer, and that the Treasurer once in two years, clear and balance all his accounts with the Colony: and that the aforesaid Treasurer's effects, both real and personal, be liable to suit at Law to satisfy the fines made due to the Country; and that no Treasurer in our Colony be capable of sustaining the office, until so cleared with the Country; and the deputies to bring a true account therof to their respective Townships."

In 1673, the Town instructed their Deputies "to move the Corte that the Law concerning sending home Deputies may be altered, so that we may know what may be the just exception against them before our choice." This had reference to the new book of laws, and also to the fact that Capt. Cudworth, one of the Deputies of Scituate, had been rejected by the Court in 1659, as well as some others in the Colony.

May 27, 1686, "The Town being met together and the New Book of Laws being read, and being sensible of our inability to undergo the Change which this new form will occasion, and what consequences thereby may accrue, if changes shall come, and being desirous to prevent what may be hurtful, chose Mr. John Cushing, Samuel Clap, Capt. John Williams, Cornet Robert Stetson, Jeremiah Hatch, Elder Thomas King and Isaac Buck, to draw up our grievances and impart their apprehensions to the Town before the next Court."

The committee reported (at the next meeting, May 27) the following instructions to their deputies:

"The Town do require their deputies to do their utmost endeavor for the repealing or altering such acts or orders as they may judge inconsistent with the well being of this Colony or Commonweale: and wheras at our last meeting the Laws of this Colony being lately revised and printed and published at said Town meeting, and upon serious consideration therof the Town did apprehend several of said laws or orders to be unsuitable to our present condition, and of doubtful consequence *how they will abide expected changes:* as first — The constituting of several Counties and County Courts and Regiments in this Government, which seemeth to have such influence in all manner of actings and transactings, as to alter the frame of our ancient Government, presages a threefold augmentation of the usual charges belonging to the Government. And it seems to deprive if not disfranchise, the freemen of their liberties, and the several plantations of their, ancient privileges: wheras before, no publick charge could be assessed on the County or any part therof, but by their own vote or that of their representatives, it is now left to the disposition of others, without their consent or knowledge.

"Besides, there are several tracts of lands in this Colony suitable for plantations, the purchasers wherof must be greatly wronged to be under a distinct power of Government over them and their estates, if that government please to raise charges on those estates, different from the free tenure on which they bought the lands, before these new constitutions creating a power in which the owners of those lands had no choice or vote, as witness Freetown, Punkateest* and Showamett.†

"Another inconvenience which they find in this model is, that it seemeth to deprive the soldiers of their wonted privileges, who being inforced sometimes by unavoidable providence to be absent from trainings, in which cases they had liberty of choice of such persons as should hear their reasonable defence, which is now left in the breast of particular men. This may produce inconveniences on both sides, impoverishing the individual without any considerable general profit.

"Another particular is a burden from which the Town desires to be relieved: that is, the Act of Court, Chap. 2. p. 6. denying any further account to be given or redress to be had, or replevin to be obtained against Rates and fines. In which Court Order there is no provision made to demonstrate how they appear to be just.

"But in the last place, as that which we conceive doth not only allow the reason of what we have said, but also requires it at our hands, is the proclamation of our gracious Sovereign made known at Plymouth, that 'we should enjoy our ancient liberties and privileges as before, not altering customs or Constitutions, till his royal pleasure be to give farther order,' which we understand nothing of as yet. If these particulars cannot be granted, we require our deputies to do their endeavor that this dissent of our town, be entered on the publick records of Court."

The expected change alluded to in the above transactions took place at the close of 1686. Sir Edmund Andros arrived with a commission which vested in him and a council nominated by the Crown, the government of all the New England Colonies. It has generally been stated that he arrived at Boston December 29, 1686. If so, there is a mistake in the records of Scituate, in the date of the first order in Council from Andros. It is as follows:

---

* Now Tiverton. † Neck north of Swansey.

"By his Excellency the Gov. & Council.
"These are to declare and publish that all Officers Civil and Military, and the Officers of his Majesty's revenue, together with all duties and imposts, as now settled in this town of Boston, and other parts of this Government, are to continue till further order, and all persons are required to conform thereto accordingly.
"Given at the Council House in Boston
"Dec. 20th, 1686.
VERA COPIA. "EDWARD RANDOLPH, Secretary."
"Mr. Cushing
"After due respects, pray be pleased to publish this in your town with convenient speed.
"WILLIAM BRADFORD, one of the
"Council."
"The above said was published at a Town Meeting in Scituate the 20th day of January, 1686-7,
per me ISAAC BUCK, Town Clerk."*

It would be hardly proper in this local history to notice further the misrule of Andros and his Council, which lasted two years and four months; we will only remark that we are happy in being able to state, that no citizen of Scituate partook in his government; and that of the eight counsellors which were selected from Plymouth Colony, seven soon deserted him, and Nathaniel Clarke alone adhered to him. Clarke in April 1689, was seized and imprisoned by the people of Plymouth, nearly at the same time that the people of Boston imprisoned the Governor. After the suppression of the tyranny of Andros, the government of Plymouth resumed their administration as usual, and continued it nearly three years. We extract from the records of Scituate, their doings in answer to the advice of the Colony Council to resume the usual functions of government,

May 28, 1689, "The inhabitants of the Town of Scituate being met together, agreed as followeth:
"Wheras the Council held at Plymouth, May 1st, 1689, advised the several Towns to provide for a general Election at Plymouth, according to former Law and Usage, the Town of Scituate accept of the advice, and do address themselves

---

* Hobart's Journal records the arrival of Andros, "Dec. 20th, 1686."

so to do, as their Law and usage was during the time of the first printed book of Laws, bearing date June 1st, 1671,* before the division of the Colony into Counties, which the Town of Scituate declares against." It seems that the new book of laws, printed 1672, had hardly been enforced, especially the division into Counties, though ordered by the Court to be of force in June, 1686.

The Charter which unites Plymouth and Massachusetts Colonies, bears date October 7, 1691.

The Warrant of Sir William Phipps, Kt., Captain General and Governor in chief, in their Majestys' name William and Mary, requiring the Town to elect two representatives for "the great and Generall Court to be convened at Boston on the eighth day of June, 1692," bears date May 20, 1692.

The qualification of electors, according to that warrant was, "a freehold of 40S per ann. or other property of the value of 40£ sterling."

In pursuance of that warrant the Town chose John Cushing and Samuel Clap. The next May the Town chose Benjamin Stetson – and a precept being issued to that effect in September, the Town chose Samuel Clap as another representative.

The following is a list of Counsellors, Senators and Representatives since 1692.

COUNSELLORS.

Judge John Cushing, from 1710 to 1729, inclusively – twenty years.

Judge John Cushing, (son of above), from 1746 to 1763 – eighteen years.

Judge Nathan Cushing, 1779 to 1789, from 1802 to 1807.

SENATORS.

Charles Turner, Esq. 1773 and 4, also 1782, 1785, 6, 7 and 8.
Nathan Cushing, Esq. 1784.
Cushing Otis, Esq. 1823.
Samuel A. Turner, Esq. 1831.

REPRESENTATIVES.

John Cushing ⎫ 1692. Samuel Clap ⎭ Benjamin Stetson 1693.	Samuel Clap in Sept. 1693. Benjamin Stetson 1694. Samuel Clap 1695 and 6.

---

* This date refers to the time when the revision was ordered.

AFFAIRS OF GOVERNMENT.

John Cushing 1697.
Nathaniel Clap 1698.
Samuel Clap 1699.
Capt. Benjamin Stetson 1700.
John Cushing, jr. 1701.
Thomas King 1702.
Samuel Clap 1703, 4 and 5.
John Barker 1706.
Samuel Clap 1707, 8 and 9.
Joseph Otis, Esq. 1710.
Thomas Turner 1711.
John Barker 1712.
Joseph Otis, Esq. 1713.
Samuel Clap 1714 and 15.
Thomas Turner 1716, 17 & 18
John Barker 1719.
Stephen Clap 1720.
James Cushing 1721, 2, 3 & 4
Thomas Bryant 1725.
Maj. Amos Turner 1726, 7 & 8
James Cushing 1729, 30 & 31
T. Bryant, extra session, 1730
Amos Turner, Esq. 1732.
Thomas Bryant 1733 and 4,
John Cushing, Esq. 1735, 6 and 7, (3 gen.)
Nicholas Litchfield 1738, 39 40 and 41.
Thomas Clap 1742.
Capt. Caleb Torrey 1743.
Thomas Clap 1744.
Cap. Caleb Torrey 1745 to 49
Thomas Clap, Esq. 1750.
Ensign Otis 1751, 2 and 3.
Thos. Clap, Esq. 1754, 5 & 6.
Joseph Cushing, Esq. 1757.
Thomas Clap 1758 to 65.
Gideon Vinal 1766 to 1774.
  Congress at Salem Oct. 1774
Nathan Cushing, Esq.
Gideon Vinal   } 1774.
Barnabas Little
  Congress at Watertown, May 31, 1775,
Nathan Cushing, Esq.

  Congress at Cambridge, February 1775,
Nathan Cushing, Esq. } 1775.
Barnabas Little, Esq.
  Representatives continued,
Nathan Cushing, Esq. 1775 & 6.
Maj. William Turner   } 1777.
Nathan Cushing, Esq.
Israel Litchfield 1778.
  Delegates to Convention at Cambridge to prepare a State Constitution 1779,
Wm. Cushing, Esq. ⎫ V. Pres.
Israel Vinal, Esq. ⎬
Wm. Turner, Esq.   ⎭
  Representatives continued,
William Turner, Esq. 1779.
Rev. Charles Turner } 1780.
Daniel Daman
  Convention to ratify State Constitution 1780,
Daniel Daman.
  Representatives continued,
Enoch Collamore 1781 and 2.
Israel Vinal, Esq. 1783 and 4.
Capt. Daniel Litchfield 1785.
Israel Vinal, Esq.   } 1786.
William Turner, Esq.
Capt. Enoch Collamore 1787,
  Convention to ratify the Federal Constitution, January 1788,
    Delegates.
Hon. William Cushing ⎫
Hon. Nathan Cushing ⎬
Hon. Charles Turner ⎭
  Representatives continued,
Capt. Joseph Tolman, 1788, 9 and 90.
Israel Vinal, Esq. 1791.
Hayward Pierce, Esq. } 1792.
Elijah Turner, Esq.
E. Turner, Esq. 1793 to 1802.
Charles Turner, jr,, Esq. 1803.
Elijah Turner, Esq. 1804.

AFFAIRS OF GOVERNMENT.

Charles Turner, jr., Esq. 1805.
Charles Turner, jr., Esq. }
Enoch Collamore } 1806, 7, 8.
Cushing Otis, Esq. }
Hayward Pierce, Esq. } 1809.
Edward F. Jacob, Esq. }
Jesse Dunbar, Esq. } 1810, 11.
Cushing Otis, Esq. }
Hayward Pierce, Esq. } 1812, 13
Elijah Turner, Esq. } & 14.
Micah Stetson 1815.
Charles Turner, Esq. }
Jesse Dunbar, Esq. } 1816.
Micah Stetson }
Charles Turner, Esq. 1817.
Vacancy 1818 and 19.
Edward F. Jacob, Esq. 1820.

William Peaks 1821.
Vacancy 1822.
Charles Turner, Esq. 1823.
John B. Turner, Esq. 1824, 5.
Vacancy 1826.
Jesse Dunbar, jr. Esq. }
Samuel Deane } 1827, 8.
John B. Turner, Esq. }
Samuel Tolman, Esq. } 1829.
Vacancy 1830.
John B. Turner, Esq. }
Samuel Tolman, Esq. } 1831.
Eben T. Fogg, Esq. }

Convention for revising the State Constitution in 1820. Delegates.

Charles Turner, Esq.
John Collamore, Esq.
Jesse Dunbar, sen., Esq.

The Town chose a Delegate to the Congress that convened at Concord 1779, on the subject of the depreciated currency, viz. William Turner, Esq. and instructed him "to use his influence that an agreement should be made through all the towns, that the necessaries of life should not bear a higher price than at present, but not to appreciate the currency as Boston recommends."

At the close of the French war in 1760, the Town seems to have been at considerable charge in supporting the French people who had been distributed amongst the towns, and the selectmen not having their full account allowed by the Provincial Government, applied to the Town for the balance; it was refused by the Town "as the proper Charge of the Province."

In 1768, the Town instructed their Representative "to do his endeavor that the Excise be laid on spirituous liquors."

In 1787, the Town chose a committee "to consult of the general good, and to prepare instructions for their Representative."

Israel Sylvester, Barnabas Little, Capt. Elisha James, Capt. Enoch Collamore, Elijah Turner, Esq., James Briggs, Joseph Benson, Constant Clap, Eli Curtis, Capt. Samuel Stockbridge and Joseph Nash, committee, reported the following instructions:

"At this critical and alarming period, it may not be unwelcome to you that your Constituents communicate to you their sentiments. While our Constitution remains unchanged as ordained by the People in the civil Compact, it is the indispensable duty of every citizen to support it. At the same time, there are grievances, as we conceive, under which the people of this Commonwealth labour, which we would instruct you, at the next Sesion of General Court, to endeavor to redress. At a time when the people feel themselves heavily pressed with public debt, wisdom, policy and justice demand, that every possible means, consistent with justice and reputation, be devised for their relief. You will therefore endeavor to render the salaries of all public Officers, suitable to the abilities of the people. It cannot be supposed that infant States, however fair and promising their prospects, should launch into the expence and pomp of old and affluent Nations, but that such a state must rise to respect, by a conduct suitable to its situation, circumstances and abilities. You will therefore, on investigation, endeavor that such retrenchments be made and such regulations be adopted, as the reputation of our Republican Government, connected with present circumstances, renders most necessary. And in order to ease the people, as much as possible from direct taxation, we think proper to instruct you, to use your endeavor, that excises may be laid on superfluities and articles of foreign luxury, and such domestic articles as are not nesessaries of life, and especially on those unnecessary articles of foreign produce, that lure to luxury and dissipation.

"And wheras, we believe there are some people in this Commonwealth, so blind to the common good as to use their endeavors that a paper currency be emitted by this Government, believing as we do, that a more fatal Engine of injustice and mischief (in our present circumstances) could not be devised, you will remember that you are instructed by your Constituents to oppose it.

"And as without the establishment of publick credit and confidence, a Nation must soon fall to contempt and ruin, you are to endeavor, to the utmost of your power, for their recovery and reestablishment, by maintaining public honor, honesty and justice.

"You are also to use your endeavor that a law may be made by this General Court, empowering Towns to raise money by taxing polls and estates, for the purpose of encouraging men to enlist in the State or Continental service, whenever called for by the Government, and providing that military officers shall not detach men from the companies, in such Towns as will seasonably procure their proportion of men in a more equitable way, by encouraging them to enlist."

In 1799, the Town instructed their Representative to use his influence in General Court "to obtain a repeal of the House and Land Tax:" and again, as times and circumstances changed. In 1808, the Town petitioned to the President of the United States that he would "suspend or modify the Embargo Law."

Municipal Regulations.

We have noticed the manner of dividing the lands under a distinct head, in the first part of this work.

Select men were chosen in 1636, and they continued to manage nearly all the concerns of the Town, save the laying out of lands until 1667, when Overseers of the Poor, as distinct from the selectmen, were first chosen. The selectmen had the sole control of the schools until 1790, except occasionally one or two were added as a committee. The first selectmen were   The first overseers of the poor were Thomas Clap and Charles Stockbridge, 1667. Before this time the poor had been disposed of to such as would engage to take care of them, in publick Town meeting.

In 1667, "The Town did enact, that if any person should entertayn any stranger, after being admonished by a committee chosen for such purpose, he should forfeit and pay 10s for each week." The preamble of this law runs thus: "Wheras some persons out of their owne sinister endes and by-respects, have too aptly been harborers or entertayners of strangers coming from other townes, by which meanes the Towne cometh to be burdened, &c." At the same meeting the Town declared by their votes, "that Mr. Black should depart the Towne presently." In what manner he had become burdensome or dangerous does not appear. We believe he was a preacher.

In 1670, "The Town did agree that the Selectmen should be moderators in the Town meetings the present year; and if any person shall speake after silence is commanded, without leave from any two of the moderators, he shall forfeit 6d for each offence."

In 1665, "Wheras the Court did require, that every Town should have two wolf Traps, and the Town did conceive that there were Traps in the Town that would answer the Court's

MUNICIPAL REGULATIONS.

order, therefore the Town did agree with Thomas Woodworth to tende them, and Thomas Woodworth did agree to baite them and tende them according as the Order of the Court doth require, and the Town is to allow him 10S for this year besides the pay for the wolves there killed."

In 1668, "The Town did agree and conclude that if any man did cut any thatch on the North River flats before the 15th day of August, he should forfeit 10S per day or part of a day to the Town's use:" also, "The Town did agree and conclude that if any man did cut more thatch in one day than would load three canoes, he should forfeit 40S to the Town's use." It is probable that many buildings and perhaps some dwelling houses were covered with the sedges of the flats at this date.

In 1690, the Town chose Thomas Woodworth "Clerk of the market," and annually to the same office till 1711. In 1712, the same person was chosen "sealer of weights and measures," which we therefore understand to be but another name for the same office.

In 1696, "The Town did enact, that every householder should kill and bring in six black birds yearly between the 12th and the last day of May, on the penalty of forfeiting for the Town's use 6d for every bird short of that number."

In 1728, "The Town allowed as a bounty for each fullgrown wild cat killed within the Town, 30S, and for each young one 10S. John Dwelly and David Hatch received the bounty that year.

In 1739, "The Town chose Capt. John Clap and Samuel Clap to prosecute the law relative to the preservation and increase of deer." Capt. John Clap was chosen annually for the same purpose until 1775 - and Constant Clap was chosen annually afterward until 1784.

We have made this miscellaneous selection, for the purpose of noting the progress of settlement.

The records of the Town are generally in a good state of preservation. A book of the laying out of land commences in 1633: but we believe these records were transcribed out of an older book in 1636, which former book is lost. The records of Town proceedings are lost previous to 1665, since which time they are perfect.

The first records before 1636, appear to be in the very beautiful hand of Mr. William Vassall: there being no Town clerk until 1636: occasionally the more beautiful hand of Edward Foster appears.

The following is a list of the Town Clerks.

Richard Garrett, 1636 to 39.	Charles Turner, jr., 1794 to 98.
Lieut. Jas. Torrey, 1639 to 44.	Augustus Clap, 1799.
Richard Garrett, 1645 to 49.	Charles Turner, jr., 1800.
Lieut. Jas. Torrey, 1650 to 64.	Augustus Clap, 1801 to 1805.
Lieut. Isaac Buck, 1665 to 95.	James Briggs, 1806 and 7.
Dea. J. Torrey, 1695 to 1701.	Charles Turner, 1808 and 9.
James Cushing, 1702 to 1706.	Augustus Clap, 1801.
Dea. Jas. Torrey, 1707 to 14.	Eben. Bailey, sen., 1811 and 12.
James Cushing, 1715 to 18.	Augustus Clap, 1813 to 15.
John Cushing, jr., 1719 to 44.	Anson Robbins, 1816 to 23.
Thomas Clap, 1745.	Ebenezer Bailey, 1824, and now in office.
John Cushing, jr., 1746 to 78.	
James Briggs, 1779 to 93.	

CHARITIES.

In 1721, "The Town, considering the distressing circumstances of the poor people in the Town of Boston, by reason of the present sickness of the small pox, agreed to advance the sum of 60£ in Bills of credit, to be sent to Col. Samuel Checkley, Mr. Daniel Oliver and Dea. Samuel Marshall, to be distributed for the relief of the poor."

In 1779 "The Town voted to support the poor of the Town in one house, under an overseer." If this was carried into effect, it was not repeated the next year.

In 1792, "The Town voted that a Hospital should be provided for inoculation with the small pox, with leave to inoculate two months." The hospital was provided at Benjamin James's house, on the south-east of Colman's hills. All suitable precautions were directed: but the infection went abroad

---

*This sum in bills of credit, was, at that time, equal to the same amount in lawful money. The first emission of bills of credit by the Massachusetts Government was ordered in 1729 (£50,000). This was proportioned amongst the towns to be loaned, and the Interest paid to the State. John Cushing, jr. and Capt. Samuel Turner were appointed trustees of the sum received by Scituate 1721. They loaned the money at six per cent in £20 notes. Many of the towns loaned at five per cent or under, according as they found a demand for the money. In 1728, £60,000 more were issued. Major Amos Turner, Thomas Bryant, Esq., John Cushing, jr., Esq., trustees in Scituate. This currency became so far depreciated, about 1750, that the rate of reckoning was 45 shillings, *old tenor*, equal to the dollar, and so shillings equal to the French crown. The Continental currency is well remembered, when in 1787 $2000 was worth but $30 in specie.

into several families, viz. those of Jonathan Hatch, widow Nichols and John Bray.* An action was commenced against Drs. Ephraim Otis, Cushing Otis and Samuel Barker, for breach of bond for faithful discharge of duty, &c., but after the panick which had seized the people was a little calmed, the action was withdrawn. The hospital was continued about two years instead of two months, as proposed at first.

In 1817, an auxiliary Society for the suppression of intemperance was established. That Society holds an annual meeting, and has a publick discourse annually. Their annual meeting was at first in May – afterward for several years on the 4th of July – and since 1826, on the first of January. The favorable influence of this association has been manifest. It is due to Mr. Joseph Tolman, to record that he originated this Society.

In 1816, the Town chose the selectmen a committee to procure some person to vaccinate, and voted to allow such person six cents out of the Town treasury, for every person vaccinated. There was a pretty general vaccination effected by Drs. Otis, James and Foster.

In 1818, the Town voted to establish an alms-house. A purchase was made of a house on the north side of the common at Herring brook hill. The house had been erected by Capt. Lane, afterward of Walpole, Mass. had been owned and occupied by Capt. Silas Morton, afterward of Pembroke, and by George Little, Esq. deceased, and by Josiah L. James, now of the city of New York. The original purchase was $1,100. The house was enlarged and furnished, and the whole cost amounted to something more than $3000. In October 1820, this house was burnt by an incendiary, John Woodward, an Irishman, being moved to this crime by the circumstance that the overseers of the poor had taken his wife whom he had cruelly treated, and placed her in the alms-house. He was convicted and sentenced to the State prison for ninety-nine years. He died in the prison in 1828. The house was rebuilt on the same spot in 1821, with additional buildings and enlarged accommodations, in lands, &c., at a cost of more than $4000. We can state in general terms, that the saving in supporting the poor in an alms-house since 1818, has more than covered all these

---

* There died of the small pox in Scituate, in 1792 and 3 – David Nash, Charles Clap, Paul Otis' child, widow Daman, Thomas Holmes, Mary Nash, widow Chittenden, Thomas Webb, Stephen Wade, John Daman, John Stetson, and Reuben, a man of colour.

expenses. The establishment is under the general control of a board of overseers, which meets once a month, and under the particular care of a master. Mr. James Barrell was the master from 1818 to 1829. Capt. Ebenezer Bailey from 1829 to the present time.

We subjoin here a list of the physicians who have been the principal practitioners. And it is necessary to remark, that for nearly a century, the ministers were the physicians here, as they were elsewhere. We find no notice of any other practice previous to 1700, save that a Dr. Chickering, from Massachusetts we believe, was occasionally called to this place, and particularly by Deacon Joseph Tilden, as early as 1670. President Chauncy practised extensively for about fifteen years.

The first regularly bred physician was Dr. Isaac Otis, who commenced practice in 1719, (see Family Sketches).

Dr. Benjamin Stockbridge commenced before 1730, (see as above).

Dr. James Otis, son of Dr. Isaac, commenced about 1760.

Dr. Ephraim Otis, Harvard College 1756, practised several years in Taunton, and afterward in Scituate, where he died 1814.

Dr. Charles Stockbridge, son of Dr. Benjamin, about 1765.

Dr. Samuel Barker, about 1787, since removed to Pembroke.

Dr. Cushing Otis, Harvard College 1789, commenced 1792.

Dr. Freeman Foster, Harvard College 1799, commenced 1802.

Dr. David Bailey, a native of Hanover, commenced 1796.

Dr. Peleg Ford of Marshfield, commenced 1805, died 1812.

Dr. Elisha James, commenced 1808.

Dr. Milton Fuller, from New Hampshire, commenced 1826.

Dr. Charles Stockbridge, practised in Boston 1815, and a few years after in Scituate.

Dr. Caleb Marsh, a native of Hingham, practised a few years about 1792.

PUBLIC GROUNDS.

The Town early reserved several landings on the North River, most of which are still used as such. The beaches from the third cliff eastward to the river's mouth, have been defended from waste, by repeated acts of the Town, forbidding the removing of stones, &c. Two landings at the Harbour have been preserved by the Town, and frequently surveyed, for the purpose of keeping their bounds. One of these is at the creek below the bridge, the other between William James's dock and the creek that marks the bounds of the Williams, alias the Barker farm. These came into the Town's possession in 1704, at that time when the Conihasset partners surrendered their highways, &c. to the Town. There has been a town landing at Union Bridge from 1645, when a ferry was kept at that place by Bisbee.

At the Chittenden place, formerly called Job Randall's building place, or ship-yard, one mile above Union Bridge, is a town landing which has been surveyed and the bounds renewed, for the last time 1799.

In 1699, "the Town ordered that the undivided land lying between the Country road and Daniel Turner's and the Barstows land and the N. River should lie for common for the Town's use." This was at North River bridge, we believe: and may have been sold or appropriated since, though we have not met with the conveyance. It is now in the Town of Hanover.

Burying Grounds, Meeting-house lots and Training fields.

There was a Meeting-house lot and burying ground reserved by the first settlers, before 1633. It was in "Meeting house lane," so called, in the earliest records that are preserved. This was the earliest of course, and the place where the pilgrims worshipped, and the place where they lie. It is a reproach to their descendants that it is suffered to lie an exposed common. This place is about three fourths of a mile from the harbour in a southerly direction.

The second Congregational Society commenced a burying ground in 1644, near their Meeting-house, (see Notes on Parishes). Here were buried the earliest generations of the Cushings, the Kings, the Torreys, the Hatches, the Robinsons, with Mr. Witherell their first pastor.

In 1673, the Town paid their high respect to General Cudworth, by granting him a family burying ground, as follows: "Feb. 26, 1673, it is agreed that Mr. Cudworth has granted to him four rods and an half of land, on the south side of the meeting house, to fence in for a burying place, and for a place to set a horse, which land is to be from the stone wall northward, one rod and an halfe for the breath of it, and to be in lengthe three rods." This place may now be easily discerned by tracing the foundation of the old Meeting-house. There are several graves on the spot, but the grave stones are rough and unlettered. These are doubtless the graves of the wife and some of the children of that venerable man. He died in England.

In 1680, the second religious Society commenced a burying ground, near their then new Meeting-house on Timothy Foster's land, a half mile north of Union Bridge. This was Society's land, as we believe.

In 1699, the Conihasset partners laid out a burying place "between the land of Thomas Hiland and John Pierce, with a way to the Country road to said burying place, not to exceed half an acre." Conihasset Rec. p. 32. This is now used by many families in the north-west part of the Town.

In 1707, the Town granted leave to the Church and Society up river to set their Meeting-house on the Town's commons.

In 1725, the Town laid out a piece of land on "herring brook hill, for the accommodation of the southerly Meeting house, a burying place, training field and other special uses." The same year a burying place and training field was laid out nearly opposite to "Meeting house lane," and east of the "Buck field." This is now used for these purposes. The same year, ten acres near drummer Setson's (Samuel) for a burying place and training field. This is the place where the Episcopal Church first stood.

In 1804, the Town chose a committee to examine and report, how much land near the south Meeting-house, it was proper to fence in with the burying ground. The fencing was not accomplished until 1828, when it was done at the expense of the south Parish.

Besides these public burying grounds we may mention that of the Wanton family, on the west bank of the North River, near the ancient residence of the family, a few rods to the north-east. No lettered stone is seen there. The family tomb of John Cushing of the second generation to the present time, may be seen on "belle house neck."

The family of Dr. Stockbridge have a tomb on their ancient place, thirty rods north-east from their venerable mansion. Another branch of the Stockbridge family has a tomb at Mount Blue, where three generations of the family are laid. The family of the late Mr. Joshua Bryant has a tomb on their place. And there is a burying ground of the family of Bowker near "burnt plain," where several generations have been buried.

Bills of Mortality.

The average number of deaths may be forty-five per annum. The climate must be considered healthy, in which so many persons reach to an advanced age. For the want of accurate records we are unable to give many instances of longevity.

Isaac Randall died 1759, aged 101.
Widow Jane Palmer d. 1810, a. 101.
Isaac Stetson d. 1811, a. 92.
Israel Sylvester d. 1812, ai. 95.
Widow Sarah Clap. d. 1812, a. 91.
Widow Zeporah Rsndall d. 1815, a. 97
Wid. Deborah Sylvester d. 1815, a. 96.
Widow Mary Brooks d. 1818, a. 101.
Hagar (color) d. 1821, a. 94.
Widow Hette Young, d. 1821, a. 91.
Rose (color) d. 1823, a. 97.
David Dunbar d. 1823, a. 93.
Lucy Whiton (color) d. 1825, a. 100.
Widow Thankful Otis d. 1826, a. 91.
Edmund Bowker d. 1827, a. 94.

Widow Meh. Jackson d. 1827, a. 92.
James Barrell d. 1827, a. 99 1-2.
Widow Eliz. Brigs d. 1828, a. 92.
Wid. Experience Stetson d. 1829, a. 92.
Mary Clap d. 1829, a. 91.
Widow Sarah Bourn d. 1829, a. 91.

There are now living.
James Briggs aged 96.
Reuben Bates a. 95 3-4.
Widow Mary Ellmes a. 93.
Seth Stodder a. 91.
Lathrop Litchfield a. 90.
Widow Grace Totman (now of Brookfield), a. 99.

Military Affairs.

In 1638, William Vassall and William Hatch were appointed by the Colony Court "to exercise the people in arms at Scituate." The year previous had been one of military operations against the Pequots, and a greater attention to discipline was now commenced. The part which Scituate bore in the war of 1637, we have not ascertained with much accuracy. The order of the Colony Court relating to that war, is as follows: "It is enacted that the Colony of New Plymouth shall send forth ayd to assist them of Massachusetts Bay and Connecticut, in their warres against the Pequin Indians, in reveng of the innocent blood of the English which the s^d Pequins have shed and refuse to give satisfaction for."* We believe

---

*The alarm excited by the Pequot War, led to the union of the Colonies, often referred to in this work. There was an informal union in 1638: but in September 1643, articles of confederation were signed at Boston, by Commissioners from Massachusetts, Plymouth, Connecticut and New Haven Colonies. In 1662, Connecticut and New Haven were united in one colony. The Commissioners chosen annually, held annual meetings at Boston, Plymouth, Hartford and New Haven, in rotation (with the exception that they met twice in succession at Boston) until 1664. The meetings were afterwards triennial, and continued to 1686, when the Charters were cancelled, and Andros was appointed by the crown General Governor.

that this expedition was conducted principally by voluntary enlistment; and we notice in the list of volunteers for this Colony, Lieut. William Holmes, George Kenrick and Henry Ewell, who were Scituate men: Lieut. Holmes however resided mostly at Plymouth,

In 1643, the Colony Court ordered a list of the men liable to bear arms that year. The list of Scituate men (liable to bear arms that year, embraced "John Hoar, John Williams, jr., Isaac Chittenden, Peter Collamore, Isaac Buck, Walter Hatch, William Curtis, Richard Curtis, Joseph Tilden, George Sutton, Samuel Sutton, Ephraim Kempton, George Moore, John Vassall, William Peaks." By what rule these were liable to bear arms that year, we have not ascertained: it is probable, however, that many were exempted that year on account of former services. The same year we observe in the Colony Census, that there were in Scituate males over sixteen and under sixty, one hundred. Scituate had offered a great reduction from her inhabitants in 1639 and 40: for we observe in the list of those liable to bear arms in Barnstable in 1643, "Richard Foxwell, Barnard Lombard, Thomas Lombard, Samuel Hinckley, Thomas Hinckley, William Cracker, John Russell, John Foxwell, Thomas Blossom," who were Scituate men three years before.

In 1652 Scituate was made "a military discipline," by act of Court, and officers commissioned, viz. James Cudworth, Capt.; John Vassall, Lieut. and Joseph Tilden, Ensign.

That a military discipline was not created earlier in Scituate, was owing to the great removal to Barnstable, above alluded to. Plymouth, Duxbury and Marshfield had been made military disciplines in 1642.

A council of war had been occasionally held previous to 1653, but in that year it was regularly established by law, and its duties pointed out. This council consisted of eleven, of which number Scituate always furnished a large part. We observe in 1665, "Cornet Robert Stetson, Serj. John Daman, Mr. Isaac Chittenden, Edward Jenkins, and Lieut. Isaac Buck." The veteran Cornet continued in the council of war until 1682. In 1654, in the expedition ordered against the Dutch at Manhatoes (New York) by the Commissioners of the United Colonies, under Major Robert Sedgwick of Massachusetts, Plymouth Colony enlisted and impressed sixty men, to be commanded by Capt. Miles Standish, Lieut. Matthew Fuller, and Ensign Hezekiah Hoar. Mr. Hoar had then removed from Scituate to Taunton.

In 1658 a troop of horse was ordered by the Court to be raised. Scituate was to furnish four men. Robert Stetson was appointed Cornet of that troop.

In 1666, the military of Scituate elected their officers, and made return to the Colony Court for ratification, viz, James Cudworth, Capt., and Michael Pierce, Lieut. The court returned an action as follows: "As to Mr. Cudworth it is directly against the advice of the Court, and as to Mr. Pierce, he is a stranger to us: therefore Serj. John Daman is directed to take the command till further orders." The reader should be apprised that Mr Cudworth having been Captain in 1652, had also been deprived of his commission in 1669, on account of his opposition to the rigorous laws against the Quakers: hence the jarring between the military of Scituate and the Colony Court. They returned their best man for the approbation of the Court, although they had previously been admonished to the contrary. The matter was accommodated in 1669, and Mr. Pierce with whom the Court had now a better acquaintance, as it would seem, was commissioned as Captain, Isaac Buck as Lieut., and John Sutton as Ensign.

From the Pequot war in 1637, to the troubles with the Narragansetts and Phillip of Pokanoket, which came to open war in the autumn of 1675, there had been peace with the Indians. This war was suspected and foreseen for several years. Neither Philip nor the Narragansetts would be faithful to their treaties of amity. It is not proper for us here to give a narrative of that war, except in so far as it had some particular connexion with this Town.

The Colony Court had put their Jurisdiction into a state of military preparation, in 1674, on account of an expected expedition against the Dutch at New York. We observe in the records of the Colony, that the military officers in each town were required to make a "search of arms," and report deficiences. We notice also, in the records of Scituate, that Capt. Cudworth was chosen to complete the Town's stock of arms and ammunition, and in particular he was ordered "to purchase seven sordes to complete the town's stock in that kinde."

In 1675, an additional garrison of twelve men was ordered to be established at the house of Mr. Joseph Barstow in Scituate. This was near the place now called Hanover Corners. The other garrisons in the Town were at the "block house" on the North River, at Charles Stockbridge's (which was the principal garrison), and at Capt. John Williams's, on farm neck.

The same year the Court ordered the Namassakesett Indians to be removed to Clark's Island near Plymouth, and not to leave the Island without license. It was also ordered that there be pressed for this war twenty-three men from Scituate, (from Plymouth fifteen, Taunton twenty, &c.)

October 4th, "At a Gen. Court held at Plymouth, Major James Cudworth was unanimously chosen and re-established in the office of General and Commander in Chief, to take charge of our forces that are or may be sent forth against the enemy, as occasions may require. Serjeant Robert Barker to be his Lieut. of his particular company."

Also, "General Cudworth, Mr. Constant Southworth, Mr. Barnabas Lothrop and Mr. Isaac Chittenden ordered to be a committee in behalf of the Country, to take an account of the charges arising by this war."

The same year the Town of Scituate chose a committee "to procure clothing, &c. for the soldiers, viz. Gen. Cudworth, Cornet Stetson, Isaac Chittenden, Joseph White."

The Colony Court also resorted to the following strong measure of precaution: "It is ordered that every man that comes to meeting on the Lord's Day, bring with him his arms, with at least six charges of powder and shot," also "that whoever shall shoot off a gun at any game whatsoever, except at an Indian or a wolf, shall forfeit 5S for such default, until further order."

It was determined, towards the close of this year, to make an expedition against the Narragansetts. It was commanded by Gov. Winslow in person, and though successful, so far as to destroy the Narragansett fort, and slay at least eleven hundred of the Indians, it was nevertheless the most memorable of all the actions in which the Plymouth forces were engaged, for the sufferings and hardships of the victors, it being on the last of December, and the country covered with a deep snow and the weather uncommonly severe. For a description of this battle see Hubbard or Church, or N. E. Memorial.

Scituate had twenty men in this battle; but we are unable to give any perfect list of their losses and sufferings. It is however due to those brave men to collect what we can, in the absence of any authentic report of killed and wounded. We learn from a letter of Gov. Winslow written from the scene of battle, that Serjeant Theophilus Witherell (son of Rev. William) was desperately wounded in storming the Narragansett Fort, December 19, 1675. We can also name John Wright, mentioned incidentally in Scituate records, as having been in that battle. We can name Joseph Turner, who had been wounded before, as it would seem, for the Town of Scituate had passed the following vote 1673: "Chose Serj. John Daman to go with Joseph Turner and procure a cure for him; also to support him at the Town's expense as long as he liveth." He recovered, it seems, and fought again. We extract from the Colony records the following particulars.

In 1678, "Ordered that William Perry of Scituate be released from military duty on account of great wounds received in the late war." The next year he was "allowed 10£ from the Colony Treasury" on the same account. In 1678, "Serjeant Theophilus Witherell, on account of his severe wounds in the late war, by which he is crippled for life, is allowed 60£ silver money." In 1681, "Joseph Turner having served in the Narragansett fight, is freed from military duty." In 1683, "John Vinal having served in the Narragansett fight is freed from military duty." It is truly affecting to observe such tributes, trifling as they were in a pecuniary view, to the brave soldiers of the "Narragansett fight."

On the opening of the campaign against Philip in 1676, twenty-five men were ordered to be pressed from Scituate early in the spring. Gen. Cudworth, Lieut. Buck and Isaac Chittenden were appointed press-masters. The Town also chose a committee "to take account of all the service of the soldiers in all their goings out, and report to the Governor," viz. Gen. Cudworth, Lieut. Buck and John Cushing.

The Narragansetts early in the spring had committed ravages in Rhode Island; parties had even penetrated to Plymouth and killed a number of inhabitants. On this alarm, Capt. Michael Pierce of Scituate, with a company of fifty Englishmen and twenty friendly Indians from Cape Cod, was ordered to pursue the Indians towards Rhode Island. He proceeded without any rencounter near to Pawtucket, in that part which has been called Attleboro Gore, when he discovered that there were Indians near him, but not suspecting that Canonchett was there, with all the collected force of the Narragansetts. He therefore ventured to cross the river and commence the attack, but soon found himself in the presence of an overwhelming force. To fly was impossible, and to retreat in order, before such an enemy, was equally desperate. His only resource was to fall back to the river's bank, in order to avoid being surrounded, and make the sacrifice of himself and of his brave men as costly as possible to the foe. But the Indians having a large disposable force, soon sent a party across the river to attack in the rear. This surprise only induced the Captain to change the front of half his company, and place them back to back; and in this position they fought until nearly every man fell, and with a bravery like that at Thermopylæ, and deserving of as great success. Capt. Pierce fell earlier than many others; and it is due to the honor of one his friendly Indians called Amos, that he continued to stand by his commander and fight, until affairs were utterly desperate, and that then he escaped by blackening his face with powder as he saw the enemy had done, and so passing through their army without notice.

Mather and others relate also pleasing anecdotes of two or three other of Capt. Pierce's friendly Indians, who escaped by equally curious artifices and presence of mind. One who was flying and closely pressed by a hostile Indian sought the shelter of a large rock. Thus the two were waiting in awful suspense to shoot each other. Capt. Pierce's Indian putting his cap on the end of a stick or his gun, gently raised it to the view of his enemy, who immediately discharged his gun at the cap, and the next moment was shot dead by the friendly Indian. Another in his flight pretended to pursue an Englishman, with hostile demonstrations, and thus escaped.

It was little consolation to learn, after this disaster, that this brave band had slain thrice their own number of the Indians. It was by far the severest calamity that befel Plymouth Colony during this bloody war, and peculiarly disastrous to Scituate.

It has generally been stated that every Englishman was killed; but we are fortunately able to furnish what may be the most accurate and authentic account of the losses in that battle, that is extant. It is a letter from the Rev. Noah Newman of Rehoboth, dated the day after the battle, to his friend the Rev. John Cotton of Plymouth. He assisted in burying the dead.

"Rehoboth, 27 ^ of the first ,76.

"Reverend and dear Sir.

"I received yours dated the 20th of this Instant wherein you gave me a doleful relation of what had happened with you, and what a distressing Sabbath you had past. I have now, according to the words of your own letter, an opportunity to retaliate your account with a relation of what yesterday happened to the great saddening of our hearts, filling us with an awful expectation of what further evils it may be antecedaneous to, both respecting ourselves and you. Upon the 25th of this Instant, Capt. Pierce went forth with a small party of his men and Indians with him, and upon discovering the enemy, fought him, without damage to himself, and judged that he had considerably damnified them. Yet he, being of no great force, chose rather to retreat and go out the next morning with a recruit of men; and accordingly he did, taking Pilots from us, that were acquainted with the ground. But it pleased the Sovereign God so to order it, that they were enclosed with a great multitude of the enemy, which hath slain fifty-two of our Englishmen, and eleven Indians. The account of their names is as follows. From Scituate 18, of whom 15 slain, viz. Capt. Pierce, Samuel Russell, Benjamin Chittenden, John Lothrope, Gershom Dodson, Samuel Pratt, Thomas Savary, Joseph Wade, William Wilcome, Jeremiah Barstow, John Ensign, Joseph Cowen, Joseph Perry, John Perry, John Rowse, (Rose). Marshfield 9 slain: Thomas Little, John Earns, Joseph White, John Burrows, Joseph Philips, Samuel Bump, John Low, More – John Brance. Duxbury 4 slain: John Sprague, Benjamin Soal, Thomas Hunt, Joshua Forbes. Sandwich 5 slain: Benjamin Nye, David Bessey, Caleb Blake, Joe Gibbs, Stephen Wing. Barnstable 6 slain: Lieut. Fuller, John Lewis, Eleazer C—, (probably Clapp), Samuel Linnet, Samuel Childs, Samuel Bereman. Yarmouth 5 slain: *John Matthews,* John Gage, William Gage, Henry Gage, Henry Gold. Eastham 4 slain: Joseph Nessefield, John Walker, John M—, (torn off), John Fits, jr., John Miller, jr. Thomas Man is just returned with a sore wound.

"Thus Sir, you have a sad account of the continuance of God's displeasure against us: yet still I desire steadfastly to look unto him who is not only able but willing to save all such as are fit for his salvation. It is a day of the wicked's tryumph, but the sure word of God tells us his tryumphing is *brief:* O that we may not lengthen it out by our sins. The Lord help us to joyne issue in our prayers, instantly and earnestly, for the healing and helping of our Land. Our Extremity is God's opportunity.

"Thus with our dearest respects to you and Mrs. Cotton, and such sorrowful friends as are with you, I remain
"Your ever assured friend
"NOAH NEWMAN."*

Note in the lower margin, probably in the hand writing of Mr. Cotton.
"from Mr Newman, March 27, 1676,
Newman, Shove, Walley, Maj. Bradford, Capt. Oliver, Keith, Fr. Mather, Moth. Mather, Sister Mather Seaborn Cotton, Walker, Moody, Mrs. Newman.
"Read."

---

* The authenticity of this letter is beyond doubt. It came into our possession in the following manner. We (the compiler of this work) remembered to

MILITARY AFFAIRS.

The greater number of the unfortunate fifteen of Scituate, were heads of families, viz. Capt. Pierce, Samuel Russell, Benjamin Chittenden, John Lothrop, Gershom Dodson, Thomas Savary, Jeremiah Barstow, John Ensign. John Lothrop was not the son of the Rev. John Lothrop, but he is called in Scituate records, an Irishman. Thomas Man, who returned "with a sore wound," was of Scituate.

Immediately after the above calamity,* the council of war decided that the danger of the crisis was such, that the utmost strength of the Colony must be put forth. The quota of soldiers to be raised by Scituate, according to their plan, was fifty. They were to rendezvous at Plymouth on the 11th April 1676, where they were to meet the council of war and receive their directions. But when the council assembled at Plymouth to meet their new raised forces, they found that it had not been possible to muster so many men as their well laid plan had contemplated. "There was a special deficiency of Scituate and Sandwich," says the New England Memorial, and the whole design was for the present abandoned. We shall do what we can to account for the unfortunate deficiency so far as Scituate is concerned. Ten days after the day appointed for the assembling of the soldiers at Plymouth, an attack was made on Scituate by a large body of Indians, which had been seen about Weymouth some days before. "They however were bravely repulsed by the inhabitants of Scituate;" so record Hubbard and Mather. We are to recollect too that Capt. Pierce with fifteen of the best men of Scituate had been slain, but a few days previous to the day of rendezvous. It was not within the compass of probability certainly, that Scituate could

---

have been shown a copy of it, several years since, by Hayward Pierce, Esq. a lineal descendant of Capt. Michael Pierce, and to have been informed by him, that the original was in the possession of Rossitter Cotton, Esq. of Plymouth, a descendant of the Rev. Mr. Cotton to whom the letter was addressed. We applied to this gentleman, who informed us that he had sent the letter, with others, to the Antiquarian Society at Worcester. By the politeness of the venerable President of that Society, the original letter was found, and copied for us by Emory Washburn, Esq. of Worcester. Rev. Mr. Newman deceased April 16, 1676.

* It may be pleasing to the reader to be informed, that Canonchett was taken prisoner a few days after, by Capt. Denison of Stonington. A young soldier of the company Robert Staunton, put some question to the Sachem, when he received this proud and disdainful answer: "You too much child – no understand matters of war – let your Capt. come – him I will answer." And when he was informed that it was determined to put him to death, he said, "I like it well – I shall die before my heart is soft, or before I have spoken any thing unworthy of myself." Hubbard's Indian Wars.

Canonchett was son of the famous Miantonomoh, chief Sachem of the Narragansetts.

MILITARY AFFAIRS.

have furnished fifty men, without leaving their homes defenceless, and their garrisons unmanned.

Again on the 20th of May following, another and the last desperate attack was made upon the Town.

They had made an attack upon Hingham on the 19th, killing John Jacob of Glad Tidings plain. The next morning, after burning five houses in Hingham, they hastened to Scituate by the Plymouth road. They came into Scituate by the "Indian path," so called, which led from Scituate to the Matakeeset settlements at Indian head ponds, by "the Cornet's mill," on the third Herring brook, near the residence of the late Major Winslow. This saw mill they burnt; and tradition tells that they wounded and burnt a man in it; but this is doubtful. They then proceeded to Capt. Joseph Sylvester's and burnt his house. It stood north of the Episcopal Church hill, (now known as such), and nearly on the same spot where stands the mansion of Mr. Samuel Waterman. There was a garrison of twelve men at Joseph Barstow's, three fourths of a mile south of Capt. Sylvester's, which they probably avoided, and proceeded down towards the Town, burning as they went.* But unfortunately we are able only to mention a few of the houses so destroyed, which we find incidentally mentioned in our Town records. The next house which they burnt (of which we have certain record) was William Blackmore's. It stood where stands the house of the late Capt. Elijah Curtis, forty rods west of the head of the lane that leads to Union Bridge, and on the north side of the street. William Blackmore was killed that day,† but whether in attempting to defend his house or not, and what was the fate of his family, we have not learned, probably however they had escaped to the "block house," on the bank of the river, but fifty rods distant. The block-house was attacked but not carried; John James, however, whose house was near the block-house, received a mortal wound, lingered about six weeks, and died. The Indians then hastened forward to attack the principal garrison at Charles Stockbridge's.

---

* We learn from Gov. Winslow's letter to Mr. Hinckley, (dated May 23, 1676), that "fourteen men marched up from Marshfield as far as Joseph Barstow's, and had sight of the enemy at William Barstow's, but being unhappily discovered by them also, they ran away, leaving some horses and cattle they were about to carry away, and those houses at that time secured from the flames." This we understand to have been on the same day, when the great attack was made on Scituate – and that this was but a small detachment of the enemy.

† Since writing this account, we have ascertained that it was in the former attack, on the 21st of April, that Blackmore was killed.

Their path may be traced directly onward towards this garrison. The house of Nicholas (the Sweede) was the next burnt, which stood on a small hill thirty rods north-east of Parker lane. We observe that the Town voted, the next year, to allow him three pounds towards rebuilding his house. In their further progress they doubtless burnt other houses, as Wm. Parker's, Robert Stetson, jr.'s, Standlake's, Sutliffe's, Holmes's, John Buck's and others were nigh their path, but unfortunately the committee's report to Gov. Winslow is not extant, at least in full. They passed over Walnut Tree hill, on the northward of the late Judge William Cushing's, and entered Ewell's house which stood at the "turn of the road, "which spot may be known in modern times, by saying, it was nearly midway between Judge Cushing's mansion and farmhouse. Ewell's wife was alone, save an infant grandchild, John Northey,* sleeping in the cradle; the house being situated beneath a high hill, she had no notice of the approach of the savages until they were rushing down the hill towards the house. In the moment of alarm, she fled towards the garrison, which was not more than sixty rods distant, and either through a momentary forgetfulness, or despair, or with the hope of alarming the garrison in season, she forgot the child. She reached the garrison in safety. The savages entered her house, and stopping only to take the bread from the oven which she was in the act of putting in, when she was first alarmed, then rushed forward to assault the garrison. After they had become closely engaged, Ewell's wife returned by a circuitous path, to learn the fate of the babe, and to her happy surprise, found it quietly sleeping in the cradle as she had left it, and carried it safely to the garrison. A few hours afterward the house was burnt. There was a considerable village around this place, and the houses of Northey, Palmer, Russell, Thomas King, jr. and some others were doubtless burnt, though we are not able to quote record for it. That Ewell's house was burnt we learn from his will, in which it was incidentally mentioned, (see Family Sketches). The garrison house of Stockbridge was pallisadoed on three sides, the fourth being defended by the mill pond. Besides this there was a small out work near the mill, on a little island between the mill stream and the waste way, where a blacksmith's shop has for several years stood. It was thought to be a point of importance to the settlement, to defend these mills. Here the Indians fought several hours, made many efforts to fire the buildings, and

---

* Whose genealogy is in this work.

sustained heavy losses, from the well directed shot from the garrison. They chiefly occupied the ground at the south end of the mill dam. They were not repulsed until night close, when nearly the whole force of the Town that was left at home, was collected for the purpose. Lieut. Buck had mustered all the men below, and the veteran Cornet Stetson had descended the river, with what people could be raised in the south part of the Town. Unfortunately, Capt. John Williams with thirty Scituate men, was absent, "ranging the woods," about Namaskett (Middleboro). A letter written by Gov. Josiah Winslow, the same week of this affair, throws out some reproaches against the inactivity of the inhabitants of Scituate about this time:* but though we give the excellent Governor all due praise for his ardor, we must suppose that he could not have been fully apprized of the circumstances at the time when he wrote. When we reflect on the amazing losses which Scituate had recently sustained, and that Capt. Williams was ranging the woods beyond Plymouth with thirty men, and that a great part of the Town was in flames, and many persons killed on the 20th of May, it is easy for us to imagine why the inhabitants of Scituate did not chase away this large force of the Indians, as Gov. Winslow would have desired. They were scarcely able to maintain their garrisons at home, with their diminished forces. The "forty smart lads from Plymouth, Duxbury and Marshfield," who are praised in the Governor's letter for venturing as far as Bridgewater, saw only a *straggling party;* the main body was ravaging Scituate. In short, we are confirmed in the opinion that the worthy Governor blamed the inactivity of Scituate at this terrible crisis, without fully knowing the circumstances, by the facts, that after this tremendous attack had been sustained, and a short breathing time had been allowed, Scituate was at the head of offensive operations against the enemy. The long persecuted Cudworth, with a magnanimity rarely equalled, though waxing old, had accepted the chief command of the Colony forces, and continued in that command until Philip was subdued. Lieut. Buck was in constant service, and his brother John the Cornet: and the veteran Cornet Stetson was constantly on horseback, either in making voluntary excursions with Gen. Cudworth, (as tradition asserts), or in returning to encourage the garrisons at home, or in guiding the directions of the council of war. In July, Capt. John Williams with a company from Scit-

---

* Dated May 23d. See Hinckley papers, Historical Society's Library.

uate chiefly, was detached to follow Philip to mount Hope, and commanded the right wing of the ambuscade, when that persevering prince was slain, (see Church's History).

In an appendix to the last edition of the New England Memorial, a paper is quoted, purporting to be a return to Gov. Winslow of the losses of Scituate. That paper was said to be thus endorsed: "13 dwelling houses burnt with their barns – one saw mill – six heads of families (Pierce, Russell, Savary, Whitcomb, Pratt, Blackmore), many others killed and made cripples." Thus far reference can be had to a part only of the war, because we have already named many other heads of families, and we will here add that we find authentic records, (incidentally), to show that Mr. Isaac Chittenden, a highly respectable citizen, a deputy to the Court, and a member of the council of war, was slain at Scituate on the memorable 20th May, 1676. The quotation from Gov. Winslow's paper continues thus, "in all 32 families, wherin are about 132 persons." By this we understand thirty-two heads of families; and this we think can embrace only the year of 1676, exclusive of the Narragansett expedition, the year previous.*

At the close of this war, the Commissioners of the United Colonies reported the state of the debt, and recommended a tax to be levied. The proportion of Plymouth Colony amounted to £3692, 16S. 2d. of which sum, Scituate paid £586, 7S. 4d. which was above £100 more than was paid by any other town in the Colony.†

In the autumn of 1676, some of the conquered lands were ordered to be sold, viz. "Showamett Neck, (between Taunton and Swanzey), Mount Hope, (Bristol), Pocassett, (Tiverton), and Assonet, (Freetown), 'for the relief of maymed soldiers and persons impoverished by the wars, and poor widows such as have lost their husbands in the wars, &c.' " The Governor, Gen. Cudworth and the Treasurer, together with one chosen from each town, were to be the committee for this purpose.‡

We notice also in the transactions of the town of Scituate in the autumn of 1676, "The Town chose a committee to join

---

* See Appendix, 2d.

† In 1663, the taxes of Scituate were as 16 to 10 compared with Plymouth, and as 16 to 4 compared with Bridgewater.

‡ Amongst the purchasers of Showamett we notice the following Scituate men (1667): Richard Prouty, Walter Briggs, Capt. John Williams, William Hatch, William Peaks, Jonathan Jackson, Lieut. Isaac Buck, Zechary Daman, Daniel Daman. The whole company was thirty. It may be proper to distinguish Showamett from Shaomet, (Warwick, Rhode Island), sometimes written Shawamett.

MILITARY AFFAIRS.

with that committee of the General Court, viz. the Governor, Gen. Cudworth and the Treasurer, according to Law, to divide the proceeds of the sales of land at Showamett amongst the soldiers, widows, &c." Thomas King was chosen.

Also in reference to the same subject, in the spring of 1677, "The Town instructed their Deputies to move the Corte, that this Town may have their part of whatsoever lands and profits have been obtained by the late warres. Also that some speedy course be taken for the relief of some wounded soldiers. Also that Capt. Williams and about 30 men which were pressed out to range the woods about Namastick and Plymouth, may be paid by the country as well as other prest soldiers."

Some of the soldiers, probably by consent, received their pay in lands, for services in Philip's war. There appears in the Colony records, and also an attested copy of the same in the town records of Scituate, the following entry:

"The persons to have land as allowed by the Court, are as followeth:

	£	s.	d.
Lieut. Isaac Buck,	10	00	00.
Zechariah Daman,	06	06	01.
John Daman,	06	05	07.
Richard Prouty,	06.	12	03.
Cornet John Buck,	08	09	05.
Jonathan Jackson,	06	05	04.
Thomas Clark,	05	05	02.
William Hatch,	02	01	00.
Richard Dwelley,	11	13	03.
Walter Briggs,	05	18	07.
Charles Stockbridge,			
for Benj. Woodworth,	07	09	07.
Joseph Garrett,	05	09	07,

Plymouth, July 22d, 1676. NATHANIEL MORETON, Sec'ry."

The wages in Philip's war were ordered by the Court to be as follows:

General 6s per day.   Ensign 4s per day.
Captain 5s   "   Sergeant 2s 6d "
Commissary 4s   "   Corporal 2s 0d "
Paymaster 4s   "   Soldier is 6d "
Lieutenant 4s   "

We notice also in the Colony records, 1680, "Serj. John Barker was freed from bearing arms for the wounds in the late war."

Also, the same year, "Job Randall was allowed 10£ for wounds in Philip's war."

Henceforth we are able to give but little account of the part borne by Scituate in the Indian wars.

We shall pass over the northern expedition of Sir Edmund Andros in 1687.

In the eastern expedition, planned and urged chiefly by Massachusetts General Court in 1689, commanded by Colonel Church, we can only state that Scituate furnished six men and two officers, viz. Capt. Joseph Sylvester, (the same whose house was burnt in Philip's war), and Ensign Israel Chittenden, (son of the very respectable Mr. Isaac Chittenden, who was killed as noticed above). This expedition, though not very successful, was not disasterous in losses, and probably all our town's men returned. Scituate paid a tax of £88 for the expenses.

In the Canada expedition in 1690, under Sir William Phipps, at the taking of Port Royal and the attempts upon Quebec, Scituate furnished sixteen men, under Capt. Joseph Sylvester, Lieut. Israel Chittenden and Ensign John Stetson. This expedition proved fatal to Capt. Sylvester (see Family Sketches) and to many of his men: but we are unable to give a list of them. We have collected a few notes from the Probate records relative to these losses. For example, the Court appointed Timothy Rogers to administer on the estate of Nathaniel Parker, who died in the Canada expedition 1690. Benjamin Stetson was appointed administrator to his son Mathew Stetson, who died in the same expedition.

The widow Mary appointed administratrix to her husband Ensign John Stetson, who died in the same expedition.

Moses Simons in his will, "being bound to Canada as a soldier in 1690; in case he shall never return," orders his property to be equally divided between his brothers: brother John to be executor. He did not return, and the will was executed by John.

Eliab Turner was appointed administrator to Lazarus Turner his brother, who died in the same expedition.

Samuel Bryant (son of John, sen.) died in the same expedition. The inventory of his estate taken by William Perry and Samuel Stetson.

Samuel Dwelley (son of Richard) died in the same expedition – inventory taken by Jeremiah Hatch and James Bowker. Thomas Hyland also – his father Thomas was appointed administrator.

Robert Sprout died in June on this expedition.

The object of the war, that of conquering and possessing Canada, was not at that time secured. Some brilliant partizan exploits were performed by the sons of Edward Wanton in 1697, (see Family Sketches), when Count Frontenac was Governor in Canada.

A second military company was established in Scituate when new regulations were ordered for the militia in 1695, three years after the union of Plymouth and Massachusetts. Our town records notice these general orders, so far as to record "that the Commands of Capt. Chittenden on the north, and Capt. Stetson on the south were to be limited by the first Herring brook, with the exception of Samuel Clap, Thomas Pincin and David Jacob, on the south side of said brook, to belong to the command on the north side." This was conformable to the division of Parishes, or nearly so. Capt. Anthony Collamore was commander of the Scituate company at the time of his decease in 1693, and an elegy on his death, which has been preserved by the family, contrives to mention that his train band consisted of two hundred. The poet must have taken some license: it may however have amounted to that number at that time, if the muster-roll included all between sixteen and sixty, as it had done under the Plymouth Colony government.

We now pass to the French war, so called, of which we shall attempt no narrative. We shall merely give a list of such men as served in that war, informing the reader that it must be far from a complete one.

Capt. John Clap, (son of Thomas Clap), at Quebec 1759.

Capt. Benjamin Briggs, in that war 1756.

Lieut. Elisha Turner, (in Capt. Keen's company 1757), and Capt. 1759.

Lieut. John Clap – a Col. in the Revol. – died in Scituate 1810.

Serjeant Barnabas Barker, in Capt. Keen's company, Colonel Thomas's regiment, 1757.

Capt. Keen's company 1757, William Carlisle, James Cushing, Samuel Bowker, Consider Cole, Stephen Lapham, Elisha Palmer, Samuel Ramsdel, Peleg Turner, Benj. Lapham.

Capt. Bassett's company 1757, John Caswell, Edward Corlew, David Marvel, Zaccheus Nash, Thomas Pearce, Gideon Rose, Luther Wade.

James Briggs, (at the first taking of Louisburg 1744).*

---

* Louisburg was taken by the *New England Troops*, the first time; it was one of the greatest achievements of the French war. Col. John Winslow of Marshfield led the New England forces.

MILITARY AFFAIRS.

Samuel Randall, died of small pox in the army 1756.
Isaac Torrey, wounded at St. John's 1757, d. in Scituate 1812.
Staunton James, } killed at St. John's 1757.
Nehemiah Randall, }
Job Cowen, at St. John's 1759, living in Scituate 1831, a. 90.
Lieut. Viney Turner, at St. John's 1759.
Lieut. Job Tyrrell, as above.
William Hayden, do.
Ezekiel Hayden, do.
William Perry, do.
Nehemiah Sylvester, do.
Seth Sylvester, } sons of Nehemiah do.
Richard Sylvester, }
Elisha Stodder, do.
Nathaniel Ellmes, died returning from Halifax 1759.
Josiah Litchfield, died at Halifax 1759.
James Tower, with Col. Bradstreet at Skenectady 1756.
John Gross, taken in a Country ship and d. at Guadaloupe 1758.
Edmund Gross, do. and returned.
Isaac Lapham, in attack on Ticonderoga 1758.
Edmund Bowker, do. died in Scituate 1826, aged 95.
Reuben Bates, at second taking of Louisburg 1758, living in
    Scituate 1831, aged 95.
David Dunbar, at Louisburg as above, also at Crown pt. 1759
Benjamin Bowker, at Ticonderoga and Lake George 1758.

The following were at Crown point in 1759.

John Foster, died in Scituate 1815.
Benjamin Palmer, died in Scituate 1820.
Elisha Barrel, died in Hanover 1829, aged 96.
Colburn Barrel, died in Rev. war.
Samuel Brooks, died in Hanover 1830, aged 95.
Nehemiah Palmer.
George Stetson.
Jedidiah Dwelley.
Henry Lambert.
Simeon Nash, died of small pox at Ticonderoga 1759.
Reuben Daman, drowned in swimming Connecticut river, on
    his return 1759.
Zechariah Lambert.
Daniel Lambert.
John Corlew, }
twins. { Edward Corlew, } sons of Edward named above.
       { Thomas Corlew, }
William Corlew, }

Elisha Litchfield.
Wilborn Hollaway.
Benjamin Collamore.
Dr. Ephraim Otis, at Fort William Henry 1757, surgeon.
Joseph Bowker, at Crown point 1759.
Luke Lambert, do.
James Woodworth, do.
Oliver Winslow, killed near Crown point 1759.
William Gould, James Orian, Thomas Pierce, Thomas Vicars, Michael Vicars, Joseph Randall, Ezekiel Sprague, William Westcott.
Dr. James Otis, surgeon's mate at Crown point 1758, Colonel Bagley's Regiment.

It will be seen, by the above notes, that two veterans of the French war survive in 1831: Reuben Bates and Job Cowen: they are intelligent men, and retain their faculties in an extraordinary degree.

Revolutionary War.

It becomes us, in the history of events so well known as those of the American war, to confine ourselves to very narrow limits, conscious that we can bring nothing new to light, and record nothing of much interest that is not already made publick. Still it may be gratifying to posterity, if haply our book may reach posterity, to see some collection of the names of their townsmen and ancestors, who acted a part in that trying time.

The first act of the Town that had a. reference to this war, appears on the record March 1774.

"It was put whether the Town would act upon the request of William Clap and others, touching the difficulties of the present times, and passed in the affirmative. The Town then chose Nathan Cushing, Esq., Doct. Ephraim Otis, Nathaniel Clap, Esq., William Turner, Doct. James Otis, Israel Vinal, Galen Clap, Joseph Tolman, Barnabas Little, Anthony Waterman, and John Clap, jr. a committee to draft such resolutions as they may think proper, and present the same to the Town at their next meeting."

May 23, 1774, the committee reported
"That we cordially join in sentiment with most of our brethren in this and other Colonies, that those acts of the British

Parliament which have a tendency to control our internal commerce and manufactures, and more especially to extort our monies, are not only disconsonant with good and lawful Government, but subversive of those rights and liberties which our Fathers have handed down to us – Therefore we advise and move that a committee be appointed to make all suitable enquiry into our public disturbances and difficulties, and lay their counsels, determinations and results before the Town, when and so often as they shall think necessary, applying to the select men to warn a meeting for the purpose.

"NATHAN CUSHING, per order."

October 3, 1774.
"It was put whether the Town would chose a committee of Inspection, to see that the Continental Association shall be strictly adhered to, and passed in the affirmative. A Committee of Inspection was then chosen, consisting of John Cushing, jr., Nathan Cushing, Esq., Charles Turner, Israel Vinal, jr., Nathaniel Waterman, Joseph Tolman, James Otis, William Turner, Barnabas Little, John Palmer, Galen Clap, Anthony Waterman, Noah Otis, Joseph Stetson, Increase Clap, Gideon Vinal, Eli Curtis, Samuel Clap, Abiel Turner, Barnabas Barker, George Morton, Ignatius Otis, Thomas Mann, Deacon Samuel Jenkins, Paul Bailey, Calvin Pierce, Amasa Bailey, Deacon Joseph Bailey, Constant Clap, John Jacob and James Briggs."

At the same meeting a committee of correspondence was chosen, viz. "John Cushing, jr., Nathan Cushing, Esq., Joseph Tolman, Barnabas Little, Israel Vinal, jr., Galen Clap, Abiel Turner, Noah Otis, Nathaniel Waterman, Dea. Joseph Bailey and Eli Curtis."

January 18, 1775, the committee of, inspection reported to the Town this "Publick Information."

"The Publick are hereby informed that on the 9th Inst. the Committee of Inspection, by request of the Town, waited on Charles Curtis and Frederick Henderson, shopkeepers, to know whether they intended to adhere to the Continental Association, the former of whom rendered the following answer: 'I shall *not* adhere to it,' and the latter replied as the former, adding, 'I don't know any *Congress,*' – whose ignorance is the more to be wondered at, seeing he has been an inhabitant of this Continent and Town several years, since quitting his marine vocation. Therefore the inhabitants of this Town do hereby resolve to break off all dealing whatsoever

with said refractory shopkeepers, until they shall give publick and absolute satisfaction to the foresaid Committee and Town, touching their open refractoriness relative to said salutary Association – trusting in the mean time that the publick will condescend to trouble their memories with their names and characters.
"JOHN CUSHING, jr., Chairman."

At a meeting of the Town, May 29, 1775.

"Voted to recommend to the inhabitants of this Town to bring their fire arms and accoutrements with them to meeting on the Sabbath, June 19, 1775."

This may have had reference to a plan concerted about that time, for capturing Capt. Balfour, who was stationed in the neighboring town of Marshfield, with the "Queen's Guards," and who, it was thought, might attempt to march through Scituate to Boston. But the British at Boston, by some means, learned the design, and took off this beautiful company of Guards by water, just in season to be annihilated at the battle of Bunker-hill, on the 17th of June.

July 1775, "Voted to choose a committee to consult with Mr. Nathaniel Waterman about *keeping* the soldiers at the Harbour."

"Voted that a guard of nine men be kept day and night, and that this guard be commanded by Capt. Noah Otis."

"Voted that a watch box be established near Eleazer Litchfield's, to be under his care – another at the Glades, under the care of Paul Bailey and Barnabas Little, and another at the 3d Cliff, under the care of James Briggs."

"Voted that if the persons who have the care of said Boxes, may fail at any time of procuring said guards, they are immediately to acquaint the committees of Correspondence and of Inspection."

June 4, 1776.

"Chose a Committee to draft instructions for our Representatives in General Court; viz. William Cushing, Esq., Major William Turner, Capt. Joseph Tolman, Capt. Israel Vinal, jr. and Mr. Anthony Waterman."

At the same meeting the committee reported these Instructions.

"The inhabitants of this Town being called together on the recommendation of our General Assembly, to signify their minds on the great point of Independence of Great Britain, think fit to instruct you on that head. The Ministry of that

Kingdom having formed the design of subjecting the Colonies to a distant, external and absolute power in all cases whatsoever, wherein the Colonies have not, and in the nature of things, cannot have any share by representation, have, for a course of years past, exerted their utmost endeavors, to put the same plan, so destructive to both countries into execution; but finding it, (through the noble and virtuous opposition of the sons of freedom), impracticable, they have had at length, a fatal recourse to that which is still more repugnant to a free Government, viz. a standing army – to fire and sword, to blood and devastation – calling in the aid of foreign troops, as well as endeavoring to stir up the Savages of the wilderness, being determined to exercise their barbarities upon us, and to all appearance, to extirpate if practicable, the Americans from the face of the earth, unless they will tamely resign the rights of humanity, and to repeople this once happy Country with the ready sons of Vassalage.

"We therefore, apprehending that such subjection will be inconsistent with the just rights and blessings of society, unanimously instruct you to endeavour that our Delegates in Congress be informed (in case that Representative Body shall think fit to declare the Colonies independant of Great Britain) of our readiness and determination to assist with our lives and fortunes, in support of that necessary measure. Touching other matters, we trust in your fidelity, discretion and zeal for the publick welfare, to propose and forward all such measures as you shall apprehend may contribute to our necessary defence in the present threatening aspect of affairs, or to the promoting of the internal peace, order and good Government of this Colony."

Campaign of Rhode Island.

September 23, 1776.
"The Town voted to pay 40S a month in addition to the Continental pay, and half a month's advance pay to such as shall go this Campaign."

Capt. Williams Barker with thirty-eight men, received the pay thus pledged by the Town.

October 14, 1776,
"A Committee was raised to draft a vote on the question whether the Town will comply with the order of Gen. Court, for forming a Constitution for this State, viz. Elisha Tolman, Nathaniel Waterman, Increase Clap, Elisha James and Dea. Joseph Bailey."

Report. "Agreeable to a Resolve of Gen. Court, the Town has taken the subject into consideration, and has voted to give their consent that the present House of Representatives, together with the Council (if they consent) in one body, and by equal voice, should prepare and agree on such a Constitution and form of Government for this State, as the House and Council aforesaid, on the fullest and most mature deliberation, shall judge most conducive to the safety, peace and happiness of this State, then to be submitted to the people at large for their ratification or otherwise." (Voted).

March 17, 1777, "The Town voted to choose a Committee of *eleven,* as a committee of Correspondence, Inspection and Safety, viz. John Bowker, Eleazer Litchfield, Ignatius Vinal, Joshua Clap, Israel Sylvester, Issachar Vinal, Josiah Litchfield, jr., Caleb Bailey, Elisha Foster and Enoch Collamore."

June 3, 1777, "The Town chose Capt. Israel Vinal to prosecute and lay before the Court, the evidence of the hostile disposition toward this or any of the United States, of any of the inhabitants of the Town of Scituate, who stand charged with being persons whose residence in the State is dangerous to publick peace and safety."

A list was exhibited by the selectmen as follows: "Elijah Curtis, Benj. James, Job Otis, James Curtis, David Little, jr., Benj. Jacob, Ebenezer Stetson, Benj. James, jr., Elisha Turner, David Otis, Prince Otis, Joseph Turner, Frederick Henderson, Jonathan Fish, William Hoskins, John Stetson, William Cole, Benj. Stockbridge, Charles Stockbridge, Samuel Stetson, Elisha Jacob, Joseph Jacob, Joseph Hayden, Jonathan Fish, jr.

"Voted that any of these persons might have liberty to be heard in this present Town meeting or at any other day, that their names may be erased on giving satisfaction, &c."

June 19, 1777, "At an adjourned meeting, sixteen of the persons charged as dangerous, &c. gave satisfaction to the Town, and their names were struck out of the list. Those remaining for trial agreeable to the law of the State are Elijah Curtis, Job Otis, James Curtis, Benj. Jacob, Elisha Turner, John Stetson, Joseph Jacob, and Joseph Hayden."

Such measures seem harsh to us who have never borne a part in such a crisis. But we are to consider that the utmost power of the Colonies was called for; and to harbour citizens within, who might turn their arms against their countrymen in their struggles, would have been a piece of criminal courtesy. Hence the necessity of committees of Safety and Inspection. It was also an important object to bring forward some who were timid, and others who looked upon the attempt to achieve independence as utterly desperate. It is well known that many of our wisest citizens and firmest patriots, belonged at first to the latter class. The ardor of many people of far less discernment, wrought up to frenzy, by the very backwardness and hesitancy of wiser men, in this case triumphed, and compelled all to pledge life and honor to the cause, or to abandon their homes. In looking over the above list of gentlemen, reported to the selectmen "as persons whose residence in the State was dangerous;" we can conceive the reasons, in most cases, why suspicions should fall upon them, even though they might be amongst the most ardent friends of independence. The spotless William Cushing did not escape suspicion, though he is not in the above list. And why? because he was a Judge of the King's Superior Court. But he soon gave his townsmen satisfaction, by drafting the instructions to the Representative of the Town, "to endeavor that Congress should be informed that we are ready with our lives and fortunes, to support independence, in case they should declare it." The worthy and intelligent Dr. Benjamin Stockbridge and his son Dr. Charles, were suspected. They were of the Church of England, as were several others in the list. Elisha Turner had been a Captain in the French war, had been somewhat distinguished for his loyalty. In short, we believe posterity now does the justice to nearly all the persons at that time suspected, to allow that they were firm friends of their country, and well wishers to independence, but coolly and discreetly calculated that it was a hopeless object – and an object it was most certainly, which all now look on with unqualified wonder that it should have been achieved. There was indeed but one in the whole list who either through despair of the cause or other more interested motives, had any known design of flying to the British; and that was Charles Curtis. As to Frederick Henderson, named in the list, we will remark that he was a Captain in the British Navy, had been wounded, and shipwrecked several years before at Nantasket: he found his way to Scituate, where he married and settled for life, and received half pay as a retired officer. He satisfied the citizens that he should take no part in the contest on either hand, and was suffered to remain. He lived several years after the Revolution, and deceased in this place. His widow (whose maiden name had been Jael Rogers) was afterward the wife of Capt. William Church, and survived until 1822. Charles Curtis was a young gentleman of liberal education and fair prospects and may have gone over to the British with ambitious views. We believe however that he was never rewarded for his mistaken loyalty.* He died in New York, where his family have since deceased. His wife was Lydia James, daughter of Deacon John James. With this single exception, the vigilant suspicions and the strong measures of the citizens, supported by law, compelled every man who had doubted, to disguise at least his doubts, and every man who had opposed by reasoning, the practicability of a successful Revolution, at least to be silent. We perhaps ought to add to our slight notice of the suspicions against the highly respectable Dr. Stockbridges above, that those suspicions did not rest merely on the circumstance that they were of the Church of England, though it is well remembered that this was considered enough at that anxious crisis to induce a visitation from the Committee of Safety. An unfortunate occurrence brought the elder Dr. into difficulty. He was at that time engaged in the practice of medicine in a wider circle than any physician in the State, at that time, or perhaps since. He had been called to Ipswich, and on his return he was unfortunately detained many days by General Gage in Boston, This was known to the authorities of the Town: and as soon as he returned to his home, they conducted him to Plymouth with the design of securing him in prison; but they were soon softened by the intercession of the people of Plymouth, and dismissed him. In the mean time his son Dr. Charles with several others, was conducted under guard to head quarters at Cambridge; but he was soon released. It was a suspicious circumstance that he had been found, with a few others, walking on the beach, between the third and fourth cliffs, apparently waiting for some communication from Boston by water.

In the summer of 1776, a regiment was encamped near the north Meeting-house, and many of them were lodged in that house. The English had landed at Hingham, and done some little injury about that time, which led to this precaution. The regiment was kept on duty until winter; and was removed to the harbour in October. Col. William Turner had the command.

We subjoin an imperfect list of officers and soldiers who served in the Revolutionary War.

Col. John Jacob.	Major Nathaniel Winslow.
Col. John Clap.	Major William Turner.

---

* He was made a forage master about New York.

Capt. Jonathan Turner.
Capt. Peter Sears, corps of Mechanicks.
Capt. Williams Barker, at R. I.

Capt. Joshua Jacob.
Capt. Amos Turner.
Dr. Lemuel Cushing, surgeon, third regiment.

Soldiers who have drawn the pension under the late war.

James Barrell, dead.
Noah Barrell, son of above.
Elisha Gross, dead.
Stephen Totman, dead.
William Hyland, drew pension at first, but not at present,
James Lincoln.
Matthew Tower, dead.
Lieut. Edward Daman, (Mechanicks), dead.
David Jordan, dead.
Simeon Grandison, colour, at taking of Burgoyne.
Thomas Church, dead.
— Hill.
John Manson.
Gideon Young.
Edward Humphries, dead.
Oliver Winslow.

Amasa Hyland, now of Winchendon.
Most of the above served during the war, as also several others who deceased long since.
William Perry.
Dwelley Clap.
Ephraim Palmer.
Consider Turner.
Benjamin Turner.
John Tower, killed at Charleston).
Lynde Tower, died in Vt.
Stephen Vinal.
Robert Cook, died 1831.
Elisha Turner.
Dea. Elisha James, (Mechanicks), living.

Besides these we might collect a long list who served in short campaigns or in the State service: — a few of whom are living, e.g.:

Jesse Dunbar.
Elisha Briggs.
Lazarus Bowker.

John Whitcomb.
Daniel Merritt.

The soldiers of the Revolution are fast dropping away. It will be seen in our list that seven only now draw pensions.

Tuesday, May 23, 1780, "The Town had under consideration the Constitution prepared by the Convention at Cambridge in 1779, and accepted every article, save the eleventh article respecting the House of Representatives, and the first article, respecting the Judiciary."

There is nothing of any interest that we can here relate, that has any connexion with this Town, during the brief troubles with Great Britain in 1794. It was altogether a maritime obstruction. Minute men were required to be raised throughout the Towns, but were never called into service. We observe in the Town records of that year: "Choose a Committee to raise minute men, according to requisition of Government, viz. Eli Curtis, Chandler Clap, Israel Vinal, Daniel Litchfield, James Clap, Calvin Daman, George Torrey, John Tolman, Joseph Jacob, Enoch Collamore." The apprehensions of a war were happily removed by Mr. Jay's Treaty in November of that year.

War with Great Britain 1812.

The war which was declared against England June 18, 1812, and which was terminated by the treaty of Ghent, December 1814, had its theatre remote from New England principally, and was scarcely felt by the people of this Town, save by the privations which were sustained in the interruption of business, and in the scarcity of foreign articles of produce. The intercourse between the States was so far interrupted in 1813 and 1814, that flour bore the price of $18 per barrel, and corn $2 per bushel, and even 2,50 cts. The war was conducted chiefly by soldiers voluntarily enlisted. No citizen of this Town bore any conspicuous part either as officer or soldier. The army raised on that occasion is well known to have been of a very different character from those in former wars of which we have been speaking, when life, honor, liberty being at stake, called forth "the lords of human kind." We mean this only as a general remark, while we acknowledge that the army was furnished with many distinguished officers.

We do not recollect that Scituate sustained the loss of a man. We will however record, that Theophilus Witherell (a lineal descendant of Samuel, the brother of the brave Serj. Theophilus, who was "crippled for life" in the "great Narragansett fight," 1675,) was wounded and crippled like his ancestor, in a northern expedition.

The militia of Scituate were called out on one occasion, viz. July 7, 1814, The British 74, called the Bulwark, had lain near Scituate harbour several weeks, and had sent a demand on shore for fresh beef and vegetables, which the citizens of course did not furnish. Early in the morning of June 11, 1814, two tenders manned with marines, had come into the harbour and set fire to the shipping, and returned without further violence. By this act, hardly to be denominated honorable warfare, ten vessels, fishing and coasting craft, were lost. The Rev. Mr. Thomas of the north Society, had the resolution, immediately to go on board the Bulwark, and to request of the commander a candid declaration, what further violence might be proposed, and received an assurance, that nothing further was intended, after having destroyed the vessels, which might bring some revenue to the Government. The regiment of militia, as we have noticed above, under Col. John Barstow, repaired to the neighborhood of the harbour, but soon returned to their homes. A guard was kept for some months, but no rencounter took place.

It is too recent and too well known to be related as history at this time that a majority of the citizens of this Town and of New England did not agree to the necessity of this war; and at its close did not believe that any advantage had been gained, which might not have been gained by negotiations without the war: and on the other hand the majority of Congress and of the citizens of the United States, declared the war to be just and necessary. It is equally well remembered, that the citizens of this country were then divided into two great parties in politicks, which denominated each other the French and English party, and accused each other with an undue partiality toward those nations respectively. The lines of these parties began to be distinctly drawn in 1792 and 3. France and England were at war. In their struggle they paid but little regard to the rights of neutral nations. England with her thousand ships of war blockaded many of the ports of France; and France declared England to be blockaded without any naval force: hence the origin of "paper blockades," in the common language of those times: England retaliated in kind, and both powers made prize of American vessels with little regard to neutral rights. In addition to this there was another and more irritating grievance of which the United States complained against England. England alleged that many of her own seamen had fraudulently obtained certificates of protection as American citizens, in the American merchant service, which was true beyond doubt. The common artifice practised in such cases was, to purchase these certificates of American seamen and adopt their names. England feeling herself strong in her right to the services of her own citizens in time of war, proceeded to search American vessels wherever they were met with, and in reclaiming British seame, the officers were not very accurate in making distinctions, so that it sometimes happened that American seamen were impressed. These subjects of irritation were agitated with increasing violence from 1806 to 1812, when the United States proceeded to declare war. A treaty negotiated by Mr. Munroe, then minister to the Court of St. James, which was thought by many to have been as advantageous as that finally obtained at the close of the war, was rejected by President Jefferson, without submitting it to the Senate, probably because he foresaw that if this treaty should be ratified, war with France would be inevitable. Had the English party, so called, been in power in the United States, this would perhaps have been the result: but the other party being in power, the election was made for war with England.

Aborigines.

Scituate, like most of the towns in Plymouth Colony, had been nearly depopulated of the natives by the small pox, a few years before the English made a permanent settlement on this coast. But there were many evidences left, that it had been thickly peopled. They were the Matakeesetts, and controlled by the chief or sachem of the Massachusetts. The principal encampment of the remnants of this tribe at the time Scituate was settled, was about the ponds in Pembroke. They visited the sea shore often for fishing and fowling, but not many resided here. Several places in the Town still retain the ancient aboriginal names, viz. Musquashcut pond, at Farm neck, and Assinippi, vulgarly called Snappet, and Conihassett. Indeed the name of the Town is the aboriginal name, derived from the brook that falls into the harbour. That brook was called by the Indians Satuit, which means cold brook, and the name of the Town has the same orthography in our earliest records in 1633 — shortly after it was written Seteat — then Cittewat, and not until about 1640, was the present orthography settled. That the population here had been considerable, appears from the facts that the English found planting lands of some extent, which were still cleared of forest trees, viz. the glades and the cliffs, which were then of greater extent than at present, the place called Greenfield, and a part of "belle house neck." On that neck, or rather a small neck connected with it called Schewsan's neck, tradition speaks of an Indian burying ground: and another burying ground is well attested at Groundsell hill, a gravelly mound, a few rods east of the residence of the late Joshua Bryant. They soon left this place after the English came. A few families made a summer residence at Wigwam neck, as late as 1700.* The family of Attaman remained in their wigwam near Spring swamp, a half century later: and somewhat later Simon was living at Simon's hill, and remembered by some of our aged people. The last of all the Matakeesetts in this Town was Comsitt, a bright and enterprising man, who enlisted into the Revolutionary army and lost his life. His family received some assistance from the Town as late as 1786.†

Though the settlers at Scituate found that region almost without inhabitants, yet they were conscientious enough to extinguish the Indian title by fair purchase of the Chief of the Matakeesetts, as by the following document may appear.

"Plymouth   June   1653.

"I Josias Wampatuck do acknowledge and confess that I have sold two tracts of land unto Mr. Timothy Hatherly, Mr. James Cudworth, Mr. Joseph Tilden, Humphry Turner, William Hatch, John Hoar and James Torrey, for the proper use and behoof of the inhabitants of the Town of Scituate, to be enjoyed by them according to the true intents of the English grants: The one parcel of such land is bounded from the mouth of the North River as that River goeth to the Indian head River, from thence as that River goeth unfo the pond at the head of that River, and from the pond at the head of the Indian head River upon a straight line unto the middle of Accord Pond: from Accord Pond, by the line set by the Commissioners as the bounds betwixt the two Jurisdictions, untill it met with the line of the land sold by me unto the sharers of Conihassett, and as that line runs between the Town and the shores, until it cometh unto the sea:‡ and so along by the sea, unto the mouth of the North River aforesaid. The other parcell of land lying on the easterly side of the North River, begins at a lot which was sometime the land of John Ford, and so to run two miles southerly as the River runs, and a mile in breadth towards the east, for which parcell of land, I do acknowledge to have received of the men whose names are before mentioned, fourteen pounds in full satisfaction, in behalf of the inhabitants of the Town of Scituate as aforesaid; and I

---

* The wigwam of the family of Tantachu was near Robert Whitcomb's farm in Beach woods, in 1700 and earlier.

† The Indian families of Opechus, Tantachu and Attaman remained until 1740.

‡ At Satuit brook which falls into the harbour.

do hereby promise and engage to give such further evidence before the Governor as the Town of Scituate shall think meet, when I am thereunto required: in witness whereof, I have hereunto set my hand in presence of

NATHANIEL MORTON,
EDMUND HAWES,   JOSIAS WAMPATUCK,*
SAMUEL NASH.   his mark."

"At the same time when Josias made acknowledgment as above mentioned, there was a Deed brought into Court which he owned to be the Deed which he gave to them whose names are above specified for the said lands, and that he had not given them another: which deed was burnt in presence of the Court.
NATHANIEL MORTON, Secretary."

The first deed, we believe, was made before 1640: the intent of this latter conveyance was to include the "two mile," which had been purchased since.

We learn from the above docmnent also, that the same sachem had sold his title in the Conihassett proprietary before this time: and probably at the time of the grant made by the Court in 1637. That original deed we have not seen. But after the decease of the sachem Josias Wampatuck, his son Josias claimed some further allowance from the Conihassett partners, and they gratified him with the sum of £14, and received a deed, dated February 3, 1686-7, and acknowledged before the Council of Sir Edmund Andros, Governor General. This deed is in the Conihassett records, signed JOSIAS WAMPATUCK, son and heir to Josias Wampatuck."

It has been very common for people to lament over the fallen fortunes of the Natives of these shores, and to criminate the forefathers for driving them from their wonted forests, and occupying their lands by force or purchasing them for an inadequate trifle. As general remarks, we believe these to be the cant of very superficial readers and reasoners, and certainly without the least truth or pertinency so far as respects Plymouth

---

* Josias was a faithful friend of the English. We find he was a minor in 1641, (see a remonstrance of the town of Braintree against the claim of Richard Thayer to lands purchased of Josias 1641, Hinckley papers). He was son of Chicatabut, chief of the Mass. The residence of Chicatabut was at Neponset river, near Squantum: but he claimed the country to the North river, and the ponds in Pembroke. He died November 1633, (Dr. Harris's History of Dorchester), Josias Wampatuck was his son, one of whose sons was Jeremy; and Charles Josiah (son of Jeremy) was the last of the race

Colony. The lands were purchased whenever a tribe could be found to allege the slightest claim. The sums paid were small, but they were a sufficient compensation to the few wandering natives whom the pestilence had spared, and who could make no use of the lands; nay, they were often above the full value of the lands to the English. These lands were a dangerous and uncultivated wilderness, and had they been received without compensation, they would have been a perilous and costly possession. Plymouth Colony claimed not a foot of land but by fair purchase, save the little districts of Pocassett, Showamett, Assonet and Mount Hope, and these were dearly won, if ever lands were so won, by conquering an unjust and unrelenting enemy. There is reason to lament that the authorities of Plymouth yielded to the imaginary necessity of executing the brave Anawon, and especially that they sold into slavery Metacomet's (Philip's) youthful son: but the justice and humanity generally shown to the natives, will be more apparent, the more we examine the subject. "Philip's Boy goes now to be sold," (see letter from John Cotton, March 19, 1676-7, Cotton papers).

TOPOGRAPHY.

The Territory of Scituate is of very irregular shape, having on its south and east a winding brook and river, and on its north the indented margin of the bay. The harbour, the river, and the principal brooks, we have sufficiently described under other heads. The four cliffs are on the margin of the bay between the harbour and the mouth of the North river, distant from each other nearly a half mile, showing sandy fronts, from one to two hundred feet in height. Colman's hills, called in early records the "high hills," are an elevated table land between the harbour and river's mouth, from the top of which a very extensive prospect is commanded, embracing the whole bay with the two capes. The glades are a point of land on the extreme north, extending to the entrance of Cohasset harbour. This tract of land is generally rocky, and shoots into beautiful and romantic shapes. There is a portion of excellent arable land, at the north point. Farm Neck is a large tract of excellent arable land near to the glades, and is nearly surrounded by marsh. Belle house neck is in the vicinity of the North river, four miles from its mouth, containing nearly an hundred acres of good arable land. Brushy hill is a round and regular eminence, a half mile south-east of the first Society's Meeting-house. Walnut Tree hill, a very early name, so called from the circumstance that the black walnut was indigenous there, is an eminence near the seat of the late Judge William Cushing. Hoop-pole hill is very elevated, being one mile west of the south Meeting-house. Cordwood hill lies three fourths of a mile south-west of the above named house: and one mile farther south is a much higher elevation called Randall hill, or in more modern times Studley hill. One mile west of the latter is Wild Cat hill, an ancient name. On the northwest border of the town are three lofty elevations, forming a triangle with a deep swamp in the centre, of a mile in extent; they are called Mount Blue (on the south), Mount Hope (on the north-west), and Mount Ararat (on the east). Two miles in a south-west direction from these, is Prospect hill, the highest elevation in the Town; it lies partly in Hingham. One mile and an half from the Town-house in a westerly direction from the territorial centre, is Black Pond hill, and on its west declivity is Black pond, a deep, cold collection of water covering about four acres: it discharges into North river by the second Herring brook. Accord pond, so called, because in early times the commissioners who settled the line between Plymouth and Charles river patents, accorded or agreed that the line should intersect that pond, lies on the extreme southwest of the Town, and lies partly in each of the four towns of Scituate, Hingham, Hanover and Abington. It is a clear and deep collection of water, covering about seventy acres.*

There is no part of Plymouth Colony so diversified with hills and vallies, rocky declivities and deep morasses as Scituate. It more nearly resembles the undulated surface of Worcester county, than any other part of these ancient territories.

The lines of the Town enclose about forty-five square miles. A survey of the outlines of the Town was accomplished, and a plan prepared by order of General Court in 1794, by Charles Turner, jr., Esq. That is in the Secretary's office.

A. D. 1830, another and more particular survey was ordered by the General Court, which is to be made, according to contract with the selectmen, by Mr. J. G. Hales of Boston: it was not completed in 1830. The General Court extended the time for completing these surveys. Mr. Hale is now (April 1831) performing the work. He is engaged to prepare a plan for the use of the State, and also to draft a Town map for engraving.

---

* Musquashcut pond and harbour named in this work, we conjecture to be a slight corruption of Mishquashtuck, "a place of red cedars or red shrubs." The red cedar grows in great abundance in that vicinity.

NATURAL HISTORY.

The early records of Scituate mention the Live Oak forests, particularly in the vicinity of Colman's hills: but whether this was a species of the oak not known here at present, or otherwise, we can by no means determine. The white oak, by name, is also mentioned nearly at the same time; from which we might conclude that the live oak was not the same tree. The black walnut was indigenous to some parts of the Town. The last of those noble forest trees was felled upon the east side of Walnut Tree hill, near the road, in 1820. Its trunk was more than three feet in diameter. We have no doubt that it was more than two centuries old. There is a frequent mention in our early records of spruce swamps. The spruce has nearly disappeared. Two varieties of the walnut are now common. The oak appears in several varieties, as the red, black, yellow, and two species of the white. The button wood grows naturally in the south part of the Town. The beach is so abundant in the north-west section, that this part of the Town has been called "the beaches," and the beach woods, from the earliest times. The white pine is the most abundant in general, and of very rapid growth, of which there are two species, the soft, upland, or pumpkin pine, and the swamp pine, that somewhat resembles the yellow pine of the west, but of inferior value to that. The white maple is rapid in its growth, and furnishes abundant fuel. The black, white, and yellow birch, and the black and white ash, and the hornbeam and elm are common. Extensive swamps of white cedar are in the westerly section of the Town, and the red cedar common to every part, but more abundant at the glades than elsewhere. That beautiful ever-green, the holly, is common to most of our woodlands – and the elegant flowering shrub, the mountain laurel, may be seen at Mount Blue, and in many other parts of the Town. It is a common and just remark, that there is and has been a rotation of forest trees, viz. when a pine forest has been felled the oak has sprung up, and when the oak has been felled it has been succeeded by the pine: as also the cedar and the maple forests have been rotatory in like manner.

As to the quantity of fuel, it is believed that it has scarcely diminished in the last half century. The ancient forests of oak have been converted to ships, but they have been followed by the more thrifty pine, so that there is no scarcity of fuel. The prices of fuel per cord vary from two to four dollars; according to the quality.

These forests abounded, in early times, with the animals common to New England. The bear was not uncommon in 1700, and perhaps later: but seems to have been a much more harmless animal than the wolf. For nearly a century the Town voted a yearly bounty for the destruction of the wolf: and in 1673, they divided out the swamps and required each man to clear a given number of acres, in order to break up the dens of the wolf. Wild cats were so common and so destructive to the sheep, that a bounty on these also was long continued. *Wolf Trap* and *Wild Cat* are well known places to this day. Deer were preserved by the law of the Colony, and this Town kept up its committee "to prosecute that law," until 1780, or later. The racoon is not uncommon in our forests now, and often plunders the corn fields in autumn. The fox still makes his burrows, and several are taken yearly.

The marshes are visited in autumn with countless varieties of birds of passage, and the river and coast with fowls of all kinds that have been here known: but they are gradually diminishing, and hardly now repay the toil of the fowler. The black bird that was so abundant a century ago as to sweep off whole cornfields occasionally, is now rarely seen.

MINERALOGY.

The rocks are all primitive granite or sienite, generally approaching to the globular form, and rarely appearing in large masses or quarries. At the glades they appear in considerable masses, and are broken into irregular fissures: but no regular layers, and no secondary rocks are seen. The soil in general is composed of the silex and argilla, in a mixture very favorable to vegetation. As a general remark, we may observe that in the northern section, the mixture is more uniform, and in the southern section silicious hills and plains and argillaceous vallies are more distinctly marked.

The beds of clay from which bricks have been manufactured we have noticed under another head.

Iron ore is found in several parts of the Town, but in no great quantities. Some has been dug for use within the last twenty years, at Spring-brook meadow, by Mr. James Torrey. Some specimens of quartz in regular crystals have been found in the neighborhood of Wild Cat hill.

Physical Changes.

The cliffs have gradually wasted by the attrition of the tides and storms. Comparing the third cliff with the number of acres of planting land originally laid out, we find that it is reduced nearly one half in two centuries. The fourth cliff wastes from twelve to sixteen inches per annum. A large rock in front of the fourth cliff that now lies at low water mark, is remembered by many, to have been at the top of the cliff, two hundred feet above its present bed, and several feet within the edge of the precipice, half a century since. The other cliffs probably waste in the same proportion. The beach between the third and fourth cliff, is composed of sand and pebbles, and resists the attrition of the tides more than the cliffs: yet it is slowly wasting, and the river probably will eventually find its outlet between those cliffs.

The great earthquake on the 18th of November 1755, is well remembered by many of our aged people. They describe the violent agitation of the earth as continuing about fifteen minutes; in which time the walls were all thrown down, the tops of chimneys broken off, and in many instances the whole chimney stacks shaken down into the rooms, and many houses disjointed and nearly destroyed. The whole surface of the earth was seen to wave like the swellings of a sea, and occasionally breaking into fissures. It happened at day dawn in the morning, and brought the people from their beds in dreadful consternation. The rumbling of the earth, and the crashing of the falling walls, &c. was like the loudest thunder, and the commotion and roaring of the sea is described as no less terrible by those who lived near its margin. Several water spouts bursted out in the Town; we can name particularly, one near the brook at Sweet swamp, on the border of Dea. Joseph Bailey's garden. It threw out a considerable quantity of reddish sand of a singular appearance, and the spring thus opened continues to run to the present time. Another fissure of considerable magnitude was made on the south side of "great swamp," so called.

Manners, Customs, &c.

Many of the fathers of Scituate were men of good education and easy fortune, who had left homes altogether enviable, save in the single circumstance of the abridgment of their religious liberty. In 1639, this Town contained more men of distinguished talents, and fair fortune, than it has contained at any period since. They were "the men of Kent," celebrated in English history as men of gallantry, loyalty and courtly manners. Gilson, Vassall, Hatherly, Cudworth, Tilden, Hoar, Foster, Stedman, Saffin, Hinckley and others had been accustomed to the elegances of life in England. It was a natural and unavoidable consequence, that in this wilderness, a less polished race should succeed; and yet many of these fathers survived the darkest period of the Colony, and gave a lasting impression of their manners upon posterity.

Slavery was practised to a considerable extent; but they had no occasion to import servants of this description, for they won them "with their sword and their bow." The wills of the first generation often make provision for Indian servants, but rarely mention an African slave. We have seen but one instance of this kind previous to 1690. Subsequently to 1700, African slaves had pretty generally been purchased by the wealthy families: and the posterity of that race is now more numerous in this Town, than in any other town of the ancient Colony.

It was a superstitious age when this country was first settled, and we are not to suppose that the fathers of Scituate were wholly exempt from the weakness of that age; and it is not improbable that the dangers of the wilderness may have contributed something towards nourishing those superstitions.

It is not an unpleasing subject of reflection to the descendants of the fathers of Plymouth Colony, that religious intolerance and her twin sister superstition, never were suffered to reign so absolutely here as in some other Colonies.

Witchcraft.

The first indictment for witchcraft in New England, was at Hartford, Connecticut, in 1647, when the first execution also took place for that offence, "against God and the King." The only indictments in Plymouth Colony for witchcraft were against two persons of Scituate, which we have extracted from the Colony records.

A. D. 1660, "William Holmes' wife was accused for being a witch. Dinah Sylvester accuser and witness sworne, said she saw a beare about a stone's throw from the path * * *

* * (blank in the records.) * *

But being examined and asked what manner of tayle the beare had, she said she could not tell, for his head was towards her," The accused was discharged. It is natural to conjecture, in looking at the manner in which this trial is entered on the original records, that the testimony was too ridiculous to be recorded in full. The bear was doubtless alleged by the witness to have been William Holmes's wife in that shape. The good sense of the Governor and assistants triumphed over superstition in a fortunate time, to check accusations of this kind. In looking at the records of the next Court, we were happy to observe that "Dinah Sylvester was summoned before the Court, and sentenced to be whipt, or to make publicke acknowledgment (paying the costs of prosecution) for false accusation against William Holmes' wife." She chose the latter, and her acknowledgment of "maliciously accusing the woman," was entered on the public records in 1661.

The other indictment was against Mary Ingham, March 1676, as follows :

"Mary Ingham, thou art indicted by the name of Mary Ingham, the wife of Thomas Ingham of Scituate, for thou, not having the feare of God before thine eyes, hast, by the helpe of the Devil, in a way of witchcraft or sorcery, maliciously procured much hurt, mischieff and paine, unto the body of Mehitabel Woodworth, daughter of Walter Woodworth of Scituate, and to some others, particularly causing her to falle into violent fits, and causing her great paine unto several partes of her body at several tymes, so that the said Mehitabel hath been almost bereaved of her senses; and hath greatly languished to her much suffering thereby, and procuring of greate grieffe sorrow and charge to her parents: all which thou hast procured and done, against the law of God, and to his greate dishonor, and contrary to our Sovereign Lord the King, his crown and dignity."

She was tried by a jury of twelve men – "Verdict, not guilty." It was natural at that superstitious day, that a person affected with nervous insanity, should look round for some one on whom to charge those sufferings. Ingham's wife was aged, and probably lived in retirement, conversing little with this world, and hence was suspected to hold converse with invisible beings. Thus, however, ended indictments for witchcraft in this colony: happy would it have been, had good sense elsewhere as soon triumphed over superstition." There is, however, some apology for the governments of Connecticut and Massachusetts, viz. that witchcraft was believed in and punished in England at the time that moral disease broke forth in this country. Even the great Sir Matthew Hale had prescribed rules for detecting witches.

The belief in the reality of witchcraft has long since been abandoned, and few persons, within the last half century, have spoken of witchcraft or ghosts or haunted houses, except as a superstition which was unworthy of their own times. The last haunted house here was that of Lathrop Litchfield, in the part of the town called the Beach woods, nearly forty years since. A knocking was heard in a closet and repeated almost daily for many months: and though several gentlemen of a good share of philosophy endeavored to investigate the cause, it could never be satisfactorily explained: it ought however to be stated, that no gentleman of the above description was found to allow that there was any supernatural cause. Dr. Barnes was invited to try his skill in the investigation, but unfortunately the ghost would not knock while the Doctor was there.

A LIST OF THE FREEMEN FROM 1633 TO 1649.

William Gilson	1633.	Isaac Robinson	
Anthony Annable		Mr. James Cudworth	1634.
Humphry Turner		Samuel Fuller	
William Hatch		John Cooper	
Henry Cobb		Henry Rowley	
Samuel House		Mr. Timothy Hatherly	1635.

* In the Massachusetts Colony records, we observe that the first indictment for witchcraft was in 1648. "Court Order. This Court (being desirous that the same course which hath been taken in England for the discovery of witches by watching, may also be taken here with the witch now in question), do order that a strict watch be set about her every night, and that her husband be confined to a private roome and watched also."

The accused was Margaret Jacob (alias Jones). Winthrop describes her confinement, and gives some details of the evidence. The persons who were appointed spies, alleged that "they saw a little child coming in and going out from her repeatedly, and when they pursued the child, it vanished."

On such testimony, the poor woman was condemned and executed.

LIST OF FREEMEN.

George Kenrick		John Williams	
Edward Foster	1636.	Mr. Thomas Dimmack	
George Lewis		John Twisden	
Bernard Lombard		Thomas Chambers	
Mr. John Lothrop	1637.	John Hews (the Welshman)	
Henry Bourne		Mr. Chares Chauncy	1640.
Mr. Thomas Besbedge		William Parker	
Samuel Hinckley		Walter Woodworth	
John Lewis		Edmund Edenden	1641.
Richard Sealis	1638.	Thomas Clapp	1645.
Edward Fitzrandle		Edward Jenkins	1647.
William Casely	1639.	Isaac Stedman	1648.
Robert Linnet		John Allen	1649.

A list of those who took "the oath of fidelity" from 1633 to 1668. Many of them were church members, but they declined taking "the freeman's oath" at first, which, however, most of them eventually did.

Nathaniel Tilden	George Moore
Thomas Bird	Joseph Tilden
Daniel Standlake	Serj. John Bryant
Mr. William Vassall	Hercules Hills
Henry Ewell	Lieut. James Torrey
William Crocker	(Richard) Beaumont
Robert Shelley	Joseph Wermall
John Crocker	James Cushman
Joseph Colman	Thomas Weyborne
Nicholas Wade	Mr. Thomas King
George Willard	John Vassall
Thomas Hyland	John Turner, sen.
Thomas Pincin	Resolved White
Thomas Prior	George Russell
Isaac Welles	Stephen Vinall
William Holmes, sen.	John Vinall
Henry Merritt	Abraham Prebble
Thomas Chittenden	Rhodolphus Ellmes
William Perry	Thomas Lapham
Robert Stetson	Henry Mason
Joseph Checkett	Jeremiah Hatch
John Stockbridge	Lieut. Isaac Buck
Edward Casely	Walter Briggs
Samuel Jackson	Gilbert Brooks
William Wills	William Curtis

LIST OF FREEMEN.

Richard Curtis
Humphry Johnson
John Hallet
William Barstow
William Brooks
Walter Hatch
William Peakes
John Hanmer
Ephraim Kempton
John Sutton
Peter Collamore
Matthew Gannett
Michael Pierce
William Randall
Stephen Tilden
Nathaniel Tilden
John Palmer
John Palmer, jr.
Thomas Palmer
Elnathan Palmer
John Turner, jr.
Thomas Oldham
Nathaniel Rawlins
George Pidcoke
Daniel Hickes
John Magoon

Jonas Pickels
Samuel Utley
Thomas Ingham
John Durand
John Whitcomb
Robert Whitcomb
Abraham Sutliffe
John Whiston
John Winter
Christopher Winter
John Cowen
John Otis   1662.
John Cushing
Charles Stockbridge   1668.
Israel Cudworth
Experience Litchfield
John James
Edward Wanton
William Ticknor
William Blackmore
Anthony Collamore
William Hatch, jr. (son of)
Thomas Hatch
Anthony Dodson
Richard Dagan
John Booth

In the above list, the present inhabitants of the Town will see the names that most commonly prevail at the present date. Some of them removed early, and left no descendants in this Town, as the reader will find noticed in the sequel of this work.

A list of "allowed and approved inhabitants," to whom portions of the common lands were assigned, by the joint committee of the Court and the Town in 1673.

Ensign John Allen
Mr. *Nicholas Baker*
Lieut. Isaac Buck
John Bryant, sen.
Walter Briggs
Joseph Barstow
William Brooks
John Booth
William Blackmore

John Buck, sen.
John Bumpus
Widow Bird
John Bryant, jr.
John Bailey
James Briggs
Isaac Buck
John Buck, jr.
John Briggs

LIST OF FREEMEN.

Isaac Chittenden
Peter Collamore
Richard Curtis
Thomas Clap
Thomas Chittenden's heirs
John Cushing
Major Cudworth
Nathaniel Church
William Curtis
John Curtis
John Cowen
Anthony Collamore
Samuel Clap
Jonathan Cudworth
Joseph Colman, sen.
James Cudworth, jr.
Israel Cudworth
Zechariah Colman
Thomas Colman
Henry Chittenden
Richard Dwelly
James Doughty
Anthony Dodson
John Daman, sen.
John Daman, jr.
Rhodolphus Ellmes
Henry Ewell
John Ensign
Widow Ensign
Widow Garrett
John Hanmer, sen.
John Hanmer, jr.
Thomas Hiland, sen.
Thomas Hiland. jr.
Samuel House
Walter Hatch
Jeremiah Hatch
Daniel Hickes
William Hatch
Thomas Hatch
Thomas Ingham
Edward Jenkins
William James
Thomas King, sen.

Thomas King, jr.
Josiah Litchfield
Henry Joslin
John Merritt
John Hews' heirs
Thomas Lapham
Thomas Nichols
Thomas Oldham
William Peakes
Michael Pierce
Matthew Gannett
Samuel Jackson
George Russell
Edward Right
Thomas Pincin, sen.
Thomas Pincin, jr.
Cor. Robert Stetson
Moses Simons
Joseph Sylvester
Benjamin Stetson
Robert Sprout
John Magoon
Joseph Stetson
Abraham Sutliffe
Thomas Stetson
Charles Stockbridge
Richard Standlake
Samuel Stetson
Thomas Perry
Thomas Palmer
John Palmer, sen.
John Palmer, jr.
John Turner, sen.
John Turner, jr.
Humphry Turner's heirs
Daniel Turner
Thomas Turner
Nathaniel Turner
Stephen Tilden
James Torrey
Widow Torrey
Nathaniel Tilden
Widow Tilden (of Joseph)
William Ticknor

CENSUS.

Jonathan Turner
Nathaniel Man
John Stetson
Stephen Vinall
Mr. *William Witherell*
John Vinall
Thomas Woodworth
Samuel Witherell
Theophilus Witherell
William Wilcome

Nicholas Wade
Robert Whitcomb
John Hallet
Joseph White
Timothy White
Jonathan Jackson
John Witherell
William Parker
Widow Young

Several others had a privilege of the commons for wood and pasture, but not in further division of land, because they had removed and still retained their farms, or because they had recently arrived. For example.

John Saffin's house. He was in Massachusetts 1673.
John Stockbridge. He had removed to Boston 1647.
Serj, William Ticknor. He was not a householder 1647.
John Rance. He was a travelling Quaker.
John Nollman. He had recently come into the plantation.
Israel Hobart. His family then in Hingham.
Henry Joslin. Recently come from Black Point.
Edward Wanton. Not a householder in 1647.
John Otis. Had temporarily removed to Barnstable.
Timothy Foster. He resided mostly in Dorchester.
James Davis. Recently arrived in Town.
Benjamin Chandler, as above.
Israel Sylvester. Had a house in Marshfield also.
Nicolas Albeson, (the Sweede, uncertain wherefore).

UNITED STATES CENSUS.

In 1790 (65 of color), 2862 souls.
1800, ... 2728.
No. of houses . . . . . 420.
1810, ... 2969.
1820, ... 3235.
1830, (60 of color), 3512.

We state the census taken in 1830, viz. 3512, according to the list of Mr. Berry the agent.

It having been suspected that the census was taken hastily and imperfectly, the Town voted in November 1830, that the school agents in each district should be requested to make a return as soon as might be, of the census in their respective districts. By that return the population amounts to 3573. This includes about sixty people of color.

ANCIENT LAND MARKS.

It may be useful to describe some of the land marks noticed in the early laying out of lands.

Asp hill, (or Mast hill), in the beach woods near Johnson's swamp.
Belle house neck, near Little's bridge, now Cushing neck.
Bound brook, falls into the gulph at Lincoln's mills.
Bound rock, the land mark of the patent line near Lincoln's mills.
Bound brook neck, north-east of Lincoln's mills.
Black swamp, on Bound brook above the mills.
Buck's rock, near the gulph meadows.
Booth's hill, near junction of the roads one mile south Lincoln's mills.
Brushy hill, three fourths mile south-east from the north Meeting-house.
Briggs's harbour, within the glades (or Strawberry cove).
Bumpas's bridge, over north branch of second Herring brook, above Dead swamp.
Burnt Plain, one mile north west of Hoop-pole hill and south-west of Mount Blue.
Bryant's bridge, over the second Herring brook.
Brook hall field, north side of Belle house neck.
Buck's corner, south-east old parsonage, (see Isaac Buck).
Barstow's hill, on the Plymouth road at Snappet Meeting-house.
Black pond and hill, one and an half mile west of Town-house.
Block-house, on North river half mile above Union bridge.
Barstow's bridge in 1650 and later, now North river bridge.
Blue bridge and island, between Hoop-pole Hill and burnt plain.
Beaver dams, on Satuit brook – on first Herring brook at the ancient fulling mill – on second Herring brook at the south of Dead swamp – on third Herring brook below old pond – also at Valley swamp above Jacob's mills – also a half mile west of Nathaniel Brooks's.
Cedar point, north of the harbour at the Light-house.
Crow point, on the south of the harbour.
Clay pits, in 1650, half mile east of "the stepping stones."

LAND MARKS.

Cold spring swamp, 1650, on Merritt's brook.
Cleft rock, back of John Pierce's, north of Conihasset burying ground.
Castle rock, the point at the gulph mill.
Cushing hill, (rather modern), half mile east of Jacob's mill.
Country road, in 1646, leading to Cohasset, in 1670, the Plymouth road.
Cordwood hill, one mile south-west of the south Meeting-house.
Clay pit cart way, south-west of Cordwood hill, and earlier south-east of old Church hill.
Cornet's rocks, in the North river opposite the Two mile mills.
Cornet's mill, 1656, at the Indian path below old pond, (Major Winslow's).
Chamberlain plain, north east of Beaver dam or Dead swamp.
Candlewood plain, between Hanover Meeting-house and Drinkwater.
Cricket hole in 1640, west of Jonah's mill (now called) or Buttonwod swamp.
Cedar swamp cart way, 1660, from Booth hill to Merritt's brook.
Capt. Jacob's cart way 1720, over Beaver dam at Valley swamp.
Drinkwater, on the west branch of Indian head river, south of Hanover.
Daman's Island, 1649, in the gulph marshes.
Eagle's nest swamp, the great swamp south-east of Beach woods.
Flat swamp, between Mount Blue and Mount Ararat.
Fox hill, one mile south-west of Wild cat hill.
Farm neck, or Great neck, north of the harbour to the glades.
Fane Island, 1646, in the marshes at Farm neck.
Great swamp, (see Eagle's nest).
Gillman plain, on Plymouth road south of Valley swamp.
Greenfield, in 1633, &c. south half mile of second cliff.
Gravelly beach, on North river, east side, two miles above Union bridge.
Gray's hill, half mile south of Cordwood hill.
Great neck, (see Farm neck).
George Moore's swamp and bridge, south branch of first Herring brook.
Groundsell brook, falls into Bound brook west of Mount Hope.
Groundsell hill, east part of Belle house neck, also east of Joshua Bryant's.
Gulph Island, at the mouth of first Herring brook.
Dead swamp, on second Herring brook, one mile from its mouth.
Dry Cedar swamp, on Merritt's brook, near ancient Studly place.

Hanmer's hook, west of Hanover Meeting-house.
Hugh's cross and brook, south branch, third Herring brook at Curtis's mill.
Hickes's swamp, east of Brushy hill.
Hoop-pole hill, one mile west of the south Meeting-house.
Hoop-pole neck, near Great or Farm neck, west of stepping stones.
Hoop-pole cedar swamp, west of Hoop-pole hill.
Halifax hill and swamp, one mile south-west mount Blue.
Horse Island, a marsh island near Farm neck.
Hatchetrock, near John Otis's, a mile south of the stepping stones.
Hollet's island, Marsh Island near the stepping stones.
Herring brook hill, on which south Meeting-house stands.
Hobart's landing, on North river a mile above Little's bridge.
Dogget's ferry, now Little's bridge.
Iron mine, or Indian head river brook, half mile south-west Hanover corners.
Indian path, over third Herring brook, foot of Old pond.
Job's landing, east side North river, below the brick-kilns.
Jenkins's meadow, east side of Valley swamp.
Johnson's swamp, west of Beach woods and mount Hope.
King's landing, half mile below Union bridge.
Long marsh, on first Herring brook above the mills, (1640).
Little marsh, east of the harbour in 1636.
Log bridge, in 1650, over third Herring brook at Elijah Barstow's.
Meeting-house lane, old burying ground south east of the harbour, 1633.
Merritt's brook, falls into Bound brook above the mills.
Musquashcut pond, at Farm neck, 1637, (near J. B. Turner, Esq.)
Man hill, 1648, east of Musquashcut pond.
Mast hill, (or Asp), in the Beach woods.
Mount Hope, on the west of the Town, near Hingham and Cohasset corners.
Mount Blue, one mile south-east of mount Hope.
Mount Ararat, one mile north-east of mount Blue.
New found marsh, on Spring brook, west of Dead swamp one half mile.
New harbour marshes, from Little's bridge to the cliffs.
New saw mill, in 1678, above Old pond at Curtis's.
Old brick yard, in 1647, south-east of Episcopal Church hill.
Old saw mill, in 1653, at Stockbridge's on first Herring brook.
Old saw mill, in 1676, on third Herring brook at Indian path, (at Winslow's).

LAND MARKS.

Old bridge, in 1670, at the east foot of Curtis hill or buttonwood hill.
Prouty's dam, 1686, at the road north of Hooppole hill.
Prospect hill, at Hingham line on the Hersey road.
Pine Island, below Little's bridge, also near Cohasset harbour.
Planting Island, south-west of Great or Farm neck.
Penguin rock, east of Farm neck.
Project dale, west part of Hanover.
Rocky swamp, south of third Herring brook below Jacob's mill.
Ridge hill, mile south-east the Town-house, also on Plymouth road.
Rotten marsh, between Stockbridge's mill and Little's bridge.
Rotten marsh swamp, south of Rotten marsh.
Satuit brook, falls into the creek at the harbour.
Savage lot, east of mount Blue, formerly property of Thomas Savage, Esq. Boston.
Spring swamp, south of Plymouth road in Hanover.
Spring brook, west branch of second Herring brook.
Slab brook, south-west White oak plain, now Margaret's brook.
Great spring swamp, near North river below Cornet's rocks.
Stepping stones, from the Cohasset road to Hooppole neck.
Strawberry cove or Briggs's harbour, within the glades.
Sweet swamp, near Cohasset road, a half mile north of north Meeting-house.
Stony brook, east branch of Merritt's brook.
Stony cove, on North river near King's landing.
Schewsan's neck, north-east of Belle house neck.
Stockbridge's old way, from Stockbridge's mill to Town-house, &c.
Sand hill, on Stockbridge's old way, one mile south-west of the Town-house.
Symon's hill, near Burnt plain on south-west.
Pincin hill, half mile north-east from the Town-house.
Round head swamp, south of Eagle's Nest swamp.
Rattle snake hill and rock, half mile west from Wild cat hill.
Till's creek, 1640, now Dwelley's creek, opposite Gravelly beach.
Taunton Dean bridge, (1680), and brook, south-west of Halifax hill and near late John Daman's.
Valley swamp, above Jacob's mill on second Herring brook.
White oak plain, one mile west of the south Meeting-house.
White oak plain bridge, on south east White oak plain.
Wild Cat hill, 1640, north side of old pond, and south of Cordwood hill one mile and a half.

Wolf Trap, near Iron mine brook in Hanover.
Wigwam neck, near the gulph and Hooppole neck.
Wanton's brook, east of Hooppole hill.
William's rock, north west of the light-house.
Walnut Tree hill, half mile south of Stockbridge's mill.
Walnut hill, west of Beaver dam on second Herring brook.
Wills's Island, a marsh island near Little's bridge.
Walter Woodworth's hill, the N. east part of Walnut Tree hill.
Fresh marsh, 1690, near Plymouth road.
Buttonwood swamp, above Jonah's mill, S. W. of Church hill.
Spruce swamp, S. of Cordwood hill and second Herring brook.
Digged hill, (1670), where William James's house now stands.
Torrey's bridge, (1690), near late Walter Jacob's.
Bardin's forge, (1704), now Curtis's anchor shop in Hanover.
Stony brook swamp, south-west of Booth hill.
Henchman's dam, (1700), near Halifax hill.
Pickell's hole, near late Galen Daman's, half mile south-east of Black pond hill,
Hickes's hole, east side of Great swamp.
Briggs's neck, at Burnt plain swamp.
Jacob's frame swamp, west of Symon's hill.
Cold west hill, fourth of mile south-east of Buttonwood or Curtis's hill, (1680).
Wolf swamp, (see Dead swamp), 1673.
Ben's hill, half mile south of Symon's hill.
Church's hill, on Plymouth road half mile west of Hugh's cross brook, (Hanover).
Wampee's swamp, south-west of Hanover Meeting-house.
Nichols' hill, mile south of the harbour, near Capt. Leonard Clap's.
Turkey plain, near Indian head river in Hanover.
Beach neck, Curtis street in Hanover,
Little Cedar swamp, near Indian head river.
Collamore's ledge, midway between Cedar point and the glades.
Egypt, a tract of land adjoining Man hill and Musquashcut pond,
Queen Ann's corner, on the Plymouth road at Hingham line; so called from Ann Whiton, who kept a tavern at that place, from 1730, many years.
Ludden's Ford, on North rivet above North river bridge on Plymouth road.

Gov. Winthrop in his pedestrian journey to Plymouth in 1632, (Winthrop I. 92), named it Luddam's Ford, "from Mr. Luddam their guide," who carried over the Governor and Rev. Mr.

Wilson on his back. We have no doubt that James Ludden," an early settler in Weymouth, was this guide, who had the honor to carry his Excellency *a-pick-back*.

POST OFFICES AND ROADS.

A Post-office was established in Scituate in 1800, and kept by Charles Turner, jr., Esq. the first Post Master. In 1805, it was removed to Augustus Clapp's, (P. M.), where it remained until 1828, Chandler Clap having been Post Master the two last years. In 1828, a Post-office was established at South Scituate, J. K. Nash, Post Master: and the same year an office was established at West Scituate, on the Plymouth road, Edward Jacob, Post Master. In 1829, the old Scituate office was removed to Shadrach B. Merritt's, Post Master, and in the same year an Office was established at the harbour, Gideon W. Young, Post Master. There are now four officers in the Town.

A mail passed through Scituate to Plymouth from the time of the establishment of the Post-Office department: and another from Boston by way of Cohasset, since 1800. These have been carried by stage coaches nearly the whole time. An accommodation coach began to pass from South Scituate to Boston in March 1828, owned by a company of gentlemen of Scituate: it is now (since January 1831) owned by Mr. Doolittle of Boston and Mr. Parker Jones. The excellent hotel in West Scituate on the Plymouth road, was first established by Eliphalet Leonard about 1800, who was largely concerned in the Plymouth stages. The masters that have succeeded in that house have been Davis Whiton, James W. Sivret and John Smith.

---

* In the Weymouth records we notice Mary daughter of James and Alice Ludden, born 1633 – Sarah 1639 – John 1656. Sarah married Daniel Fairfield 1659. The name is written Louden in Plymouth county at this time.

FAMILY SKETCHES.

PREFACE.

In presenting to the publick the following Family Sketches, it may not be improper, by way of preface, to observe, that though many of the families in our Catalogue cannot exhibit a line of illustrious names, yet they are such as partook in the perils of founding and defending this country, in times when courage, constancy and patience were indeed common virtues, but not the less admirable to us for being common at that time. There needs no apology for attempting to preserve the genealogies of those families, who occupied these hills in those early times: it is all the nobility we have; and it is nobility enough, when we can trace our descent from the fathers of New England.

Nature is wonderfully impartial in the distribution of intellectual talents: and it seems to be the fixed order of Providence, that families, in this respect, should flourish and decline: nay, often, that an individual should spring forth into eminence, whose "origin was as obscure as that of the spark, which by the collision of steel and adamant, is struck out of darkness."

It is highly instructive to learn the character, opinions, and manners of those men, and to follow them in their transaction of the concerns of their young communities, and to observe what an impress they were giving to the character of future generations, and how, almost unconsciously, they were preparing the foundation for a free and illustrious empire. This is the philosophy of history. But the muse of history is a sister and inmate of that of Poetry. Few subjects are more agreeable (at least to many minds) than that of contemplating the characters of the men who first broke the soil which we now cultivate, and few things can more excite the imagination, than to muse upon the spot where they lighted their domestic fires, or to walk over the green turf that covers their remains.

It would, however, be weakness in us to hold the memory of our ancestors in undiscriminating admiration. They were men, and had their faults, for which it is hardly apology enough to say, that they were the faults of the age. In their opposition to the Church of England, they were often found contending against the most unessential forms, as if they involved the deepest principles of religion: and their nonconformity, even in these, degenerated to obstinacy. But then it was defensive obstinacy;

and the contest, though nominally relating to so trifling a question, as whether a cap should be round or square, in reality, involved the question of liberty or subjection.

It was their object to found a pure and harmonious Church; and in pursuing that object, they committed mistakes rather than crimes. In the first place they had not profited by their own example in England, as well as the example of all Christendom, to learn that a community or church of perfectly harmonious sentiments was a vision and not reality. Then after having defended, with a martyr's zeal, the liberty of interpreting the Scriptures for themselves, they hastened to the inconsistency of claiming a right of interpreting the Scriptures for others. And again, in order to preserve the greatest practicable degree of unity of opinion, instead of the true policy of toleration, they embraced the mistaken policy of persecution. Yet it was in some degree defensive, because they were rather desirous to remain unmolested by others, than to invade their faith or practice. This furnishes some apology for their desires to keep out the Quakers from their communities: but the apology would go farther, had they not manifested both a vindictive spirit towards foreigners who came to disturb their peace, and a censoriousness nearly as rigorous, towards the members of their own Churches, who dared to hold an opinion not approved by the majority. They ought to have been aware that their own example of resistance against the Church of England had fostered and encouraged the resistance which they themselves met.

But after all these abatements, our admiration of their virtues, their sufferings and their achievements is deservedly high. Many of them, if they had not stood in the ranks of power and nobility, had certainly stood in the ranks of the most learned and enlightened people of England: and their integrity, their piety, and the purity of their morals in general, were unimpeachable.

It would be filial impiety in us, not to honor their memories: it would be the part of ignorance, not to confess, that the spirit of freedom which dwelt first in them, has gradually grown up to that more enlightened spirit of liberty which is our present glory: and especially would it be the part of ingratitude, not to honor their memories for their labours in subduing this wilderness, and their sufferings in defending and preserving a home for us their posterity. We love to speak of the patriots of the Revolution; but we ought to know that we owe less, if possible, to the patriots of 1776, than to those of 1676. The one was a contest for liberty: the other a struggle for existence.

"— — egregias animas, quæ sanguine nobis,
Hanc Patriam peperere suo, decorate supremis
Muneribus." AEN. xi. 24.

Ministers of the First Church.

Previously to the gathering of a Church under Mr. Lothrop, January 18, 1634, O. S.* we have found few records that relate to the teachers of religion, who may have visited and occasionally officiated at Scituate.

Mr. Giles Saxton

was undoubtedly the first who officiated for any considerable term of time. We find his name on the list of freemen in Massachusetts in 1631. We have no record to show when he came to Scituate, nor how long he resided in the plantation: we can only infer from incidental dates and facts, that it must have been between the years 1631 and 1634.

Mather, in his Magnalia, furnishes us with all the notice which is extant, of Mr. Saxton; and he was ignorant of his Christian name. It is our conjecture that it was Giles, and the same who took the freeman's oath in 1631.

Mather thus speaks of him: "Mr. — Saxton was a Yorkshireman, a studious and learned person, and a great Hebrician. The unsettled condition of the Colony, and some unhappy contention in the plantation where he lived, put him upon removing from Scituate, first to Boston, and so unto England, in his reduced age. I find in honest Mr. Ryther's devout book, entitled 'a plat for Mariners,' this passage concerning him. "An old Puritan Minister, Mr. Saxton, of Leeds in Yorkshire, in a storm coming from New England, when they were all expecting the vessel to sink, said, 'Oh! who is now for heaven? Who is bound for heaven?' " Mag. I. 536.

The "unhappy contention in the plantation," of which Mather speaks, may have been nothing more than that alluded to in Mr. Vassall's letter to Mr. Wilson, (see Ecclesiastical History), viz. concerning the removal of their Meeting-house nearer to the North River. A discussion respecting the mode of baptism had not yet agitated the plantation, that we can learn.

---

* The second centennial anniversary will fall on January 7, 1835, N. Style. See note on *double dating*, at the close of this work.

Mr. John Lothrop.

By the industrious researches of a descendant of this worthy man, (the late Rev. John Lathrop, D. D. of Boston), we are furnished with many interesting notes of Mr. Lothrop, the first regularly settled minister of Scituate. He is particularly noticed also in Neal's history of the Puritans. He had been a minister at Egerton, in Kent in England; and having imbibed the principles of the Puritans, he renounced his orders under the Church of England, and removed to London, where he found the same sentiments gaining ground. This was in 1623. Mr. Henry Jacob had established the first Congregational Church in England, at London, in the year 1616: it was on the plan of Robinson's at Leyden, he having consulted with Mr. Robinson on the subject. Mr. Jacob having removed to Virginia in 1624, Mr. Lothrop became his successor in London. That Church has held their meetings privately, and escaped the vigilance of their persecutors for some time: at length, April 29, 1632, they were discovered by Tomlinson, the pursuivant of the bishop, holding a meeting for religious worship, at the house of Mr. Humphrey Barnet in Blackfriars. Forty-two of them were apprehended, and eighteen only escaped. Mr. Lothrop, with others, was imprisoned, where he remained until April 1634. two full years, and was then set at liberty, on condition of departing from the kingdom. Morton, in the New England Memorial, remarks, that "during the time of his imprisonment, his wife fell sick, of which sickness she died. He procured liberty of the bishop to visit his wife before her death, and commending her to God in prayer, she soon after gave up the ghost."

He embarked for Boston, with about thirty of his Church and people, and arrived September 18, 1634, in the ship Griffin: and on the 27th of the same month he proceeded, with his friends, to Scituate, where a considerable settlement had already been made by "the men of Kent," and who received Mr. Lothrop as a former acquaintance. A considerable accession had been made to the settlement in the autumn of the same year, as we observe in the records of Plymouth Church, November 23, 1634, Anthony Annable, Henry Cobb, George Kenrick, George Lewis, and several others, were dismissed from the Plymouth Church, "in case they join in a body at Scituate." The Church was gathered on the eighteenth of the January following, and Mr. Lothrop "elected into office." The ceremonies of induction into office, were the laying on of the hands of the elders with prayer. Those elders had probably been elected previously and ordained by the Church on the same day.

During Mr. Lothrop's residence in Scituate, he lived on a farm, granted by the Court and laid out by their committee, on the south-east side of Colman's hills. The place is accurately marked by deeds of conveyance, viz. nigh the first Herring brook where it approaches nearest to the sand hills: bounded by Josiah Checket's land west – by John Hewes' and the highway south – and by Humphry Turner's east. This place with the buildings, was sold to Mr. Hatherly (who was always ready to accommodate in affairs of the plantation, with his purse) in 1640: and by Mr. Hatherly to Christopher Blackwood in 1641: and by Blackwood to Mr. Charles Chauncy in 1642. Mr. Lothrop had shares in the New Harbour marshes, between his house and the North river.

His ministry here was not prosecuted with great sucess or in much peace. The difficulties with which he was embarrassed, early inclined him to seek another residence for himself, and such of his friends as might choose to accompany him, and application was made to the Governor accordingly. In the memoir prepared by his descendant, above named, two letters to Gov. Prence are preserved,* dated at Scituate in 1638, touching his proposed removal. In these letters he observes, "Many grievances attend me, from the which I would be freed, or at least have them mitigated, if the Lord see it good." But he so cautiously avoids naming those grievances, that we are obliged to seek an explanation from other sources. He remarks also, "Your worthy self, together with the rest joined and assisting in the Government with you, having gratuitously and freely, upon our earnest and humble suits, granted and conferred a place for the transplanting of us. – Wherefore let me entreat and beseech you to do this further greate curtisye for us, to make composition with the Indians for the place, with what speede you can, and we will freely give satisfaction to them, and strive to be the more enlarged in thankfulness to you," The place to which removal was contemplated at that time, is not named; but we have no doubt that it was Seipican, (Rochester), because an order of Court, 1638, grants "Seipican for

---

* The originals were found amongst Governor Winslow's papers by Hon. John Davis.

the seateing of a township for a Congregation, to Mr. Thomas Besbeech, Mr. James Cudworth, William Gilson, Anthony Annable, Henry Cobb, Henry Rowley, Edward Foster, Robert Linnet and others." The place of destination was changed however the next year, and the removal made to Barnstable in 1639 and 40. The records of Scituate show that more than half the Church removed with their pastor. The author of the New England Memorial observes, "He was a man of a humble heart and spirit – lively in dispensation of the word of God, studious of peace, furnished with godly contentment, willing to spend and be spent for the cause and Church of Christ. He fell on sleep in the Lord, November 8, 1653."*

The troubles which affected his peace at Scituate, were in part, the dissensions amongst his people on the subject of removing their Meeting-house, but chiefly, we believe, their dissensions on the subject of baptism. The mode of baptism was a subject which had shaken and divided his Church before he left England, in 1633; and the controversy followed him and divided them again; this appears from the fact that many of those who remained at Scituate after his removal to Barnstable, brought in Mr. Chauncy for their pastor, against the remonstrances and opposition of nearly one half of the Church; and eagerly adopted his mode of immersion.

The first wife of Mr. Lothrop died in England in 1633, while he was a prisoner, as related above. There were four sons of that wife who came with him, viz. Thomas, Samuel, Joseph and Benjamin.

He married a second wife, (whose name we have not learned), whose sons were Barnabas and John. He had also two daughters, Jane and Barbara of the first wife, and Abagail of the second.

Thomas settled in Barnstable, and his posterity are numerous in Plymouth County. We believe also that the families of this name in Cohasset are his descendants.

A Thomas Lothrop of Barnstable married Deborah Loring of Hingham, in 1736; he died early in Boston. His only son was the late venerable Col. Thomas Lothrop of Cohasset, born 1738, whose sons are John, Capt. Peter and Capt. Anson.

Samuel settled in Norwich, Connecticut, and his descendants are numerous in that State and in New York.†

---

* Mr. Lothrop was educated at Oxford in England.

† A record made by the descendants of Samuel, varies somewhat from that of the most authentic records that have fallen under our notice. Proba-

MINISTERS OF THE FIRST CHURCH.

Joseph, Barnabas and John settled at Barnstable, and have descendants surviving at Bridgewater and elsewhere, John was in England in 1653, but we believe he returned. Benjamin settled at Charlestown, and has left posterity in Essex County.

Of these sons, Barnabas was the most distinguished. He was an assistant in the Government of Plymouth Colony, also, a member of the first Council in 1692, after the union of the Colonies under the Charter of William and Mary. His wife was Susan Clark. He died at Barnstable in 1715, aged 79. He was born at Scituate, as we believe were all the children of his mother, save Abigail, who was the first child baptized at Barnstable, October 1639. – John married Mary Cole of Plymouth 1671.*

The will of Rev. John Lothrop is dated in 1653. We trust that it is not improper to subjoin an abstract of that will, for historical purposes.

"To my wife, my new dwelling house. To my oldest son Thomas, the house in which I first lived in Barnstable. To my son John in England and Benjamin here, each a cow and 5£. Daughter Jane and Barbara have had their portions already. To the rest of the children, both mine and my wife's, each a cow. To each child one book, to be chosen according to their ages. The rest of my Library to be sold to any honest man who can tell how to use it, and the proceeds to be divided, &c."

The inventory estimates the remainder of his library at £5.

The removal of Mr. Lothrop's family was October 11, 1639. Barnstable Records.

There was a Thomas Lothrop free in Massachusetts 1633. This must have been another family. It was probably his son Thomas, who was killed by the Indians at Deerfield in 1675.

In the papers of the Historical Society, (Vol. IV. 2d series, Anno 1816), it is mentioned that Adam Blackman officiated

---

bly names and order of the ages of Mr. Lothrop's children were as follows: Thomas, Samuel, Joseph, Benjamin, Jane, Barbara, Barnabas, (born at Scituate 1635), John born 1637, Abagail born 1639. *Samuel* of Norwich had sons, Samuel, Israel, *Joseph* and five daughters. *Joseph* had sons, Joseph, Barnabas, *Solomon* and four daughters. *Solomon* had one son *Joseph*, D. D. of West Springfield, and one daughter. Dr. *Joseph* has sons, Solomon, Seth, Joseph, Hon. Samuel and Dwight. The late Rev. John Lothrop, D. D. of Boston, was also a descendant of Samuel of Norwich.

* A John Lothrop died in Boston 1716, and gives in his will "to wife Esther, to son Joseph, to brother Barnabas, and sisters Mary, Martha, Elizabeth, Hannah, Abigail and Experience." We notice also, "Abigail, widow of Barnabas Lothrop, late of Barnstable, died in Boston 1715." This may have been a second wife of Mr. Barnabas Lothrop.

for a time in Scituate. It has been repeated by Farmer and Baylies. But as we ourselves were the author of that mistake, we take this opportunity to correct it. It was not Blackman, but Christopher Blackwood. He officiated a short time in 1640; but soon disappears, having deceased or perhaps removed from the country.

Mr. Charles Chauncy

was born in Hertfordshire, England, A. D. 1589, and baptized at Yardley, November 1592. He was the fifth son of George Chauncy, who died in 1627. He was prepared for the University at the celebrated Westminster school. While he was a student there, the gun powder plot was discovered, which, had it taken effect, must have destroyed the seminary with the pupils, if it had blown up the Parliament house, as was interided, the buildings being contiguous.

He was matriculated of Trinity College, Cambridge, from which, he proceeded B. D. after a distinguished course. He was afterward Hebrew professor, and subsequently Greek professor of the same College. Cotton Mather asserts that "he was incomparably well skilled in all the learned languages, especially in the oriental, and eminently in the Hebrew." In a few years he became a very popular preacher, first at Marston and then at Ware. While he was at Ware, Archbishop Laud issued his famous Licences for Sports on the Lord's day, and prohibiting preaching in the afternoon, that the people might engage in amusements. Mr. Chauncy endeavored to evade these pitiful laws, by catechising in the afternoon. But this, said the bishop, "was as bad as preaching." Shortly certain spies upon his words, reported to the bishop certain objectionable expressions in his sermons, relating to the errors of the times, and he was called before the High Commission Court; the Court referred his cause to the bishop of London, and the bishop adjudged him to make a publick recantation in Latin. The worthy Mr. Chauncy was seized with terror and complied. But this weakness of his, afterward filled him with poignant regret, to which he was wont to allude on all publick occasions. But he soon found that there was no rest for him in England, and he joined some of those who were flying to this wilderness. He arrived at Plymouth on the latter end of December 1637, a few days (says Mather) before the great earthquake, which happened January 1, 1638. He remained in Plymouth nearly three years, as an assistant in the ministry to Mr. Rayner. We observe that the Colony Court assigned him certain grants of land, and particularly ten acres of meadow at Jones's River in 1640, (now in Kingston). In 1641, he was elected pastor of the Church at Scituate. At the "renewing of his ordination," as Mather terms it, he preached from Prov. IX. 10. "Wisdom hath sent forth her maidens," – and in alluding to that regretted recantation which he had made in England, he said, "Alas! Christians, I am no maiden; my soul hath been defiled with false worship: how wondrous is the free grace of Christ, that I should still be employed amongst the maidens of wisdom." Mather intimates that Mr. Chauncy alludes in his expression, "false worship," to the English Prayer book, the ordination of Priests, &c. Neal, in his account of his recantation, (Vol. II. Ch. 5.), represents his crime and his recantation to relate principally to his opposing the custom of enclosing the communion table with a rail, and of kneeling at the communion service.

His ministry in Scituate was a scene of constant agitation. (See Ecclesiastical History in the former part of this work). These vexations were owing in a great measure to his own ardent temper and impatience of opposition. He met with an opponent in Mr. Vassall, who was at least his equal in argument, and who early entered into a controversy with him on the subject of the *seals,* and particularly on the mode of baptism: and as they could come to no terms of concord, Mr. Vassall and nearly half the Church and Society withdrew and formed another Church. There seemed to be three parties in Scituate at this time: one of which held to infant sprinkling – another to adult immersion exclusively – and a third (of which was Mr. Chauncy) to immersion of infants as well as adults.

Winthrop remarks, (Vol. II. p. 72), "Mr. Chauncy persevered in his opinion of dipping in baptism, and practised accordingly, first upon two of his own, which being in very cold weather, one of them swooned away. Another having a child about three years old, feared it would be frightened (as others had been; and one caught hold on Mr. Chauncy, and had nearly pulled him into the water). She brought her child to Boston, with letters testimonial from Mr. Chauncy, and had it baptized there." Several children were afterward carried to Boston for baptism.

Winthrop also names another error of Mr. Chauncy which gave offence at Scituate, "That the Lord's supper ought to be administered in the evening, and every Lord's day." Vol. I. p. 331.

Now this latter practice truly, so far as we can discern, is of as much importance as is the particular mode of applying the water in baptism. No one can doubt that the Lord's supper was instituted in the evening, and few, if any, will deny that baptism may have sometimes been administered by immersion, in the times of the Apostles. But that these modes should be adhered to in all climates and all seasons, seem to us to *put a yoke* upon Christians *which they are not able* or bound *to bear.* The discretion of Christians may very properly lead to such modes of administering these ordinances, as may seem to them to be most decorous and most useful.

Though Mr. Chauncy persevered in these practices so long as he remained in Scituate, he suffered only from individual opposition. The government of the Colony never took up the controversy, as was done in Massachusetts. In 1644, that government began to enact penal laws against "Anabaptistry," and a few years later, under Endicott and Dudley, the Baptists were whipped, imprisoned and banished. An order of Court in Massachusetts in 1651, enacts "banishment to such as obstinately oppose the baptism of infants." Mr. Chauncy, on his election to the Presidency of the College, made a compact with the Overseers, to be quiet on the subject of the mode of baptism. It would seem, therefore, that his opinions were much relaxed from their former rigour.

There are many evidences on record, that Mr. Chauncy was unhappy at Scituate. The circumstances by which he was surrounded, together with his ardent temperament, make apology in part, for his uneasiness. He was a studious man, beyond what is often known, and was subject to all the nervous sensibilities peculiar to hard students. He was consciously endowed with great talents and eminent learning. He was devoted to his profession, and he was too much inclined to accept it as an indignity, that his powers should not keep down all opposition, and his labours bring him at least the comforts of life in temporal things. There lay his weakness — in not being able to make allowance for the poverty and hardships of his people in the new settlement, and in imagining that his opponents in religious principles and usages, were his personal enemies. He was constantly chafed by the opposition: his Society had become divided and weakened, and his apprehensions in regard to a livelihood were of a most melancholy kind. In 1649, Mr. Chauncy made known the poverty of his circumstances to the Governor and assistants, probably with the expectation of some grant for his relief, though we do not find that any grant was made with reference to this application. It is a well known historical fact, that about that time there was a question started, whether it were right to pay taxes for the support of religious teachers; and many withdrew their assistance in their support. From this circumstance Mr. Chauncy may have met with embarrassment, as did his successor. The list of his property above named, is a curious document, which we have here extracted from the Colony records.

"I. The house of Mr. Hatherly, bought of Mr. Vassall, with the enlargements. A new building and barn and other out houses.

II. All the ground about it, being six acres.

III. An enclosed stony field, near the marsh.

IV. An orchard behind the house.

V. The barn close, compassing the barn.

VI. Twenty acres upland – ten of it enclosed called the New field.

VII. Twelve acres of Conihassett marsh.

VIII. Twenty acres at Hooppole island, with undivided lands among Conihassett purchasers.

CHARLES CHAUNCY, 1649."

Now it is obvious, that in those times, this could not have been a very productive estate, and yet, while his people were suffering all the hardships of newcolonists, it is doubtful whether many of them were better provided for than their minister. It is certain that he had warm friends. The people of Plymouth (at least a part) would have made great sacrifices to have enjoyed his services there, and those people of Scituate who tolerated or who embraced his sentiments on the subject of baptism, were strongly attached to him. In 1654, Mr. Hatherly, the untiring patron of the plantation, offered to make a deed of gift to Mr. Chauncy, of a house and land on "Satuit brook," (see notes on the first Parish), on condition that Mr. Chauncy agree to spend his life in Scituate, which offer he declined. Mr. Hatherly then makes the deed to the Church, and submits the farm to their disposal. The same year the Church conveys it to Mr. Chauncy, by deed of gift, signed probably by most of the male members, viz. Timothy Hatherly, Thomas Chittenden, Richard Sealis, John Williams, Humphry Turner, John Allen, Edward Jenkins, Rhodolphus Ellmes, Thomas Clap, William Wills, Isaac Chittenden, Henry Ewell, Walter Woodworth, John Hewes, George Pidcoke, Samuel Jackson, Thomas Ensign, Joseph Colman, Samuel House, John Daman.

Though. this was given, without any condition to be performed on Mr. Chauncy's part, at least, specified in the deed, yet, on his retiring at the close of the same year, the farm seems to have been relinquished to the Church.

The time of Mr. Chauncy, while at Scituate, must have been spent with his accustomed diligence in business. Besides performing his ministerial labours, he practised to a considerable extent as a physician, for which, Mather informs us, he was eminently qualified: and moreover was engaged in instructing his own sons, and preparing young men for the ministry. We can state for a certainty, that the celebrated Mr. Thomas Thatcher, who had come out of England before his Theological education was completed, was under the care of Mr. Chauncy at Scituate. This was the ancestor of the eminent ministers of that name. He was settled in Weymouth in 1644, and in Boston 1669.

In the autumn of 1654, Mr. Chauncy received an invitation from his former people at Ware in England, to return to them; he had concluded to comply with their request, and had proceeded to Boston with his family in order to embark for England, when the overseers of Harvard College offered him the Presidency of that institution, and he accepted. His inauguration took place November 27, 1654. He entered upon his office with his wonted energy. Having softened in his opinions concerning the mode of baptism, he became also pastor to the Church in Cambridge. Mather gives us an account of his labours in words that astonish us, "He rose at 4 o'clock, both winter and summer – he spent his first hour in secret prayer – then visiting the College Hall, he expounded a chapter, with a short prayer before, and a long prayer after – he then did the like, with a prayer before and after in his family – and when the bell rang for nine at night, he retired for another hour of secret prayer. On the Lord's day morning, he preached a sermon in the College Hall. Beside all this, he often set aside whole days for prayer with fasting, alone by himself, and sometimes spent whole nights in prayer. Many days of prayer with fasting, he also spent with his religious consort: and many such days he kept with his family, calling in the assistance of three or four godly neighbors. Moreover, every day, morning and evening, after he had expounded a chapter, he used to examine his children and servants, with some fit questions thereon."

In terms equally high, this singular historian commends his ability and diligence in teaching the liberal arts, and in conducting the government of the Institution. He acknowledges that he suffered the disadvantages of a *hasty temper;* but adds,

that these were presently corrected by his *holy temper.* Though his life was thus spent in labours, which sooner than all others are wont to impair the human constitution, yet the elasticity or vigour of his mind was not relaxed until extreme age. "After age had enfeebled him, (says Mather), the fellows of the College, once leading him to preach a sermon in a winter day, they, out of affection to him, to discourage him from so difficult an undertaking, told him, *Sir, you'll certainly die in the pulpit* – but he laying hold on what they had said, as if they had offered him the greatest encouragement in the world, pressed more vigorously through the snow drift, and said, *how glad should I be, if what you have said might prove true.*"
When his friends used to press him to abate his vast labours, he used to reply, "oportet imperatorem stantem mori." His labours were scarcely remitted to the last. At the Commencement in 1671, he took leave of his literary friends and his public labours, in a farewell oration, and "illness growing upon him," he did not live to see another of those anniversaries. He died February 19, 1671, in the eighty-second year of his age. He was buried February 21st, with appropriate honors. The Rev. Urian Oakes, his successor as pastor to the Church of Cambridge, and (after Dr. Hoar) his successor as President of the College, preached his funeral sermon, one passage of which is noted by Mather as being singularly beautiful. The preacher having made some allusion to his hasty temper, turned from the subject, saying, "The mention therof is to be wrapped up in Elijah's mantle." He was thirteen years minister of the first Church in Scituate, (not sixteen, as Mather and Elliot and others state), and seventeen years the President of the College. We believe he was provided for to his satisfaction, after he had been elected President of the College, and learned not to oppose the overseers in the matter of baptism. We observe that the Massachusetts Colony Court in 1659, ordered five hundred acres of land to be laid out for him, near Charles river.

We add a short notice of his family.

His wife was Catharine, the daughter of Robert Eyre, Esq. of Wiltshire: Mather commends her as a person of extraordinary piety. She died January 4th, 1668.

Their children were eight, Isaac, Ichabod, Barnabas, Sarah, Nathaniel and Elnathan, twins, Israel and Hannah.

Isaac was born in England, August 23, 1632, and graduated at Harvard College in 1651, He went to England, was settled in the ministry, and ejected from office at the restoration, and afterward settled in Berry street in London, where he died

February 28, 1712. The celebrated Dr. Isaac Watts was his colleague in 1698, and his successor at his death. His children were Isaac, Uzziel, Charles and Elizabeth.

Ichabod was born in England in 1635, and received his degree at Harvard College also in 1651. He went to England, and was appointed chaplain of Sir Edward Harley's regiment at Dunkirk, 1684. He afterward practised as a physician in Bristol, England, where he died in 1691, July 25th.

Barnabas was born in England in 1637; he graduated at Harvard College in 1657. He was admitted a member of the Church in Cambridge, (Farmer), December 10, 1656. He was a preacher, according to Mather, and died in rather early life, not settled. Sarah was admitted a member of the Church in Cambridge, December 10, 1656. She was afterward the wife of Rev. Gershom Bulkley, of New London, 1659. Nathaniel and Elnathan, twins, were probably born at Plymouth, though baptized at Scituate, December 1641. We believe it was the baptism of these children to which Winthrop alludes. Nathaniel was a fellow of the College, and afterward minister of Hatfield, Connecticut, where he died November 4, 1686. Elnathan, with his twin brother, received his degree at Harvard in 1661; was a preacher, but not settled in the ministry, and afterward a physician in Boston.

Israel was born at Scituate in 1644, and graduated at Harvard in 1661. He was ordained minister of Stratford, Connecticut, 1665, where he deceased March 14, 1703. He left two sons, Charles and Isaac, whose posterity are in England. Dr. Elliot informs us, that at his ordination at Stratford, the laity insisted on their right of "laying on hands," and that one of the lay brothers forgot to take off his mitten, and hence the Episcopalians endeavored to turn it to ridicule, by styling it "the leather mitten ordination." It is a well known historical fact, that at this time, a sharp controversy was agitated respecting the validity of Congregational ordination, and also respecting the right of laymen to bear a part in ordaining ministers. It was gradually yielded up by the laymen, but it may still be made a question, whether they ought not to have retained it, as an original right, both by the early practice of the Congregational churches, and the practice of Apostolic times.

Of Hannah, the youngest daughter of President Chauncy, we have met with few notices.

Of the descendants of President Chauncy, the most distinguished has been the late Dr. Charles Chauncy of Boston. He was the great grandson of President Chauncy, was born

1705, January 1st, – received his degree at Harvard in 1721, was ordained as colleague with Mr. Foxcroft 1727, of the first Church in Boston, whom he survived many years, and in 1778, received the Rev. Dr. Clark as his colleague. He died Feb. 10, 1787. As an author and a divine, not another perhaps in this country has been more extensively known, both here and in Europe. His mother was Sarah Walley probably, as we notice in the records of Boston, "Charles Chauncy married to Sarah Walley 1699." His father was Charles, a merchant in Boston, who was son of Rev. Isaac, of Berry street, London.

MR. HENRY DUNSTER

arrived in Boston A. D. 1640, and took the freeman's oath in 1641. Mather records him amongst the ministers of his "First Class," i. e. those who had been ministers in England before coming to this country. But neither Mather nor Morton nor any other historian has informed us where he exercised his ministry in England. He was acknowledged to be an eminent scholar, and a place seemed to have awaited him on his arrival. Dr. Eaton had been removed from his preceptorship of the Grammar school at Cambridge, (then Newtown), and the school, by means of a legacy from John Harvard, the minister of Charlestown, had been erected into a College, and a President was wanting. At this conjuncture Mr. Dunster arrived, and was chosen President August 27, 1640.

A cotemporary historian remarks, "over the College is Master Henry Dunster placed as President, a learned, considerable, and industrious man, who has so trained up his pupils in the tongues and arts, and so seasoned them with the principles of Divinity and Christianity, that we have, to our great comfort, and in truth beyond our hopes, beheld their progress in learning and godliness also," (see New England's First Fruits).

He was particularly eminent for his Hebrew learning. He had the happy endowment of personal manners and of temper which peculiarly qualified him for governing; and he continued in the Presidency about fourteen years, with great acceptance to the pupils, and likewise to the Overseers, save in one point. In the controversy of that day, he sided in opinion with those who opposed infant baptism; and though he was confessedly mild and tolerant, allowing others to hold a different opinion and practice, yet (as Mather observes) "he filled the Overseers with uneasy fears, lest the students, by his means, should come to be ensnared." They honored him for "his learning and excellent spirit, and laboured with extreme agony, to rescue the good man from his mistakes;" but finding it impracticable, "they did quietly procure his removal." In short, his friends advised him to retire, and he accordingly tendered his resignation to the Overseers October 24, 1654. He immediately repaired to Scituate, where we find notices of him the same autumn, employed in the ministry, and in which he continued nearly five years; we have not been able to ascertain, however, that he was regularly inducted into office. Morton in his New England's Memorial remarks, that while in Scituate" he opposed the abominable opinions of the Quakers," (p. 283. Judge Davis's Edition), and Mr. Baylies in his history of Plymouth Colony, (Vol. II. p. 50), adopts the same idea, and more, even that "he was vindictive" in his persecution of the Quakers. We know not from what authority these remarks are derived. Morton's remark could have scarcely been sufficient to authorize the severity of that of Mr. Baylies, and that Morton, though a contemporary, may not have been an impartial historian in this case, we fully believe. In the first place, it was entirely foreign from the character of President Dunster to be bigoted and persecuting: and in the next place, we can quote as good authority as any other, that if he opposed their opinions, it was only by argument and persuasion, and that he equally opposed the persecution of the Quakers, (see General Cudworth's letter, in the Family Sketch of Cudworth).

Elliot is in an error respecting the date of Mr. Dunster's death; it is on record in Scituate February 27, 1659. "He was embalmed and removed to Cambridge, and honorably buried," (New England's Memorial). "He died in such harmony of affection with the good men who had been the authors of his removal from Cambridge, that he, by his will, ordered his body to be carried to Cambridge for its burial, and bequeathed legacies to those very persons." (Mather).

He left but few printed works. There is a monument of his literary labours in the New England Psalms, which were sung for nearly a century in some of the Churches. This translation of the Psalms was first printed at Cambridge in 1640, and was the united labour of the Rev. Thomas Weld and John Elliot, ministers of Roxbury, and of Richard Mather of Dorchester: "but afterwards it was thought that a little more art was to be employed upon them, and they were committed unto Mr. Dunster, who revised and refined this translation," (Mather's Mag.) We cannot but wonder what the work could have been at first, since that which was used in the churches until 1700, and indeed subsequently, is called a *refined translation*. But this was before Milton's works were much read, and before Dryden and Pope had exemplified how capable was the English language of the rythm and melody of verse.

Mr. Dunster's wife was Elizabeth, the widow of the Rev. Jesse Glover, who died on his passage to New England in 1639.

His children were David, born May 16, 1645, Henry, born 1650, Jonathan, born 1653. Some of his descendants are in Boston.*

Mr. Nicholas Baker.

This gentleman was one of the first settlers of Hingham, from which circumstance we presume that he came from Hingham in Norfolk, England, as did most of the early inhabitants of that town. He received a share in the first division of house lots in Hingham in 1635, as did also Nathaniel Baker. He afterward became an extensive landholder in Hull, and resided there. He seems to have been employed chiefly in agriculture for several years, though a man of more than ordinary qualifications, and often employed in publick affairs. He was a deputy to the Massachusetts Colony Court (the May session) in 1636, it being the sixth Court that had been holden, but the first in which Hingham was represented. Again, he was a deputy at the May Court in 1638. The practice then, was to choose a deputy for each session. In 1642, he seems to have entertained a purpose of removing: for we observe in the Plymouth Colony records of that year, the following entry: "Nicholas Baker and three others of Hingham, made application to the Court for lands at Seekhonk." But the grant, we believe, was not made: at least, Mr. Baker did not remove.

After the death of President Dunster, he was invited to preach at Scituate, first Church. Where and when he had qualified himself for the ministry we have not learned: but the probability is, that without a regular education, by the force of his own talents, he had acquired a respectable degree of theological knowledge, and by the virtues of his life he had recommended himself to the publick.

He was ordained in Scituate in the year 1660. He left here no memorable name for great powers or great success

---

* Henry J. Dunster, a descendant, performs the press work of this book.

in his ministry, but records are not wanting to show his peaceful and godly influence. He was especially instrumental in bringing to pass a reconciliation of the two Churches at Scituate, which had held no communion with each other for thirty-five years. By the consent of the first Church he signed an instrument of reconciliation with the second Church, April 1, 1675. His Church had now returned to the practice of infant sprinkling, from which they had been led away by President Chauncy.

Cotton Mather, in his quaint style, characterizes him thus: "Honest Nicholas Baker of Scituate, who, though he had but a private education, yet being a pious and zealous man, or, (as Dr. Arrowsmith expresses it), *so good a logician, that he could offer up to God a reasonable service, so good an arithmetician, that he could wisely number his days, and so good an orator, that he persuaded himself to be a good Christian;* and being also one of good natural parts, was chosen Pastor of the Church there; and in the pastoral charge of that Church he continued about eighteen years, until that horror of mankind and *reproach of medicine,* the *stone,* (under which he preached patience by a memorable example of it, never letting fall a worse word than this, which was an usual word with him, 'a mercy of God it is no worse'), put an end to his days." (Magnalia I. 542). He died August 22, 1678.

He was twice married: the first time doubtless in England, and the second time during his ministry in Scituate. We find no record of the marriage, however, in Scituate, and conclude it probable that he was married at Hull. All that we have discovered respecting it, we owe to that curious miscellany, the journal of Mr. Peter Hobart of Hingham, viz. "Mr. Nicholas Baker's wife died at Scituate 1661. Mr. Nicholas Baker married 1662." The births of his children are not found on record at Scituate, and the baptisms in the first Church during his ministry are deficient. The births may have been recorded in Hull.

An abstract of his will, dated 1678.

"To my wife Grace, half my dwelling house at Hull, and the lands adjoining Thomas James' lot. Also a swamp at Allerton's hill – a lot on Strawberry hill – a lot at Sagamore hill – a lot upon White head – a lot on Duke's Island – half my right to commons in Hull – and all my upland and meadow in Hingham during her life: provided my son Samuel, or any of my children at Hull, have liberty of fire wood.

To my son Samuel half my house at Hull, with lands, &c.
To daughter Elizabeth 10£.
To my son Nicholas a share in Conihassett lands at Scituate, he paying to my daughter Sarah 10£.
To daughter Deborah 10£. To daughter Mary 10£.
My wife Grace to be executrix. Brother Nathaniel Baker and kinsman John Loring overseers of this my will."

We can give but little further account of this family.

Samuel, it appears, settled in Hull. Mary was married in Scituate to Stephen Vinal 1661, and has left posterity. Elizabeth married John Vinal of Scituate, brother of Stephen, in 1664, and has also left posterity. Sarah married Josiah Litchfield of Scituate in 1671, and her posterity is almost countless. Deborah married Israel Chittenden of Scituate in 1678, and left posterity. Nicholas inherited a share of Conihassett lands in Scituate, but we find no further trace of him here. We believe there was also a son Nathaniel, though not named in his father's will. He probably settled in Hull.

We observe in the will of Nathaniel Baker of Hingham, dated 1682, that he gives to the children of his son in law John Loring, (his grand children), large tracts of land at Ware river, Turkey hill and elsewhere – and also makes provision for his wife Sarah – and his two Indian servants – and also 10£ apiece to the children of his brother Nicholas late of Scituate.

There was a Samuel Baker of Marshfield, who may have been the son of Rev. Nicholas, named in his will. He married Ellen, daughter of Kenelm Winslow 1656, and had children, Kenelm 1657, Lydia '59, Elizabeth '61, Mary '62, Alice '63, Ellen (or Eleanor) '65: and by a second wife Patience Simmons, married 1677, a son Samuel, who married Sarah Snow 1699.

MR. JEREMIAH CUSHING.

This gentleman was born at Hingham, July 3, 1654. He was the son of Daniel Cushing, Esq. and Lydia his wife, the daughter of Edward Gillman. Daniel, Esq. was the son of Matthew Cushing, one of the early settlers of the town of Hingham. To Daniel Cushing, that town is indebted for the first accurate records of the proceedings of the town. His clerkship commences in 1669, and the method and neatness of the records for many years, does him much credit. Jeremiah his son received his degree at Harvard College in 1676. He was educated for the ministry under the direction of Mr. Norton of Hingham. He was not settled immediately in the ministry. He received an invitation to become the pastor of Haverhill in 1682, which he declined. He began to preach in Scituate in February 1691, and was ordained there on the 27th of May the same year. His salary was £60. Besides this, the Conihassett partners made him a gift of twenty acres of land. It was laid out in 1694, adjoining the lands of John Curtis and Henry Merritt. He purchased John Curtis's house in 1698, and probably resided in it, and rented the parsonage. It stood between Timothy White's and the harbour.

We have few materials for composing a life of Mr. Cushing, and no data by which we may compare the success of his ministry with that of his predecessors or successors, all the Church records during his time being lost. For the want of another Cotton Mather, obscurity must rest upon many ministers of that period. Mather could swell the lives of ordinary men into very respectable dimensions.

The term of Mr. Cushing's ministry was short, he having deceased March 22, 1705, in the fifty-first year of his age and the fourteenth of his ministry. There is a monument to his memory in the old burying ground near the harbour. He suffered a lingering illness, having been obliged to suspend his labours for several months.

He was married to Hannah, the daughter of Thomas Loring of Hingham, June 1, 1685. Their children were Hannah born 1687, Ignatius born 1689, Jeremiah born 1695, and Ezekiel born 1698. His widow was married to John Barker, Esq. a lawyer, in 1706, and the same year Hannah the daughter, was married to Samuel Barker, the son of John, Esq. They resided at the ancient Williams farm, one mile north of the harbour.

None of the sons of Mr. Cushing settled in Scituate. Ezekiel settled at Cape Elizabeth, (Casco Bay). His daughter Lucy, born 1736, was the wife of Dr. James Otis of Scituate, and the mother of Hon. Cushing Otis.

Mr. Nathaniel Pitcher

was born at Dorchester, we believe, and a descendant of Andrew Pitcher, an early settler in that town. He was born in 1685, and received his degree at Harvard College in 1703.

MINISTERS OF THE FIRST CHURCH.

Under the care of Mr. Danforth of Dorchester he received his theological education. He first preached in Scituate in March 1705, during the illness of Mr. Cushing. Again in May 1706, the Church and Society voted to invite him to preach, which he did for a few Sabbaths; and again in the summer of 1707, when he was invited to become their pastor. He was ordained on the 4th Wednesday of September 1707. In 1710, he married Sarah, the daughter of John Cushing, Esq. Their children were Nathaniel born 1711, Samuel born 1713, Sarah born 1715, and Mary born 1716.

This family has long since disappeared from our records. The ministry of Mr. Pitcher was rather short, he having deceased September 27, 1723, and in the thirty-eighth year of his age; as we learn from his monument in the old burying ground. His children were young; and they probably removed to Dorchester, as we find no further notice of them here. Mr. P. attempted to write verses, some of which may be preserved, more for the sake of antiquity than for their merits, (see Appendix).

There was a Joseph Pitcher who came to Scituate nearly at the same time with Rev. Nathaniel, and tradition (perhaps uncertain) speaks of him as a relation. He married Mercy Stetson, 1714. We find the birth of one child only on record, viz. Lydia, born 1717. His wife deceased the same year; and from that time, further traces of the family are lost.

There was also an Ezra Pitcher,* who appears in Scituate in 1730, and who was a relative of the foregoing. He married Zeruiah Booth 1732. His children were Desire born 1733, Ezra born 1735, John born 1736, Nathaniel born 1738, Elisha born 1740. Some of this family removed to Broad Bay in Maine. Nathaniel was in Scituate in 1761, when he married Experience Jones. We believe he was a physician, and removed to Stonington, Connecticut.

A sister of the Rev. Nathaniel Pitcher (Abigail) came with him to Scituate, and was married to David Tilden in 1710.

These are all the notices of value respecting this family that have fallen in our way. Tradition speaks of the Rev. Mr. Pitcher as a gentleman of very agreeable person and manners, a preacher of more than ordinary talents, and remarkable for promoting peace and union amongst his people. Union of religious sentiment very generally prevailed at that time. The

---

* Mr. Ezra Pitcher was chosen deacon in 1754, at which time he is mentioned as having been a member of Brattle street Church, Boston.

controversy on baptism and the opposition to the Quakers had ceased, and Whitefield's excitement had not been spread. It was a mild form of Calvinism into which the general sentiment had settled. Mr. Eells of the second Church, was a cotemporary with Mr. Pitcher, and they are said to have maintained a very remarkable friendship. At the ordination of Mr. Pitcher, the Rev. Peter Thatcher of Milton gave the charge – Rev. Mr. Norton of Hingham, the right hand of fellowship – The Rev. John Danforth of Dorchester preached, (Phil. ii. 20), and Mr. Little and Mr. Eells joined in laying on of hands.

Rev. Shearjashub Bourn.

After the decease of Mr. Pitcher, Mr. Nathaniel Leonard, afterward of Plymouth, was invited to become the pastor of the first Church in Scituate, but declined. Mr. Bourn, who was eventually the successor of Mr. Pitcher, was the son of Bourn, of Sandwich, and a lineal descendant of Mr. Richard Bourn, a preacher to the Cape Indians in early times. He received his degree at Harvard 1720and was ordained in Scituate December 3, 1724. In 1725, he married Abigail, the daughter of the Rev. Roland Cotton of Sandwich. Their children were Elizabeth born 1726, Abigail 1727, Desire 1728, Bathsheba 1730, Shearjashub 1732, (died early). His wife deceased 1732. In 1738, Mr. Bourn married Sarah Brooks of Medford. By her he had one son, Shearjashub, born 1739. His second wife deceased in 1742. He married Deborah, the daughter of Mr. Samuel Barker, in 1750, by whom he had one son, Roland, born 1750. His third wife deceased the same year. He married again in 1757, Joanna Stevens of Roxbury.

His health had become impaired in 1755, by paralytic affections. Through life he had been struggling against the infirmities of an unfortunately feeble constitution, and depressed and melancholy spirits, by which his usefulness was in some measure impaired. Especially after 1755, he proceeded in his labours with such painful efforts, that he was soon induced altogether to withdraw from his publick services. Accordingly he tendered his resignation and was dismissed August 6, 1761. He retired to Roxbury, the native place of his wife, where he deceased August 14, 1768, aged sixty-eight.

The Society testified their great regard for Mr. Bourn and their regret at foregoing his very acceptable services, and generously voted to give him £100 and the use of the parsonage for a year and an half.

We can give very little account of his family. Shearjashub, his son, married Sarah Woodworth, the daughter of James Woodworth of Scituate in 1769. He spent the greater part of his life in Boston, but returned and died at Scituate in September 1819. His children were Sarah born 1770, Lydia 1772, Abigail 1775, Elizabeth 1777, and Bethia 1781. Two of these daughters are living in Scituate, Sarah the wife of William Corlew, and Bethia the wife of Charles Corlew.

At the ordination of Mr. Bourn, Mr. Eells of Scituate gave the charge – Mr. Daniel Lewis of Pembroke gave the right hand of fellowship and preached, (2. Cor. xii. 15). Mr. Brown of Abington and Allen of Bridgewater joined in laying on hands.

Rev. Ebenezer Grosvenor

was born in Pomfret, Connecticut, in 1739. His father was the master of a well known tavern in that place, for a long series of years. Ebenezer received his degree at Yale College in 1759. He preached first at Scituate near the close of 1762, and was ordained April 1763. He married Elizabeth, the daughter of Rev. Mr. Clark of Danvers in 1764. Their children were Deborah born 1765, Lucy born 1766, Ebenezer born 1768, Elizabeth born 1769, (died early), Peter Clarke born 1771, and Nancy born 1773. His ministry was not very quiet. His religious tenets were the moderate Calvinism of that day, and a straiter sect in his Society were disposed to give him some trouble. It is certain that he was not a zealot of Whitefield's school, and hence they suspected him of Arminian heresy, but probably without foundation. He was undoubtedly too mild and catholic in his faith and practice, to give universal satisfaction at that time.* It is said that his wife was much more vexed with the contradictions and oppositions which he met with, than Mr. Grosvanor himself, and was finally instrumental in deciding his determination to retire. It may be added that his poverty and embarrassments during the American war were so great, that it was difficult for him to procure even subsistence for his family. Those who remember the hardships of those times, the scarcity of the necessaries of life, and the wretched

---

* A remonstrance signed by seven, was handed to the council that ordained him.

condition of the paper currency, can give full credit to this account.

He offered his resignation in April 1780, and was honorably dismissed, having officiated as pastor seventeen years. He is now remembered by some of the aged people with great affection and very tender regret. His person is described as rather remarkable for beauty, of middling stature but of noble and commanding presence, but of singular benignity of countenance. As a preacher, he is not said to have risen above mediocrity in power and eloquence, but as a man and a Christian to have excelled in the finest and gentlest traits.

After retiring from Scituate he was invited to preach at Harvard, where he was installed in 1782, and where he deceased May 28, 1788, aged forty-nine.

His son Ebenezer was matriculated of Harvard College in 1784, and is remembered as a youth of great dignity and uncommon promise. Unfortunately he was attacked with a severe fever, while in the last year of his college course, was carried to his father's house for attendance, and there died. The same disease attacked others of the family, of which Mr. Grosvenor himself died, and also a daughter.

After Mr. Grosvenor retired from Scituate, a wider distinction began to appear between the religious parties, and for several years defeated every attempt to settle another pastor. Many candidates were employed, who either were unable to give general satisfaction, or were discouraged with the prevailing disunion. We can name Mr. Daniels of Medfield, who preached in 1780. Mr. Fuller, who received a call to settle in 1781. Mr. Paul Litchfield, (afterward of Carlisle), who supplied for a term of time in 1781. Mr. Merrill also in 1782.* Mr. Judson (afterward of Taunton and Plymouth), who received a call in 1783. Mr. Hazlett, an Englishman, who preached in 1784, and Mr. Zachariah Howard of Bridgewater, who received a call in 1786. This unhappy state of the Society continued seven years, the liberal party gradually gaining strength, until they found themselves able to settle a minister without offending a large minority.

---

* Afterward of North Haverhill.

Rev. Ebenezer Dawes

was a native of Bridgewater, the son of Samuel Dawes, jr. of the East Parish. He was born in 1756. He received his degree at Harvard College in 1785, and was educated for the ministry under the direction of Dr. Wigglesworth of the University. He began to preach very early after receiving his degree, and was ordained at Scituate in November 1787. In 1789, he married Elizabeth Bailey, daughter of Col. Bailey of Hanover, a lady of very pleasing personal accomplishments. Their children were William born 1790, and Ebenezer born 1791.

This situation was laborious and perplexing to Mr. Dawes beyond measure, and his office truly a crown of thorns, owing to the violence of the opposition. His constitution was never firm, and his health sensibly declined after the second year of his ministry. He deceased September 29, 1791. His person was pleasing, his complexion fair, his manners such as might disarm enmity, and in all the gentleness and meekness that adorn the Christian character, he was nobly accomplished. Perhaps there has rarely occurred a separation of a pastor and people by death, which has occasioned more poignant grief, to a majority at least. He had been called into the ministry through great and anxious efforts of his religious friends: he had been their pastor long enough to give them a surety that they had not overrated his talents and virtues: and now, in the blooming of life, at the age of twenty-six, and in the ascendancy of his reputation, he was suddenly withdrawn from them. The day of his death became almost an anniversary of sorrow, and for a long time no company of mourners followed the remains of a friend to the tomb, without paying honours to the lamented Dawes, sighing as they passed his grave, and pausing to read again, what they had often read before, the inscription on his monument.

We believe that his family are all surviving at the time of our writing, (1831). His widow has been twice married since the loss of the husband of her youth, and is now a widow for the third time. Her second husband was Mr. Lucas of Boston, and her third husband was the late venerable Dr. Williams of Deerfield. William, the eldest son, married the daughter of the late William Torrey, Esq. of Pembroke, and has resided in Taunton. Ebenezer, the younger son, is a physician of good reputation at Taunton.

Rev. Nehemiah Thomas.

The present pastor of the first Church and Society, is the son of the late Nathaniel Thomas, Esq. of Marshfield. He was born A. D. 1768, and received his degree at Harvard College 1789, and was educated for the ministry at the University. He was ordained at Scituate November 1792. We shall not write his history while living, and long may it be, before his decease shall permit it to be written. We may however, venture to add, that in 1794, he married Hannah the daughter of Dr. James Otis of Scituate.* Their children – Henry born 1796, Harriet 1798, Lucy Otis 1800, Francis 1804. Henry was matriculated of Harvard University in 1813, and unfortunately deceased in College the next year. He was a youth of uncommon acquirements and of great promise. His classmates erected a beautiful monument, as a testimony of their respect to his memory, in the churchyard at Cambridge; and his College friend, the Rev. Ira Henry Thomas Blanchard of Harvard, paid the respect to his lost friend, of procuring legal permission to assume his name.

Francis received his degree at Harvard University in 1829, and is, at present, a student and assistant attendant with Dr. Wyman at the Insane Hospital.

Ministers of the Second Church and Society.

Mr. William Witherell

was born in the year 1600, but we have not been able to trace this worthy man into England, or to learn any thing of him before his arrival in this country, except, on the authority of Cotton Mather, who places him in the list of ministers who had been in that office in England. But we suspect this to have been an error, (see Mr. Vassall's letter to Mr. John Elliot, in our Chapter in Ecclesiastical history). There is a tradition here which has been handed down for truth, that his mother was the daughter of John Rogers, the Smithfield martyr. He arrived before 1634. The first notice which we find of him is, that he was employed in a grammar school at Charlestown

---

* It is our melancholy office to record her death, while we are in the act of writing the above brief notes. She deceased March 28, 1831.

in 1635, and also in Cambridge the two years following. In 1638, he removed to Duxbury, where he purchased a house and land of Edward Hall; it is described in the deed as lying "between the farms of Mr. Ralph Partridge and Nicholas Robinson." As the town of Duxbury was provided with a pastor (Mr. Partridge) at this time, it is probable that Mr. Witherell was employed in agriculture, and perhaps school teaching: he however was but poorly provided for, as we presume, in the latter calling at that day. In 1640, he (with Thomas Weyborne) received a grant from the Colony Court, of a considerable tract of land in Duxbury, "on the north-west side of North hill."

In 1644, affairs at Scituate had become ripened for the settlement of a minister in the second Church; and Mr. Witherell, being of the moderate party, as it regarded the refusal to commune with members of the Church of England, and also an advocate for infant sprinkling, and withal an educated and a worthy man, was invited to preach, and made himself so acceptable to Mr. Vassall and the rest of Mr. Chauncy's opponents, that he was ordained pastor September 2, 1645. His ordination had been delayed for some time by the influence of Mr. Chauncy and the elders of Plymouth Colony who sided with him, and also by the Church at Duxbury which refused to dismiss him; but at length, by advice of the elders of Massachusetts Bay, the Church proceeded to ordain him in the face of all opposition, (see Ecclesiastical History).

Mr. Witherell probably built or purchased a house on his removing to Scituate. It stood a few rods south-east of the second Society's Meeting-house at that time, on what is called in modern times Wilson hill, where he continued to reside during his life. A record of the baptisms in the second Church commences September 7, 1645, and is kept in Mr. Witherell's hand until 1674, when it appears that some paralytic affection compelled him to borrow the assistance of another hand. From 1674, the records appear in the hand writing of Mr. Mighill, though he was not in Scituate until 1680: he probably copied them. Mr. Mighill had been procured to assist Mr. Witherell in 1680; but the baptisms were administered by Mr. Witherell until March 16, 1684. He died April 9, 1684, as we find in Hobart's journal. He had been in the ministry nearly thirty-nine years, and had administered six hundred and eight baptisms. Several persons from neighboring towns had brought their children hither for baptism, probably because their own ministers were opposed to infant sprinkling. Amongst whom were the families of Rogers of Marshfield and Nathaniel and Josiah Winslow, (the Governor) and Kenelm Winslow, (brother of Gov. Edward Winslow), from Yarmouth.

Mr. Witherell had lived to see the two churches in this town brought to a happy reconciliation, after a long variance; to see the long disputed lines between his parish and the first parish amicably settled; to see a new and more commodious house of worship erected by his Society, and the wasting and sanguinary Indian wars at an end. It was a peculiar season of calm when he closed his useful life.

We have heard of but few printed works of this venerable man. Cotton Mather commends a certain little book of Mr. Witherell's, (in which he was assisted by Mr. Baker), viz. "the life of John Clap of Scituate." This was a son of Mr. Thomas Clap, remarkable for his understanding and his piety, and who died on his approach to manhood. We presume it is not now to be found in print.

Mr. Witherell wrote verses, some of which are extant, and we can say of those which we have seen, that they were vastly superior to those of Dunster who wrote a little earlier, particularly in point of versification. An elegy on Mrs. Sarah, the wife of John Cushing, Esq. is extant: as also an elegy on the death of Gov. Josiah Winslow, written in 1680, when Mr. Witherell was eighty years of age. For the gratification of the curious, we have inserted it in Appendix.

An anecdote is handed down by tradition, which may serve to illustrate the manner of conducting his ministry, and in short the prevailing manner in those times. Mr. Bryant entered the church after the services had commenced, and Mr. Witherell at the close of his prayer, thus addressed him: "Neighbor Bryant, it is to your reproach that you have disturbed the worship by entering late, living as you do within a mile of this place, and especially so, since here is goody Barstow, who has milked seven cows, made a cheese, and walked five miles to the house of God in good season."

Mr. Witherell had probably married before he left England. His sons were Samuel, John, Theophilus and Daniel: his daughters, Mary, Elizabeth, Sarah and Hannah, the two latter being all that were born in Scituate, viz. Sarah baptized in 1645, and Hannah 1646.

Most of these children, though some of them had deceased, are mentioned in his will in 1684, as may be seen in the following abstract.

"To Samuel Witherell, son of my oldest son Samuel, my house and orchard and ten acres of land, when he shall arrive at the age of twenty-one, he paying (a certain sum) to his brother Joshua: also to Joshua a lot of marsh next to Israel Hobart's: also to Hannah, daughter to my son Samuel, two cows.

"To my two sons, John and Theophilus, my wearing apparel. As to Daniel and daughter Sarah Hobart, they have had their portions.

"To Isabel, the widow of my son Samuel, the improvement of the house and orchard until her son Samuel shall come of age."

The inventory of his estate amounted to £165, his books valued at thirteen shillings.

Samuel, the oldest son, deceased in 1683. His children were Samuel born 1678, Hannah 1680, Joshua 1683.

Isabel, his widow, married Josiah Torrey in 1684.

John, the second son of Mr. Witherell, left a family, viz. John born 1675, William 1678, Thomas 1681, Joshua 1683.

Theophilus, the third son, married Mary Parker, the daughter of William Parker, in 1675: their children, Mary born 1677, (died early), Elizabeth 1679, Mary 1681, Lydia 1683, (the wife of Edward Shove 1704), Ruth 1687, Judith 1689. His place of residence was on the west of Dead swamp, and he built the first house on the place, now owned by Mr. Lot Litchfield. He was a serjeant in the "Narragansett fight," (see Chapter on Indian wars).

Daniel, the fourth son, was living in Scituate when his father deceased. He married earlier than his brothers; his daughter Hannah was baptized in 1660: no other children of his appear on record.

Mary, the daughter of Mr. Witherell, married Thomas Oldham of Scituate in 1656: her descendants are in Pembroke.

Elizabeth, married John Bryant of Scituate 1657, and left posterity. (This was the gentleman whom Mr. Witherell reproved – he was Deacon in 1669).

Sarah married Israel Hobart in 1676, and left posterity.

Hannah probably died early.

We believe the posterity of the oldest son only of Mr. Witherell have preserved the name in this Town; and it is nearly extinct in that line. Samuel his son, named in the will of his grandfather, left ten children, born from 1699 to 1720, several of whom removed. – The late Theophilus and Anson now living, sons of Simeon of Hanover, we believe are his descendants. Hannah born 1720, married Nathaniel Robbins of Marshfield. William, the son of John, also left a family. He had a son William born 1702, a daughter Sarah, who married Abner Dwelley 1721, and a daughter Hannah, who married Samuel Eells in 1729, the son of Rev. Nathaniel Eells.

The people of this name in this vicinity, are not all descendants of Rev. William Witherell. There was a John Witherell (probably a brother) in Cambridge in 1635, and afterward in Watertown. There was also a William Witherell in Taunton in 1645, or earlier, who left descendants. Judge Witherell of Detroit, Michigan, is said to be of his posterity.

Mr. Thomas Mighill

was the son of Thomas Mighill of Rowley, one of the early settlers of that place, and who was their representative in 1648, in General Court. Thomas, the second son, was born October 29, 1639, and received his degree at Harvard College 1663. He had been a preacher for some years before he came to Scituate. We observe in the records of the second Society the following entries.

"Sept. 7, 1680, Thomas King, sen., John Bryant, sen. and Charles Stockbridge were chosen a committee to procure a minister. Mr. Mighill came to us Sept. 19, 1680.

"Voted to allow 60£ a year for a minister, and 10£ to our Pastor Mr. Witherell.

"At a meeting of the Church Feb. 6, 1681, a committee was chosen to agree with Mr. Mighill for his coming and for his transportation, and to get a house for him, so as we do not exceed 60£ and his firewood. July 3d, 1681, the Church did give the vote that they desired Mr. Mighill, to give him a call."

Mr. Mighill, however, declined receiving ordination at that time, but continued to assist Mr. Witherell till his decease. He was ordained October 15, 1684.

The children born to him after his coming to Scituate, were Mary born 1683, Samuel 1685, Grace 1688.

His ministry was short, he having deceased August 26, 1689. There is no record of his death in Scituate, and no monument to mark his grave: we are indebted to Hobart's journal for the date of his decease.

Of his brief ministry few notices can be found, and no relick of his literary labours. His family probably returned to Massachusetts; the name is extant in Essex county.

In the inventory of his estate is named "a quarter of a sloop, valued at 15£ the quarter."

Abstract of his Will dated 1689.

"To my daughter Elizabeth 60£.

To my wife Bethia the remainder of my estate, to bring up the other three children, Samuel, Mary and Grace: and after my wife's decease to be divided to these three, Samuel having a double portion.

To Samuel my Library.

And I entreat the worshipful Mr. Samuel Sewall and Mr. Isaac Addington of Boston, and my loving cousin Mr. John Wells of Roxbury, to take the oversight of this my will and assist my wife, &c."

There was a Mr. Mighill who erected Iron works at "Drinkwater," about 1710, and owned a considerable tract of land in that vicinity.

After the decease of Mr. Mighill, Mr. John Cotton (son of Mr. Cotton of Plymouth) preached several months Anno 1690-1.

Mr. Deodate Lawson.

This gentleman may have been the son of Christopher Lawson, an early settler in Boston, though we do not find his name on record in that family. Thomas, the son of Christopher Lawson, was born in Boston in 1643, and Mary 1645. Deodate may have been of the same family, and born in New Hampshire, as Mr. Farmer informs us that Christopher Lawson was afterward in New Hampshire. Deodate not being found on the Catalogue of Harvard College, however, leads us to suspect that he may have been born and educated in England. He was a preacher in Danvers in 1688, says Mr. Farmer. We find he had lived in Boston with a family, previous to that date. In 1682, the birth of Deodate, the son of Deodate Lawson and Jane his wife, appears on the records of Boston: also his second marriage to Deborah Allen in 1692. A hiatus in our records prevents our giving the date of his ordination here, but it must have been in November of the year 1694.

His children born here were Deborah 1694, Richard 1696, (and we believe John), and Mordecai Hewitt 1700.

It is singular that we can find so few traces of his ministry, not even of the baptisms or marriages solemnized by him. It is probable that whatever records he kept, he carried away on his removal. Touching his removal, we find the following documents.

"September 26, 1698, the Church and Society up the N. River in Scituate, being met together, and considering their unsettled state, by reason of the long absence of their Pastor, Mr. Deodate Lawson, did make choice of Capt. Benjamin Stetson, and Dea. Thomas King, to go to the neighboring Elders, and acquaint them with their present state and condition, and entreat their advice what said Church and Society may and ought to doe, being under such circumstances as they at present are.

Per order { JAMES TORREY, ELISHA TURNER."

"At a meeting in Weymouth September 28, 1698. The Church and Society of the N. River in Scituate according to their vote of the 26th, having sent messengers to advise with us the Elders of their neighboring Churches, concerning their present case and duty, considering their unsettled estate, by reason of the long and still continued absence of their Pastor: after solemn invocation of the name of God, and consultation about his mind and will, we do offer our opinion on their case as followeth, viz. that a Pastor, without express consent of his people, desisting of the duty of his charge and function, merely for secular advantages, and taking no heed to the ministry which he has received of the Lord to fulfill it, nor to the flocke over which the Holy Ghost hath made him overseer, to feed the flock of God, &c. for two years together delaying his return, notwithstanding many faire advantages offered him for the same, and signifying unto his people neither any justifiable reasons of his absence, nor any resolved intention of speedy return, is faulty before God: and his people are not to blame if they use all Evangelical endeavors to settle themselves with another Pastor, more spiritually and more fixedly disposed.

SAMUEL TORREY, (of Weymouth),
MOSES FISK, (Braintree),
NEHEMIAH HOBART, (Newton),
ZECHARIAH WHITMAN, (Hull),
PETER THATCHER, (Milton),
JOHN DANFORTH, (Dorchester),
JOSEPH BELCHER, (Dedham),
JOSEPH BAXTER, (Medfield)."

In November 1698, the Church and Society "voted to accept the advice of the Elders," also "chose Capt. Benjamin Stetson and Dea. Thomas King to procure a Minister in order to ordination and settlement."

We find no further traces of Mr. Lawson or of his family, unless John Lawson was his son, who married Mary Leach in 1721, and whose son John was born in 1722, as appears by our records.

REV. NATHANIEL EELLS

was the son of Samuel Eells, Esq. of Hingham. His mother was Anna Lenthal, the daughter of the Rev. Robert Lenthal of Weymouth." Capt. Eells, afterward Major Eells, commanded a garrison at Ponagansett (Dartmouth) in Philip's war, and we understand it to have been the same gentleman as above named. He is found to have been a resident in Hingham soon after the close of that war. He there married a second wife, called Sarah North in Hobart's journal, and the widow Sarah Peck in the Clerk's records of that town. We reconcile these records by supposing that the lady had been Sarah North before her marriage to Mr. Peck, and family tradition confirms this supposition. She was doubtless the widow of Mr. Joseph Peck. We find no records of births of this family in Hingham, and where their children were born we have not discovered. Major Eells died in Hingham in 1709, and his widow died in Scituate in 1711. We have discovered that two of his daughters married in Hingham, viz. Anna to Thomas Wilder in 1704, and Elizabeth to John Stowell in 1710.

Rev. Nathaniel of Scituate, was born 1678, and received his degree at Harvard College in 1699. The first notice of him in Scituate is January 12, 1702-3, when "the Church and Society chose a Committee to discourse with Mr. Eells concerning his settling with us in the work of the ministry." Again in July 1703, "The agents before chosen are directed to apply themselves to Mr. Eells, at his return to Hingham, concerning his settlement in the work of the ministry." We conclude that in the interim between the above dates, he had preached in other places. August 18, 1703, "Voted to invite Mr. Eells to settle, and to allow him for his maintenance 65£

---

* Rev. Robert Lenthal left Weymouth in 1640: he was in Newport in 1641, where he was engaged in a controversy against Nicholas Easton, Coddington and Coggeshall, who had begun to hold forth the doctrine that God is the author of sin. (Winthrop II. 40).

per annum, and the use of the Parsonage." He was ordained June 14, 1704. The marriage of Mr. Eells is recorded in Hingham, viz. "Mr. Nathaniel Eells of Scituate to Hannah North of Hingham, by Samuel Eells, Jus. P. Oct. 12, 1704." She was the relative of the wife of Samuel Eells, Esq. and both were descended of the noble family of that name in England. She was the aunt of Frederick Lord North, Prime minister of England during the American Revolution. Some of Mr. Eell's descendants, viz. Nathaniel and Richard Williams of Taunton, his grandsons, visited England after the Revolution, with the hope of obtaining some fraction of his lordship's estate, as he was childless, but we believe they did not meet with success.

Mr. Eells resided in the parsonage-house at first, after his marriage. April 1704, "The Society voted to repair the parsonage-house, and make it tenantable and convenient for Mr. Eells to dwell in." He had been a boarder in the family of the widow Lydia Barrell previous to his ordination. He resided at the parsonage until 1715, when he purchased a spacious house of Mr. Joseph Henchman. It stood on the north side of the way, a few rods east of the parting of the two roads that lead from the south Meeting-house, the one to Boston, and the other to mount Blue, (see Henchman, Family Sketches). Here he resided until his decease, August 25, 1750, aged 72. There are a few aged people now living who remember him. They describe his person to have been of a stature rather above mediocrity, of broad chest and muscular proportions, remarkably erect, somewhat corpulent in his late years, of dark complexion. with large black eyes and brows, and of general manners rather dignified and commanding than sprightly and pleasing. He had an influence and authority amongst his people that none of his successors have exercised, and which may have been in some measure a peculiarity of earlier times than these. The controversy with which his predecessors had been agitated had ceased. The Quakers, by not being persecuted here, had become quiescent. Whitefield's New light, and his spirit of denunciation had been kept out of his society, by the determined stand which he took against him; and the times were prosperous and happy.* His people were delighted to see him at their doors, as he rode up on horseback to inquire after their health, and to hand his pipe to be lighted. We mean no satire by recording this trifle; for he was a venerable man, and so

---

* See Appendix.

beloved, that every parishioner would take pleasure in performing such an office for him. He was also a leader amongst the neighboring clergy – well acquainted with the constitution and usages of the Churches, weighty in counsel, and often called to distant parts of the State, and to other States on Ecclesiastical Councils. As a preacher, there is reason to believe that he did not so much excel as in his dignity of character and soundness of understanding. We have seen a volume in manuscript of nearly an hundred sermons, which he used to carry with him when he travelled abroad. They embrace a considerable variety of subjects, and enabled him to preach at any time and on any occasion. They begin with his own ordination sermon, which he himself preached, according to ancient custom, and include the sermons which he composed during the few first years of his ministry. Were we to judge of his talents from these alone, we should not do him justice. There are a few discourses in print which are very respectable productions, and in particular those delivered at the ordinations of his two sons. He preached the Election sermon in 1743, (Deut. xxxii. 47.)

His sentiments were the moderate Calvinism of that day: we have seen one sermon on the doctrine of election, which had many explanations closely bordering on Arminianism. In the latter part of his life he continued to speak of Arminian free will as an error, but with no asperity. Mr. Lemuel Bryant of Quincy, who had gone somewhat before the age in liberal speculations, preached for him on a certain day, and delivered a sermon which he afterwards printed, (on the text, "all our righteousnesses are filthy rags,") and explained the text in the manner which would now be generally acceptable, showing that the formalities of a corrupt generation of the Jews were therein described, and not the moral virtues of true worshippers, which led Mr. Eells to say, "Alas! Sir, you have undone to-day, all that I have been doing for forty years," and Bryant with his accustomed wit and courtesy replied, "Sir, you do me too much honor in saying that I could undo in one sermon, the labours of your long and useful life." An aged and highly intelligent gentleman, who related this anecdote to us twenty years since, also remarked that Mr. Eells preached a series of sermons afterward, with a view to correct Mr. Bryant's errors, but it was not easy, remarked the same gentleman, to discern much difference between his doctrine and that of Mr. Bryant. On the whole, we believe there has rarely been known a ministry of forty-six years which so many circumstances conspired to render successful and happy. There are a few now living that remember the solemn day of fasting and prayer, kept by his people, on account of his death.

Mr. Eells prepared his own sons and several other young men for College, and also for the ministry: amongst whom we can name President Clap of Yale College, Rev. David Turner of Rehoboth, and Rev. Thomas Clap of Taunton, afterwards Judge Clap.

There is no man of eminence, but who suffers detraction for the very reason that he is eminent. Thus it has often been told as a satire upon Mr. Eells, that in his simplicity, he one day directed his scholars to dig for a thunderbolt at the foot of a tree, where the lightning had made an excavation. We have no great confidence in the truth of the story: but if it were true, it was but a specimen of the general ignorance at that time, in a certain branch of philosophy, for it was before Franklin had made his discoveries in Electricity.

We have no doubt that Mr. Eells had disciplined himself into an extraordinary self command. His less placid partner (whose name had been North) did not so well endure the disagreeable events of life, and when chafed with family vexations, she would say, "It is wonderful that so good a man as my husband should have such wayward children." He would pleasantly reply, "True, and you seem to be sensible that the mischief lies in the *North* side of the family."

His children were *Sarah* born 1705, and who married Benjamin Turner, (son of Thomas Turner of Hanover), 1726.

Samuel born 1706, who married Hannah Witherell (granddaughter of Rev. William) in 1729, and settled in Scituate. From him have descended Robert Eells, Esq. and others of Hanover.*

John born 1709, who married Abiah Waterman 1730, and lived in a house fifty rods east of his father's. He had a son Waterman.

Nathaniel born 1710, received a degree at Harvard College 1728, and was ordained pastor of Stonington, Connecticut 1733. The same year he married Mercy, the daughter of Hon. John Cushing of Scituate.

Edward born 1712, received a degree at Harvard College 1733, and was ordained pastor in Middletown, Connecticut, 1737. Both Edward and Nathaniel, we believe, have posterity in Connecticut and New York.

---

* Robert, Esq., Joseph, Edward and Samuel are sons of Robert Lenthal Eells, and grandsons of Samuel. Their mother Ruth Copeland, (see Copeland).

MINISTERS OF THE SECOND CHURCH.

Hannah born 1714, married Anthony Eames of Marshfield, and has left posterity.

Mary born 1716, married Seth Williams of Taunton, 1738, and has left descendants,

North born 1718, married Ruth Tilden 1741, and has left descendants in Scituate. His grandson Nathaniel, son of Nathaniel, deceased 1831.

Anna Lenthal born 1721, married Zechariah Daman 1748, and has left posterity in Scituate and Hanover: Edward Galen, &c.

The widow of Mr. Eells survived him about four years, having deceased May 2, 1754.

The family of Eells came to New England early. There was a John Eells, freeman in Massachusetts, 1632, who may have been the grandfather of our minister. The Rev. Nathaniel we know had a brother John, whose daughter Frances deceased at the house of her uncle in Scituate. She is called "the daughter of John Eells late of Milford." She died 1718.

There was a John Eells of Sandwich, whose sons Bennet and Mordecai were born 1648 and 1650; but whether the same who was freeman in Massachusetts in 1632, we have not ascertained. Perhaps his family have changed the name to Ellis. There was also a Roger Eells of Yarmouth, whose son John was born 1648.

REV. JONATHAN DORBY

was the son of Capt. Eleazer Dorby of Boston, and Mary his wife, who was the daughter of John Cushing, Esq. married in 1721. Capt. Dorby lived for a short time in Scituate, and Eleazer his first son was born here 1772. Jonathan was born in Boston in 1727, and received a degree at Harvard College 1747. He came to Scituate in the spring of 1751. In July following the Church and Society voted to invite him to settle, offering "for his maintenance 80£ lawful money and the use of the Parsonage:" and in September following "5£ in addition to what had been voted before."

He was ordained November 13, 1751. But his ministry and his life were very brief. He had gone to Hingham to exchange pulpit services with Mr. Gay, and was there attacked with a fever at the house of Mr. Lincoln, (father of General Benjamin Lincoln), which terminated his life after a sickness of five days. He died April 22, 1754, in the twenty-eighth year of his age and the third year of his ministry. He had been an inmate of the family of Judge John Cushing, his maternal uncle, and was about to be married to his daughter Mary, when his bright course was arrested.* His remains were placed in the family tomb of the Cushings.

Mr. Dorby is described as of moderate stature, fair complexion, round features and blue eyes: in his manners graceful and winning: using much familiarity in his intercourse with his people, without disgusting, and entering their dwellings like a son or a brother. As a preacher, we have a sufficient testimony of his lively and interesting manner, in the memory of many who knew him: but of his talents as a writer we have less decisive proof. We have seen but one sermon (in manuscript) of his, and that was of course an early production. It however might be considered as a respectable performance.†

---

* Their bans were published April 13, 1754. She married Rev. Ebenezer Gay of Suffield, 1763. The first ancestor of Rev. Mr. Dorby in this country, we believe, was Edward of Boston, whose children were Mary, Eleazer and others, born from 1660 forward. Eleazer was the father of Mary, born 1688, and of Capt. Eleazer, father of Rev. Jonathan. Capt. Eleazer was a mariner.

† Since writing the above, we have discovered that Dr. Gay of Hingham preached at the ordination of Mr. Dorby, November 13, 1751, from Rev. i. 16. "And he had in his right hand seven stars." In his address to the people in that discourse, he thus alludes to the late pastor Mr. Eells, and to the pastor elect:

" 'One star differeth from another star in glory.' That, with the comfortable and enlivening rays of which ye were favored for the space of forty-six years, was of distinguished lustre: and its influences, how sweet and extensive! The neighboring Churches, yea, the *Land* rejoiced with you in the light therof. There never was in this country, if in the Christian world, a minister so frequently sought to, as your late deceased Pastor, when the Churches wanted light and peace: and his coming to their help, in the way of Ecclesiastical counsel, wherin he, for the most part, *moderated,* might seem as the welcome approach of Mazaroth in his season, or the kindly aspect of a benevolent planet with his satellites. Ye are witnesses, and God also, how holily and justly and unblameably he behaved himself among you: as ye know how he exhorted, and comforted and charged every one of you, as a father doth his children. But alas I that burning and shining light, little dimmed or diminished by age, was suddenly extinguishing from your eyes.

" 'But lo! he that is in the midst of the Churches, hath another star in his right hand, which he this day giveth you.'

"I can from intimate acquaintance, bear this young man witness, that he hath taken laudable pains to be thoroughly furnished unto the good, but arduous work he is designed for, and by the blessing of God on his preparatory studies, hath acquired those desirable qualifications, which have justly recommended him to your well advised choice. And I may, with little variation, say to you of him, as Paul did to the Philippians concerning his son Timothy: 'I know no man like minded, who will naturally care for your state.' 'See that he be with you without fear, for he worked the work of God.' Let not his light be obscured by poverty or reproach that he shall

His death was deeply lamented. But perhaps, as it regarded himself, we ought not to pronounce his lot an unfortunate one. So far as his memory on earth is concerned, it can hardly be esteemed unfortunate – and no man of elevated mind can disregard wholly what shall be said of him after his death:

"Servi igitur, iis etiam judicibus, qui multis post sæculis, de te judicabunt," was Cicero's advice to Caesar, and may well be regarded even by the Christian. Every idea or image of Dorby, which memory has called up since his decease, has been one of a fair model of the human species in its vigor and and not in its decline, or of increasing, not of waning honors, nor the remnants of manhood and of mind, which age is constantly rendering less valuable and lovely. Certainly, in the light of Christian faith, we cannot imagine that Dorby should shine the less "as a star," for having been transferred in his brightness from earth to heaven.

Rev. David Barnes, D. D.

was the son of Daniel Barnes of Marlboro, a substantial farmer. Daniel was the son of John Barnes, and probably the grandson of Richard Barnes, who settled in that town as early as 1660; having taken the freeman's oath that year. Dr. Barnes, whose mother was Zeruiah Eager, was the fifth in order of twelve children, and born March 24, 1731. He received his first degree at Harvard College 1752. He began to preach at an early season after leaving College, for we find that he received an invitation to become the pastor of Quincy in 1753. This invitation was declined: it was afterwards renewed with more favorable proposals, and again declined. He preached first at Scituate in June 1754, and on the 15th of August the same year, received an unanimous invitation to become the pastor of the second Church and Society. The salary proposed was "80£ and the use of the Parsonage so long as he shall continue in the ministry in this place." He was ordained November 27, 1754. He continued to reside at the parsonage until 1770, when he purchased a farm of John Turner's heirs, near the

---

suffer from you. Let not your minds be so blinded by the god of this world, or the mist of prejudice, or the dust of perverse disputings, that their darkness should be impenetrable to the rays of Gospel light. The brightest star is not ordained in the firmament of the Church, merely for people to gaze upon, to observe its motions and admire its glitterings, but to travel by, as did the wise men, in the way to Christ and, Heaven."

north-west side of the parish common, and erected a house. The parish Meeting-house was built the same summer, and meetings were held in Dr. Barnes's unfinished house, during the erection of the Meeting-house. This house and farm was purchased by Mr. John Nash, after Dr. Barnes's decease; and the house and ten acres of land were soon sold again to Capt. Isaac Whittemore.

Dr. Barnes entered upon the ministry with fair prospects, his people being united and prosperous. We have heard something of his privations and difficulties during the Revolutionary war. His salary, paid in the depreciated currency of the time, was of very little value. Fortunately his wife had property, which afforded his family a subsistence. It was a time of universal privation and suffering, and this was duly considered by Dr. Barnes: for he was not known to complain, unless indeed, it may be said, that after days of prosperity returned to his people, he felt wounded that no consideration was made to him, on account of the almost total deficiency of his salary in previous years. His ministry continued in a good degree of quiet from the troubles of religious dissensions almost to the last. A short time before his death, the spirit of faultfinding began to move, and a stricter mode of Calvinism began to call for a separation, but had produced no great effect during his life. We believe he was remarkable for his meekness in "instructing those that opposed," and by parables, rather than by direct argument, he was accustomed to converse with such. A neighbor who was a Calvinist of the *straitest sect,* having frequently spent long sittings in arguing with Dr. Barnes, was finally answered by the following parable.

"You, Sir, are a gentleman to whom the publick feels and acknowledges much obligation for your mechanical skill and inventions. Now we will suppose that your powers should be so far increased that you could make intelligent beings, and that you should produce thousands each day, formed with all the endowments of the human race. Then suppose that your neighbours should enquire, what destination you proposed for these beings; and you should reply, that you had also prepared a place of torment to which you proposed to condemn the greater part – not for any personal offence against you, but because you had made them for that end: and that the remaining few you had destined, in the same arbitrary manner, to another place of perfect happiness, which you had also prepared. Now, Sir, suppose that your neighbors were furnished with the common sense of mankind, concerning justice and goodness in the administration of one being, who has a controlling power over other beings, would they not knock your shop down, and say that such a wicked trade should not go on?"

He was an acceptable preacher to his people from the commencement of his ministry, but near the middle of life, he is said to have come forward with new powers, and to have become a popular preacher throughout a considerable circle of the churches. He preached the Dudleian lecture at Harvard College in 1780, (John xx. 31), and he was honored with the degree of D. D. in 1788.

His ministry may be said to have been long, for very few have exceeded fifty-seven years. His health had never been robust, but he preserved it with great care and skill. He laboured in his fields with a view to health: and at one period of his life was a great walker, and in short took a fancy to run, and would continue it, at a moderate pace for miles. When about forty years of age, he was affected with an asthma, and (as he has told the writer) during one entire year, he did not sleep a single night in his bed: he used to sit and sleep, and wake and read alternately. He often observed that he had a tendency to fever in his constitution, and he had been thereby "condemned to an abstemious diet." For the last three years of his life, his voice had failed, and a general weakness of muscles rendered his walk tottering and unsafe: in short, he was in a degree paralytic, as his features occasionally indicated. He was extremely deaf for ten years, which led him to talk the more without listening to others, and it was often both amusing and instructive to hear the dialogues which he would carry on by himself in the midst of company; for, not like the generality of aged people, would he ever sit silent, or speak only in monosyllables.

He was a Christian philosopher of so elevated a kind, that it was not every one that could fully appreciate his feelings and conversation. It was a matter of surprise to some, that he would speak so familiarly of his own death, and therefore they unjustly attributed it to an obtuse sensibility. It was far otherwise – even the resignation of Christian faith. He never sighed "Oh! mihi præteritos referat si Jupiter annos:" but with onward views, he would often say, "that were it not the fixed design of Providence that nothing should go back, it would be his voluntary choice to go forward, and to see for himself, what is to come in other modes of existence." He had, in a remarkable degree, overcome the fear of death, by making it a subject of constant meditation, in the light of Christian faith. His only painful prospect, in his late years, was that he might survive his usefulness; but in this respect his prayers were nearly answered. Fifteen months before his decease, a colleague was ordained, from which time he attempted but few public performances: but those were not only interesting, as being the last efforts of an uncommon mind, but excellent in themselves; for when he would allude to his own waning light, and to the increasing light of those who were rising behind him, his audience were melted in tears, not so much of tenderness perhaps, as of admiration at his magnanimity. He deceased, with all the Christian philosophy with which he had lived, April 26, 1811, having completed eighty years, of which fifty-seven had been the term of his ministry. He gave directions to his son, that his remains should be laid in a grave, by the side of those of his consort, (who had deceased October 22, 1805, aged 78), and that both graves should be covered with one plain monument of granite.

In person, Dr. Barnes was of rather slight form, of middling stature, and erect: his complexion had approached to the florid in his youth: his eyes were grey, his forehead and brows prominent, and his nose aquiline. His form is the more distinctly remembered, and not with the less veneration, for his having retained the ancient fashions of dress, and worn the last of the grey wigs.

As a preacher, it would be difficult to describe him, for he was like none other. His voice, we believe, was never remarkable for sweet tones, and his skill in varying its tones was but ordinary. He would sometimes startle his audience with a high note, and then fall rather abruptly to a low one. His manner might be called familiar, and the whole, though unique, was never displeasing, but always calculated to keep up attention. It was, however, the matter of his discourses which constituted their chief excellence. Perhaps no preacher has lived, who treated his audience with a greater variety, which circumstance gave fault finders an occasion to accuse him of not being evangelical. He was too much a man of genius to be confined to a narrow round of subjects, and too much a man of piety to touch any subject, without leading the mind to important lessons in religion. For instance, his sermons on "the east wind – on the lightning – on making salt – on bees – on the basket of summer fruit, (Amos viii. I.)" seem not to have been evangelical, at the first thought, but they were beautiful defences and illustrations of divine Providence. But, though he preached in a great variety, during his long ministry, evangelical subjects, in a more strict sense, were his favourites. Dr. Barnes did not practise frequent exchanges, though he was always ready to accommodate his brethren. It was his familiar maxim, that "a minister's stock is of that nature, that the more he uses, the more he has left."

His style is remarkable for a sententious brevity, which gave rise to a common remark, that his discourses were *clusters* of *maxims*. The writer of this can never forget the charge, given by the venerable Doctor to him, when ordained his colleague. It was never published, for it could never be found – perhaps it was not written but in part. It was full of pointed sayings like the following: "In attempting to instruct your people, be careful not to preach what they will not understand, and especially careful not to preach what you don't understand yourself."

He was a great admirer of Dr. Gay of Hingham, for those pithy sayings, in which he himself excelled. He once remarked to the writer, that at the funeral of Dr. Gay's wife, there was much touching eloquence displayed; but that one sentence of the Doctor at the grave, was of more value than all the rest, viz. "I thank you; my friends, for burying the poor remains of my wife out of my sight." Ignorance might mistake the purport of this quotation from the words of Abraham, but Dr. Barnes could see in it the reach of an elevated mind. It was like himself, whose maxims and apt quotations were and are in the mouths of every one who knew him.

People of straiter sects used to remark that Dr. Barnes had formed too good an opinion of human nature, and always avoided the accusing strain, even towards the most worthless of mankind. It may have been a trait in his character. But while his heart was full of tenderness, and his words full of prudence, those words were often of the deepest import, and like parables, of the keenest application.

"Tam unice vituperat, ut laudare videtur."
PLINY.

As Dr. Barnes was a Christian philosopher, so he was a philosopher in the affairs of life, and looked at every thing with a view to practical uses. He was a farmer, not more in theory than in practice, not more in experiment, than in following the best examples already struck out, and seeing at once, how to turn his fields and his labour to the best account. He studied the qualities of domestick animals – the adaptation of crops to soils – and the curious economy of bees, and was successful in their management.

But in no qualification was he more amiable, than in his spirit of hospitality. His house was a favorite resort of his clerical brethren, and of an extensive acquaintance, beside the people of his own charge. Had the ancient literary trick been in fashion, of transposing the letters of one's name to make out a sense expressive of character, we believe that many an anagram would have been made upon his name, with reference to his hospitality; and nothing could have been more suitable than that witty saying, recorded by Mather of Mr. Ward, the first minister of Ipswich, (the simple cobbler of Agawam, as he styles himself in the title page of a curious book), who, when anagrams were called for on the name of the venerable John Wilson of Boston, said with great humour, "the anagram of John Wilson is, I pray you come in, you are heartily welcome."

Dr. Barnes left in print several ordination sermons, a discourse at the Derby Academy, a sermon on the death of his daughter, Mrs. Cotton, a sermon on the love of life and fear of death – a sermon on the death of Washington. There is also extant a posthumous volume, published by the Society for promoting Christian knowledge, piety and charity.

The following notice appeared in the publick papers at the time of his decease, which, I shall be pardoned for saying, was from Dr. Allyne of Duxbury.

"Dr. Barnes was distinguished amongst his brethren for much thinking, though not for much speaking. His mind. was seldom inert. In small circles he was communicative, and never wanted topicks of useful reflection and conversation. His company was highly instructive and entertaining. Altogether free from pedantry and envy, a friend to all men, and a hearty lover of good men; he would have been delighted in the society of such men as Mr. Locke, Bishop Watson and Dr. Paley. One biographical remark on the last mentioned writer may be justly appropriated to Dr. Barnes: 'At no time of his life was he a hard student, according to the common acceptation of that word, which is used rather to describe one who reads, than one who thinks much. His writings do not display any very profound or extensive acquaintance with books: they are valued, not for discussing or deciding upon the opinions of learned men, but for original and enlightened reflections on the transactions of human life, such as may be supposed to have passed before him, or to have come to his knowledge, without any laborious enquiry.'

"The subject of this obituary notice was a firm enemy to all hierarchical principles, as well among protestants as papists – a warm advocate for the liberty of private judgment – averse to common theological controversies, and above all to the usual temper of disputants: and if prevailed on to enter the lists, his way was to begin with acute discriminations and precise definitions. He was tolerant without religious indifference – candid, without forgetting to be severe against folly and vice – and devout, without any 'mysterious carriage of the body to cover the defects of the mind.' His prayers seemed to be dictated by the emotions of his heart on the occasion, and were extemporaneous in an unusual sense. The want of solemnity in his manner of speaking, a similarity of vocal inflection, and the abruptness of his cadences, might suggest to a stranger, the idea of levity and indevotion; but the starting tear and faltering tongue would soon remove the false impression. The wisdom and goodness of God in the permission of evil – the evidences of Christianity – the philosophy of social life – the doctrine of habits and association of ideas – the excellency of nature's laws, were among his favorite topicks of preaching and conversation; and what appeared strange to some, he would often connect maxims of frugality, temperance and industry with his ideas of religion. He was popular with those capable of appreciating "words so fitly spoken as to resemble apples of gold in pictures of silver." The most rational and judicious delighted to hear him. His sermons were transcripts of his mind, and his mind was always exhibited without any disguise. He inculcated no lessons which he did not practise, and dwelt much on the virtues for which he was distinguished, viz. candor, humility, patience, meekness. In this last particular, he may be compared to Moses. Had he lived in the Apostolic age, with Thomas, he would probably have doubted – in kind affections, he would have emulated the character of John: but he would have stood aloof from those disciples who were desirous to call down fire from heaven upon the Samaritans. To extirpate heresy by consuming hereticks, was a thing equally abhorrent to his judgment and feelings.

When such men die, the living are to be compassionated. Dr. Barnes, in his latter years, was solicitous lest he might survive his ability to do good, and his usefulness not be prolonged with his days. He suffered much from the apprehension of being cast by as a "broken vessel." But it was only for the space of one or two years that his friends had cause to lament the wreck of a wise and a good mind.

In the circle of his acquaintance, a rich and unfailing fountain of intellectual improvement and social enjoyment is closed up.

The flock of his charge may recollect and parodize the words of the sentimental journalist, and with an application to their deceased pastor, say, "we thought we duly respected him when he was alive, but now he is dead, we fear it was otherwise."

Dr. Barnes married Rachel, the daughter of Hon. George Leonard of Norton, 1756. His children, were *Rachel,* born July 11, 1757. She was married to Josiah Cotton, Esq. clerk of the Courts of Plymouth, 1789. She deceased in middle life, leaving a son and a daughter.

Hon. *David L. Barnes,* born January 28, 1760. He was a lawyer of distinction in Taunton and Providence, and Judge of the United States Court for the district of Rhode Island. He married Mrs. Russell of Providence. He deceased in 1814, leaving a son and several daughters.

Anna, born September 26, 1765. She married William Jackson, Esq. of Plymouth, 1788, and deceased in middle life, leaving two sons and one daughter.

One brother of Dr. Barnes, viz. Solomon, deceased December 1830, in Marlboro. He was ninety years of age on the 20th of June, 1830.

When Dr. Barnes retired from the labours of the ministry in 1809, he compounded with his parish for £100. Assistance was procured for him in June of that year. The only candidates employed were Mr. William Torrey, Mr. Ezekiel Rich, and the present pastor, who was ordained February 14, 1810.

FAMILY SKETCHES

IN ALPHABETICAL SERIES.

JAMES ADAMS.

was the son of John Adams, who came to Plymouth in the Fortune in 1621, and whose widow Eleanor married Kenelm Winslow. James married Frances, the daughter of Mr. William Vassall of Scituate, 1646. He was a member of the second religious Society in Scituate, though his farm was on the Marshfield side of the river, probably near the place of the late Capt. George Little. His children were William born 1647, Anna 1649, Richard 1651, Mary 1653, Margaret 1654, all baptized in the second Church in Scituate. It is stated in the Historical Society's papers, that he died on board the ship James of London, 1651. This mistake (at least in date) is adopted by Mr. Farmer also. John Adams, jr. of Marshfield married Jane James 1654, and left a family.

HENRY ADVERD, (or ADFORD).

was a householder in Scituate 1640. His farm was south of John Bryant's, and west of the "block-house," on the second Herring brook. He married Tamsen Manson 1643. His children were Mary, Elizabeth and Sarah, baptized in the second Church 1651, and Experience 1652. He died 1653. That year "the Town allowed for the buryall of Henry Adverd 8S."

NICOLAS ALBESON, "the Sweede."

This name is not to be found written in full in our records: "Nicolas the Sweede," is the uniform manner of writing it. The committee which made report to Gov. Winslow of the losses of Scituate in Philip's war, write it as we have done at the head of this article. He was early here; had lands. in

1636 – was a householder before 1647, (see division of lands), and was entitled to a share in the division of common lands. His house stood forty rods north of Parker lane, and west of the farm of Rawlins, (now Col. James Curtis's), on a small hill. It was burnt by the Indians May 20, 1676. The next year, the Town "voted to raise 3£ toward rebuilding the Sweede's house." Several anecdotes concerning him are handed down, such as his baptizing his own children, &c.: but they preserve his memory only as a wild and singular man. His children are not on record, and the name has not been continued in this Town.

ISAIAH ALDEN, JR.

of Scituate Harbour, often employed in the publick business of the Town, is the son of Isaiah Alden, Esq. of Duxbury, and a descendant of Mr. John Alden, who first landed upon the Plymouth rock. He married Mercy, the daughter of Lemuel Vinall, and has a family.

JOHN ALLEN.

was one of the Conihassett partners in 1646. Probably the same person had lands in Plymouth in 1633.

His house in Scituate stood twenty rods south of the bridge at the Harbour.* He died 1661, and his widow Ann administered.

There is no record of the births of his children here. He had a family connexion with Lawrence Litchfield, and probably came from Barnstable with him 1645, to Scituate.

His son John succeeded to his father's lands. He was an Ensign in 1670, and Captain 1686. He kept a garrison in Scituate in Philip's war. He was living in Scituate 1698, but left no posterity here. His daughter Jeane was born in Scituate 1669. She married John Marshall of Boston, 1697, who was the son of John and Ruth, married in Boston 1664, which latter was the son of John and Sarah Marshall, married 1643.

This family disappears from our records about 1700.

There is no trace of this family in Scituate in 1633, as Farmer's Register states. We conjecture that the Allens of Barnstable, and Dr. Allyn of Duxbury, are of this family.

---

* He occupied the house of Edward Foster and John Allen, Jun. purchased it of Timothy Foster 1679.

GEORGE ALLEN.

of Scituate Harbour, is the son of Rev. Morrell Allen of Pembroke, and Hannah his wife, daughter of Hon. Josiah Dean of Raynham. George married Hannah Ensign, the daughter of Ensign Otis, jr. in 1828, and succeeded to the mercantile business of his father in-law. This family descended, as we are informed, from Rev. John Allen or Allin, the first minister of Dedham, who came to New England 1638, was ordained 1639, and deceased 1675, aged seventy-five.

ANTHONY ANNABLE.

arrived at Plymouth in the ship Ann, 1623. He sold his house in Plymouth to Daniel Ray, 1630, and came to Scituate that year. His house here was on Kent street, the sixth lot from Satuit brook, between Elder Henry Cobb's on the north, and the Meeting-house common on the south. He had also eighty acres of land on Stony cove at the North river, between that Cove and Edward Fogter's land on the south. He was a useful and exemplary man. He was deputy (with Edward Foster) to the first Colony Court 1639. In 1640, he sold his lands to Thomas Rawlins, and removed to Barnstable. His daughter Sarah married Henry Ewell 1638, of Scituate.

Hannah married Thomas Bowman of Barnstable, 1644.

Susanna married William Hatch of Scituate, 1652.

Anthony, jr. had married Jane Alcock, who died early, (in 1643), and 1644, he married Ann Clark of Plymouth. He had children, Samuel born 1646, Esek 1648, Desire 1652. Of these, Samuel married the daughter of Thomas Allen, and deceased 1678, leaving sons. Anthony Annable, sen. deceased at Barnstable 1673. We believe there are a few descendants of this family in Boston.

JOHN BAILEY.

appears first in Scituate, as tenant to Capt. John Williams before 1670, at Farm neck. He married Sarah White (perhaps of Weymouth) 1672, also Ruth Clothier 1699. He deceased 1718, and names in his will, "To sons John, Joseph, Benjamin,

William and Samuel 4£ each in addition to what they have already received. To daughter Mary Perry 60£, son William Executor." His farm had been a gift of Capt. John Williams, (see his will).

These children were born as follows: John 1673, Sarah 1675, Mary 1677, (wife of James Perry 1700), Joseph 1679, Benja. 1682, (who was resident at Marlboro 1713), William born 1685, (who married Judith Booth 1714), Hannah born 1687, (wife of James Briggs, jr. 1714), Samuel born 1690, who probably removed after his father's decease.

John married Abigail, daughter of Dea. Samuel Clap, 1700; children, Jane born 1700, John 1703, Jacob 1706, Capt. Israel 1708, Timothy 1709, (who married Sarah Buck 1731, and probably removed), Abigail 1712, (wife of John Bates 1733), Sarah 1714, (wife of Thomas Jenkins 1731), Deborah and Hannah 1717, Rachel 1719, Naomi 1722.

Joseph left a family, viz. Dea. Joseph born 1704, Martha 1707, Ruth 1709, (wife of Dea. Josiah Edson of Bridgewater 1737), Benjamin 1712, Ebenezer, 1714, Seth 1717, Caleb 1720, Adams 1722.

Capt. Israel married Keziah Perry 1730, children, Rhoda born 1731, Israel 1732, Keziah 1734, Hannah 1736, Abigail 1738, Rachel 1740, Ward 1742, Sarah 1744, Elizabeth 1746.

Dea. Joseph married Elizabeth White 1732, children, Elizabeth born 1733, (second wife of Eli Curtis, sen. 1777), Joshua 1735, Caleb 1738, Joseph 1743, Rebecca 1746, Miranda 1749, (Rebecca was wife of Constant Clap).

Benjamin (son of Joseph, sen.) married Ruth Litchfield 1735, children, Jerusha born 1736, (wife of Capt. John Clap 1752), Martha 1738, Benjamin 1747, (who lived at Merritt's brook), Nathaniel Tilden was also of this family, who probably died early: also Mary, (wife of Rev. Paul Litchfield 1778), also Roland, who removed westward, and Ruth, (wife of Lemuel Dwelley).

Ebenezer (son of Joseph, sen.) married Mary White 1736, children, Ebenezer born 1740, Paul 1743, who married Ann Holmes of Kingston 1769 – his son Paul now inherits the paternal estate at Farm neck.

Seth (son of Joseph, sen.) married Rachel Cudworth 1744. He died early, and his widow married Joseph Briggs 1750.

Caleb (son of Joseph, sen.) married Philippa Peaks, children, Lydia born 1762, Ebenezer 1764, Martha 1766, Caleb 1768, Joseph 1771, Israel 1773. Caleb now lives in Scituate.

Adams (son of Joseph, sen.) married Sarah –, children, Seth born 1747, Capt. Adams 1748, Joseph 1749. Capt. Adams was the late master of the Marine Hospital, whose son Adams resides in Boston, born 1780.

Joshua (son of Dea. Joseph) married Abigail Clap 1756, his son Ebenezer was Town clerk several years – and Ebenezer, the son of the latter is the present Town clerk.

Joseph (son of Dea. Joseph) graduated at Harvard College 1765, and removed to Chesterfield, where his posterity may now reside.

William (son of John, sen.) married Judith Booth 1714 – his children were William, (who married Elizabeth Nichols of Hingham, 1736, and left one son William), Job, who died single, Amasa, who married Elizabeth Bourn 1748, and whose children were Amasa, Abner, (whose son Abner, jr. removed eastward), Job, Judith, (wife of Hayward Pierce, Esq.), and Abigail, (wife of Caleb Pierce). Judith, (daughter of William, sen.), married Issachar Vinal 1750, and Susanna married Thomas Curtis 1759. The late Roland (of Booth hill) was son of Abner, jr., also Mary (daughter of William, sen.) married Nathaniel Turner 1748, and was the mother of Elijah Turner, Esq., Job and Nathaniel.

The families of Bailey at Hanover, are probably all descended from Jacob, (son of John, jr.), who married Ruth Palmer 1716.

BENJAMIN BALCH.

came from Boston. He married Nazareth, the daughter of Judge John Cushing, and resided in Scituate several years, near the north Meeting-house, fifty rods south. His daughter Deborah born 1727, his son Hart 1731. He removed to Boston, where he had other children born, one of whom was Nathaniel, of facetious memory. This family probably descended from John Balch, an early settler in Salem.

ABRAHAM BARDIN.

was from Scotland. He married Mary Booth in Scituate, 1697. His son conducted Iron works at Hanover for many years.

JOHN BARKER, Esq.

was the son of John Barker of Duxbury, and Anna, the daughter of John Williams, sen. of Scituate, (married 1632), John Barker, sen. was at Jones's river (now Kingston) 1638. He was drowned 1652.*

John Barker, jr. was a serjeant in Philip's war, and freed from bearing arms at the close of that war, "on account of wounds received." He was afterward a Justice of the Peace, and is mentioned as a lawyer in the Colony records in 1674. His brother-in-law, Capt. John Williams, having no children, gave his farm in Scituate, 1694, to Williams Barker, his grandnephew, son of John, Esq. This is the well known Barker farm north of the Harbour. It is now owned by Benjamin Barker, descendant of Robert Barker, (we believe) a brother of the first John Barker, by purchase of Capt. Williams Barker, the last of John Barker's family in Scituate.

John Barker, Esq. lost his first wife Desire, 1705, and married Hannah Cushing, (the widow of Rev. Jeremiah), 1706.

Samuel, Esq. born 1684, the only son of Williams of which we have any knowledge, married Hannah, the daughter of Rev. Jeremiah Cushing, 1706, and succeeded to the family residence. His sons were Samuel, Ignatius and Ezekiel, born from 1707 to 1714, and daughters Hannah and Deborah.

Capt. *Samuel,* son of the above, succeeded to the family residence. He married Deborah Gorham of Barnstable. His sons were Capt. Williams, Dr. Jeremiah, and Dr. Samuel, born from 1744 to 1762. This family is extinct in this Town; Capt. Williams removed to Wiscasset, Dr. Jeremiah to Portland, and Dr. Samuel is living in Hanson.

We will add that Robert, the son of Robert Barker, lived in Scituate in 1698, where his son Isaac was born March 10, 1698-9, and who settled in Pembroke, and was the grandfather of the present owner of the Barker farm named above.

There was another family of this name in Scituate distinct from the above, viz. Barnabas Barker, who married Hannah Turner in 1719. His house at Beach woods near Johnson's swamp was burnt 1739, and the Town voted to exempt him from taxes that year. His sons were Barnabas and Thomas.

---

* He had purchased the ferry (now Little's Bridge) of John Brewster, son of Elder Brewster, 1641, and was there drowned.

Barnabas was an active man in the Revolutionary war. He resided near Halifax hill, and was succeeded in his residence by Ignatius Otis. His wife, Sarah Green 1750, and a first wife Mary Neal 1740. His son Joshua lived in Boston: he married Mary Copeland, and has posterity in Hanover.

WILLIAM BARRELL.

appears in Scituate in 1676. He was the son of William Barrell, who died in rather early life in Boston in 1639, and who with his brother George and John settled in Boston and Charlestown 1636. William of Scituate married Lydia, the widow of John James 1680 and resided at her residence near "the block-house." His children were William born 1683, Lydia 1684, Mary 1686, James 1687.

We trace the descendants of two only of these in Scituate.

William married Elizabeth Bailey 1706. His children were Hannah born 1706, Lydia 1709, (the wife of Joseph Young 1726), William born 1714, James 1727, Elisha 1735, and Colburn.

Lydia (daughter of William, sen.) married Samuel Stockbridge in 1703, who resided on mount Blue in Scituate.

The family of William, jr. have been remarkable for longevity.

William (we believe) lived to advanced age in Bridgewater.

James, had been a soldier and a laborious man, but by the strength of his constitution and temperance, he retained sufficient vigour to perform the labour of an ordinary man at ninety, and to walk three miles up Church at ninety-six. He died April 17, 1827, having nearly completed a century. His sons were James, William, Noah and Bartlett.

Elisha (son of William, jr.) completed his ninety-fourth year, and died 1829.

The descendants of William Barrell are in Scituate, Hanover, Bridgewater; in the State of Maine, and also near Albany in New York.

Colburn was also a man of extraordinary strength and activity. He died, we believe, about the close of the American war, in which he was a soldier, as also in the French war.

WILLIAM BARSTOW.

was a brother of Michael Barstow, a representative of Watertown 1653. He settled for a time at Dedham, where Joseph his son was born, and probably John also. He was a freeman in Scituate in 1649. His house was about one hundred rods north-west of Hanover corners, on the east side of the Plymouth road. He built "Barstow's bridge," 1656, (see Bridges).

Beside the children above named, there were born to him in Scituate, Deborah 1650, William 1652, Martha 1655. There was also a son Jeremiah, born probably at Dedham.

William Barstow died 1668, and Anna his widow administered. His descendants are many in Hanover, Rochester, Fairhaven and Salem.

Joseph, his son, lived in a house thirty rods north-east of Hanover corners. It was a garrison in Philip's war. He married Susanna Lincoln of Hingham, 1666. His children, Susanna born 1667, Joseph 1675, Benjamin 1679, Deborah 1681, Samuel 1683. He died 1712.

John was a householder in Scituate 1678. A considerable tract of land was laid out to him west of the south Meetinghouse common, extending to Jordan lane. His house was fifty rods south of the present road, and was afterward the house of John Ruggles, on the land now owned by Pickles Cushing.

He married Lydia Hatch 1678, daughter of William Hatch, who removed to Swanzey. His children were Job born 1679, Jeremiah 1682, John 1684, and several daughters.

Jeremiah was killed by the Indians with Capt. Pierce at Rehoboth, 1676. His widow Lydia was married to Richard Standlake of Scituate, 1677. We observe in the Colony records, that John administered on his brother's estate: also that "Lydia, the wife of Richard Standlake, was appointed (1677) guardian to her two sons, John and Jeremiah Barstow, and to recover a legacy to each of them from Michael Barstow, their great uncle, late of Watertown deceased, for their use when twenty-one years of age."*

We believe most of the people of the name of Barstow may thus trace their descent from William. Those at Hanover descended from his son Joseph. William, jr. succeeded to his father's residence, and to him succeeded Benjamin his son, born 1690. Deacon Samuel of Hanover is son of Samuel, and grandson of Joseph.

---

* The younger of the sons, Jeremiah, had been a captive amongst the Indians.

GEORGE BARSTOW.

was also a brother of William, sen. and Michael. He was a member of the artillery company in Boston, 1644. In 1652, he was a householder in Scituate, and a member of the second Church. He had here one son, George, born 1653. The same year he removed to Cambridge, and deceased immediately after. We notice the following entry in the Plymouth Colony records, 1653: "A suite was commenced against William Barstow by Mr. Charles Chauncy, (afterward President), for saying that he (Mr. Chauncy) was the cause of the death of his brother George Barstow, late deceased: and for saying that the s^d Mr. Chauncy sent his bulls abroad to the Church at Cambridge, whereby the s^d George Barstow was hindered from communion with s^d Church, which hastened his death through griefe." The court ordered William Barstow to retract. The explanation of this is, that George Barstow was a member of the second Church in Scituate, with which Mr. Chauncy was at variance.

JAMES BATES.

was in Scituate 1642. We believe he was a son of James Bates of Dorchester. His name appears also in Hingham. He married Ruth Lyford 1643. His son John was born here 1649. The family returned to Hingham. But the grandson of John, whose name was John, resided in Scituate in 1733. He married Abigail Bailey 1733. His sons were Reuben born February 4, 1735, Simeon 1737, Levi 1738, Judah 1740, John 1746, Caleb 1749, and daughter Aquilla born 1743. Reuben is now living at Scituate Harbour. His son Simeon is keeper of the light-house. He has sons Simeon, Joseph and others.

There was a Joseph Bates in Scituate in 1695, whose sons were Joseph, Solomon, Amos and Clement, born from 1696 to 1710. From this family we understand Neal Bates to have descended, now living. They descended from Clement Bates, who was in Weymouth 1633. The descendants of this family are in Hanover, viz. the late Col. Bates, and Benjamin of Scituate, concerned in the Plymouth stages. The late Gen. Benjamin Bates of Mansfield was a descendant of Clement.

JOSEPH BATTLES, from Hingham.

was the first of the name in Scituate. He married Susanna Studley 1738. Joseph, his son, married Rebecca Burbank 1759. He has descendants living at Hoop-pole neck. Robert Battles of Boston, 1658, was the common ancestor of this family. There was David Battles of Leominster, 1796, of the Scituate family, we believe.

JOHN BEAL.

of Scituate Harbour, a gentleman of great enterprise in the fisheries, is son of John of Cohasset, and Catherine Kimball, his wife. He married Jane, daughter of Ensign Otis, sen. and has a family. He is descended from John Beal, an early settler in Hingham, a representative 1649.

JOSEPH BENSON.

was the son of Joseph Benson of Hull. He settled in Scituate in 1743. His farm was on the south of Hoop-pole hill, near Margaret's brook, where his descendants now reside. He married Abiel Stockbridge 1743. Joseph, his son, born 1744, was his only child, he having deceased 1745. His widow married John Bryant.

Joseph married Susanna, the daughter of Nathaniel Clap, Esq. 1770. He was a useful and worthy man, often employed in the business of the Town, and clerk of the second parish for many years. His sons John and Joseph are deceased. Stephen and Artemas are living in Scituate, and Gorham in Charleston, South Carolina. Joseph of Hull, above named, was a son of John of Hull: His first wife was Prince, his second Mary Curtis of Scituate, 1727, and his third Alice Pickels 1739. He died in Scituate.

MR. THOMAS BESBEDGE, (now Bisbee or Bisby).

was in Scituate in 1634, and a freeman in 1637. He was a Deacon in the first Church at its first institution. We have found few notices of him: he probably deceased early.

Elisha Bisby, whom we suppose to have been his son, kept the first ferry where Union Bridge now stands, in 1644. His house stood near the bridge on the west side of the river, and the south side of the way. His son Elisha kept a tavern at the same place for many years. His children were Hopestill born 1645, John 1647, Mary 1648, Elisha 1654, Hannah 1656, (wife of Thomas Brooks 1687), baptized in the second Church. Martha was also probably his daughter, who married Jonathan Turner 1677. *Elisha,* the son of Elisha Bisby, died in Hingham 1715. The descendants of Mr. Thomas Besbedge are now at Plympton, and write the name Bisby.

THOMAS BIRD.

was one of the earlier settlers of Scituate. He cultivated land on the third cliff, before 1628, and (tradition says) in 1623. There is a deed in the Colony records dated 1628, by which Henry Merritt conveys to Nathaniel Tilden, "planting land which he had of Thomas Bird." His name is amongst the first freemen in 1633. There is no record of his family. He or his son Thomas was in that part of the Town called the Two mile, 1649, when he had a law suit with George Russell, (Colony Records). A widow Bird (no doubt of Thomas) had a part in division of common lands in Scituate 1673. There were several early settlers of the name of Bird in Dorchester and other parts of Massachusetts.

HUDSON BISHOP, from Duxbury.

The first of the name in this place in 1711. There are few records of the family.

WILLIAM BLACKMORE.

came from England 1665. He was a nephew of Peter Collamore, and (as tradition relates) came with an expectation of being his heir, (see Collamore). A farm was laid out to him by the freemen, (in part), where the late Capt. Elijah Curtis, resided. His house occupied nearly the same place, a few rods east. He married Elizabeth Bankes 1666. His children were Peter born 1667, John 1669, Phebe 1672, William 1675.

In 1669, he was freed from military duty, "for the loss of an eye." He however lost his life in repelling the Indians in 1676, April 21. His widow married Jacob Bumpus 1677.

Peter died 1692, leaving two children, Joseph and Jane.

Phebe married Ebenezer Holmes.

William died without children 1698. In his will, he gives legacies to "brother John – sister Phebe Holmes – brother Peter's two children Joseph and Jane, and brother in-law Ebenezer Holmes."

MR. CHRISTOPHER BLACKWOOD.

purchased the farm that had been that of Rev. John Lothrop, east of Colman's hills, in 1641, of Mr. Hatherly. He was employed for a short time as a preacher. But in 1642, he sold his farm to Mr. Chauncy, whom the Church had chosen for their pastor, and retired. He probably returned to England, as we find no further trace of him.

JOHN BLOSSOM.

was in Scituate 1728, where his son Thomas was born the same year. He probably returned to Barnstable, from whence we believe he came. He was a descendant of Dea. Thomas Blossom, who died in Plymouth 1633. (Colony Records).

JOHN BOOTH.

was in Scituate as early as 1656. He purchased lands in the Conihassett proprietary, and settled near the hill which now bears his name. His house was where that of Rowland Bailey now stands. He had several sons, Joseph born 1659, John born 1661, Benjamin 1667, Abraham 1673, and four daughters, Elizabeth, Mary, Grace and Judith.

Joseph, the eldest son, lived in Pennsylvania in 1710.

John married Mary, the daughter of Anthony Dodson 1687, and had a son Anthony born 1689.

Mary married Abraham Barden.

Rev. Chauncy Booth of Coventry, Connecticut, may be a descendant of this family. The name has here been extinct for more than half a century.

HENRY BOURN

was a freeman in Scituate 1637, but not an householder that we can learn. He removed to Barnstable 1639. His descendants may be there and in Rhode Island. He was brother of Richard Bourn, the first preacher to the Marshpee Indians. John of Marshfield may have been his son, whose children were Elizabeth born 1646, Thomas 1647, Alice 1649, Anna 1651, Martha 1653, Sarah 1663. Thomas had a son Thomas whose daughter Hannah married William Wilson of Scituate.

JAMES BOWKER, (from Sweden).

was in Scituate 1680. His farm was laid out on the east of Burnt plain and west of Samuel Bryant's land. His house was near the corner of the field, a few rods west of the house of his late grandson Edmund Bowker. His wife was Mary. His children James, Mary and Lazarus, the two last being baptized in the second Church 1686: also Richard, Edmund and Benjamin.

James succeeded to his father's residence. He married Hannah Lambert 1717. His children were five sons and seven daughters. Four of the sons settled near the original farm, viz. Lazarus, James, John and Edmund. Joseph removed to Maine. This family has been remarkable for longevity. Edmund born August 20, 1732, reached his ninety-fourth year. Lazarus, son of Lazarus, is now in active life at the age of eighty-eight.

Benj. has left descendants here, viz. Major Joshua and others.

Richard lived in Pembroke, and left sons.

WILLIAM BROOKS.

was a householder in 1644. His farm was south of Till's creek, latterly called Dwelley's creek, and his house near that of Capt. William Brooks, his descendant of the sixth generation. The spot seems to have been selected on account of the sweet spring of water near it. His wife was widow Susanna Dunham of Plymouth, His children were *Hannah* born 1645, Nathaniel 1646, (who married Elizabeth, daughter of Richard Curtis, 1678, and succeeded to his father's residence), Mary born 1647,

Sarah born 1650, (who married Joseph Studley), Meriam born 1652, (who married John Curtis, son of Richard Curtis), Deborah born 1654, (who married Robert Stetson, jr. son of the Cornet), Thomas born 1657, who married Hannah Bisby 1687, and Joanna born 1659.

The people of this name in Scituate have all descended from *Nathaniel.* His sons were William, Gilbert and Nathaniel. William's posterity remain on the ancient seat of the family.* Gilbert had a son William, born 1714, (who removed or died early), Gilbert 1718, and Benjamin 1720. Nath'l, 2d. married Mary Taylor 1717, and purchased lands of Michael Wanton, a half mile west of Hoop-pole hill, where the fifth Nathaniel Brooks now resides. His children are of the seventh generation. Nathaniel, 3d. married Elizabeth Benson 1744, Nathaniel, 4th. married Deborah Brooks 1783, and Nathaniel 5th. married Charlotte Lapham 1821.†

Thomas, the son of William, sen. had one son Thomas, born 1688, and a daughter Joanna born 1695. Thomas had no family. Joanna married John Ruggles, who succeeded to the farm of Thomas Brooks. It lies a half mile east of the residence of William above described. It was the farm of William Richards 1640.

GILBERT BROOKS

was a brother of William Brooks, sen. and came into Scituate at the same time. His residence was on the south of Colman's hills. He sold his house to Robert Crossman of Taunton, 1652. It was afterward the residence of Joseph Otis, Esq. The earliest notice which we have seen of him, is, that he was in the family of Mr. William Vassall 1638. He married Elizabeth, the daughter of Gov. Edward Winslow. He had sons

---

* The late Capt. William, who deceased 1821, on the paternal spot, was his grandson, (and son of William, who married Mary Braman 1737). His children are Capt. William, who lives on the paternal farm, Sarah, (wife of Dea. Loring of Duxbury), Philenda, (wife of Capt. Luther Tilden), Temperance, (wife of Capt. Reuben Drew of Duxbury), Betsey, (second wife of Capt. Jotham Tilden), Gilbert of Medford, Lucy, Seth and Nathan of Duxbury. Their mother Betsy Stodder.

† Nathaniel, 2d. had also a son Taylor, who married Miriam Curtis 1740. Capt. Noah was his son, born 1744, and died at sea. His son is Capt. Noah of South Boston, and his daughters the wives of William Bradford of Kingston, Samuel Kent, late of Scituate, and Hon. John Holmes of Maine.

Gilbert (son of Gilbert) was father of late Samuel of Hanover, born 1742.

Nathaniel, 2d. had sons Noah, Michael, Simon and Stephen, who died early or removed, born from 1723 to 1737.

Gilbert and John, probably born in Marshfield. His children born in Scituate were Elizabeth, born 1645, Sarah 1646, Mary 1649, Rachel 1650, Bathsheba 1655, Rebecca 1657, Hannah 1659, all baptized in the second Church.

In 1675, he kept a garrison at Gov. Josiah Winslow's house in Marshfield. We observe that John, son of Gilbert Brooks, had a legacy in the will of his uncle, Gov. Josiah Winslow.

Gilbert was in Rehoboth 1683, and one of a committee "to treat with the Rev. Samuel Angier, concerning his settlement in the ministry there." (Colony Records),

WALTER BRIGGS.

appears in Scituate 1651, when he purchased a farm of Mr. Hatherly, on the north side of Farm neck. The cove within the *glades* still bears the name of Briggs's harbour. He was long a useful man in the plantation.

His will dated 1684, gives

"To my wife Frances one third of my estate during her life, also a gentle horse or mare, and Jemmy the Negur shall catch it for her. To son John my homestead, bounded south-west by Mr. John Saffin's farm. To son James the easterly side of my farm (bounds named). To daughter Hannah Winslow (certain movables). To son Cornelius one freeman's share in the town of Swanzey, and 30£. Son John Ex."

Capt. John married   and left on record Hannah born 1684, Deborah 1685, John 1687. Hannah married John Alden of Duxbury, 1709: their son John Alden was baptized in Scituate second Church, December 10, 1710, and Samuel, May 17, 1713. The venerable Judah Alden, Esq. of Duxbury is a descendant, being the son of Briggs Alden, another son of John. Deborah, we believe, married Dea. Thomas King 1705. Capt. John, jr. married Deborah, the daughter of Hon. John Cushing, sen. 1712. Their daughter Deborah born 1713, John 1714. Deborah, last named, married Thomas Savage, Esq. of Boston, (see John Cushing). The family of Capt. John Briggs removed or became extinct probably.

Lieut. James married Rebecca, daughter of Dea. Joseph Tilden, 1678. His children were Joseph born 1678, Mary 1682, James 1687, Benjamin 1695, (and perhaps others).

Joseph married Deborah Holbrook 1703, and had children, Cornelius 1705, (who married Lydia Stodder 1741, and probably removed), Mary 1707, John 1709, Joseph 1714, Thankful, Hannah and Ezra, (who married Lydia Neal 1764). James (above) married Hannah Bailey 1706, and left no family on record. Benjamin married Leah Merritt 1719, and left daughters Leah, Deborah, Rachel, and sons Capt. Benjamin born 1722, and James born November 16, 1735. Capt. Benjamin married Rebecca Curtis 1758, and was the father of Capt. Benjamin now living, whose children are James of Watertown, Billings of Boston, Paul of Scituate, and daughters: and James, the veteran Town clerk, married Rhoda Nash 1763, and had sons Shadrach, Bartlett, Joseph, George and daughters. James Briggs is living, aged ninety-six.

Cornelius married the widow of Samuel Russell 1677, (she was daughter of James Doughty, and granddaughter of Humphry Turner). He was an Ensign in Philip's war, with his two brothers who were his superior officers. He had sons Cornelius 1678, Joseph 1679, James 1683. Cornelius married Ruth Barker, and removed, we believe, to Swansey. Joseph married Mary Garrett 1709, and left daughters, Mary born 1711, Hannah, the wife of Dea. Joseph Clap 1732, Judith, (the wife of Wm. Collier 1748), and no son we believe. James (son of Cornelius, sen.) has a numerous posterity. He married Elizabeth Garrett 1713, by whom he had one daughter. Elizabeth 1715. His second wife was Hannah Stowell 1716, and her children were John born 1718, James 1719, Seth 1721, Job 1722, Elisha 1723, Hannah 1724, Cornelius 1728, and William 1731. Of these John married Abigail Neal 1751, and left children, John, Abigail, Anna, Joshua, Sabera, Rebecca, Elisha, (now living), Lydia (widow of Elisha Turner) and Deborah, born from 1751 to 1767.

James married Hannah Barker 1745, and had children, Hannah, Sarah, Lucy, James, and Thomas Barker, (who married Lucy, daughter of Dr. James Otis, and left children, Thomas, Cushing Otis, Henry, Deborah and Charles).

Seth married Abigail Church 1745, and was the father of Elisha, and Alden, Esq. of Pembroke, and the late Thomas of Milton.

Cornelius married Jerusha Church 1753, and had children, Mary, Cornelius, Samuel, Joseph, Charles, from 1753 to 1768.

William married Elizabeth Copeland 1754, and had children, Rachel, Ruth, William, Elijah, Lemuel, Elizabeth, John, Charles, Cornelius, Hulda, (wife of Major Pratt of Scituate), born from 1754 to 1780: most of whom are living in Scituate, Milton and Salem.

Though the descendants of Walter Briggs are numerous,

there are some of the name in the Old Colony who descended from Clement Briggs, an early settler in Weymouth. His son Thomas born 1633, we think, settled in Taunton soon after 1650; from him probably descended the people of this name at Taunton, Norton, and Mansfield: also the Rev. Ephraim Briggs, late of Halifax, (son of Dea. Briggs of Mansfield) who left sons Ephraim, William, Isaac, Richard and Charles in the ministry, and John a physician at Dedham.

Cornelius Briggs, alias Wade, (a son of Sarah Wade, daughter of Thomas Wade), and Jane his wife, removed to Maine before 1750. They had children born in Scituate, John 1737, Jane 1739, Reuben 1741, Sarah 1742.

JOHN BRYANT, house carpenter.

was a freeman in Scituate 1639. His farm was on the second Herring brook, ten rods east of the mill, an ancient orchard now marks the place. His son John built the first saw mill on that brook, 1690, and shortly after a grist mill.

John, sen. was an active and useful man, always employed in division of lands and other publick concerns. He married Mary, the daughter of George Lewis, (then of Barnstable), 1643. His children, John born 1644, Hannah 1645,* Joseph 1646, died early, Sarah 1648, Mary 1649, Martha 1651, Samuel 1653. In 1657, he married a second wife, Elizabeth, daughter of Rev. William Witherell, who died early. In 1664, he married Mary, daughter of Thomas Hiland, by whom he had another family of ten children, viz. Elizabeth born 1665, Benjamin 1669, Joseph 1671, Jabez 1672, Ruth 1673, Thomas 1675, Deborah 1677, Agatha 1678, Ann 1680, Elisha 1682.

Lieut. *John jr.* had children, John, 3d. born 1677, Jonathan 1679, Mary 1682, David 1684, Joshua 1687, Samuel 1689, Martha 1691. This branch of the family possessed a large tract of land, extending from Spring brook to James Bowker's, on which the sons settled. Joshua settled near the place where his descendant Snow Bryant lives. Samuel near him on the west, David on the east, Jonathan on the south, and John on third Herring brook at Cornet's dam.

Joseph, son of John, sen. settled on the east of White-oak plain, by the brook. He was the uncle of Peleg Bryant, the last of the name who lived on that place, Peleg was, son of Thomas, Esq.

---

* Wife of John Stodder of Hingham, 1665.

Benjamin, son of John, sen., lived at Spring brook, near the place now occupied by Rev. Mr. Jewett. His family removed to Chesterfield.

Thomas, Esq., son of John, sen., succeeded to his father's farm, and built the house now occupied by the heirs of Dea. Thomas Cushing. It was built in 1698. He was an able and useful man as a magistrate, but tradition speaks of some singularities. He was the father of Rev. Lemuel Bryant of Quincy, a man of extraordinary powers and singularities, who died 1754, and was buried at Scituate.

Samuel son of John, sen., died in Phips's expedition to Canada, 1690.

John Bryant, sen. gives in his will, (date 1684),
"To sons Samuel and Daniel my lot of land near Barstow's tree at grass pond, (now Old pond). To Benjamin 20S when 21, in trust of his grandfather Hiland. To Joseph and Thomas the house where I live: also to Joseph a lot at white-oak plain. To daughter Mary a bed. To Ruth a bed when 18. To Deborah, Agatha and Ann each 5£ at 18. To youngest child Elisha 10£ at 21. To son John 10S. To daughters Hannah, Sarah and Martha 20S each. To wife Mary all other property not named in this will."

SAMUEL BROWN.

married Hannah Nash 1731. Jonathan Brown was also in Scituate 1740, he had a son Abner born 1741. There was a Hannah Brown, a member of the first Church 1746. There are descendants of this family in Town, but we find no record of the early generations.

JEREMIAH BURROUGHS.

was in Scituate 1647, but not a freeman here. He had a house on "Bell house neck," probably the house in which Resolved White had lived.* His son Jeremiah had an assignment of common lands in Scituate, in the last division of 1699. And Jeremiah, son of the latter, married Hannah, daughter of Henry Ewell (of the second generation) in 1710; he is then called of Marshfield.

---

* He had children Jeremiah born 1651, John 1653, Elizabeth 1655, Mary 1657, baptized in second Church.

FAMILY SKETCHES.

HENRY BURDITT.

married Lydia, the daughter of Richard Dwelley 1712. Their children born here were William 1713, and Elizabeth 1717, Thankful, Joshua, Francis, Ruth, and Deborah, who married Benjamin Healy 1759. Elizabeth married Peter Curtis 1747.

CORNET JOHN BUCK.

appears in Scituate before 1650, and may have been the son of James Buck of Hingham. He was the first proprietor of Walnut tree hill, at least the west part of it, in 1651, and his house was on the west side of that hill. He succeeded the veteran Robert Stetson as "Cornet of the Troopers," before Philip's war, in which war he was constantly in service, (see Indian wars). His children were Elizabeth born 1653, Mary 1655, Joseph 1657, John 1659, Hannah 1661, Susanna 1664, Benjamin 1665, Deborah 1670, Robert 1672, Rachel 1674. Some of this family have descendants in Easton.

John Buck's will dated 1697, gives legacies

"To daughter Chandler – To Isaac Randall's children – to John Garrett's children – to all my grand children living at Yarmouth and Sandwich." His wife was Elizabeth, daughter of Samuel Holbrook of Weymouth.

LIEUT. ISAAC BUCK, Blacksmith.

was a brother of John, and was in Scituate before 1647. He purchased the house of Jeremiah Burroughs, which had been that of Resolved White at Belle house neck. In 1660, he built a house near the Harbour, on the Buck field, so called even now. The house of Anthony Waterman, lately deceased, occupies the spot. He was a very useful man, often engaged in publick business, and the Clerk of the Town for many years. He was a Lieut. in Philip's war, and repulsed the Indians with great bravery from Scituate in March 1676. He died intestate 1695.

Commissionerws divided his estate as follows:

"To Frances the widow the house in which she now lives.
To Thomas, the land where his house stands.
To the heirs of the second son James, &c.

To Joseph – to Jonathan and Benjamin, (sons of Lieut. B.)
To Elizabeth, wife of Robert Whitcomb.
To Mehitabel, wife of Stephen Chittenden.
To Ruth, wife of Joseph Garrett, and Deborah wife of Henry Merritt."

Beside these children there is a son Isaac amongst the baptisms: but he may have died early. A son John is also incidentally mentioned in other records. He left a son Dea. Isaac, who was the last of the name in Scituate. He lived at the north-east of Hoop-pole hill, thirty rods south of late Judge Nathan Cushing's residence. He deceased more than seventy-five years since.

JACOB BUMPUS, (originally Bonpasse).

lived north of Dead swamp 1676. He married Elizabeth, widow of William Blackmore 1677. Children, Benjamin born 1678, Jacob 1680. There was also John Bumpus, whose children were Mary born 1671, John 1673, Samuel 1676, James 1678. This family went to Middleboro and Rochester. They descended from Edward Bonpasse of Plymouth, 1633: He was of Marshfield 1640, when his son John was born: Jacob was born 1644, and we believe there were other children.

JONATHAN BADCOCKE.

married Mary, the daughter of Richard Curtis 1677, and had children baptized in the second Church, Jonathan 1678, Mercy 1679, Caleb 1680, Mary 1681.

OLIVER CALLOWAY (or Callow).

(a very rare name) received grants of land in Scituate in 1647. He left no family here. Capt. Israel Chittenden succeeded to his right in common lands.

WILLIAM CARLISLE.

came from Marblehead 1750. He married Elizabeth Davis 1755. He was a soldier in the French war. He had a son William who removed.

EDWARD CASELY.

was in Scituate 1638, removed to Barnstable 1639.

NATHANIEL CHAMBERLAIN.

probably from Hull, received grants of land 1693, on the east of Dead swamp. Chamberlain plain is the well known name of those lands. His children were Freedom born 1697, Eunice 1698, Joseph 1699. Some of this family were Quakers and went to Rhode Island.

THOMAS CHAMBERS.

was in Scituate 1640. His house lot was on the top of the hill, opposite to the Meeting-house of the second Society. It was afterward the place of William Holmes, and more recently of the Wilson family. He had a share in Conihassett lands 1646, which he sold to Gen. Cudworth 1653. He disappears from our records after 1658. We believe he removed to Charlestown.

BENJAMIN CHANDLER.

was probably son of Edmund Chandler of Duxbury, (and who also was in Scituate 1650, when he sold his lands to Thomas Bird). Benjamin had a farm on the west of Brushy hill, near Nicholas Wade's. His wife was daughter of Cornet John Buck. His children born here were Benjamin born 1672, Martha 1673, Samuel 1674, John 1675, Mary 1678.

JOSEPH CHECKETT.

had a farm on the east of Colman's hills, adjoining that of Rev. John Lothrop 1638. He probably went to Barnstable, as he disappears from our records 1640.

ISAAC CHITTENDEN.

was one of the men of Kent. His house lot assigned in 1633, was on Kent street. He bore arms 1643. He came with his father Thomas Chittenden, who was one of the Conihassett partners in 1646. Thomas deceased in 1669, leaving legacies to his sons Isaac and Henry, and to Benjamin, son of Isaac.*

Isaac, jr. married Martha, (daughter of widow Anna Vinall), 1646. His children, Sarah and Rebecca born 1646, Mary 1648, Israel 1651, Stephen 1654, Elizabeth 1658, Isaac 1663. Isaac, jr. was an active and useful man, often a deputy to Court. He fell in repulsing the Indians from the Town 1676.

Benjamin, son of Isaac, sen. fell with Capt. Pierce in the battle of Rehoboth, 1676, and left no family.

Sarah, daughter of Isaac, sen., married Capt. Anthony Collamore 1666.

Israel, son of Isaac, jr., married Deborah, daughter of Rev. Nicholas Baker 1678. His sons were Nicholas born 1678, Isaac 1681, and Israel 1690.

Stephen, son of Isaac, jr,, married Mehitabel Buck 1679. His son Thomas born 1683.

Thomas, son of Stephen, married Elizabeth Woodworth 1707, his sons Thomas born 1718, Stephen 1722.

Israel, son of Israel, married Mary Pickels 1713, (and afterward the widow of Benjamin Turner and mother of, Capt. Elisha Turner). His sons were Israel born 1715, Isaac 1719, Nicholas 1721, Nathaniel 1724.

Isaac, son of Israel above, had a son Calvin 1746, and removed to Malden.

Nathaniel, son of Israel, had a son Nathaniel born 1751, and Isaac 1753, who removed to Princeton. Nathaniel last named lived at the mouth of the second Herring brook, and married Ruth Foster, (now the wife of Dea. Elisha James).

Israel born 1715, (son of Israel), married Deborah Vinal 1741. His son Israel married Abigail Turner 1763. He was the sixth generation, and the last that occupied the original house lot on Kent street. He sold to the family of Vinal in 1800, and removed, we believe, to Charlestown.

---

* Thomas's son Henry left a family, Joseph born 1656-7, also Susanna, Elizabeth and Ruth, and Joseph had a son Nathaniel born 1694, his grandfather Henry lived to a great age. He died 1713, leaving legacies to "gr. son Nathaniel my Conihassett lands – to gr. daughters Mary Morton, Ruth Stetson and Alathea Chittenden 20S each. Daughter Elizabeth Executrix."

ANTHONY CHUBBUCK.

a descendant of Thomas Chubbuck, an early settler in Hingham, resides near Scituate Harbour. He married Lucy, daughter of Ensign Otis, sen., and has a family. He was son of David Chubbuck, who deceased at Quincy. David had three other sons, Melzer, Martin and Thomas, who were lost at sea at one and the same time.

NATHANIEL CHURCH.

was born in Plymouth or Duxbury, and the youngest brother of Col. Benjamin the warrior. He was in Scituate 1666. His farm was laid out on the North river, south of Cornet Stetson's, including the *bald hills.* His house stood near the river, opposite nearly to Job's landing. His children, Abigail born 1666, Richard 1668, Nathaniel 1670, Alice 1679, Joseph 1681, Charles 1683, Sarah 1686.

Richard (whose wife was Mary - of Scituate) had one son Richard, born 1697.

Nathaniel had sons, Nathaniel born 1698, Joseph 1709, Caleb 1712.

Joseph and *Charles* left no families here. Some of this family removed to Watertown, (tradition).

Nathaniel (son of Nathaniel, jr.) married Jerusha Perry 1719, and left a family on record. *Caleb* married Sarah Williamson 1735, and lived probably in Marshfield.

Lemuel Church, who deceased on the paternal lands in 1829, was the son of Nathaniel and Jerusha Perry, (born 1742) and one of fifteen children. His son, Capt. Cornelius, is his successor.

Thomas Church, (a Revolutionary soldier), who deceased 1830, on a part of the same lands, was son of *Thomas,* the eldest son of Nathaniel and Jerusha above named.

We think proper to add, that since preparing these notes on the family of Church, we have had reason to doubt whether Nathaniel first named was brother of Col. Benjamin, though we had the opinion of the late Samuel Davis, Esq. to this effect. Richard Church, early of Hingham, had a son Nathaniel, as Hobart's journal testifies, and he may have been the Nathaniel of Scituate. Richard of Hingham was probably a brother of

Joseph, (the father of Col. Benjamin), at least there has been a tradition in the family here, that their first ancestor was his relative.

Nathaniel of Scituate deceased 1700, intestate. His property was divided "to his widow Sarah – to the three children of his son Richard deceased – to Nathaniel – to the child of Joseph deceased – to Charles – and to daughters Abigail, Alice and Sarah." Plymouth Probate Records.

Hobart's journal records that Richard Church, sen. died at Dedham, 1668. His will, however, is dated at Hingham that year, giving "all his estate to his wife Elizabeth during her life, and then to be divided equally to his children, (without naming them), save, to Joseph a double portion on account of the lameness of his hand." Massachusetts Probate Records.

MR. THOMAS CLAP.

was born in Dorchester, England, 1597. He came to New England with the early settlers of Dorchester, where his brothers John, Richard and Ambrose tarried. Thomas proceeded to Weymouth, where his first son Thomas was born 1639. He had grants of land in Hingham, 1637, but never resided there. His farm in Weymouth was near the present residence of Hon. Christopher Webb. He came to Scituate 1640. We find no record of his children born here, but we learn from incidental records, that he had Eleazer, Samuel, Elizabeth, Prudence, John born 1658, and Abigail born 1659. His farm in Scituate was on the south-west of Stockbridge's mill pond, and now owned by Calvin Jenkins, sen. He was a Deacon of the first Church 1647. He was an active, useful, and venerable man.

His son Thomas lived at Dedham, and is the ancestor (we believe) of the Claps of Walpole. Eleazer lived at Barnstable, and left no family. Elizabeth married Dea. Thomas King, (son of Elder King), 1669. John died early, as Abigail also.

From Samuel descended the distinguished family of this name in this vicinity. He succeeded to his father's residence. He married Hannah, the daughter of Thomas Gill of Hingham 1666. His children were Samuel born 1667, Joseph 1668, Stephen 1670, Hannah 1673, Bethia 1675, John 1677, Abigail 1679, David 1684, Deborah 1686, Jane 1689.

Joseph had land at Black pond hill 1700, where his son Deacon Joseph settled, and Elijah, son of the latter, now resides.* Stephen settled on the west of White-oak plain 1690. John lived near the residence of late Augustus, east of the mill pond. Some of David's sons, Noah and perhaps others, went to Norton. Galen of Scituate was his grandson, son of David, jr.

Amongst the most distinguished of Samuel Clap's family, we may name Dea. Stephen, whose house above mentioned at White-oak plain is now standing: It was erected before 1686, and in that year is called, in a survey of the road, "Samuel Clap's new house." Dea. Stephen occupied it 1690. It is now owned by the fifth generation from Dea. Stephen. Of the children of the venerable Dea. Stephen, *Thomas* born 1703, and graduated at Harvard College 1722, was one of the most distinguished men of his time. He was ordained at Windham, Connecticut, 1726: chosen President of Yale College 1740, and continued in the chair until 1764, when he resigned, and on a visit at Scituate 1765, he deceased.

President Stiles, his successor, speaks of him as standing in the first ranks of the learned men of the age. "He studied (says he) the higher branches of mathematicks, and was one of the first philosophers America has produced, and equalled by no man, except the most learned Professor Winthrop."

As a theologian he is equally praised. As a President, most indefatigable and successful in promoting the interests of learning, and raising the rank of his College.

He wrote many books, or rather pamphlets, in defence of the New England Churches in Whitefield's time, from 1734 to 1755. That he was a powerful opponent to Whitefield, and did much to counteract his disorganizing measures, we may easily conceive, when, in looking over these pamphlets, we find him quoting Whitefield's own words, and declaring himself ready to testify as to the correctness of the quotation, viz. "I intend to turn the generality of the ministers of this country out of their pulpits, (who are half beasts and half devils), and bring over ministers from England."

He wrote also a valuable history of Yale College, which we could wish to see reprinted.

His brother Nathaniel, Esq. born 1709, was a respectable and useful citizen and magistrate. He married Desire Bourne of Barnstable, 1736. His son Sylvanus deceased in the ancient house of his grandfather 1811, whose son Stephen

---

* Dea. Joseph married Hannah Briggs and Sarah Perkins – Elijah married Martha Turner.

afterward occupied the same mansion, and deceased 1825, leaving a family; Nathaniel, the only surviving son of Sylvanus, is now living near Margaret's brook, on lands which the family have possessed from the year 1660: the widow of Charles Lapham, the wife of Mr. Hall of Chelsea, the wife of Job Loring of Hingham, and the wife of Isaac Totman of Boston, are daughters of Mr. Sylvanus Clap.

Col. John Clap, an officer in the French war, and also in the Revolution, was the son of John, the eldest of Dea. Stephen's sons. John Clap now occupies the place of his father's (the Col's.) residence, near the second Herring brook, and Elijah the place of his grandfather John. Col. John married Chloe Stowers of Hingham, 1761. The family also of *John,* son of the first Samuel Clap, has been distinguished. He married Hannah Gill (his cousin) 1702, (she was a widow 1730, and married Major Amos Turner).

Thomas (son of the latter John) born 1705, graduated at Harvard College 1725. He was the minister of the first Church of Taunton a few years; afterward a Judge of the Court of Plymouth County, and a Colonel of the militia. He was the father of Capt. John Clap, an officer in the French war; Augustus, Esq., Town Clerk and Post-master for many years, who deceased 1826; Mary, who died 1830, aged ninety, a remarkably accomplished woman; also Chandler, Hannah and Rufus now surviving. Capt. John was the father of Capt. Leonard Clap, and the only one of the family that married. His wife Jerusha Bailey 1752. The first wife of Judge Clap was Mary, the daughter of Judge George Leonard of Norton,* and his second was Esther, the daughter of Hon. John Chandler of Worcester.

By way of illustrating the early history and connexions of this family, we add a few extracts from the Colony records.

Plymouth, 1676, "At this Court Thomas Clap of Dedham claimed to be heir to his brother Eleazer deceased, and the Court being satisfied that he is the eldest son of Dea. Thomas Clap of Scituate, ordered that Samuel Clap of Scituate, Administrator, forbear to dispose of any of the lands of the s^d Eleazer, unless all concerned shall agree."

Dea. Thomas Clap's will is dated 1684, and mentions that he was then eighty-seven years old. He gives legacies "To

---

* The wife of the first Judge George Leonard was Rachel, daughter of Dea. Stephen Clap, and mother of the Rev. Dr. Barnes's wife, married November 9, 1721.

wife Abigail – To son Samuel – To son Thomas at Dedham and to daughter Elizabeth King."

The will of John Clap of Dorchester, dated 1655, gives "My house and land to my wife during her life, and after her decease to the support of the ministry and a school in Dorchester – To my brother Ambrose Clap what is due me from my brother Richard, now in England. To my brother-in-law Edward Clap 3£. To Richard and Elizabeth, children of my brother Richard, (certain moveables named), and to Deborah, daughter of brother Richard, a silver spoon. To Nathaniel, Ebenezer, Sarah and Hannah, children of my brother Nicholas Clap, 4S each. To Elizabeth, Prudence, and Samuel, children of my brother Thomas, (of Scituate), 8S each, and to the rest of his children 5S each."

We add, that Noah, who removed to Norton, as mentioned above, had a son Eleazer, who deceased at Uxbridge, leaving descendants: and a son, Capt. Abiel of Mansfield, who was the father of Hon. Asa Clap of Portland, and Capt. Elkanah deceased.

George Clap, (son of John and grandson of Dea. Stephen), born 1726, removed to Northampton. Rev. Mr. Clap of New Orleans, we are told, is his descendant.

THOMAS CLARK.

was in Scituate 1674. He came hither from Plymouth, and was probably the son or grandson of Thomas Clark, the mate of the May-flower in 1620. His farm in Scituate was on the west of Walnut tree hill, (a half mile west of late Judge William Cushing's mansion), and adjoining that of Cornet Buck. He married Martha Curtis 1676, and had children, Thomas, Joseph, David, Samuel, Nathaniel, Marcy, Deborah, Rachel, Ann, Charity and Mary, born from 1676, to 1704.

His son Thomas, jr. succeeded to his father's house, and had children, Thomas, John, Mary, Joseph and Seth. This family intermarried with the Parkers, and also with the Palmers. The wife of Thomas, jr. was Alice Rogers 1705 – and also Alice Parker 1719. Thomas, sen. was a soldier in Philip's war, and received a grant of land for his services, of the value of £5, 5S, 2d.

This family disappears from Scituate after 1740. Thomas Clark, jr. and Alice his wife removed to Rochester 1731.

ELDER HENRY COBB, in Scituate 1633.

was one of the men of Kent, and settled on Kent street. He had also eighty acres on North river, which was afterward the farm of Ephraim Kempton, and then of John James. Elder Cobb removed to Barnstable with his pastor Mr. Lothrop, 1639. Two of his children were born at Plymouth, one at Scituate, and eight at Barnstable. His first wife Patience died 1648, and he married Sarah, the daughter of Samuel Hinckley, and sister of Governor Hinckley. He was a useful and valuable man, often deputy to the Court, and other publick employments. His son John settled in Plymouth, Gershom in Middleboro, Edward in Taunton. His posterity is almost countless. He deceased 1679. His sons were John, James, Gershom, Eleazer, and daughters Mary and Patience, of his first wife: his sons Samuel, Jonathan and Henry, and his daughters Mehitabel and Sarah of his second wife. These children born from 1632 to 1662. Matthew Cobb, Esq. of Portland, was of the Barnstable family.

ROBERT COCKE, (now Cook).

was in Scituate 1690, and lived east of the Great swamp. His children (born in Scituate) were James born 1693, William 1695, Jane 1697, Margaret 1698. His wife was Mary Jenkins, (see Jenkins). Robert (probably, jr.) of Scituate, married Agnis Kent of Boston, 1703. William, brother of Robert, sen. married Sarah Curtis 1705. Robert, a great grandson of the first Robert, deceased in Scituate 1831. He had been a Revolutionary soldier. William (son of William), married Mary Ramsden 1726, and lived in Hanover.

AMBROSE COLE.

purchased lands of Capt. Stephen Otis, in the Conihassett 1695. His house stood on the Cohasset road, forty rods southeast of Bound brook bridge, on the north-east of the way.

His first wife's name was Silence – and his second Abigail Sutton, 1715. His children, William born 1693, Ambrose

1695, Ensign 1698, Ann 1701, David 1704, Jonathan 1707, James 1716.

Ambrose married Elizabeth Lincoln 1721. Children, Elizabeth born 1721, Amos 1722.

Ensign married Sarah Peaks 1726. Children, Desire born 1732, Ruth 1734, Ensign 1737, Lucy 1742.

David married Sarah Balch 1732. Children, Lydia born 1733, Wm. 1735, David 1737, Elizabeth 1739, Abigail 1743.

Jonathan married Sarah Gannett 1732. Children, Mary born 1733, Sarah 1736, Jonathan 1739.

James married Sarah White 1745. Children, Mary born 1746, Sarah 1748, James 1750, Mehitabel 1753, Desire 1756, Charles 1759, Nabby 1763, Enoch 1766. Charles is now living, and has a numerous family here and in Boston.

William (son of David) left a family, viz. William born 1766, Charlotte 1768, Oliver 1771, Elizabeth 1774, David 1776, (died 1830), Ambrose 1779, Rachel 1782, Gridley 1784, Bradock 1787. Ambrose is of Charlestown.

Ambrose, sen. died 1738, and names in his will "sons Ambrose, Ensign, David, James, Jonathan, and daughter Ann Sutton."

There was a James Cole in Scituate 1653. He removed to old York, soon after that date. Ambrose may have been his son. There was a Job Cole in Plymouth 1634, who married Rebecca Collier.

PETER COLLAMORE, (early Collamer).

was on the list of those liable to bear arms in Scituate, 1643. His house lot was on the east part of Belle house neck, adjoining Mr. Vassall's. It is now called the "Collamore place." He had no children, and sent to England for some relative to inherit his estate. William Blackmore, his sister's son, accordingly came. But desiring an heir of the name of Collamore, he gave but little to Blackmore, and made his nephew, Capt. Anthony Collamore, who afterwards came, his principal legatee.

The will of Peter Collamore is dated 1684, and bequeathes "To wife Mary one third of the income of my estates. To the children of William Blackmore, deceased, viz. to Peter a lot of marsh on the first Herring brook – to John all my lands at Sowamack* – to Phebe a cow – to William 50 acres of land at

---

* Probably Shaomet, north of Swansey.

Seconett. To Mary, daughter of Anthony Collamore, 56 acres in Scituate – to Sarah (do.) 10£, and to Martha and Elizabeth the like sum. To my man William Clift a 10 acre lot at Seconett. To nephew Anthony Collamore all other property.   Peter Collamer."

Capt. Anthony Collamore married Sarah, one of the twin daughters of Mr. Isaac Chittenden, 1666. His children were Mary born 1667, Peter 1671, Sarah 1673, Martha 1677, Elizabeth 1679.

Peter married Abigail Davis of Roxbury, 1695. His children, Abigail born 1695, Sarah 1697, Anthony 1699, Peter 1701, Mary 1703, John 1704, Isaac 1707, Thomas 1709, Samuel 1712. Isaac married Thankful Curtis 1733, and left posterity. Samuel removed to Maine. Capt. Thomas to Pembroke.

Most of these left descendants. Many have removed to distants parts. Jacob Collamore, Esq. of Royalton, Vermont, is a descendant of Anthony.* The only branch of the family which preserves the name in Scituate, is that of John, who married Margaret Whiton 1732, and settled at Gillman plain. His son, Capt. Enoch, kept a well known tavern there for many years: and the sons of Capt. Enoch, viz. John, Esq. and Enoch reside on the same plain, and Dr. Anthony, (graduated at Harvard College 1805), and Horace reside in Pembroke.

We add that Capt. Anthony Collamore, on a coasting voyage from North river to Boston, was wrecked and lost on Scituate beach, December 16, 1693. On the Probate records of 1695, appears an agreement of his heirs in the division of his estate, in which the parties concerned were "Sarah the widow – Peter, the only son – Mary, the wife of Robert Stetson – Sarah, Martha and Elizabeth Collamore."

The rocks where Capt. Collamore was wrecked are called "Collamore's ledge." He was the commander of the militia of the town, and was buried "under arms."

---

* Anthony (son of Peter) married Susanna Oakman of Marshfield, 1731, and had children, Anthony born 1735, Samuel 1737, (of Maine), Susanna 1740, Abigail 1745. He died 1744. Anthony, son of Anthony, married Mercy Barker 1757, and removed to Vermont, 1778: he was grandfather of Jacob, Esq. of Royalton. Isaac (who married Thankful Curtis abovenamed) had children, Peter 1735, Joseph 1737, Thankful 1739, Joshua 1740, Rebecca 1742, Davis 1743. Thomas married Hannah Gross of Hingham, 1737, and had a son Thomas born 1738, and daughters Lydia, Martha and Hannah. *John* above named, had children, Sarah born 1733, Betsy 1740, John 1742, Capt. Enoch 1744.

FAMILY SKETCHES.

THOMAS COLLIER, (from Hull).

married Bridget Bosworth 1735 — children, Thomas born 1736, Gershom 1738, Bridget 1740, William 1742, Jane 1744, Mary 1746, Ephraim Bosworth 1748.

ISAAC COLLIER.

married Tamsen Hayden 1770 — children, Rev. William born 1771, sometime of Charlestown, Isaac 1773, James 1775, Moses 1777, Elizabeth 1779, Fanny 1782, Peleg and Judith 1784, Anna 1786, Elisha 1788, Mary 1792, Cynthia 1794. He lived on the beach, between the Barker farm and the glades. He died 1817.

WILLIAM COLLIER, (called of Boston).

married Judith Briggs 1748, and was father of Isaac above, born 1749, and three daughters, Sarah, Judith and Elizabeth. He had large tracts of land south of the glades.

JOSEPH COLMAN, (shoemaker).

was in Scituate 1638. His house was on the west side of Colman's hills, where several generations of the family dwelt. The original house lot is now deserted. There is no record of his family in the Town or Church books. From incidental record we find he had sons Joseph, Zechariah, Thomas, and several daughters. Most of these children belonged to the society of Friends, and some of the daughters were married and removed to Newport, Rhode Island.

Joseph removed to Connecticut before 1690, and probably to Norwich. The high hills between the Harbour and the North river, derived their name from this family,

JOHN COOPER.

was in Scituate 1634. In 1638, "tongue island," so called, was granted to him by the committee for laying out lands.

This is one of the marsh Islands near Little's bridge, and has been known by the name of Cooper's Island. In 1639, he sold the island to William Wills, and the island bears the name of Wills's island to this day.

He married Priscilla Wright 1634, (of Plymouth). He removed to Barnstable, 1639. We believe he left no children. He deceased at Barnstable, dividing his estate between the Church at Barnstable and Nathaniel Morton's wife, (being Lydia, his sister). Mrs. Alice Bradford of Plymouth was also his sister.

JOSEPH COPELAND.

came into Scituate from Bridgewater, 1730, a descendant of Lawrence Copeland, an early settler in Braintree. He married Elizabeth, daughter of Capt. Benjamin Tolman 1735, and succeeded to the family residence of Capt. Tolman. It is the place occupied by the family of Ebenezer Copeland, late deceased, forty rods east of the Episcopal church hill. Here he built a tannery.

The children of Joseph Copeland have been remarkable for longevity.

Elizabeth, born May 6, 1736, died August 1828, aged ninety-three. She was the wife of Mr. William Briggs, and the mother of several sons surviving at Milton and Salem.

Ruth, born August 16, 1738, the mother of Robert Eells, Esq. of Hanover, is now living, (1831). She married Robert Lenthal Eells 1757.

Mary, born November 3, 1740, is Mrs. Joshua Barker of Hanover, now living.

Hannah, born February 24, 1743, single, living in Scituate.

Rhoda, born April 22, 1745 - Mrs. Ford, living in Scituate.

Lydia, born July 20, 1747, single, living in Scituate.

Joseph, born August 22, 1749, living in Turner, Maine.

William, born September 21, 1751, living in Scituate, has a son William, and daughters.

Ebenezer, born October 20, 1753, died in Scituate 1810, and left three daughters.

Rebecca, born August 30, 1755, wife of Samuel Tolman, living in Scituate.

Sarah, born January 2, 1758, wife of Micah Stetson, living in Scituate.

Elisha, born December 20, 1759, living in Fairhaven. These all, save two, have families.

EDWARD CORLEW.

was in Scituate 1730, and purchased lands in the north part of the Town. He married Abigail Russell 1732. He came from the north of England with a considerable company, bound for Boston, but who were unfortunately wrecked on the beach near the mouth of North river: many of the company were lost. He had children, John born 1732, Edward and Thomas 1736, William 1744, Daniel 1746.

Thomas married Mary Russell of Pembroke, 1763, and removed to Vermont. His son Thomas married Abigail, the daughter of his uncle Daniel Corlew, 1792, and lives in Vermont.

Edward also removed to Vt. and probably left descendants.

John died of the small pox in Scituate, and left no descendants that we have learned.

William married Margaret Humphreys, and has children, William, Elijah, (whose son Elijah is an officer in the Suffolk Bank), Charles, Anna, Joseph, Polly (now Mrs. Colman of Scituate) and Jane.

Daniel married Deborah Price 1769. He had a son Noah, who was lost at sea, and a son Reuben, who married Elizabeth Burbank, 1794. It is an extraordinary fact, that Edward Corlew, sen. and his first four sons, were soldiers together in the French War.

JOHN COWEN, from Scotland.

appears in Scituate 1656. He purchased lands in Conihassett, north of Sweet swamp, and east of Michael Pierce's farm, (late Hayward Pierce, Esq. His house stood where the house of Stephen Litchfield now stands. We notice in the Colony records a curious evidence of his Scottish spirit, viz. "1670. John Cowen appeared in Court to answer for contemptible words against Royal Authority; to wit: that he scorned to be in subjection to an Englishman – and that there never was any King in England that was an Englishman, save one crooked back'd Richard – a crooked Rogue, just like such an one, (naming a well known hunch back)." Cleared.

John Cowen married Rebecca, the widow of Richard Man, 1656. His children, Joseph born 1657, Mary 1659, John 1662, Israel 1664, Rebecca 1666, He lived in Richard Man's house until 1670, (see Appendix).

Joseph was killed in the Rehoboth battle, 1676.

John married Deborah Litchfield 1687. His children, Sarah born 1688, Joseph 1690, John 1692, Joshua 1694, Caleb 1696, Israel 1701, Mary 1705.

Israel married   His children, Mary born 1691, Hannah 1694, Elizabeth 1697, Israel 1699, Jonah 1704, (died early), Gethelus 1708, (no family), Job 1713, Joseph 1715, Sarah 1717.

Of this latter family, Israel married Howland of Pembroke, and removed to Weymouth. His sons born in Scituate, Israel 1724, Balch 1728.

Job had sons, Job born 1742, Gethelus 1745, Israel 1750.

Joseph removed to Bridgewater, and married Howard 1736.

Capt. Job, son of Job, is now living in Scituate, (no sons).

Gethelus left sons David and Job. He married Mary Gill of Hingham, 1735.

Israel left Israel, Charles and others.

JOHN CROCKER.

was in Scituate 1636. In 1654, he sold land south-west of the burying ground, near the Harbour, to John Whiston, and removed to Barnstable, probably. His brother William was in Scituate 1636, or earlier, and removed 1639. John Cracker's children were William born 1637, Elizabeth 1639, Samuel 1642, Job 1644, Jonah, 1647, Eleazer 1650, Joseph 1654. There are many descendants in Barnstable, Rev. Joseph of Eastham, Rev. Josiah of Taunton, (1742), and Rev. Nathan Bourn Cracker of Providence, were descendants.

FRANCIS CROOKER*

was in Scituate 1648, and soon removed. He has posterity in Hanover. He married Mary Gaunt of Barnstable, 1647.

JAMES CUSHMAN.

was in Scituate from 1639 to 1649.

---

* "Upon petition of Francis Crooker, who desires in marriage Mary Gaunt, kinswoman to Mr. Coggin of Barnstable – the Court having heard both parties, and seriously weighed the circumstances, doth order that if the s^d Croaker bring in to the Governor a certificate under the hands of Mr. Chauncy, and some other approved phisition, that that disease with which he is sometimes troubled, be not the falling sickness, that then he the s^d Croaker shall, in convenient time, have in marriage the s^d Mary Gaunt." Colony Records.

GEN. JAMES CUDWORTH, (salter).

was a freeman in Scituate 1634. We think it probable, that he came from London to Boston, 1632, in company with Mr. Hatherly, as he was Mr. Hatherly's particular friend. His house in 1640, was near the bridge at the harbour, which he sold to Thomas Ensign 1642, and removed to Barnstable. He returned before 1646, when he became one of the Conihassett Partners. After his return from Barnstable he resided for a time on the south-east of Colman's hills: which house he sold to Thomas Robinson before 1650. He then resided during life near the little Musquashcut pond. Ward Litchfield now possesses the land and house lot. In 1652, he was Capt. of the militia of Scituate. He was deputy to the Colony Court 1649, and several succeeding years. He was an assistant of the government in 1656, 7 and 8. Also a commissioner of the United Colonies, 1657. In 1658, he fell under the displeasure of those commissioners because he would not set his hand to the severe laws which that board propounded to the several General Courts, to be enacted against the Quakers, and also under the displeasure of Gov. Prence and the Court of Plymouth, for the stand which he took in favour of toleration. Occasion was sought to displace him. A letter was produced which it was suspected he was the author of, sent to England, and describing the bigotry of the government. Another letter to the Governor was produced, in which some expressions were so construed, that he was judged to be "a manifest opposer of the government," and he was left out of the magistracy and the board of Commissioners, and deprived of his military command 1658, and disfranchised 1660. In 1659, the town of Scituate returned him a deputy to the Court, and the Court rejected him. In all the passages of the life of this admirable man, he never manifested his magnanimity more signally, than by his dignified silence and quiet demeanor under these persecutions. He remained at home, prosecuting his agricultural pursuits, and employed in the municipal concerns of Scituate, without railing at the government. The Colony was at peace with the natives, and his commanding talents could be spared from the government. The letter above alluded to, as sent to England, was addressed to (Mr. Brown?) then in England, and who had been an assistant in Plymouth Colony.

We insert an extract. It is dated at Scituate, 1658.

"As to the state and condition of things amongst us, it is sad, and so like to continue. The antichristian, persecuting spirit is very active, and that in the powers of this world. He that will not lash, persecute and punish men that differ in matters of religion, must not sit on the bench, nor sustain any office in the Commonwealth. Last Election Mr. Hatherly and myself were left off the bench, and myself discharged of my Captainship, because I had entertained some of the Quakers at my house, thereby that I might be the better acquainted with their principles. I thought it better to do so, than with the blind world to censure, condemn, rail at, and revile them, when they neither saw their persons nor knew any of their principles. But the Quakers and myself cannot close in diverse things, and so I signified to the Court; but told them withal, that as I was no Quaker, so I would be no persecutor.

"This spirit did work those two years that I was of the Magistracy, during which time, I was, on sundry occasions, forced to declare my dissent in sundry actings of that future: which altho' done with all moderation of expression, together with due respect unto the rest, yet it wrought great disaffection and prejudice in them against me: so that they themselves set others to frame a petition against me, so that they may have a seeming ground (though first moved by themselves) to lay me under reproach. The petition was with nineteen hands: it will be too long to make rehearsal. It wrought such a disturbance in our town, and in our military Company, that when the act of Court was read at the head of the Company, had I not been present and made a speech to them, I fear there would have been such actings as would have been of sad consequence. The Court was again followed with another petition (counter) of fifty-four hands: and the Court returned the petitioners an answer, with much plausibleness of speech, carrying with it great show of respect to them, readily acknowledging with the petitioners my parts and gifts, and how useful I had been in my place, professing that they had nothing against me, only in that thing of my giving entertainment to the Quakers.

(Here follow extracts of the laws against the Quakers, &c.)

"All these carnal and anti-Christian ways, being not of God's appointment, effect nothing to the hindering of them in their course. It is only the word and the Spirit of the Lord that is able to convince gainsayers. They have many meetings and many adherents; almost the whole town of Sandwich. And give me leave to acquaint you a little with their sufferings, which is grievous, and saddens the hearts of most of the precious saints of God: it lies down and rises up with them, and they cannot put it out of their minds, when they see poor families deprived of their comforts, and brought into penury and want. As for the means by which they are impoverished – they were, in the first place, scrupulous of an oath: why then we must put in force an old law: they must all take the oath of fidelity – this being tendered they will not take it – then they must pay five pounds, or depart the Colony in such a time; when the time comes, the Marshall goes and fetcheth away their cows, and other cattle: another court comes, they are required again to take the oath – they cannot – then five pounds more. A poor weaver that had 7 or 8 small children, had but two cows, and both were taken from him. The Marshall asked him what he would do – and the man said, that 'God who gave him them, he doubted not would still provide for him.'

"The last Court of Assistants was pleased to determine fines on Sandwich men for meetings, one hundred and fifty pounds, wherof W. Newland is twenty-four pounds, for himself and wife, at ten shillings a meeting – W. Allen forty-six pounds – the poor weaver, afore spoken of twenty pounds. Brother Cook told me, one of the brethren of Barnstable was in the weaver's house, when cruel Barloe (Sandwich Marshall) came to demand the sum, and said he was fully informed of all the poor man had, and thought it not worth ten pounds. What will be the end of such courses and practises the Lord only knows. – – I am informed of three or four score, last Court presented, for not coming to publick meetings: and let me tell you how they brought this about. You may remember a law once made called Thomas Hinckley's law, 'that if any neglect the worship of God in the place where he lives, and set up a worship contrary to God and the allowance of this Government, to the publick profanation of God's Holy Day, and ordinances, he shall pay 10 shillings.' This law would not reach what then was aimed at, because he must do all things therein express'd, or else break not the law. In March last a Court of Deputies was called, and some acts touching Quakers were made, and then they contrived to make this law serviceable to them, by putting out the word (*and*) and putting in the word (*or*), which is a disjunctive, and makes every branch to become a law; yet they left it dated June 6, 1651; and so it stands as an act of the Gen. Court, they to be the authors of it seven years before it was in being; and so yourselves have a share in it, if the Record lie not.

"We are wrapped up in a labyrinth of confused laws, that the freeman's power is quite gone, and it was said last June Court by one, that he knew nothing the freeman had there to do. Sandwich men may not go to the Bay lest they be taken up for Quakers – warrants lie in ambush, to apprehend and bring them before a Magistrate, to give an account of their business. Some of the Quakers in R. I. came to bring them goods, and that on far more reasonable terms than the professing and oppressing Merchants of the County – but that will not be suffered. And truly it moves bowels of compassion in all sorts, except those in place, who carry it with a high hand towards them. Through mercy, we have yet among us, the worthy Mr. Dunster, whom the Lord hath made boldly to bear testimony against the spirit of persecution.

"Our bench now is Thomas Prince, Gov., Mr. Collier, Capt. Willet, Capt. Winslow, Mr. Alden, Lieut. Southworth, W. Bradford, Thomas Hinckley. Mr. Collier, last June, would not sit on the bench if I sat there, and now will not sit the next year, unless he may have thirty pounds to sit by him. Our Court and Deputies last June, made Capt. Winslow Major. Surely we are all mercenary soldiers, that must have a Major imposed upon us. Doubtless, the next Court, they may choose us a Governor, and Assistants also: a freeman shall need to do nothing but bear such burdens as are laid upon him. Mr. Alden hath deceived the expectations of many, and indeed lost the affections of such as I judge were his cordial Christian friends, who is very active in such ways as I pray God may not be charged upon him to be oppressions of a high nature.

"JAMES CUDWORTH."

On the election of Josiah Winslow Governor, 1673, he endeavored, and with success, to make honorable amends for the abuse and neglect which Cudworth had suffered from his predecessor, Gov. Prence. We notice in the Colony records, July 1673, "Capt. Cudworth, by a full and clear vote, is accepted and reestablished, in the association and body of this Commonwealth." He was chosen an assistant again from 1674 to 1680 inclusively. In 1675, he was chosen "General and Commander in Chief of all the forces that are or may be sent forth against the enemy," and he continued in that office until Philip's war was ended. In 1681, he was appointed an agent for the Colony to England. He was also Deputy Governor the same year. On his arrival in London in the autumn of 1682, he unfortunately took the small pox, of which he died.

We cannot forbear to quote from another interesting letter of his to Gov. Winslow, modestly declining the office of Commander in Chief, which had been, as it were, unanimously pressed upon him in 1673, when an expedition against the Dutch at New York was projected.

"Sir, I do unfeignedly and most ingenuously receive the Court's valuation and estimation of me, in preferring me to such a place. It is not below me or beneath me, (as some deem theirs to be), but is above me, and far beyond any desert of mine; and had the Court been well acquainted with my insufficiency for such an undertaking, doubtless I should not have been in nomination; neither would it have been their wisdom to hazard the cause and the lives of their men upon an instrument so unaccomplished for the well management of so great a concern. So being persuaded to myself of my own insufficiency, it appears clearly and undoubtedly unto me, that I have no call of God thereunto: for *vox populi,* is not always *vox Dei.* Beside, it is evident unto me, upon other considerations, I am not called of God unto this work at this time. The estate and condition of my family is such as will not admit of such a thing, being such as can hardly be paralleled; which was well known unto some: but it was not well or friendly done as to me, nor faithfully as to the country, if they did not lay my condition before the Court. My wife, as is well known unto the whole town, is not only a weak woman, but has so been all along; and now by reason of age, being sixty-seven years and upwards, and nature decaying, so her illness grows strongly upon her.

"Sir, I can truly say that I do not in the least waive the business out of any discontent in my spirit arising from any former difference: for the thought of all which is and shall be forever buried, so as not to come in remembrance: neither out of any effeminate or dastardly spirit; but I am freely willing to serve my King and my Country as any man, in what I am capable and fitted for: but I do not understand that a man is called to serve his country with the inevitable ruin and destruction of his own family.

"These things being premised, I know your Honor's wisdom and prudence to be such, that you will, upon serious consideration thereof, conclude that I am not called of God to embrace the call of the General Court. Sir, when I consider the Court's act in pitching their thoughts' upon me, I have many musings what should be the reasons moving them thereunto; I conceive it cannot be, that I should be thought to have more experience and better abilities than others; for you, with many others, do well know, that when I entered upon military employ, I was very raw in the theoretic part of war, and less acquainted with the practical part: and it was not long that I sustained my place in which I had occasion to bend my mind and thoughts that way; but was discharged therof, and of other publick concerns: and therein I took *vox populi* to be *vox Dei* and that God did thereby call and design me to sit still and be sequestered from all publick transactions, which condition suits me so well that I have received more satisfaction and contentment therein, than ever I did in sustaining any publick place."

    The magnanimity of Gen. Cudworth has rarely been equalled; and when we couple with it the mildness and humanity of his demeanor, his character reaches the sublime. If he was ever reproached, it was for virtues which his coevals failed to attain.

    He accepted the command in Philip's war, as we have stated above, and acquitted himself with honor. He had undoubtedly the talents of a brave and able commander, different indeed from those of Church, who shone in the darings of partizan warfare, but such as were proper for his place. When he took the field in Philip's war he was past seventy years of age; there is therefore little propriety in drawing a parallel between him and Church.

    Of General Cudworth's family connexions in England, we have no certain information. It has been suggested by some that he was the brother of that distinguished man of learning, Professor Ralph Cudworth, whose work on the philosophy of of the mind has been a foundation for all subsequent writers: but this we have not made certain.

    It appears that Gen. Cudworth did not proceed to England on his mission, to obtain a new charter which should include Narragansett, (for this was the object of the mission), until the summer of 1682. His will is dated in the spring of that year, at Scituate, and orders his estate "to be divided into six equal parts – James two sixths – Israel one sixth – Jonathan one sixth – daughter Mary's four children (Israel, Robert, James and Mary Whitcomb) one sixth – daughter Hannah Jones one sixth.

        "THOS. HYLAND, } witnesses."
        RICH'D. CURTIS,

    It appears that his wife had deceased.

Capt. James, the oldest son, had lands in Freetown, in his father's right, and may have resided there for a time, but most of his children are recorded in Scituate. They were Mary born 1667, Sarah 1669, Capt. James 1670, who deceased at Freetown, 1729, Joanna 1671, (wife of Zachary Colman 1696), Elizabeth 1672, Abigail 1674, John 1677. John (last named) settled in Scituate, and left sons, John born 1706, James 1715, both of whom left sons.

Capt. James, sen. deceased before 1699. His widow Mary deceased 1699, leaving legacies "to sons James and John, and daughters Mary, Sarah, Joanna Colman, and Eliz. and Abigail."

Israel (son of Gen. Cudworth) removed to Freetown, (as is said), but he retained an interest in Conihasset lands in Scituate as late as 1700. He had one daughter born in Scituate, Mary 1678, (wife of Jacob Vinal 1695).

Jonathan (son of Gen. Cudworth) resided in Scituate. He married Sarah, the daughter of Jonathan Jackson. His children, Nathaniel born 1667, Bethia 1671, Hannah 1674, (wife of Thomas Hatch. 1695), Sarah 1676, Jonathan 1679, James 1682, Israel 1683, Rachel 1689. Of these sons, most of them had families. – The sons of Nathaniel were Israel born 1706, Jonathan 1710, Nathaniel 1712. The sons of James were James born 1714, Zephaniah 1719. The sons of Zephaniah were Noah, Melzar and James.

John (born 1706, above named) married Mary Briggs, 1731, his sons were John, jr. and Capt. Joseph. John, jr. married Elizabeth Clap 1772, and had sons John, Job, Charles, Abiel, Arvin. This family resided on Hooppole neck. Capt. Joseph married Elizabeth Souther 1775, and has sons Elijah of Scituate and Peter of Boston.

RICHARD CURTIS

was one of four brothers who came early to New England, viz. Richard, Thomas, John and William. John left no family.*

Richard had lands at Marblehead in 1648, and in the same year he purchased lands in Scituate, and built a house between Gowin White's and the Harbour. He married Lydia, daughter of John Hollet, 1649, and had children, Anna born 1649, Elizabeth 1651, John December 1, 1653, Mary 1655, Martha 1657, Thomas, March 18, 1659, Deborah 1661, Sarah 1663.

---

* He had a house at Curtis's hill, which was burnt in Philip's war.

He died 1693. His will, dated 1692, gives "To oldest son John two thirds of my real estate, he providing for my wife Lydia during her life. To son Thomas one third, &c. To daughters Hannah Curtis, Elizabeth Brooks, Mary Badcocke, and Martha Clark."

John married Miriam, daughter of William Brooks 1678, and had children, Mercy born 1678-9, Hannah 1681, William September 15, 1683. His only son William married Rachel, daughter of Dea. Samuel Stodder, 1707, and had children, John born 1708, Samuel 1711, Rachel 1712, William 1714, Rachel 1717, Samuel 1719, Elizabeth 1722. The last son, Samuel married Rachel Briggs 1745, and his son Samuel married Ruth Nash 1777, and Ammiel, son of the latter, is living in Scituate.

Thomas (the younger son of Richard) settled on the tract of land called Egypt, where he had a house 1693. He married Mary, sister of Robert Cooke, 1694, and daughter of William Cooke: and had children, Deborah born 1697, Ruth 1699, Mary 1701, Thomas, March 5, 1703-4, Ruth 1711. The only son, *Thomas, jr.,* married Ruth Wade 1729, and had children, Thomas 3d, born December 8, 1729, Jael 1732, Eli 1733, Ruth 1735, Simeon 1739, Abner 1742, Beriah 1745. Charles, who occupies the farm of three generations of his ancestors, is son of the last named Thomas, whose wife was Susanna Bailey 1759. Eli has also posterity in Scituate. He married Desire Turner 1758, and Elizabeth Bailey 1777. Eli, jr. married Bathsheba Nichols 1782.

From this family have descended some of the name in the west of Scituate, Hanover and Abington. Abner, son of Thomas, jr., married Sarah Ford 1766, and lived in Hanover. *Beriah* removed to Chesterfield. He married Desire Litchfield 1783.

THOMAS CURTIS, (brother of Richard).

was in Scituate 1649. He had previously lived at Georgiana, and is called of York, in our records. He returned to York, where he was living in 1684, at which date he gave a deed to his son Samuel, of lands on Curtis or Buttonwood hill, where Samuel and several generations of his family lived.

Two children of Thomas Curtis were born and baptized in Scituate second parish, Elizabeth 1649, and Samuel 1659. He had also a son Benjamin of Portsmouth. We have seen a deed (preserved here) from Robert Tufton Mason to Benjamin Curtis, conveying a lot of land "on Great Island in the Piscataqua River," dated 1681.

Samuel married Elizabeth — and had children, Elizabeth born 1694, Samuel 1695, Benjamin 1699, Abigail 1703.

Benjamin married Rebecca House 1723, and had children, Samuel born 1734, Job 1736, Benjamin 1737, Rebecca 1738, James 1739, Elijah 1740, Mary 1742, Charles 1744. Of these sons, *Samuel* married Rachel Briggs 1745. His children were Samuel born 1750, and several others. Samuel last named deceased at Marshfield, and was the father of Samuel Curtis, the present Clerk of that town. James died unmarried in Scituate in 1820. *Elijah* lived on Curtis hill, married Abigail Sole 1756. His children Zynthia Bartlett, Capt. Elijah, (and by a second wife Zeporah Randall), Nehemiah and Col. James.

Charles (youngest son of Benjamin) graduated at Harvard College 1765, married Lydia James, and died at New York.

WILLIAM CURTIS, (brother of Richard).

bore arms in Scituate 1643. His farm was on North river, next south of the Wanton farm. His children were Joseph born 1664, Benjamin 1666, William 1668, John 1670, Miriam 1673, Mehitabel 1675, Stephen 1677, Sarah 1679, Samuel 1681.

Joseph married Rebecca — 1692, and had children, Joseph born 1693, Josiah 1696, Rebecca 1699, Martha 1701, Richard 1702, Elisha 1704, Thankful 1707, Jesse 1709.

Benjamin married Mary Sylvester 1689. He first built the Curtis mills on the third Herring brook. His children were Mary born 1691, Benjamin 1692, Ebenezer 1694, Lydia 1695, Sarah 1697, Ruth 1700, Susanna 1702, Deborah 1704, William 1706, David 1708, Peleg 1710. The descendants of this family reside near the Curtis mills. Peleg married Experience Ford 1749.

John married Experience Palmer 1707, and settled near Hugh's Cross in Hanover. His children were John born 1709, Bezaleel 1711 — his descendants, Samuel and others, reside near the same place.

Samuel (youngest son of William, sen.) resided on his paternal farm. He married Anna Barstow 1707. His children were Samuel born 1708, Anna 1711, Martha 1713, Miriam

1715, Deborah 1717, Simeon, June 1, 1720, Amos 1722, Mehitabel 1726.

Simeon settled in Hanover, a half mile south-east of Hugh's Cross. He married Asenath Sprague of Duxbury, and had children, Simeon, (now Capt. Simeon of East Bridgewater), Melzar, (the father of Melzar, Esq. of Hanover, and others), James, (of Freeport, Maine), Asenath, Susanna: and by a second wife (widow Lucy Macomber, whose maiden name was Barker of Hingham), Lucy, Asenath, Mary, and Barker, (of Maine). Mary married Job Young.

Amos (son of Samuel) settled on the paternal farm. He married Mary Faunce of Kingston, 1744. His children were Samuel born 1745, Amos 1747, (died young). Amos, sen. died 1750. His widow married Nathaniel Church 1758. Her daughter Mary Church was the first wife of William Copeland, sen. 1782.

Samuel succeeded to the paternal farm. He married Mehitabel Young 1778. His children are Sophia, Samuel, Mehitabel, who all reside on the ancient farm, and Mary, the wife of Peter Cudworth of Boston.

JOHN CUSHING, SEN.

came into Scituate from Hingham, 1662, and purchased the farm on "Belle house neck," of Capt. John Vassall, son of William Vassall, to whom it was laid out 1634. He was the son of Matthew Cushing, and Nazareth Pitcher his wife. Matthew was born in England 1588, the son of Peter Cushing of Norfolk, whose grandfather had possessed large estates in Lombard street, London. Matthew Cushing, with his wife and five children, viz. Daniel, Jeremiah, Matthew, Deborah, and John, sailed from Gravesend, April 26, 1638, in the ship Diligent, John Martin of Ipswich master, and arrived at Boston on the 10th of August. They appear in Hingham in the autumn of the same year. Matthew deceased at Hingham, September 30, 1660, aged seventy-two. His widow survived to 1681, aged ninety-six. His children were all living at his decease, save his daughter, who had been the wife of Matthias Briggs. His will bequeaths legacies "to my wife Nazareth my house, &c. - to son Daniel (lands described) - to son-in-law Matthias Briggs 150£ - to son Jeremiah 2£, 2S, 10d, - to Matthew and John each (a sum named)." Of these children, Deborah and Jeremiah left no children. Daniel and

Matthew left families in Hingham, whose posterity is very numerous.

We return to John, sen., who settled in Scituate. He was born 1627. He married Sarah, the daughter of Nicholas Jacob of Hingham, 1656. He was a deputy to the Colony Court many years, and first in 1674: an assistant of the Colony Government 1689, 90 and 91, and representative to the Court at Boston, the first year after the two Colonies were united in 1692, and several succeeding years. He died 1708. His wife died 1678, aged thirty-eight. Their children were John, jr. born April 28, 1662, and died 1737, He resided at "Belle house" neck. He was Chief Justice of the Inferior Court of Plymouth, from 1702 to 1710. – Counsellor of Massachusetts, from 1710 to 1728, inclusively – Judge of the Superior Court from 1728 to 1737. A cotemporary journalist (John Cotton) says "he was the life and soul of the Court." He married Deborah Loring of Hull, May 20, 1687, who died 1713. Children, Sarah born 1687, (a son 1692, who died in infancy), Deborah born 1693,* John, 3d. born July 17, 1695, Elijah 1697, Mary 1700, Nazareth 1703, Benjamin 1706, Nathaniel 1709. By a second wife, Sarah Holmes, married 1714, Josiah born 1715, Mary 1716. Of some of these children we only give a brief notice. Elijah[†] settled in Pembroke.

Nazareth was the wife of Benjamin Balch, (see Balch).

---

* Deborah, daughter of John, jr., Esq. married Capt. John Briggs, jr., December 2, 1712. Deborah Briggs, her daughter, (and the only one on record here), was baptized in the North Parish, February 20, 1714, She was the wife of Thomas Savage, Esq., of Boston, and the grandmother of Hon. James Savage. She died at Judge John Cushing's, when here on a visit, and her remains lie in the Cushing tomb, with those of an infant child, which was born and which expired on the same day as the mother's death.

† Elijah (son of John, jr., Esq.) settled in Pembroke. He married Elizabeth Barker 1724. His sons were Elijah, Nathaniel, and Judge Joseph, and his daughters were Mary, wife of Gen. Benjamin Lincoln, Deborah, wife of Rev. Dr. Shute, Elizabeth, wife of Major Cushing, all of Hingham. The sons of Elijah, Jr. were Elijah, who deceased at Natches, Thomas and Nathaniel, of Hanson. The sons of Nathaniel, 1st. were Nathaniel, Esq., Capt. Benjamin and Charles. The son of Joseph (who was Judge of Probate many years) is Horatio, Esq. of Hanover.

Nathaniel, Esq. was father of Dr. Ezekiel, who graduated at Harvard College 1808, was educated in the science of Medicine in Paris, practised several years in Boston, and deceased at Hanover 1827. He was highly accomplished as a physician and a gentleman, and left few equals behind him. His brother George deceased at New Orleans; and his brother Elijah resides in Hanson.

Josiah (son of John, jr., Esq.) married Ruth Thomas 1738, and settled in Pembroke. The late Capt. Josiah was his son.

Nathaniel graduated at Harvard College 1728 – married Mary Pemberton of Boston, 1729, and died one month afterward.

John, 3d. resided at "Belle house" until 1743, when he built the mansion south-east of Walnut tree hill. He lived eighty-two years, having died 1778. He was a representative from Scituate 1721, and several succeeding years. He was Judge of Probate from 1738 to 1746 – Judge of the Superior Court from 1747 to 1771, when he resigned, and also a counsellor of the province, from 1746 to 1763, inclusively. He married Elizabeth Holmes, (of Boston, we believe), daughter of his father's second wife, 1718, she died 1726. Children, Deborah born 1718, (wife of David Stockbridge, and mother of David, Esq.), Sarah born 1720, (not married).

John, 4th. born 1722, who resided at Belle house, and whose sons, John removed to Berwick, Dea. Francis to Maine, and Nathaniel deceased on the paternal estate 1825.

Nathaniel, (son of John, 3d.), born 1724, died early, as also William, born 1725, the last of the children of Elizabeth Holmes. The second wife of Judge John, 3d. was Mary Cotton, daughter of Josiah, Esq. of Plymouth, married 1729, whose children, Mary born 1730, the wife of Rev. Ebenezer Gay of Suffield), William born March 1, 1732, and died September 13, 1810. Charles born 1734, died 1810, Edward 1736, died early, Hannah born 1738, (the wife of Rev. Samuel Baldwin of Hanover), Bethia born 1740, (the wife of Abraham Burbank, Esq. of West Springfield), Lucy born 1745, (the wife of Thomas Aylwin, Esq. of Boston), Abigail born 1748, died 1824, not married, Rowland born February 26, 1750, died 1789. He graduated at Harvard College 1768, was bred to the law, practised several years at Pownalboro, Maine; he left no family. He is remembered as a gentleman of distinguished talents, and remarkable for his personal beauty and gracefulness.

Col. Charles born 1734, (as above noted), graduated at Harvard College 1755, was bred to the law, and was many years the Clerk of the Courts in Boston, and a gentleman worthy of his distinguished ancestors. His wife was Elizabeth, (sister of Gov. Sumner). His only son, Charles, Esq. resides at Portsmouth, New Hampshire, and his daughters are the wives of Charles Paine, Henry Sheafe, Stephen Codman, and Elisha Doane, Esquires.

William, LL. D. (son of John, 3d.) was prepared for the University under the care of Mr. Richard Fitzgerald, a Latin schoolmaster in this vicinity. He graduated at Harvard College

1751, and was educated for the bar under the care of the celebrated Jeremy Gridley of Boston, many years (previous to 1761) Attorney Gen. of the Province of Massachusetts. He commenced practice at Pownalboro, Maine, 1755, was Judge of Probate for the County of Lincoln in 1768 – appointed Judge of the Superior Court of Massachusetts, (under the crown), 1772, in which office he was the only member of the Bench that adhered to the American cause. At the re-organization of the Court, 1777, he was appointed Chief Justice of that Court, in which office he laboured with great success in establishing our Judicial system on a firm basis. At the organization of the United States Government in 1789, he was selected by Washington for one of the Justices of the Court of the United States, in which office he eminently shone. During the mission of Chief Justice Jay, envoy extraordinary to the Court of Great Britain, Judge Cushing presided; and after Judge Jay's resignation in 1796, Judge Cushing was nominated to the Chief Justice's office, and unanimously confirmed by the senate: but notwithstanding this extraordinary expression of confidence, he declined the office on account of infirm health; but he continued on the bench until 1810, when he had prepared an instrument of resignation, but was called to resign life.* In person he was of middling stature, erect and graceful: of form rather slight, of complexion fair, of blue and brilliant eyes, and aquiline nose. His oratory was ready and flowing, but not of that overawing description with which some native orators of more fiery mould have transported audiences: but its excellence consisted in cool, deliberate judgment, and logical and lucid argumentation, which gave him eventually an advantage over those of more ardent temperament. As a Judge, he was eminently qualified by his learning, and not less by his unshaken integrity and deliberate temper. The writer of this notice first saw him on the bench in 1801, when his zenith brightness had probably abated, but he still remembers how forcibly his youthful mind was affected by the order and perspicuity with which he performed the duties of his high office, and the mild though commanding dignity with which he guided the bar. In private life, he was all that was amiable, always ready to instruct by useful discourse, and to make his friends happy by his cheerfulness. He diligently collected works of taste, and (if we

---

* See Appendix IV.

may judge by the numerous notes written with his own hand in margins) he read with the greatest care. He was a learned theologian – well acquainted with the controversies of the day, and though far from gathering heat in those controversies, he was conspicuously on the side of liberal Christianity. He used to speak of his acquaintance with Dr. Priestley, as a happy era of his life, and to read and talk of his works with approbation. In short, as an exemplary Christian, he was irreproachable, and as a publick character, he is universally acknowledged to have stood in the first rank of his countrymen, with Washington, and Adams, and Henry, and Jefferson, either in times of awful hazard, or in times of those prodigious civil labours, which laid the foundations of our country's policy. He left no children. He married Hannah Philips of Middletown, 1774, and this highly accomplished lady, who partook so largely in her husbands cares and journeyings, still survives. He resided southeast of Walnut tree hill.

We return to the children of the first John Cushing. His second son *Thomas* born 1663, settled in Boston. He was Ensign of the Ancient and Honorable artillery 1709, and was of his Majesty's Council for several years. His son Thomas, born 1693, graduated at Harvard College 1711, resided in Boston. He was speaker of the House of Representatives from 1742 to 1746, inclusively, when he deceased. And his son Thomas, graduated at Harvard College 1744, was the well remembered patriot in the Revolution – a member of the Congress at Philadelphia, 1774 – Commissary General from 1775 to 1779, and Lieut, Governor from 1779 to 1788, when he deceased.

Matthew (son of John first) born 1665, and Jeremiah born 1666, we believe, left no families.

James born 1668, was several years Clerk of the Town of Scituate. He resided in the north parish. His son James married Sarah House 1710, and Lydia Barrell 1713, and settled at Cushing hill, as did his son James after him, whose daughter, Mrs. Lapham, resides at the same place.

Joshua (sixth son of John first) born 1670, left no family.

Sarah (daughter of John first) married Dea. David Jacob, 1689, (son of John Jacob of Hingham).

Caleb (son of John first) born 1672, graduated at Harvard College 1692, was ordained at Salisbury 1697, married Elizabeth, daughter of Rev. John Cotton, (widow of Rev. James Alling of Salisbury). Of his children we remark that James was minister of Plaistow, New Hampshire, and John, minister

FAMILY SKETCHES. 259

of Boxford, Massachusetts.* Rev. Caleb died 1752. Hon. Caleb Cushing of Essex County, is his descendant – son of Judge Caleb.

Mary (daughter of John first) born 1676, died single 1698.

Deborah also born 1674, left no family, that we can trace.

Joseph born 1677, married Mary Pickels 1710, and settled near Henchman's corner, three quarters of a mile west of the south Meeting-house. He was a deacon of the second Church, a Justice of the peace, and a venerable man. His only son, Dea. Joseph, (graduated at Harvard College 1721), succeeded him, married Lydia King 1732, and had fifteen children.† He was long employed as grammar schoolmaster, and was Justice of the peace. He prepared his own sons and several others for College. Of his children, we name George, who succeeded his father, and whose son George resides on the paternal spot. Pickels, who inherited a part of the estate of the family of Pickels, from the brother of his grandmother. Lemuel, who graduated at Harvard College 1767, was a surgeon in the thirteenth regiment Revolutionary army, and deceased 1779. Alice, (the widow of Nathaniel Cushing), born 1756, now

---

* Rev. John of Boxford had sons Hon. John, who graduated at Harvard College 1761, and who was a Judge and member of the Council many years. (His residence was Freeport, Maine), and Rev. James of North Haverhill. Rev. Giles Merrill was his successor, and married his daughter. James C. Merrill, Esq. of Boston, is his son.

† The fifteen children of Dea. Joseph, jr. were as follows: Joseph born 1733, George 1736, Mercy, 1739, Nathan 1741, (died early), Judge Nathan 1742, Pickels 1743, Hawkes 1744, Dr. Lemuel 1746, Thomas 1748, (died early), Thomas 1749, (died early), Caleb 1750, (died early), Nathaniel 1751, (died early), Deborah, 1752, (the wife of Josiah Cushing of Pembroke), Caleb 1754, (died in middle life, single), Alice 1754.

We add to the notices of this family that George married Lydia, the daughter of James Cushing. and left children, Hannah, the widow of Perez Turner, George, (his successor), Robert, late of Hull, Rachel, the wife of Pickels Cushing, jr., Mary, the wife of Dea. James Loring of Boston, and Lydia.

Pickels married Abigail Hatch 1768, and left sons Joseph, Pickels, jr., Bela, Charles, Martin, Roland, and daughters Lucy, Abigail, Sarah.

Hawkes married Ruth Cushing, daughter of Josiah of Pembroke, 1770, and left children, Dea. Thomas, who died 1825, (a man whose amiable qualities were above all praise), Ruth, Major Isaac, who deceased in Boston, Sarah, (wife of Samuel Waterman), Capt. Lemuel of Roxbury, Nancy, (wife of George Cushing, jr.), Clarissa, (wife of Dea. Joseph Stevens of Boston), and Charlotte, (the wife of Col. Vose of the United States' army).

Alice, the widow of Nathaniel Cushing, (who came from Hingham), had children Nathaniel, of Scituate, whose wife is Jane, daughter of Hayward Pierce, Esq. Deborah, (the late amiable consort of Mr. John Nash), Betsey, Warren of New Bedford, Samuel, late of Boston, Mary, (the wife of Bela Cushing, late of Boston), and Chauncy, who died at nineteen, in 1813.

Dea. Joseph, jr. educated three sons at Harvard College, viz. Joseph graduated 1752 and died early, Judge Nathan and Dr. Lemuel mentioned before.

survives, and Judge Nathan, born September 24, 1742, graduated at Harvard College 1763. He was at first a preacher, and afterward a lawyer. In 1776, he was appointed Judge of admiralty, and with great firmness condemned the capture British vessels, which brought him into notoriety as a patriot He was appointed Judge of the Supreme Court in 1789, in which office he continued until 1801, when he resigned. He was afterward a Counsellor of the State. He was a gentleman of noble form, commanding countenance and courteous manners; distinguished more for solid judgment and discretion than for eloquence. He deceased 1812.

He married Abigail Tilden 1777, the daughter of Christopher Tilden, Esq. of Boston. That highly accomplished lady deceased 1810: They had three children, *Abigail,* the wife of Hon. Cushing Otis. *Christoper, Esq.* graduated at Harvard College 1794 – married Lucy Nichols of Scituate, 1817, and deceased 1819: His widow married Hon. Wilkes Wood of Middleboro, 1828. And *Frances,* the wife of Capt. Lemuel Cushing of Roxbury.

The residence of Judge Nathan Cushing was at the east foot of little Hoop-pole hill, three fourths of a mile west of the south Meeting-house.

Benjamin, the last son of John first, born 1679, settled in Boston. He was a member of the Honorable Artillery 1700, and at that time Lieutenant in another corps. We have not learned that he left any family.

RICHARD DAGAN.

had lands in the Conihassett as early as 1690, by purchase of the family of Jackson, in the right of Richard Sealis. His farm was west of "cedar swamp cart way," and adjoining Bound brook. His house was near to John Sutton's and John Booth's, being on the west side of the way, a few rods south of Booth hill. He sold to John Booth, jr. 1696, and removed, we know not whither. Two children were born here. Elizabeth 1693, and Thomas 1694.

JOHN DAMAN.

with his sister Hannah, came into Scituate before 1633. They were then minors, and under the guardianship of Mr. William Gillson, their uncle. We understand that they were very young at that time, from the circumstance, that having been made the heirs of Mr. Gillson, they were not established in their inheritance by the Court until 1649. "John and Hannah Daman are allowed by the Court to be lawful heirs of William Gillson, it being proved by diverse persons that Gillson had often said that he intended to make these (his sister's children) his heirs." (Colony Records, 1649). John Daman succeeded to the residence of his uncle, on Kent street, the second lot from Satuit brook, (Edward Foster's being the first). He married Katharine, daughter of Henry Merritt, 1644, whose children were Deborah born 1645, John 1647, Zachary 1649, (died early), Mary 1651, Daniel 1652, Zachary 1654: and, by a second wife, Martha Howland of Plymouth, married 1659, his children were Experience (a son) born 1662, Silence 1663, Ebenezer 1665, Ichabod 1668, Margaret 1670, Hannah 1672.

John Daman died in 1677. His widow Martha executrix. In the division of his estate John, Experience and Ichabod are named, and also Ebenezer, "a weake childe," (whose land was ordered to be improved by Peter and Martha, his mother and father-in-law), also Silence, Martha, Hannah and Margaret – also Daniel. These were living 1679. Martha, the widow, had married Peter Bacon of Taunton: We notice also in the Town records of 1680, that "they instructed their deputies to move the Court for a rehearing touching the land of Ebenezer Daman being ordered to be improved by Peter Bacon, lest the child be outed of his inheritance." The Court, however, did not order a rehearing.

Of these sons, John was a soldier in Philip's war, and received a grant of land for his services, 1676: but we find no record of a family. Lieut. Zachary was also an officer in Philip's war, and received lands. He married Martha Woodworth 1679, and left a numerous family. He died 1730, aged seventy-six. His son Zachary settled on the lands granted to Lieut. Zachary for services in the war, north of Symon's hill. His house was near the spot now occupied by that of Deacon Joshua Jacob. He married Mehitabel Chittenden 1711. Daniel, his brother, married Jemima Stetson 1721, and settled near him on the same side of the way. Daniel, his son, born 1716, (by a first wife), was a man of distinction, often employed in the business of the Town, and also a representative. The posterity of this family remain in that neighborhood. That of Zachary, 3d. (whose wife was the daughter of Rev. Mr. Eells), are also in the Town, viz. the families of Edward and Galen, late deceased.

Experience (son of John, sen.) lived near Pincin hill; he had a son Experience, and a grandson Seth. Ichabod also had a family – a son Ichabod, and grandsons Israel, Caleb, Ichabod and Reuben. Some of this family removed to Chesterfield, as we have been told, viz. Ichabod last named.

JAMES DAVIS.

was in Scituate 1673, when he had lands in the Conihassett laid out. He married Elizabeth, daughter of William Randall, and removed to Boston.

TRISTAM DAVIS.

son of Robert of Yarmouth, born 1654, was in Scituate 1695. He married Sarah Archer of Braintree, 1694. His daughter Elizabeth was born 1695; from which date the family disappears from our records: save that Hannah Davis of Scituate, married John Hatch, jr, 1709, whom we suppose to have been his daughter.

JONAS DEANE.

was in Scituate 1690. He undoubtedly came from Taunton in England, as he is frequently styled Taunton Deane. He first possessed the land on the west of the brook now called Taunton Deane brook. His house was near where stands that of late John Daman. His children were Thomas born 1691, and Ephraim 1694. He deceased 1697, and his widow Eunice married (1701) Dea. James Torrey, Town Clerk.

BENJAMIN DELANO.

was a descendant of Philip De La Noye,* who was born in England, 1602, came to Plymouth in the ship Fortune, 1621, married Hester Dewsbury 1634, and Mary, widow of James

---

* In our researches, we often find cause to regret the changes in the orthography of some early names. Thus, Bonpasse is unfortunately changed to Bumpus – Blancpied to Blumpy – Jaques to Juckett – Roncevalles to Rounseval – Pincin to Pinchin and Pynchon.

Glass of Duxbury, (and daughter of James Churchill), 1657. Benjamin Delano came from Pembroke, 1770. His place of residence was on the east side of the road, and north side of Dwelley creek brook, on an ancient seat of the Dwelleys. He conducted the business of ship building for forty years, at the ancient Wanton's ship-yard. He married Mary, daughter of William Brooks, 1774. His children were *William* born 1775, who conducted the business of ship building with great spirit. He married Sarah Hart of Boston, and deceased 1814, leaving three sons and four daughters.

Mary born 1776, (the second wife of Rev. Elijah Leonard of Marshfield).

Sarah born 1782, (the wife of Samuel Foster, who resides on the paternal spot).

SIMON DELIS.

"a member of the French Protestant Church in Boston," was in Scituate 1716, and several years subsequently. He married Eunice, daughter of Anthony Dodson, 1717.

THOMAS DIMMICK.

was a freeman in Scituate 1639. We believe he was at Hingham a year earlier. He removed to Barnstable, 1642, where he had a family. Capt. Dimmick was his son, who was killed by the Indians in a battle at Casco Bay, 1697.

ANTHONY DODSON.

was in Scituate 1650. He married Mary, the daughter of John Williams, sen. 1651. His land was on the east of John Cowen's and his house near where the house of late Rowland Litchfield stands. He had, Conihassett lands in the right of John Williams, and was much employed as a surveyor, by the partners. His children were Sarah born 1652, Gershom 1653, Mary 1656, Jonathan 1659, Patience, Bethia and Eunice.

Sarah married Thomas Stetson 1671, Margaret married Nathaniel Tilden 1693, Mary married John Booth, jr., Patience married John Pierce, Bethia and Eunice living single 1695, when their mother deceased, and named them in her will.

Gershom was one of the unfortunate men who fell with Capt. Pierce in the Rehoboth battle, 1676.

Jonathan married Abigail, daughter of Matthew Gannett, and left a family, viz. Jonathan, Anthony, Deborah, Mary, Sarah, Hannah and Gershom, born from 1695 to 1704. This family name has long since been extinct in this Town.

CAPT. JOHN DOGGET, born 1730.

kept Doggett's ferry (now Little's Bridge) 1755, and subsequently. He married Abigail House 1748. His son Abner born 1749. His father had kept the ferry in 1730. He was also Capt. John, a mariner, and had another son David born 1734. The descendants may be in Middleboro. Capt. John Doggett, sen. married Jemima, the daughter of "Mr. Lawyer Thomas Turner," as he is often denominated in our records. His first ancestor in this country was Thomas Doggett of Marshfield, who married Mary Chillingworth 1654. He had sons Samuel and John, the father of the first Capt. John. He had also a brother John in Marshfield.

JAMES DOUGHTY.

was early in this Town, having married Lydia, daughter of Humphry Turner, 1649. His children were Mary, James, Elizabeth, Martha, Lydia, Sarah, Samuel, Robert, and Susanna, born from 1650 to 1670. He was a soldier in Philip's war, and 1678, was paid by the Town for nine weeks' campaign in 1676. This family may have removed to Connecticut, where the name is extant.

DAVID DUNBAR.

was born in Halifax, 1734. He was son of Joseph, who was son of David of Hingham – David, sen. had other sons, viz. David, who married Bathshua Stodder of Scituate, 1728, and lived near Accord pond in Hingham, and Samuel Dunbar, the father of late James Stockbridge's wife, of mount Blue in Scituate.

David Dunbar of Scituate married Margaret Bennet 1756. His children, David born 1756, who married Elizabeth Ellmes

1779, Jesse 1760, Elisha 1762, Bennet 1766, Reuben and Lucy 1769. Of these sons, Jesse, Esq., who married Sally Witherell 1785, is now living at the harbour; his mansion at the head of William James's dock. He has been enterprizing in navigation and the fisheries. He has been frequently a representative in General Court, and was a member of the Convention for revising the State Constitution, 1820.

His son Jesse Dunbar, jr. Esq., also a representative and a useful man, deceased in 1830, greatly lamented. He left no family. His two sisters are, the wife of Capt. Webb, and Sarah – John deceased single 1820.

BENJAMIN DUNBAR.

we believe from Hingham, also has left descendants in the north Parish. His sons were Seth, Elisha, Obed, Ezekiel, Amos, Melzer, and Peleg, born from 1737 to 1755.

RICHARD DWELLEY.

was in Scituate 1665, or earlier, probably the same that was in Lancaster 1654, and in Hingham a few years afterward. His farm was on the road leading from the third Herring brook to the harbour, about one mile north of said brook, and his house stood where stands the house of Capt. Seth Foster, late deceased. In 1676, he was a soldier in Philip's war, and received a grant of land for his services, between Cornet's mill and the Plymouth road. He had meadow land at Till's creek, which subsequently is known as Dwelley's creek. He died 1692. There is no record of his family here. Mary was baptized in Hingham, (see Hobart's journal), 1664. Richard his son married Eamie Glass, daughter of Roger Glass of Duxbury, 1682, and Elizabeth Simons 1690, and died 1708, leaving sons Richard, Joshua, Samuel, and daughters Mary, Elizabeth, Ruth, Lydia, Margaret, born from 1684 to 1696.

Richard his son married Grace Turner 1712, and left a family.

Samuel, son of Richard, sen. died in Phipp's expedition to Canada, 1690.

John (son of Richard, sen.) married Rachel Buck, daughter of Cornet John Buck, 1693, and left fifteen children, principally in Hanover. His daughter Thankful, born 1706, married William Fobes of West Bridgewater.

EDMUND EDENDEN.

was freeman 1641. In 1643, "granted by the Freemen to Edmund Edenden six acres of marsh in the long marsh on that end of the marsh next the Town." He removed to Boston, probably, as we notice his name as witness to Thomas Weyborne's will at Boston, 1656.

RHODOLPHUS ELLMES.

was one of the Conihassett partners 1646. His farm was between Gowen White's (afterward Timothy White's) and Man hill. His aged and respectable descendant Robert Ellmes occupies the paternal spot. The first house in that pike was built by Thomas Tart, and sold to Rhodolphus Ellmes 1659. His wife was Catherine, the daughter of John Whitcomb, 1644. His children, Sarah born 1645, Mary 1648, Joanna 1651, Hannah, 1653; John 1655, Joseph 1658, Waitstill 1660, Jonathan 1663, Rhodolphus 1668. Some of this family went to Middleboro, Rhodolphus and perhaps others. Jonathan settled between Great swamp and mount Hope, which farm has been since occupied by his son Joseph, born 1701: and Joseph, son of the latter, born 1732, and died 1821 – and his son Nathaniel – and now by Thomas and Nathaniel sons of Nathaniel, who are the fourth generation on that place. The relict of Joseph who died 1821, is now living, more than ninety years of age. Her name was Lincoln, (see Lincoln). Joseph his father married Elizabeth Sutton 1731.

THOMAS ENSIGN.

purchased the third cliff of Mr. Hatherly 1640, also Mr. James Cudworth's house, and five acres adjoining the bridge, on the north, at the Harbour, 1642. He was one of the Conihassett partners, 1646. He married Eliz. Wilder of Hingham, 1638. Thomas, sen. deceased in 1663, and John administered. *Hannah* married Thomas Shepherd of Cambridge or Charlestown. Elizabeth married Nicholas Wade.

John succeeded to his father's mansion, He had lost his wife before 1676, and had but one daughter Hannah, born

1669. She married Capt. Stephen Otis 1685, the ancestor of the distinguished physicians of the name of Otis in Scituate and Bridgewater. Ensign Otis (three of the name) occupied the original Ensign house lot.

John Ensign went out with Capt. Michael Pierce 1676, and was one of the heroes that fell in the Rehoboth battle.

His will, dated March 1676, was signed and witnessed on the eve of their march. We subjoin an extract.

"Being to go forth in the present Expedition against the barbarous Natives, I commit my soul to the hands of God my Creator: and I give to my mother Elizabeth all the lands which my father gave me in his will dated 1663, during her life – and afterward the same to my daughter Hannah – To my sister Hannah Shepherd's son Thomas Shepherd, jr. 20 acres of land next to Isaac Chittenden's. To sister Elizabeth Wade's son Jacob, the 1st cliff, he to pay his sister 10£, and his brother Joseph 5£. – To Sarah Underwood two cows."

HENRY EWELL

was a soldier in 1637, in the Pequod war, and was freeman 1638: removed to Barnstable 1640, and returned before 1647. His farm was on the east side of Walnut tree hill. The stately black walnut tree that was felled a few years since at the turning of the road between Judge W. Cushing's mansion and farm house, marks the place of Ewell's house. This house was burnt by the Indians 1676, and another erected on the spot. His wife was Sarah Annable, 1638. The children born in Scituate were Hannah 1649, Gershom 1650, Bethia 1653, Ichabod 1659, Deborah 1663. Besides these he had several children born at Barnstable. John, his eldest son, lived in Boston. There is a letter of attorney in the Colony records, 1687, "from Mary, the daughter of late John Ewell of Boston, to her uncle Ichabod of Scituate, authorizing him to settle her claims to the estate of her grandmother Sarah Ewell." John died in Newbury, 1686. Gershom in 1680, had a share in Conihassett land (by purchase) in the right of John Hoar of Concord. The lands at a place then called Cold spring, (now Dea. Seth Merritt's), were first owned by him. His son John resided at that place after him: and John his son removed to Chesterfield. Ichabod lived at the paternal farm. His sons settled in Marshfield.

The will of Henry Ewell, dated 1681, gives legacies "to wife Sarah – to son Gershom and Ichabod – to daughters Sarah Northey, and Hannah, Eunice and Deborah Ewell. And wheras my daughter Sarah Northey has received a legacy formerly from goody Woodfield, viz. a cow and some moveables, my will is that the legacy be made good to her, except what goods were burnt, when my house was burnt by the Indians."

BENJAMIN FARROW.

was in Scituate 1720. He was the son of John Farrow of Hingham, who married Persis Holbrook of Scituate, 1696. Benjamin resided near the Ridge hill, south of Valley swamp, on the Plymouth road, where his grandson Capt. Abiel Farrow resides. His children were Thomas born 1721, who succeeded to the paternal residence, (the father of Capt. Abiel), Sarah born 1722, Benjamin, Tamar, (wife of Carryl), Christiana, (wife of David Foster), Leah, (wife of Samuel Hatch, an itinerant Baptist preacher, and father of Col. Israel Hatch of Attleboro), Capt. Abiel, the ingenious agriculturist who lives on the paternal farm, has several sons, viz. Abiel, Rufus, James, Benjamin, in Scituate, and one in New York."

JONATHAN FISH.

was the first of the name in this Town: he came from Sandwich. His residence was near the training field, one mile south of the Harbour. His children, Jonathan born 1744, Mary 1747, Nathaniel 1749, (died 1831). He married Mary Merritt 1743.

RICHARD FITZGERALD.

a veteran Latin schoolmaster, resided principally in Hanover. He married Margaret Snowdon of Scituate, 1729. Of the family of Snowdon we have few traces.

---

* John Farrow, sen. was in Hingham 1636, the common ancestor of the people of this name. He lived to a great age, "Old John Farrow died 1678," Hobart's journal.

EDWARD FITZRANDLE.

resided in Scituate from 1638 to 1649. He probably went to Georgiana.

JOHN FLOYD.

was in Scituate 1640. He purchased of Mr. Hatherly the house that Samuel Hinckley left 1639, on Kent street. In 1653, he was a merchant in Boston, at which date we find the town of Scituate bartered with him, "boards for powder." He was afterward in England, and probably the same John Floyd who promoted the Society for propagating the Gospel among the Indians in New England. He had a son Nathaniel born 1658. There was also Richard Floyd in England, who was probably brother of John.

PELEG FORD.

from Marshfield, had lands in Scituate, near the Harbour. His daughter Hannah born 1717. He sold his lands to Ensign Otis 1720.

Dr. Peleg Ford, some time a physician of enterprize in Scituate, and who died rather young in 1813, was of Marshfield. His residence was at the ancient Stedman place, (see Stedman). His widow (who was sister of Dr. Elisha James) and children survive.

MICHAEL FORD (shipwright).

(a descendant of William of Marshfield, the common ancestor), came into Scituate from Marshfield, and married Rhoda Copeland 1778. He purchased the farm of Ebenezer Stetson, a part of the original plantation of the venerable Cornet Stetson, a half mile above Cornet's rocks on the North river. His widow and children survive. His son Michael conducts the business of ship-building near the mouth of the second Herring brook. James resides in Medford – there are also daughters.

William Ford, the common ancestor of this family, was born in England in 1594. He settled on the east side of the North river, in Marshfield, near "Gravelly beach," before 1640. He died 1676. We have had little opportunity of taking notes of his family. We can state, however, that his eldest son William married Sarah Dingley 1658, and had children, John born 1659, Mercy 1662, Josiah 1664: also that his second son Michael married Abigail, daughter of Anthony Snow, 1667, and Bethia Hatch 1683. His children were Lydia born 1668, Hannah 1670, William 1672, (whose son Samuel was born 1701), James 1675, Abigail 1679, Patience 1682, (twin daughters 1683), Thomas 1685, (whose son Amos was born 1714), Susanna 1688, Bethia 1691, Ephraim 1693, Elizabeth 1694, Elisha 1696.

James (son of Michael) married Hannan Dingley 1698, and had children, Hannah born 1705, Michael 1710, and probably others. The latter had a son James, who was the father of Michael, the first of the family in Scituate, at the head of this article.

EDWARD FOSTER, Lawyer.

was one of the men of Kent, and settled in Kent street, at the corner near Satuit brook, (now Capt. Webb's), 1633. He was freeman 1636. He had also sixty acres on the North river, between Annable's lot and Humphry Turner's lot. (now owned by John and Timothy Foster, near King's landing). Timothy, his only son, was born 1640, Elizabeth 1645, (married Ephraim Hewitt of Hull, we believe, 1666). Timothy sold a part of his house lot to Edward Jenkins, 1662, and removed to Dorchester, but retained the farm at North river. He sold the west part of the house lot and the house at the Harbour, to John Allen 1679.

The children of Timothy Foster born at Dorchester were Ruth born 1664, Elizabeth 1667, Naomi 1668, Hatherly 1671, Rebecca 1675, Timothy 1681, Edward 1682, Thomas 1686, Elizabeth 1688. Of these children we trace Edward, who married Jemima, the daughter of Jonathan Turner of Scituate, 1705, and resided in Dorchester. His daughter was the grandmother of Edward Foster Jacob, Esq. of Scituate.

Dea. Hatherly Foster was in Scituate 1698, when he married Bathshua, the daughter of Joseph Turner, and settled on the farm at North river. The house in which his great grandson Timothy now resides, was built 1697, and is now in good repair. His children were Margaret born 1699, Joseph 1702, Ruth 1704, (wife of Richard Turner 1735), Timothy 1706.

Elisha 1708, John 1711, Elizabeth 1721, wife of Joshua Barstow of Hanover, 1741.

Joseph married Abigail Steel 1733. His children were Margaret born 1734, Hatherly 1737, Abigail 1738, Elizabeth 1741, Joseph 1742, Timothy 1744, Steel 1750. This family removed to Topsham, Maine. A daughter of Steel Foster is the wife of Peter Green, Esq. high sheriff.

Dea. *Elisha* (son of Dea. Hatherly.) married Temperance Freeman of Harwich, 1739. Children, John born 1740, Bathshua 1742, Elisha 1745, Temperance 1747, wife of Dea. Francis Cushing, who removed to Maine: Sarah 1749, first wife of Dea. Elisha James: Mary 1751, wife of Elijah Turner, Esq.: Ruth 1754, wife of Nathaniel Chittenden, and second wife of Dea. Elisha James.

John (son of Dea. Elisha) married Sarah Jacob 1765 – children, Abigail born 1766, wife of Elisha Briggs: John 1768, who resides on the land laid out to Edward in 1636, Jacob 1770, of Roxbury, Joseph 1772, of Roxbury, Timothy 1775, who resides also on the lands of Edward 1636, Sarah 1778, Josiah 1780, of Roxbury.

Elisha, son of Dea. Elisha, married Grace Barstow of Hanover, 1769. Children, Capt. Seth 1770, an enterprising ship wright and valuable man, who deceased 1826, leaving a family: Margaret 1772, wife of Capt. Samuel Tilden, Capt. Elisha 1775, Dr. Freeman 1777, Samuel 1779, Charles 1781, Temperance 1782, died early, Daniel 1787, Walter 1789,

It may be proper to add some further notices of Edward Foster. We notice in the records Lettice Foster married to Samuel Thompkins, 1639, (of Bridgewater afterwards). This was doubtless Edward Foster's sister. It appears also that his mother had married Dea. Richard Sealis, probably before they came from England. Her name was Eglin Hatherly, the sister of the venerable Timothy Hatherly. She was first married to a Mr. Hanford, then to Edward Foster's father, and a third time to Dea. Sealis. Edward Foster had also a sister who married Isaac Robinson, the son of the founder of Congregationalism. Edward Foster had practised law, we believe in England, and is named as a Lawyer in the Town records. He was (with Anthony Annable) deputy to the first Colony Court, 1639. He was constantly employed in publick affairs, and doubtless would have risen to importance, had he not died early.* His will, dated 1644, gives "To wife Lettice all my cattle and

---

* He was an assistant 1637, and deputy 1639.

moveable goods, (except my books, which are to be my son Timothy's), and also the use of my house and three parcels of land, viz. at the North River – at the 2d Cliff – and at Satuit brook, until Timothy come of age. To son Timothy one third of all my property at 21 years of age. To an infant yet unborn another 3d part, whether male or female, at 21 years of age. Timothy Hatherly, Father Richard Sealis, Edmund Edenden, and brother Isaac Robinson to hold the same in trust."

By way of illustrating the connexion of these families we add an extract from the Colony records, Anno 1666: "Mr. Thomas Hanford, Pastor of Norwalk, Con. being the only son of Eglin Sealis, the sister of Mr. Timothy Hatherly, relinquishes his claim to the estate of his uncle Mr. Hatherly for the consideration of 20£, to Nathaniel and John, sons of Dea. Joseph Tilden."

RICHARD FOXWELL.

a man of Kent, settled in Kent street 1634, on the fourth lot south of Meeting-house lane. He had meadow also at New Harbour marshes. In 1643, he was in Barnstable, and we hear of him at Georgiana, 1646. But he died at Barnstable, 1668, Intestate: Hugh Cole and Samuel Bacon administrators. His children born in Scituate were Mary 1635, (wife of Hugh Cole 1656), Martha born 1638, (wife of Samuel Bacon 1659), and Ruth born 1641. In 1659, Richard Foxwell, John Philips, George Lewis, Henry Josselyn, Robert Jordan, Francis Neal and others, gave in an acknowledgment that they belonged to the Jurisdiction of Massachusetts, (Colony Records). They resided occasionally in Georgiana, and the country between Portsmouth and the Kennebec.

SAMUEL FULLER.

a man of Kent, was freeman 1634. His house was on Green field, 1635, the first lot abutting on Kent street. He also had twenty acres on the east of Belle house neck, afterward Peter Collamore's. He was doubtless one of the company of the Mayflower, and came with his uncle Dr. Samuel Fuller, 1620.

Samuel Fuller left no family here; he went to Barnstable, where he died 1683. He was in Plymouth 1638.

We notice in the Colony records, the will of that Dr. Samuel Fuller, who made himself so useful to both Plymouth and

Massachusetts Colonies in their early times; it bears date 1638, and gives "To my son Samuel my house at Smelt River, (and farm). Also my cousin Samuel shall be allowed to go freely away with a certain stock of swine and cattle which he was allowed to call his own." His cousin Samuel was said in his will to be "then in his house." There was a Samuel Fuller, who died at Rehoboth, 1677. Robert Fuller and Nicholas Ide administrators. This may have been Dr. Fuller's son.

MATTHEW GANNETT.

was born in England, 1618. He settled first in Hingham, from whence he came to Scituate, 1651, when he purchased a half share of the Conihassett lands of Anna Vinal. His house was at the west end of the dam at Lincoln's mills, near where Capt. Wallis's now stands, but within the line of Scituate. He had a brother Thomas at Bridgewater, who died 1655, and left Matthew a legacy of lands in Bridgewater, (Colony Rec.) Matthew had two sons, Matthew and Joseph. Matthew, jr. erected a house a few rods north and near his father's, 1675. He also had two sons, Matthew and Joseph. The former of whom, Matthew 3d. married Mary Chapin 1712, and left sons Matthew, Seth (who died early) and Samuel, born from 1712 to 1721. *Joseph,* son of Matthew, sen. married widow Sharp, who had before one son, Benoni Sharp). His children, Hannah born, 1684, Joseph 1686, Matthew 1688, (who married Mary Bacon 1708), Deborah 1690, Joseph 1693. Of these Joseph and Matthew settled in Bridgewater, from whom are derived the respectable families of the name there, as also at Boston and Cambridge.

Matthew Gannett, sen. died 1695. His will dated 1694, gives legacies "to wife Hannah – to sons Matthew and Rehoboth Gannett – to daughters Hannah Adams, Abigail Dodson, Elizabeth Leavitt. To grand daughter Esther Palmer – To the sons of my son Joseph, deceased, (Matthew and Joseph), all my right to undivided land in Bridgewater." Rehoboth Gannett deceased in – Morristown, New Jersey, and left no children. Samuel married Sarah Cole, and his sons Samuel and Joseph are living in Scituate. Matthew (son of Matthew, 3d.) had sons in Vermont, Prince and Amos – and Elkanah of Scituate.

SAMUEL GARDNER.

was in Scituate 1707. His house was west of Margaret's brook. He married Lydia Oldham 1707. His son William succeeded him.

DEA. RICHARD GARRETT.

was a householder before 1646. He was the first Town Clerk, 1636, also clerk of the Conihassett partners ten years, though not a partner himself, being a skillful penman. His land was nearly in front of the north or first Society's Meeting-house, as it now stands, which was probably his house lot. Also east of Eagle's nest swamp, where his sons John and Joseph settled.

He married Lydia, the daughter of Elder Nathaniel Tilden. His children, Joseph born 1648, John 1651, Mary 1655, Richard 1659, (who married Persis Pierce, daughter of Capt. Michael Pierce, 1695).

Joseph had one son, Joseph born 1680, and four daughters. His wife was Ruth, daughter of Lieut. Isaac Buck. Joseph was a soldier in Philip's war.

John had one son, Richard born 1689.

Richard, jr, had one son, John born 1706, and two daughters, Anna and Deborah.

We find no record or note of the death of Richard, sen. He may have deceased in Boston, where we observe the record of the death of a Richard Garrett, 1662. He is supposed to have been the son of that Capt. Richard Garrett whose loss is described in Winthrop's journal, (Vol. I. 39.), and brother of Capt. Robert Garrett of Boston whose will dated 1660, is as follows: "Being bound on a voyage to Barbadoes, &c. I give to my wife Mary my house in Boston, to my children John, Robert, Mary and Sarah, the rest of my estate to be equally divided."

Joseph Garrett, the son of Dea. Richard, died at Scituate, 1714. His will bequeathes "to wife Ruth, to daughters Ruth Wade, Mary Briggs, Elizabeth Briggs, and Jael Garrett, (certain legacies), to son Joseph Garrett two tenths of a thousand acres, which Mr. John Saffin gave me."

JOHN GIBBS

was in Scituate 1719, when his daughter Ann was born. John his son had a son, John born 1760.

MR. WILLIAM GILLSON.

settled in Kent street, 1633. His house lot was the second from the corner, near the bridge. He had land also at the north-east end of the second cliff, and also a lot on the south-east end of third cliff, where he erected a wind mill, 1636, the earliest mill in the Plantation if not in the Colony." He had a lot of eighty acres upland and marsh, from "stoney cove eastward," on North river, in which lot he was succeeded by several purchasers, Thomas Robinson the west part 1640, Thomas Nichols the centre 1645, Israel Hobart east part somewhat later. We observe an act of Court respecting his mill, 1637: "It is enacted that the miller of Scituate shall not take above the twelfth part for the toul of grindinge corne." We observe also that he was a contractor (with others) at a very early date to improve the navigable passage at Green's Harbour, near Gov. Winslow's in Marshfield, (then called Rexham). Colony records 1633, "It is ordered that unless Mr. Gillson, John Shaw and others, that undertook the cutting of the passage between Green's Harbour and the Bay, finish it before October next ensuing, according to covenant, they be amerced in 10£." He was an assistant in the government from 1633 to 1638, excepting 1635. He is noticed in all the transactions of those times as a man of education and talents: but he died early. His will dated 1639, gives legacies "to my wife Frances, &c. to nephew John Daman my lot on the third cliff after the next crop is taken off — To niece Hannah Daman 20£ in money. To nephew Daniel Romeball 40S money — to my Pastor Mr. John Lothrop 5£ in money." He left no children. After the decease of his widow 1649, John and Hannah Daman were made the sole heirs of the estate, (see Daman).

JOHN GRANGER.

was in Scituate 1640, or earlier. His farm was south of the training field, and north-east of Hick's swamp, John Whiston's

---

* Stephen Deane erected a mill for pounding corn in Plymouth 1632. Gillson's was the first grinding mill in the Colony.

being on the north. These lands were Peter Worthlike's 1660, and Joseph Colman's 1690. He left no family here. Grace Granger, a widow, who seems to have owned a farm near the mouth of North river, on the Marshfield side, in 1648, was his widow. She deceased 1648, and gives in her will, "To son John my house and land, also a share of Conihassett land to indemnify him for 10£ of his money in England, which has been paid for land here – also a saw, broad axe and narrow axe at 21 years of age. To daughter Elizabeth a bed and bedding – also one heifer with the increase – also one great mortar and pestle, and one great kettle." This son may have gone to Connecticut. There was a Launcelot Granger in Ipswich 1648: also John, of Andover, at the same time.

THOMAS GRAY.

(called of Dublin) owned a tract of land in Scituate, on the south of Cordwood hill, in 1730. His house stood a half mile south of that hill, at a small eminence, now well known by the name of Gray's hill. The name of his wife was Sarah. His children were George born 1730, who removed to Pownalboro, Maine. He died early, and left, we believe, no family. He was about to be married to Sarah Woodworth, afterward the wife of Shearjashub Bourn, the son of Rev. Mr. Bourn of Scituate.

William born 1732, married Abigail Perry of Scituate, 1753, and Sarah Hayden 1765: he is then called of Boston. He had three children. Lucy, who married Mr. Lane of Cohassett, Abigail, who married Dwelley Clap of Scituate, and James, who resided some time in Hingham, but who settled in Scituate, and married Bethia Curtis 1785. He died in middle life, leaving children, Abigail, (wife of Mr. Dunbar), William, who died at Amelia island without a family. Harrison, bookseller, of the firm of Hilliard, Gray and Co., Boston – Bethia, (wife of Thomas Simmons), Rebecca and Elizabeth (died early).

Elizabeth, (daughter of Thomas), born 1736, was the wife of Samuel Brooks of Hanover, and died 1830. *Sarah* born 1738, died single 1827. Mary born 1740, died single 1827.

JOSEPH GREEN.

was in Scituate 1690. He married Ann, daughter of John Turner, jr. in 1695, he is called in our records "of Weymouth."

EDMUND GROSS.

from Hingham, was in Scituate 1730. His farm was west of Simon's hill, on the road from Assinippi to Prospect Hill. He married Olive, the daughter of Richard Sylvester, 1736. She deceased 1816, aged ninety-five. He had eleven children, two of whom, Elisha and Thomas, were soldiers, remarkable for their bravery in the American war. The father was a soldier in the French war. Elisha succeeded his father in his residence, and deceased 1829, whose son resides now at the same place. This family descended from Edmund Gross, who was in Boston 1642, and whose son Isaac, born 1642, probably came to Hingham.

JOHN HALL.

married Abigail, the daughter of Timothy White, 1705, and settled at Scituate Harbour. His children were Mary, Abigail, Elizabeth, John born 1712, Timothy 1714, Susanna, Sarah, Rachel, Katharine.

This family removed probably to Marshfield.

Capt. Robert P. Hall, who deceased at Scituate Harbour, 1814, was from Cape Cod. His wife was a sister of Capt. Moses Rich.

JOHN HALLETT, Planter, (Early written Hollet.)

was one of the Conihassett partners, 1646. His house stood at the harbour, near where stands that of Jesse Dunbar, Esq. perhaps a little south-east. In 1691, "Capt. Stephen Otis's new house" is mentioned, which is now Young's tavern and Post-office), and as bounded to John Hollet's house lot on the north. He was an extensive landholder. Hollet's island, near "the stepping stones," now retains his name. He was in Scituate, or rather had lands assigned to his right, in 1668. He was probably at Yarmouth in 1650, in which year his son John was there born. Richard Curtis of Scituate, married Anna his daughter, 1649. His descendants are at Cape Cod, and at Boston. His brother Andrew was of Sandwich, 1638.

WILLIAM HAMANS.

was in Scituate 1636. He soon deceased or removed.

JEDIDIAH HAMMOND.

probably from Middleboro or Rochester, was the first of that name in this place. His residence was thirty rods west of the north Meeting-house, near the four corners. He married Elizabeth, daughter of Joseph Parker, 1712. His children, Agatha born 1713, Joseph 1714, Benjamin 1718, Joanna 1721. Joseph was the father of twelve children, born from 1738 to 1764, some of whom are living. Seth, his son, married Mary Buck, (the last of the name of Buck in the Town), and left a family.

JOHN HANMER.

was in Scituate 1639. His house was south of Colman's hills, next to Isaac Robinson's. He seems to have had another west of those hills, which he sold to Joseph Colman, jr. 1660. He had also a large lot of land in that part of Scituate now Hanover, south-west of Hanover Meeting-house. This was sold by his sons to Jeremiah and Walter Hatch before 1680. "Hanmer's hook" was the name of this lot, and it still bears the name. He was living 1673. There is no record of the births of his family. His daughter Rebecca married Daniel Hicks, 1659. He had also daughters Bethia and Hannah, and sons John, Joseph and Isaac. Isaac had a son Benjamin, who married Abigail, the daughter of Henry Josselyn, 1715, and Jane Wright 1724. The name has been extinct in this place for near a century.

CONSIDER HOWLAND.

came from Marshfield. He married Ruth Church 1795, and settled at the ancient Amos Perry place, on the north-east of the Episcopal Church hill. He has a family: a son Luther.

SAMUEL HARLOW.

from Plymouth, resided a short time in Scituate. He married Mary Barstow 1716. His daughter Mary born 1717.

ELDER WILLIAM HATCH.

settled in Kent street 1634. His house lot was the first south of Greenfield lane. He was the first ruling elder of the second Church, 1643. He was an active and useful man in the settlement of the Town. His children probably were born in England. His wife's name was Jane. *Walter,* his son, bore arms 1643, when he was, of course, over sixteen years of age. He settled on a point of land north-east of Stoney cove, and south-east of the second Society's Meeting-house. He married Elizabeth, daughter of Thomas Holbrook of Weymouth, 1650. His children, Hannah born 1651, Samuel 1653, Jane 1655, Antipas 1658, Bethia 1661. His posterity are in Marshfield. Mr. Samuel Hatch of Scituate, near Stockbridge's mill, is also his descendant.

William, jr. lived in the house at Kent street. He married Susanna Annable, (daughter of Anthony), 1652: his children, Lydia born 1653, (who married John Barstow 1678). He removed to Swanzey, where he was living 1690; and his posterity may be found in that vicinity.

Jeremiah (son of Elder William), settled near his brother Walter, with whom he was engaged in ship building for many years. He was often a deputy to Colony Court, a surveyor, selectman, and in short a man of great usefulness. He married Mary, daughter of John Hewes, "the Welshman," and had fourteen children, born from 1658 to 1678. His sons Jeremiah, John, Israel, Joseph, Thomas and James. Jeremiah succeeded his father in his residence and his calling. Several descendants are in Vermont.

Hannah (daughter of Elder Hatch) married Samuel Utley, 1658. Ann married Lieut. James Torrey, 1643. Jane, the widow of Elder Hatch, married Elder Thomas King, 1653.

Elder Hatch died 1651. His will bequeaths "To wife Jane 2 cows, with keeping for the same, half my house, half the fruits of my orchard, 16 bushels of corn, 4 of wheat, and 4 of rye per ann. – To daughter Jane Lovell [probably of Weymouth] one cow – to gr. son John Lovell a cow calf: and if the Lord give my daughter Jane more children, the next child shall have the first calf of the cow given to John, and the next child the next, and so on successively. To daughter Ann Torrey one cow – to her son James Torrey the first calf of that cow, the next to Joseph, her son, and the next to Damaris, her daughter. All of the rest of my property to my sons Walter and William, they paying the legacies.

"Attest, { WILLIAM WITHERELL, JAMES TORREY, WILLIAM HATCH," (son of Thomas).

THOMAS HATCH.

was an older brother, probably, of William. He settled in a part of the Town at that time but little cultivated, viz. three fourths of a mile west of the present Town-house, near a small brook that runs in the meadow, and twenty rods west of the road. He died early. His widow had an infant Hannah brought to baptism 1646, which was probably near the date of his death. His other earlier children were William and Thomas.

William was a soldier in Philip's war, and received a grant of land 1676. He left daughters, Mary born 1652, Lydia 1654, Phebe and Hannah, but no son probably.

Thomas married Sarah, daughter of Rhodolphus Ellms, 1662, and had eleven children, born from 1664 to 1684. His descendants now living are Marshall Hatch, and Jonathan, who lives near the first settlement of the family.

Alice, who married Jonas Pickels 1657, was probably daughter of Thomas, sen.

Thomas, jr. deceased 1686. His will gives "To eldest son Thomas, land at Long marsh – to Rhodolphus, Joseph and Jeremiah, (the youngest child being two years old), land at Stonnington, Conn. To daughter Sarah, Lydia, Caturah, Hannah; Mary, Margaret, Abigail, 8£ each."

There was a Samuel Hatch, a volunteer soldier in the Pequod war, 1637.

MR. TIMOTHY HATHERLY.

arrived at Plymouth in the ship Ann, 1623. He there erected a house, which was soon destroyed by fire. He went to England 1625, and did not return hither until 1632. Winthrop says "in the Charles from Barnstable, Eng., which sailed April 10, and arrived June 5." He came in by way of Boston, proceeded to Plymouth, where he tarried a year or more. We notice in the Colony records, 1633, "ordered that the whole tract of land between the brook at Scituate on the north-west side, and Conihassett, (the gulph), be left undisposed of until we know the resolution of Mr. James Shirley, Mr. John Beauchamp, Mr. Richard Andrews and Mr. Timothy Hatherly," (see Conihassett). The grant was made to these gentlemen 1637: but we find Mr. Hatherly here in 1634. This territory as we have elsewhere remarked, was purchased of the other three to whom the grant was made, by Mr. Hatherly, and sold in shares, he retaining one fourth of the whole: and by agreement that fourth consisted of four hundred acres north and west of the Harbour, two hundred acres at Musquashcut harbour, (afterwards Briggs's harbour), and 10£ in money. The first land which he cultivated was west of great Musquashcut pond, where he had "a herring wear," and where he had a house 1638. In 1651, he sold a farm on Musquashcut harbour to Walter Briggs. He married Lydia, the widow of Elder Nathaniel Tilden, 1642, and changed his residence to Kent street. He was ever ready to purchase the lands and houses of those who were desirous to remove, and to accommodate others who came into the settlement. He built several houses, one of which was afterwards the parsonage. He purchased Mr. Lothrop's house on his retiring to Barnstable, and sold it again to Mr. Chauncy. In short, he was the pillar and supporter of the plantation — always ready to advance money for the Town in times of difficulty, or to aid individuals with his wealth. His large tract of land west of Accord pond, he sold but in part, and gave the remainder to the Conihassett partners: it consisted of nine square miles, and was laid out to him by order of government, 1663. The line of this land is called "the share line." He gave a share in Conihassett lands to Rhodolphus Ellmes — a house lot to Eglin Hanford, (north of Thomas Ensign's, at the Harbour), his sister's daughter. He gave the parsonage house and land to the Church, 1654, and seven years afterward his Musquashcut farm and buildings to the Church and Society. No man deserved so well of the plantation, and we believe he was generally considered as the guardian and patron of Scituate. We have often regretted that the Town was not called after his name. Morton, in the New England's Memorial, observes: "He was one of the first beginners, and a good instrument to uphold the Church and Town of Scituate." We may add that he was also an important member of the government, having been an assistant thirteen years — treasurer of the Colony — and a commissioner of the United Colonies three years.

In 1658, he fell under the displeasure of Gov. Prince and his assistants, by reason of his taking a firm stand against the oppression of the Quakers, and was afterward suffered to remain in retirement from the cares of government. General Cudworth, his friend and fellow sufferer in "persecution for righteousness sake," lived to see the veil taken off from the eyes of government, and to find his proper station in society: not so the venerable Hatherly. In 1666, he made over the remainder of his estate to Dea. Joseph Tilden, and took a bond in £100, "for the peaceable possession of it to himself and his wife Lydia during their lives." He deceased the same year, leaving no children of his own: but for the children of Nathaniel Tilden, he made a bountiful provision before his decease, by deeds of gift.

Mr. Hatherly was a merchant of London: but it is probable the seat of his family had been in Devonshire, there being a town of Hatherly in that shire. Few of the name have come to this country, and those probably not nearly connected with him: for example, Arthur Hatherly in Plymouth, 1660, left no family that we have learned, unless Thomas Hatherly of Boston, 1670, was his son, whose son Thomas married Lydia Green 1693. Dea. Hatherly Foster, of Scituate, was the great grandson of Mr. Hatherly's sister. It is a name worthy to be perpetuated.

JOHN HAYDEN.

came into Scituate from Hingham, 1720. He married Mary Vinal 1723. His sons were William, Ezekiel and Joseph. William left sons William, Ezra, Peleg, and Elisha, and two daughters, viz. Anna, (wife of Abner Sutton, and the wife of Collier).

Elisha married Deborah Pierce, his son Elisha is the sole survivor of the name in this Town, except Elisha's children.

JOSEPH HENCHMAN, (or Hinckesman).

appears in Scituate 1680. He owned a considerable tract of land at Henchman's corner, half mile west of the south Meetinghouse, adjoining Dea. Joseph Cushing's and Philip Turner's land. His house stood twenty rods east from the parting of the roads, on the north side of the street. He sold it to Rev. Mr. Eells 1714. It was a spacious house. Thirty years since it was taken down, and a slight habitation built with its ruins: and the whole removed 1826.

The family of Henchman on record are Elizabeth born 1685, (married Amos Sylvester 1706), Mary 1689, Thomas 1691, Deborah 1692, Joseph 1694, William 1696, Hannah 1698, Edmund 1700, Sarah 1702. He had also a sister Elnathan, who married Eliab Turner 1694. This family came from Massachusetts and returned thither; probably to Chelmsford. We take him to have been the son of Thomas Hinchman, Esq. of Chelmsford. There was, however, a Mr. Hinckesman in Marshfield, 1653, who may have been his father.

JOHN HEWES, "the Welshman."

was in Scituate 1632. We trace him previously at Plymouth: the name is sometimes written *Hewghs*. He was freeman 1639. His house was on Kent street, the second south of Meeting-house lane. There are few notices of his family. He was living 1673. His daughter Mary married Jeremiah Hatch 1657. His son John, who had been a freeholder, died 1661, leaving no family here. John Hughs of Hingham, in 1665, who left sons John, Samuel, and others, may have been his son. He died 1672.

EPHRAIM HEWETT.

son of Thomas of Hingham, was born 1639. (Hobart's journal). He had brothers, James born 1643, Thomas 1644, Timothy 1647. Ephraim was a short time in Scituate. He married Elizabeth Foster, the only daughter of Mr. Edward Foster, 1665. Their children were Thomas born 1667, Ruth 1669, Susanna 1672, Jael 1673, Ephraim 1676. This family returned to Hingham, and probably resided some time at Hull. Thomas ("an unfortunate insane young man") was kept by his guardian, Thomas Jenkins of Scituate, 1690.

Ephraim Hewett, minister of Windsor, Connecticut, was brother of Thomas of Hingham. There was a John Hewett of Marshfield, who married Martha Winter 1668.

THOMAS HICKES, from Plymouth.

was in Scituate 1640. He was probably brother of Robert, and came in the ship Ann, 1623. His house lot was northeast of Hickes's swamp, a well known place a mile south of the Harbour. There is no record of his family. Daniel Hickes, his son, succeeded him, and married Rebecca, daughter of John Hammer, 1659. The family soon disappears after this date. In 1652, Thomas Hickes died, "and his aged widow being unable to at tend Court, Mr. Hatherly was authorized to take evidence of his will, his inventory, &c." This family came from Bermondsey street, Southwark, (Colony Records).*

Robert Hickes (brother of Thomas) had lands also in Scituate. In 1662, "Margaret his widow confirms a sale of 50 acres on the North river, sold by her husband in his life time, to Elnathan, youngest of the sons of President Chauncy." Colony records. Samuel (son of Robert) was a deputy from Nauset, (Eastham), 1647 and 8. He married Lydia Doan 1645. *Ephraim* (another son) married Elizabeth Howland 1649, and died 1650. Lydia and Phebe were also daughters of Robert Hickes.

HERCULES HILLS.

was in Scituate 1636: a soldier in the Pequod war, 1637, afterward returned to England. We learn the place of his residence in England, 1666, to have been Rochester, in Kent, from the conveyance made of certain lands in Scituate, to Edward Goodwin, shipwright of Boston. He had a lot at Kent street.

SAMUEL HINCKLEY.

came into Scituate probably with Mr. Lothrop, 1634. He was a freeman 1637. His house was on Kent street, the second south of Greenfield lane. He also owned the marsh between

---

* By way of showing our authority for asserting that this family came from Southwark, England, we subjoin the following deposition of Clement Briggs, from the Colony records, Anno 1638:

"This deponent saith that about 22 years since, this deponent then dwelling with Sam'l. Latham, in Bermondsey street, Southwark, a fellmonger, and Thomas Harlow then dwelling with Robert Hickes, in the same street, fellmonger – the s[d] Harlow and this deponent had often conference together, how many pelts cache of theire masters pulled a weeke – and this deponent saith, that the s[d] Robert Hickes did pull three hundred pelts a weeke, and diverse tymes, six or seven hundred and more, a weeke: and that the s[d] Robert Hickes sold his pelts for 40S a hundred, at the same tyme that Sam'l. Latham sold his for 50S."

his house and the third cliff. He had also land near Rotten marsh, on the south-east, next to Mr. Vassall's "brook hall field." He removed to Barnstable, 1640. His son Samuel was here with him, and removed to Barnstable: his children were Sarah born 1642, John 1644. His wife Sarah died 1656, and he married Bridget Bodfish 1657.

Thomas, the son of Samuel, sen. was born in England, 1618. He married Mary Richards 1644, and had one daughter Mary, same year. He married a second wife, widow Mary Glover, 1659.* He was an assistant and magistrate many years. He was elected Governor 1680, and continued annually in that office until the charter of the Colony was cancelled, and the union with Massachusetts took place in 1692: with the exception of 1686 and 7, (under Andros, General Governor), when he was one of the Council; and too good a patriot, we may add, to approve of the tyranny of Andros. He died 1706. Hubbard says he was seventy-three years of age. Prince says eighty-eight: and from hence other writers have been misled. But we ascertain the probable correctness of those who state his age at eighty-eight, by recurring to the facts that he was married in 1644: and bore arms in Barnstable 1643: and of course he could not have been born in 1633, as some state.

Joseph Hinckley of Barnstable married Mary Otis of Scituate, 1725, daughter of Joseph Otis, Esq., who removed to New London.

JOHN HOAR.

bore arms in Scituate 1643. In 1646, he was one of the Conihassett partners. His farm was on the west of little Musquashcut pond. This farm adjoined General Cudworth's in 1658. We find he was always engaged while here, in the business of the Town, and draftsman of deeds, bonds, &c., and is mentioned occasionally as a lawyer, though the practice must have been small in those days. He removed to Concord, 1659 or 60. His mother deceased in Braintree, 1661. He had a brother Hezekiah Hoar in Scituate for a time, and afterwards of Taunton. He was an Ensign in the expedition to New York against the Dutch, 1654. He was then of Taunton. He had sons born, Nath'l, 1656, Edward 1663, Hezekiah 1678.

---

* She was widow of John Glover of Dorchester, and daughter of Lawrence Smith: she had a son Ebenezer and five daughters, of whom Mary married Samuel Prince, Esq. of Sandwich and Middleboro, and was the mother of Prince the Chronologist.

Richard Hoar of Yarmouth, 1641, was probably a brother of John: as also Daniel of Concord, who deceased in London. President Leonard Hoar was also his brother, who died at Braintree, 1675. By way of illustrating the family connexions, we subjoin an abstract of President Hoar's will, dated 1675:

"To daughter Bridget 200£ at 21, or marriage with her mother's consent. To my brother Daniel, whose real and perpetual kindness I can never remunerate, my stone signet and my watch. To my dear brother John a black suit – To my dear sisters Flint and Quinsey, each a black serge gown. To cousin Josiah Flint, out of my Library, Rouanelli Bibliotheca. To my cousin Noah Newman, Aquinas' Sermons, and to them both the use of any books and manuscripts of mine on Divinity, they giving a note to return them on demand. My medical writings to my wife's custody, till some of my kindred addicted to those studies, shall desire them, and especially John Hoar's or any other of my brothers' or sisters' sons or grandsons."

ISRAEL HOBART, shipwright.

son of Rev. Peter Hobart of Hingham, (born 1642, died 1731, aged eighty-nine), came into Scituate 1676. His house at Hingham had been burnt by the Indians in the spring of that year. He settled here on the North river, at the well known place, since called Hobart's landing. His house stood near the ship-yard: it is remembered by some of our oldest inhabitants, as a spacious mansion, adorned with two carved cherubs over the door. He married Sarah, daughter of Rev. Mr. Witherell, 1674, his children, Nathan and Abigail born 1678, Jael 1680, Israel 1682, Abigail 1683, Israel 1686, were born in Scituate. In Hingham had been born Nathaniel 1675, Rebecca 1676.

Israel Hobart's will, dated 1729, gives legacies "To son Israel – to daughter Abigail – to Mary Witherton, Grace Davis, and Bathsheba Bradford, daughters of my daughter Sarah Brock – and to my daughter Jael, executrix."

Israel, jr. was a householder 1723. He had two daughters, Patience and Grace.

CAPT. WILLIAM HOLBROOK

came into Scituate 1660, and purchased lands in Conihassett, adjoining the farm of Capt. Michael Pierce, on the south-west.

His house was on the south side of the Cohasset road, a half mile west of Capt. Pierce's. His father Thomas had lands in Scituate 1649, but resided in Weymouth: Capt. William died here 1699. His sons settled here, viz. Samuel, whose son Samuel was born 1683, (which latter married Jane Clap 1708). John (son of Capt. William) had a son John born 1686: he had six daughters: John, his son, married Sarah Chittenden 1709. Persis, daughter of Capt. William, married John Farrow 1696.

THOMAS HOLBROOK.

was brother of Capt. William. He married Deborah Daman 1666, and removed shortly to Weymouth.

Thomas, sen. deceased at Weymouth 1673. His will gives "To wife Jane all my estate during her life, (requesting sons John, William and Thomas to be helpful to her, as she is ancient and weak of body), afterward to be divided to those three sons, and my three daughters, Ann Reynolds, Elizabeth Hatch and Jane Drake. To my grandsons John Holbrook my sword, to Peter my gun and grey mare's colt, and to William my musket: and to each grandchild at my wife's decease 2S. each."

Samuel, sen. deceased at Weymouth, 1696. His will gives to son Cornelius lands in Weymouth, also to son William, and legacies to daughters Elizabeth Buck, (wife of John of Scituate), to Mehitabel Sprague, (wife of Jonathan), to daughter Jane Balcome, and daughter Hopestill Holbrook."

WILLIAM HOLMES, planter.

was one of the Conihassett partners in 1646: and a householder before 1647: his right to common lands descended to his heirs as late as 1703. He was a freeman in 1658. Before 1662, he removed to Marshfield side of the North river; where he died before 1690, and where Elizabeth, his widow, died 1693. His children were Abraham born 1641, Israel 1642, Isaac 1644, Sarah 1646, Rebecca 1648, Josiah 1650, Mary 1655, Elizabeth 1661, all baptized in Scituate second Church. We have met with few records of this family after their removal. Abraham had a family in Marshfield: (his daughter Elizabeth was born 1666): he had a second wife, we believe, viz. Abigail Nichols of Hingham, 1695, (see Hingham Records).

Israel (with Joseph Trouant) was shipwrecked and lost, "sailing into Plymouth harbour, Feb. 24, 1684," Marshfield Records. Joseph was in Marshfield 1671, when he sold lands in Scituate to Caleb Lincoln of Hingham. There are many descendants of this family in Plymouth County. Some, however, of this name descended from John Holmes, a freeman 1634, and who had lands "at Reed pond," in Plymouth, the same year. We notice in the Colony records that he was often the messenger of the General Court. The Rev. John Holmes, minister of Duxbury, who died 1675, may have been his son; but this we have not ascertained. Some of the families in Plymouth County derive their descent from him, viz. those of Rochester. And some derive their descent from yet another source. In A. D. 1718, Judge John Cushing (second generation) married a widow Sarah Holmes of Boston, who had several children, viz. Elizabeth, who became the first wife of Chief Justice John Cushing, 1718 – Nathaniel, who resided in Boston, and John, who married Susannah Briggs of Scituate, and had children; some of whom were Deborah and Ruth, twins, born 1719, Abigail 1720, and John, who married Hannah Briggs 1746.

We had conjectured that William Holmes, at the head of this article, was the son of Lieut. William Holmes, who was freeman in Plymouth 1634 – "appointed to instruct the people of Plymouth and Duxbury in arms, 1635," – commander in the Pequod war, 1637, and afterward Major in Massachusetts: but we are not certain. Major Holmes died in Boston, 1649, and it does not appear that he left a family. We notice in the Plymouth Colony records 1654, "Job Hawkins of Boston, claimed as heir, the lands of the late Major William Holmes, at North River, on Marshfield side, and was allowed to take possession, giving security to give them up, in case an heir of better claim should appear.

WARD HOLLOWAY

came from Hingham in 1730. He married Mary, the daughter of Benjamin Studley, 1734. His children were Mary born 1737, now living, William, who was drowned in early manhood, and Wiborn, a soldier in the French war, lately living in Boston.

JOHN HOSKINS.

was in Scituate 1695. His residence was south-east of Great swamp. His children, Samuel born 1699, Martha 1706, he had also a son Benjamin, who married Charity Sergeant of Hingham, 1725. We believe Mr. Lemuel Hoskins, who now resides in the south part of the Town, is descended from this family. There was a William Hoskins in Scituate, freeman in 1634, probably ancestor of John.

SAMUEL HOUSE.

had lands assigned by the committee for laying out lands, in 1684, south-east of Colman's hills, between the lots of Rev. Mr. Lothrop and Richard Foxwell. He probably was one of Mr. Lothrop's church, who came with him from London. He died in Scituate, 1661. Son Samuel and daughter Elizabeth administer; it is said in the Historical Society's papers, (Vol. IV. 2d. series), that he removed to Cambridge, but this does not appear.

Samuel, his son, was a shipwright, and his place of residence was near Hobart's landing, on the north-east of the ship-yard. He married Rebecca, the daughter of Thomas Nichols, 1664. His children, Samuel born 1665, Joseph 1667, Rebecca 1670, John 1672, Sarah 1678, (who married James Cushing 1710).

Samuel, 3d. married Sarah Pincin 1692, and lived probably near Curtis's mill, west of the third Herring brook. The last of this family in the Town was Coombs House, who removed to Pembroke ponds, 1808. Samuel, 3d. died 1718, and left sons, Joseph, David, James, Samuel and John.

GOODMAN – HOYT, probably Simon.

was a freeman in Massachusetts, 1631. In Scituate 1633, and probably earlier, he had a lot of planting land on the third cliff, as also Thomas Bird and Henry Merritt. He had a house lot also on Kent street, the third lot on the Green field, west of Barnard Lombard's lot. Traces of him here disappear after 1636.

EDWARD HUMPHRIES, (from Ireland).

was in Scituate 1740. He married Anna Sandlin 1739. He purchased land of the Randall family, one quarter of a mile west of Wild cat hill, where he resided. His children, Margaret born 1741, Edward 1742, Richard 1744, Mary 1748, John 1749. Edward, a very worthy man, resided on the paternal place, and deceased 1825, not married. He had been a Revolutionary soldier. Margaret married William Corlew, and left a family in Scituate. She died 1826. Richard has recently been living in Littleton. John also resided and deceased in Littleton.

THOMAS HYLAND.

was freeman in Scituate 1638. His farm was on the fourth cliff, principally, but his house was on Kent street, nearly opposite to the lane called "the drift way." He came from Tenterden in Kent, England. There is no record of the birth of his children. It, however, appears that his daughter Deborah was the second wife of Serjeant William Ticknor, 1666, and a daughter Mary, the third wife of John Bryant, sen. 1664, and Ruth, single, 1664, and Sarah, wife of Thomas Turner, 1652. He mentions these daughters in his deeds of settlement, 1664. He had a son Samuel, who died a soldier in Philip's war, 1676. His wife Elizabeth executor, and Serjeant John Bryant bondsman.

His son Thomas succeeded to his father's residence. He married Elizabeth, daughter of John Stockbridge, 1661. His children, Thomas born 1662, Elizabeth 1665, Mary 1667, John 1669, Ruth 1673. Of these children,

Thomas, died in Phipps's Canada expedition, 1690. (Thomas, sen. appointed administrator, Probate Records).

John married Elizabeth James 1693. His children, Ruth born 1695, Elizabeth 1697, James 1701, John 1704, Sarah 1706, Thomas 1708, Ann 1710, Benjamin 1711.

Mr. John Hyland, who now resides on the fourth cliff, (land which the family has possessed since 1633), is the grandson of John, born 1704. William Hyland, a Revolutionary soldier, is now living one fourth mile south-east of mount Blue.

THOMAS INGHAM.

was a weaver, as we observe in the Colony records. "1663, Thomas Ingham was presented for detaining yarn of those who brought it to be woven," (cleared). He bought lands on the south side of Stockbridge's mill pond, of Abraham Sutliffe, 1640. His house was about forty rods from the mill dam, near Northy's. He had lands on the south-east of Brushy hill, and elsewhere. Both he and his wife were guilty of being old and solitary, and therefore suspected of witchcraft, (see witchcraft). He had a daughter Mary born 1647, Thomas born 1654, John 1663. John left no family on record. *Thomas* had a pleasant farm south of George Moore's swamp. He sold it before 1720, to Anthony Stetson, and removed to the south. Isaac, the son of Anthony Stetson, succeeded to this place, 1750, and it is now owned by his son, David, Esq. of Charlestown.

SAMUEL JACKSON.

came from Plymouth 1638. He married Hester, the daughter of Dea. Richard Sealis, 1639, and succeeded to his residence, (see Sealis). He had but one son, Jonathan born 1647, who was a soldier in Philip's war, and received a grant of land for his services. He succeeded his father, and had but one son, Jonathan born 1685, and daughters Sarah and Hannah. Jonathan married Sarah Daman 1728, and Deborah Stetson 1732. He had but one son, Jonathan born 1733, and one daughter, Sarah born 1730. Jonathan married Mehitabel Hyland 1757, and had several children; of whom Roland resides in Scituate, and Dea. Ward Jackson in Boston.

CAPT. DAVID JACOB,

was the son of John Jacob* of Glad Tidings plain, Hingham. He was born 1664. His mother was Mary, the daughter of George Russell, sen. of Hingham, a second wife: he was

---

* "John Jacob slain by the Indians near his father's house, April 19, 1676, and about the same time of day, Serj. Pratt at Weymouth. April 20th. Joseph Jones's, Anthony Sprague's, Israel Hobart's, Nath'l. Chubbuck's, and James Whiton's houses burnt down by the Indians." (Hobart's journal).

grandson of Nicholas Jacob, who was amongst the first settlers of Hingham. David came into Scituate 1688, when he purchased the lands of George Russell, (his uncle), on the south-east of Stockbridge's mill, the ancient Stedman place. His house stood near where stands the house of Mr. Samuel Hatch, his descendant. That Russell house was burnt 1712, and another erected near the same place, which has been succeeded since by the spacious mansion of Mr. Hatch. Dea. David Jacob was an active and useful man, always employed in publick business, and often also as town schoolmaster, there being but one school at that time. He married Sarah, the daughter of John Cushing, Esq. 1689; she was his cousin. His children were David born 1690, Elisha 1692, (died early), Lydia 1700, died early, Joshua 1702, Joseph 1707, Benj. 1709, Elisha 1711. Besides these, he had daughters Mary, Sarah, Deborah and Hannah. Of these sons Benjamin succeeded to his father's residence, and was the grandfather of Mr. Samuel Hatch, above named. David, Joshua, and Dr. Joseph settled in the west part of the Town, at Assinippi, (Snappet), David on the Plymouth road, half mile south-east of the mill. Dr. Joseph at the foot of Barstow's hill on Plymouth road, at the east of Gillman plain, (now Col. Collamore's), Joshua sixty rods north-east of the mill, where Richmond Jacob, his grandson, resides. Col. John Jacob, a Revolutionary officer, was his son: as also Capt. Joshua: and James, who succeeded to his father's residence.

Nicholas Jacob, the first of the family, died at Hingham, 1657, and gives in his will legacies, "To wife Mary 30£, to Joseph, Hannah and Deborah Loring 10£ each – To son John a double portion – To son Joseph, to daughter Mary, wife of John Otis, to daughter Elizabeth, wife of John Thaxter, to daughter Sarah, wife of John Cushing, to daughters Hannah and Deborah equal shares."

WILLIAM JAMES.

was in Scituate 1673. He came probably from Marshfield, where there was a widow Anna James and family as early as 1650. William settled at Scituate harbour 1673. His house lot was "north of Job Otis's ware-house," a part of which he sold to Capt. Stephen Otis, for the place for "a new house," 1697, (now Young's Tavern). He conducted ship-building, and dug a dock for launching his vessels, which now bears the name of "Will James's dock." He was also engaged in a coasting trade and fishery. He succeeded to a share in Conihassett lands in the right of John Woodfield. There is no record of children. His wife's name was Mehitabel. Elizabeth James married John Hyland 1693, and Mehitabel to Samuel Tuell 1700, which we conjecture to have been his daughters. Also Ann James to John Turner, jr. 1649; probably his sister.

There was a Samuel James mentioned in our records, who may have been his father: and a Samuel James married Hope Chamberlain of Hull, 1711, he was from Hingham, and a son of Francis James.

JOHN JAMES.

so far as we have discovered, appears to have been of a different family from William above, and probably was the son of Thomas James of Dedham, 1740. John was a freeman in Scituate in 1668. He purchased the farm of Ephraim Kempton's heirs, at "the block-house," on the North river, where his descendant Dea. Elisha James now resides. He married Lydia, daughter of John Turner, Sen. in 1675. He had but one son, viz. John born 1676, (see William Barrell), and he deceased about the time of the birth of that son, having been wounded by the Indians.

Dea. John married Eunice Stetson 1700, and Lydia, daughter of Nathaniel Turner, 1719, and succeeded to his father's residence. His children were Eunice born 1703, Mary 1704, Eunice 1706, John 109, Benjamin 1711, Lydia 1713, Elisha 1715, Zipporah 1717, (wife of Elisha Randall: she died 1815.)

Dea. John jr. married Rhoda, daughter of Dea. George King, 1730, by whom he had John born 1731, and by a second wife, Prudence Staunton of Stonington, Connecticut, he had Staunton born 1738, Prudence 1740, (wife of Capt. Elisha Turner), Rhoda 1742, (wife of Mr John Beal of Hingham), Elisha 1744, William 1746, Eunice 1747, Lydia 1749, (wife of Charles Curtis, Lucy 1751, Thomas 1753. – Of these *Dea. John 3d.* married Sarah Jacobs 1758, and succeeded to the residence of Dea. George King, his grandfather. His children were Sarah, John, (late Major James of Medford, whose sons are Capt. Galen, Joseph and others), Hannah, George, Joseph and Charles, born from 1759 to 1775.

Staunton was killed in the French war.

Dea. Elisha succeeded to the residence of his grandfather, his father having resided at the place now owned by Mr. Lemuel Jacob. He married Sarah, daughter of Capt. Elisha Foster, 1774, by whom he has children, Staunton, Sarah, (widow of Capt. Thomas Southworth), Elisha, of Roxbury, Temperance, (wife of Mr. Wild of Hingham), and Dea. Joshua of Scituate. The second wife of Dea. Elisha is Ruth, widow of Nathaniel Chittenden, and sister of his first wife.

William married Mary, daughter of Capt. Benjamin Randall, 1780, and has children, Lydia, (wife of Capt. Bass of Quincy), Betsey, (wife of Rev. William Torrey), William of Scituate, Hannah, (wife of Mr. Briggs Alden of Duxbury), and Josiah Leavitt of New York. Thomas married Sarah Clap, and deceased at Londonderry, leaving sons and daughters, one of whom is the wife of Dea. Joshua James of Scituate.

Capt. Benjamin (son of the first Dea. John) settled on the east of Colman's hills. His children were Mercy born 1738, Benjamin 1740. The latter was the father of Benjamin, John and Doctor Elisha of Scituate.

EDWARD JENKINS.

was one of the Conihassett partners in 1646, and a freeman 1647. He purchased a part of Edward Foster's house lot 1647, and built his house at the corner of Kent street, near the bridge, where the house of Capt. Lemuel Webb now stands. He had a lot also near where the Methodist chapel now stands, where his son Thomas settled 1678. Edward Jenkins kept an ordinary many years: licensed first 1677. He deceased 1699. His will gives legacies, "To my wife Mary – to son Thomas – to grandson Daniel 20 acres near Valley swamp – (note: this is now called the Jenkins meadow, on the north of Jacob's mill pond) – to grandson Edward – to granddaughters Hannah Turner and Mary Bacon – to daughter Mary Cooke, to granddaughter Mary Jenkins. *Item,* it is my will that bread and beer be given at my funeral: also that a sermon be preached at my funeral by Mr. Jeremiah Cushing, or some other minister whom my Executor shall think meet: also I give to the minister that shall preach my funeral sermon 20S." By way of explanation, we remark, that Edward Jenkins seems to have belonged to the liberal party of the puritans: the more strict party forbade sermons, and even prayers at funerals, because the Church of England "said prayers at funerals," and the Church of Rome "prayed for the dead." See Neal's History.

FAMILY SKETCHES.

We have not learned who was the first wife of Edward Jenkins, and the mother of his children: his second wife was widow Mary Ripley of Hingham, 1684. His daughter Mary married Marmaduke Atkinson, 1670, and in 1674, "being deserted, was divorced," Colony Records. She afterwards married Robert Cooke. His daughter Hannah married Thomas Turner, Esq. a lawyer, 1693, and his daughter Sarah married Mr. Bacon, probably of Taunton.

Thomas married Martha - 1678. Children, Hannah 1679, Thomas 1681, Edward, 2d. 1683, Daniel 1685. We find no families of these sons here except of

Edward, 2d. who married Martha Daman 1705, and Abigail Merritt, 1728, and left children, Mary born 1706, Thomas 1707, Anna 1708, Samuel 1710, Thankful 1712, Edward 1713, David 1715, Mary 1717, James 1718, Martha 1724, Content 1726, Daniel 1728. Of these,

Thomas married Sarah Bailey 1740, and had children, Thomas, who married Hannah, the daughter of Dea. Joseph Clap, of Black pond hill, and whose son Bailey Jenkins is living, and has a family. Gera, who married Lillis Colman, 1766, and has sons Gera, Capt. Colman, Capt. Elijah, Capt. Oliver, (of Quincy), and Israel. Dea. Samuel (son of Edward, 2d.) married Rebecca White, 1740, his children, Edward born 1741, Samuel 1742, Joshua 1744, Ebenezer 1745, (died young), Rebecca 1747, Nathaniel 1748, died early, Martha 1750, Nathaniel 1752, died young, Caleb 1754, died early, Joseph 1757, Caleb 1758, Abigail 1759, Sarah 1761. Dea. Samuel lived nearly a century. Of his sons:

Edward, 3d, married Jerusha Neal 1764, and left a son Charles, who married Jane Collier 1785. He was then of Bridgewater, and his sons William and Noble Everett are of Boston.

Samuel (son of Dea. Samuel) married Abigail Cole 1771. Children, Samuel born 1772, Abigail 1774, Nathaniel 1776, George 1779, Sarah 1782, Nancy 1784, Sophia 1786. Capt. Joshua (son of Dea. Samuel) married widow Ruth Sparrell, 1778: his son Capt. Davis Jenkins, by a first wife, was lost at sea, 1819, and Joshua by his second wife, was also lost at sea, and Capt. Joshua himself.

Joseph (son of Dea. Samuel) removed to Sandy river, Maine, where he has a family.

Caleb (son of Dea. Samuel) married Elizabeth Tilson of Plymouth, 1791, and had sons Peres, Peleg, (of Bridgewater), and Nathan, who died young.

David (son of Edward 2d.) removed to Abington, where he has posterity. He married Elizabeth Merritt 1741.

James (son of Edward, 2d.) married Mary Vinal 1746, and left children, Mary born 1747, James 1749, Peleg 1751, (died early), Gideon 1753, Calvin 1758. Of these James, jr. married Ruth Lincoln 1774, and had children, Polly born 1775, Ruth 1777, James 1779, Cummings 1782, Isaac 1784, Ruth 1788. Gideon married Mercy Lincoln of Cohasset, 1777, and left children, Capt. Peleg of Scituate Harbour, born 1779, Luther 1780, Nancy 1783, (widow of Capt. Davis Jenkins), Gideon 1785, Mercy 1789, Josiah 1791, Solon 1793, (who married Hannah, daughter of Charles Cole), Shadrach 1796, Clarissa 1799, Chloe 1802. Calvin married Elizabeth Litchfield 1781, and has sons Calvin and others.

Daniel (son of Edward, 2d.) married Elizabeth Nichols 1759, and had children, Daniel born 1760, Elizabeth 1761, Paul 1762, (now living in Scituate), Silas 1764, died early, Bathsheba, (wife of Dr. Benjamin Stockbridge), Elizabeth 1768, Ruth 1772, Noah 1776.

SERJ. HUMPHREY JOHNSON.

was in Scituate 1651, and purchased lands of William Hatch, on the north of Cornet Stetson's farm, a deep ravine dividing the two farms. His house stood near the bank of that ravine: it was afterward owned by Joshua Lincoln. He had also several houses by purchase, and claimed to be successor in division of common lands, to Resolved White and Josiah Holmes. His wife's name was Eleanor, probably of Hingham: and Johnson removed to Hingham 1673. His children, John born 1653, Joseph 1655, Benjamin 1657, Margaret 1659, Mary 1663, Isaac 1667, born in Scituate, and Joseph 1676, born in Hingham. Serj. Johnson was a capable man in publick affairs, and often employed in Town business, in the early part of his life: but he had an uncommon inclination to law suits, and few men have left on the records of the Court, so many evidences of his litigious disposition – some of which we select, In 1683, he commenced a suit against the Town for three shares in common lands. He had removed his residence out of the Colony ten years before, and the Town considered that his right to common lands was thereby cancelled. He, however, recovered an execution, and John Cushing, Samuel Clap and Jeremiah Hatch, were appointed to set off lands to satisfy the execution.* Again, 1687, when Sir Edmund Andros, Governor General, and his Council had the sole control of affairs, Johnson went with complaints to the Governor, "that he had not had his full rights in Scituate." The Town being notified, thus remonstrated and answered that Johnson's claims had all been satisfied: "that the original writ and process thereupon was altogether tortious and wrong, and yet what was obtained by judgment of Court had been satisfied." Nevertheless, Johnson was furnished with a warrant from Andros, and came with his surveyor, and laid out one hundred acres at the head of Richard Dwelley's lot – one hundred acres at Burnt plain, and one hundred acres at Halifax cedar swamp. On this the Town address the Governor (by John Cushing and Samuel Clap, agents,) in a very spirited declaration, showing that much of the land laid out by Johnson had already been appropriated to others – that Johnson "had already been accommodated with thrice sixty-five acres to the full amount of his claim as principal and successor to two others." We believe this grant was never confirmed, and probably the overthrow of Andros and his miserable oligarchy, a few months after the date of the above declaration, put an end to Johnson's hopes and projects. Johnson's swamp in Scituate, (near Hingham line, in the beaches), derived its name from Johnson's trespass, for which the Town recovered damages. We observe in Colony records, 1673, "Humphry Johnson being convicted of removing a land mark, near the land of Thomas Hyland, sen. for the boldness and insolency in coming into this Government to do this act, is fined 5£." Also same year, "Humphry Johnson having come into this Government without leave of the Governor and two of the Assistants, (contrary to law), is now ordered to remove his dwelling and cottage erected within the town of Scituate, within one month from the date hereof, or else order shall be given for the pulling down therof."

JOHN JONES.

Thomas and Robert Jones were amongst the first settlers of Hingham, having lands assigned them in 1637 and 8. There was a John Jones of Cambridge, 1640, and afterward of Concord, who was brother (according to tradition) of Thomas and

---

* See Appendix II.

Robert. Robert had a family in Hingham, viz. Robert, born probably in England. Ephraim born in Hingham 1649. John 1652, Lydia 1655, Joseph 1658, Thomas 1659. Most of these removed. Robert, jr. had a son Robert, born in Hingham, 1666.

Thomas (the eldest of the three) left a numerous posterity in Hingham, viz. Joseph, born probably in England, Benjamin in Hingham, 1637, Thomas 1640, Mary 1643.

Joseph married Patience – 1659. Children, Joseph born 1660, Benjamin 1662, Patience 1665, Anna 1667, Ruth 1669, Sarah 1771, Ephraim 1773, Mary 1776, Thomas 1779. The house of Joseph was "over the river," that is, towards mount Blue. It was burnt by the Indians 1676.

Joseph, jr. married Sarah – 1689, and had children, Joseph born 1690, Patience 1693, Abigail 1694, Ebenezer 1695, died early, Ebenezer 1698, Elisha 1700, Amos 1702, John 1704: the latter removed to Marshfield, married Ruth Hatch 1738, and had sons, Samuel born 1739, Amos 1742, baptized in Scituate second Church.

Benjamin (son of Joseph, sen.) married Susanna Real 1686, (she died 1689, and her son Benjamin was born same year), Thomas born 1697, by a second wife, Patience. Benjamin, jr. married Mary Jordan, and had sons, David born 1721, Jonathan 1723, Daniel 1726.

Ephraim (son of Joseph, sen.) married Margaret Fearing 1708, and left a family.

Thomas (youngest son of Joseph, sen.) married Katharine Caswell 1703, and had children, Joanna born 1705, Lydia 1706, Thomas 1711, died early, Thomas 1714, Sarah 1717.

Thomas (only son) married Mary Marsh 1737, and had sons, Thomas born 1739, and John, at the head of this article. He married Lucy Wilder of Hingham, 1779, and removed to Scituate, 1799, His wife deceased 1831. The place of his residence is a half mile south of Cushing hill. His children, John, who married the daughter of Michael Lapham, and resides at Cushing hill: Charles, who married Betsey Nichols, and resides at the seat of the late Judge Nathan Cushing: Isaac of Boston, Thomas of Scituate, and daughters Bathsheba, widow of Melzar Daman, Elizabeth, wife of Elijah Randall, Lydia, and Lucy, wife of John Ewell of Medford.

There was an Isaac Jones, called of Boston, who married Hannah Perry 1716, and lived at Wild cat hill. His family removed. Isaac, his son, was baptized 1717.

JOHN JORDON.

was in Scituate 1750. His last house was at the south end of Jordan lane. His sons David and Nathaniel are deceased. Peleg is living. Jonathan was drowned at the mouth of the North river, July 4, 1776. The wife of Luther Daman, sen. was the daughter of Nathaniel. John Jordon occupied a house at Gillman plain in 1755, and in 1775, he occupied the place where Judge Nathan Cushing's mansion stands.

HENRY JOSSELYN.

came into Scituate 1669, and family tradition asserts, from Black point, now Scarboro: he is therefore supposed to have been the son of Henry Josselyn, who had been an important man in the government of Georgiana, and nephew of "John Josselyn, Gentleman," the author of "New England's Rarities," and other books. Henry Josselyn married Abigail, daughter of Charles Stockbridge, 1676. His residence was in the field fifty rods east of Judge William Cushing's farm house. His children, Abigail born 1677, Abraham 1678, Anna 1680, (died early), Charles 1682, Mary 1684, Nathaniel 1686, Rebecca 1689, Jabez 1690, Jemima and Keziah 1695, Henry 1697, Joseph 1699, Thomas 1702.

Nathaniel married Frances Yellings 1711. Children, Mary born 1712, Nathaniel 1722.

Henry, jr. married Hannah - 1721, daughter Lydia born 1722. He was in Hanover after that town was incorporated.

Jabez married Sarah Turner 1722, and removed to Pembroke. Thomas and Charles settled in Pembroke. Joseph deceased in Abington, 1726, leaving "a widow Sarah, sons Joseph, Ebenezer and Abraham, daughters Hannah, Beatrice, Mary Bates and Sarah Porter." (Probate Records).

EPHRAIM KEMPTON ("Taylor").

was the son of Ephraim of Plymouth, and came probably with his father in the ship Ann, 1623. He purchased Elder Henry Cobb's eighty acre lot on the North river, at the block-house. He married Joanna, the daughter of Thomas Rawlins, 1645. His children, Joanna born 1646, Patience, 1648, Ephraim

1649, Manasseh 1651. He died in Scituate, 1655, and his wife Joanna 1656. The farm was sold to John James a few years after. Some of the descendants may be in New Bedford. There was a Manasseh Kempton, who had lands in Scituate 1643: he probably lived in Plymouth.

GEORGE KENDRICK.

was one of the members dismissed from Plymouth Church, 1634, "in case they join in a body at Scituate." He had lands in Scituate 1633: was a freeman 1635. His house lot was on Kent street, the second south of the drift way, between Elder Tilden's and Isaac Stedman's. He had a lot on third cliff, between the lots of John Hanmer and William Dauckinges: also marsh near Stony cove. He was a volunteer soldier in the Pequod war. He disappears from our records 1638. In 1645, when he sold one hundred and sixty acres of land on North river to William Randall, (near Till's or Dwelly's creek), he was in Boston. There is no record of his family here. In Boston there is the record of Joseph, born 1639, and Deborah 1646. George Kendrick, who took the oath of fidelity in Rehoboth, 1658, may have been his son, but was not the same who had lands in Scituate 1633. George of Rehoboth had a son Isaac born 1675. There was also Thomas Kendrick of Rehoboth, whose daughter Mary was born 1680.

JOHN KENT (shipwright).

was in Scituate 1698. He probably came from Charlestown. His wife was Sarah, His children Ebenezer, Benjamin, Sarah, Samuel, Ezekiel, Nathaniel, born from 1699 to 1705. Ebenezer, his brother, was in Scituate, and had two sons, Ebenezer and Isaac born 1712, and daughters Abigail, Mercy and Elizabeth.

David Kent, the last of the name in Scituate, married Lydia Daman 1773. He was son of David of Boston, who married Abigail Daman 1744. He deceased 1825. His son was Samuel of South Boston, also deceased. His daughters the wives of Thomas Lapham and Perkins Clap.

Joseph Kent of Charlestown married Rebecca Chittenden of Scituate, 1702.

ELDER THOMAS KING.

came into Scituate with Mr. William Vassall, 1634 or 5, and built his house a few rods south of Mr. Vassall's, on the top of the hill at Belle house neck. He also had lands on the north side of Rotten marsh, where Dea. Thomas his son had a house 1666. His children were Rhoda born 1639, George 1642, Thomas 1645, Daniel 1647, Sarah 1650, and John 1652. His wife Sarah died 1652, and he married Jane, the widow of Elder William Hatch, and was chosen to succeed Elder Hatch in the second Church. His second wife deceased the same year. The name of his third wife was Anne. Of these children John died early, Daniel settled in Marshfield, Rhoda married John Rogers, Sarah married Elisha Bisby, jr. George died early or removed.

Dea. Thomas continued the name in Scituate. He married Elizabeth, daughter of Dea. Thomas Clap, 1669. She deceased 1698, and he married Deborah Briggs 1699: she deceased 1711, and Des. Thomas the same year. He purchased Nathaniel Rawlins' farm, at Stoney cove brook, before 1680. His children, Sarah born 1669, Thomas 1671, Jane 1673, Daniel 1675, John 1677, Mercy 1678, Ichabod 1680, George 1682, Anna 1684. Of these, Thomas died early, Ichabod had a son Thomas born 1703, and removed soon after. John married Sarah Whiton of Hingham, 1706, and lived, we believe, in Marshfield, as did Daniel and Ichabod. Daniel had two sons and two daughters, Elizabeth, Daniel, Robert, Mehitabel, born from 1702, to 1709. This family removed. *Dea. George* inherited the farm south of Stoney cove brook, which had been originally Anthony Annable's land, then the farm of Rawlins, then Dea. Thomas King's. Dea. George King married Deborah Briggs 1710. Deborah, Rhoda, (wife of John James), Lydia, (wife of Joseph Cushing), and Sarah, were his children. He died in Scituate. Some descendants of Elder King are in Abington.

Elder King's will, dated 1691, gives "to wife Anne – to daughter Sarah Besby land at Gravelly beach – To grandsons John and Thomas Rogers 10£ each. Item: it is my will that Robin, my negro, be set free, and receive of my estate a bed and 5£ in money – Item: to son Thomas all my property not otherwise disposed of in New and Old England."

Dea. Thomas King's will, dated 1711 gives "to son Daniel the homestead; (of Elder Thomas King, late deceased, on the neck); he allowing daughter Anne to live in the house. To son John a farm in Marshfield. To son George the farm where I now dwell, also a lot adjoining my brother Samuel Clap's land. To daughter Mercy Winslow 30£. To daughter Anne King 30£. To son Ichabod, &c."

There was a John King in Weymouth, whose daughter Mary was born 1634."

JOHN LAMBERT.

from Hingham, was in Scituate 1693, when his son John was born. Some descendants of this name have remained until within a few years. Henry, Daniel and Zachariah were soldiers in the French war. These were sons of Thomas. Edmund Bowker, late deceased, married his daughter.

THOMAS LAPHAM.

was in Scituate 1640. His residence was near the harbour. He married Mary, daughter of Elder Nathaniel Tilden. His children, Thomas born 1643, Rebecca 1645, Joseph 1648, Elizabeth, Mary and Lydia: the latter was the wife of Samuel Bates of Hingham, 1666.

Thomas, jr. settled in Marshfield, where several generations of his family have lived. His children were Joseph born 1670. Samuel 1676, Lydia 1677, (and by a second wife), Mary born 1704.

The sons of Joseph were Joseph born 1709, Ichabod 1711.

The sons of Samuel were David born 1706, Joshua 1710, Amos 1717.

David (of Marshfield) was father of Thomas, who settled at Studley hill in Scituate, and whose sons were Thomas, Israel, Michael and Charles, and whose daughters were the wives of Noah Barrell, Ashur Sprague and Nash (of Hanover).

Daniel Lapham removed to Pittsfield, and David to Norwich, (sons of David). This was a numerous family. Stephen, another son of David, has a son Isaac of York. Thomas (son of Thomas) has sons Thomas and Israel at South Boston. Michael married Sarah, daughter of the last James Cushing, of

---

* There was Samuel King in Plymouth 1649, whose sons were Samuel and Isaac. The Kings of Taunton probably are descendants.

Cushing hill, and left daughters, viz. the wife of John Jones, the wife of Allen Cushing of Hingham, and another. Israel deceased many years since, his widow married Dea. John Jacobs of Hingham. Charles left sons William and Henry, and daughters, viz. the wives of Nathaniel Brooks, Theophilug Cushing of Hingham, and Elijah Clap, 3d.

GEORGE LEWIS (clothier).

was one of those dismissed from Plymouth Church in 1634, "in case they join in a body at Scituate." He had lands here in 1633. His house lot was on Kent street, the first south of Meeting-house lane. He came from East Greenwich in Kent. He married Sarah Jenkins in England, sister of Edward Jenkins. There is no regular record of his children: some having been born in England, others in Plymouth, others in Scituate, and two in Barnstable. They were Mary, born as early as 1623, (married John Bryant of Scituate, 1643), Thomas, George, James, John 1637, Ephraim* 1641, Sarah 1643, Nathaniel 1645, Joseph 1647. The last four born at Barnstable, whither George Lewis removed in 1640. He died intestate, 1662. Probate records.

Thomas married Mary Davis 1653. His children were James born 1654, Thomas 1656, Mary 1659, and probably others at Barnstable. He removed to Swansey, where were born Samuel 1672, Hepzibah 1674.

George, jr. married Mary, daughter of Bernard Lombard, 1654: we have seen no record of his children.

James lived at Barnstable, and married Sarah Lane 1655. He was a selectman of Barnstable in 1660, and subsequently. He had sons John born 1656, and Samuel 1659, and eight other children.

John was killed with Capt. Pierce in the Rehoboth battle, 1676.

Joseph married Mary Jones 1671, and had children, Joseph born 1672, Sybil 1674. The next year he was killed at Swansey by the Indians. Hon. James Lewis of Pepperell, Massachusetts, descended from this branch of the family.

Nathaniel also removed to Swansey, where his son Nathaniel was born 1673. Nathaniel deceased at Swansey 1683, October 13th. Joseph Lewis "of Barnstable," married Sarah

---

* So recorded in the Colony records – but we think it should be Edward.

Marsh, daughter of Thomas Marsh of Hingham, February 3d, 1702-3, and resided at Hingham. We suppose this to have been the son of Joseph, who was killed at Swansey. His children, Joseph born 1705, died early, Thomas 1707, who married Mary Lawson 1736: Paul born 1710, who married Hannah – 1733, and had a son, Urbane 1736: James 1712, Jonathan 1714, who married Lydia Stodder 1740: and (by a second wife Elizabeth) Hannah born 1723, died early, Samuel 1724, died early, Israel 1727, died early, Hannah 1731, Joseph 1736.

John (son of James born 1656) settled in Hingham: married Hannah Lincoln 1684, and had nine children, of whom Rev. Daniel, minister of Pembroke, was born 1685. Rev. Isaiah, minister of Wellfleet, married into the family of Winslow: from the latter have descended Winslow Lewis, and other respectable families in Boston.

JOHN LEWIS.

a brother of George, sen. was freeman in Scituate 1637, and had a house lot on Kent street, the fourth south of the drift way. He disappears early from our records, and we have discovered no traces of a family.

MORDECAI LINCOLN.

son of Samuel of Hingham, born 1651, settled at Bound brook bridge, 1700. He built a spacious house east of the brook, and erected Lincoln's mills. At this place Caleb Lincoln lately deceased, son of Jacob, and the grandson of Mordecai. The widow Mary, of Joseph Eellmes, another of his grandchildren, is now living, more than ninety-three years of age, born June 1, 1738. Their father was Jacob. Mordecai, jr. married Abigail, the daughter of Rev. Nathaniel Eells, 1756, and removed to Taunton.

Isaac, another son of Jacob, had Solomon, Isaac, William, Jacob, John, George, and James, (the latter a Revolutionary soldier, born June 20, 1752, and now living).

ROBERT LINNET.

was a freeman in Scituate 1639, and the next year removed to Barnstable. We notice in the Colony records, 1669,

"Penninah, the widow of Robert Linnet, entered a complaint that her son Robert had kept back property given her by her husband." Abigail, the daughter of Robert, sen. married Joshua Lombard of Barnstable, 1650.

LAWRENCE LITCHFIELD.

was in Barnstable, where he bore arms 1643. His children were Experience, Remembrance, Josiah and Dependance, the last being the only birth of the family on our records, (1646), we conclude the others may have been born at Barnstable.

Experience was a freeman 1668, but we find no record of his family. Remembrance married Lewis of Barnstable.

Josiah born 1647, (Colony Records), married Sarah, the daughter of Rev. Nicholas Baker, of the first church in Scituate, 1671. His children were Hannah born 1672, Sarah 1674, Josiah 1677, Nicholas 1680, Experience 1683, Judith 1687, Samuel 1690: of these children,

Josiah married Mary Briggs 1712. Children, Mary born 1715, Josiah 1716.

Nicholas married Bathsheba Clark 1704. Children, Experience born 1705, Josiah 1706, Nicholas 1707, Bathsheba 1709, James 1711, John 1712, Israel 1714, Eleazer 1715, Susanna 1717, Isaac 1719, Thomas 1721.

Samuel married Abigail Buck 1712. Children, Samuel born 1715, Abigail 1716, Sarah 1718, Judith 1720, Hannah 1721, Experience 1723, Deborah 1725, Nathaniel 1727, Remember 1728, Ruth 1730. This may enable most of the present generation to trace their descent.

Rev. Paul Litchfield, late of Carlisle, was of the sixth generation, having descended from Lawrence through Josiah, Nicholas, Thomas and Paul. Rev. Joseph Litchfield, late of York, was of the fifth generation, having descended from Lawrence, through Josiah, Josiah and Josiah.

Dea. Israel Litchfield is of the fifth generation, having descended from Lawrence, through Josiah, Nicholas and Josiah.

Two of the sons of Nicholas (Israel and John) settled in Canterbury, Conn. 1743, and have many descendants. No family perhaps in the country has increased to a greater extent, Dea. Israel, named above, had prepared a genealogical table in 1820, of one hundred and ten families.

We illustrate the early history of this family, by a few notes from the Colony records.

1657, "Judith, the wife of William Peaks testifieth that her former husband, Lawrence Litchfield, lying on his death bed, did send for John Allen and Ann his wife, and desired to give their youngest son Josiah, to be their adbpted child – whereunto all consented.

Signed, "JOHN ALLEN,
ANN ALLEN,
JUDITH PEAKS."

1662, "Judith, the wife of William Peaks, petitioned that her son Josiah Litchfield, the adopted son of John Allen, might be allowed to choose two guardians," (granted).

1665, "The Court did sanction an agreement between Lieut. James Torrey and Robert Stetson, guardians to Josiah Litchfield on one side, and Anna his mother, (wife of Lawrence Litchfield, and some time the wife of John Allen), concerning the improvement of his property." Here is undoubtedly a mistake in the records; Anna was the wife of John Allen, and the mother of Josiah Litchfield by adoption: Judith Peaks was his natural mother, some time the wife of Lawrence Litchfield, and some time a wife of John Allen, and separated or divorced in England.

1668, "Josiah Litchfield having become of age, Major Josiah Winslow is appointed to see him put in possession of his land, a legacy from John Allen."

1673, "Verdict – that Experience Litchfield came by his death in attempting to carry a heavy stick of timber on board a boat, at Rhodolphus Eellme's landing place, at Hoop-pole neck, his feet slipping up, and he falling on a plank, and the timber on his head, he dying at his father's house [perhaps late father's] the same day."

Same year, "The Court ordered that Josias Litchfield, brother of Experience Litchfield, deceased, shall have his land, and the remainder of his estate shall be divided equally between his two sisters, Remember Lewis and Dependance Litchfield."

DAVID LITTLE, ESQ.

was from Marshfield, 1700. He often laboured in publick affairs in the Town, and practised as a lawyer. His children Ephraim, David, Nathaniel, Elizabeth, Mary and Barnabas, born from 1708 to 1731.

Ephrain graduated at Harvard College 1728, was minister of Hebron, Connecticut.

David resided in Scituate, was often employed in publick business: left no family. He married Deborah Clap 1734.

Barnabas was a public spirited and useful man, and distinguished for his zeal in promoting the American cause in 1776: he left no family.

The family residence was north of "Hatchet rock," now the residence of Mr. John Otis.

Capt. James Little, a man of enterprise, at the Harbour in 1800, and whose daughters were married to Ensign Otis, and Dr. Elisha James, was from Marshfield, and a connexion of the family above. They were descendants of Thomas Little, of Plymouth, until 1650, (at which date his son Ephraim was born), and afterward of Marshfield. He married Ann Warren 1633. He died 1671.

BARNARD LOMBARD.

one of the men of Kent, was in Scituate 1633, and freeman 1636. His house lot was on Kent street, the second on the Green field, adjoining Samuel Fuller's, which was on his north side. He removed to Barnstable, 1640. He was an ensign of the military company of Barnstable, 1652. His son Jabez born 1642, at Barnstable, Mary and Martha, and Joshua, were probably born in Scituate.

Jabez married Sarah, daughter of Matthew Darby, 1660, Joshua married Abigail Linnet 1650, and had sons Jonathan born 1657, Joshua 1660. *Mary* married George Lewis, jr. 1654. Ma&a married John Martin 1657.

---

* Thomas Little, who married Ann Warren 1633, had sons Ephraim and Isaac, and perhaps others. Ephraim married Mary Sturtevant 1672. His son Ephraim born 1673, graduated at Harvard College 1695, and was a minister of Pymouth.

Lieut. Isaac had sons, David, Esq. born 1680, (of Scituate, as noted above), Thomas born 1676, graduated at Harvard College 1695; he was a lawyer, and died early, as has been the tradition; Capt. Isaac born 1677, was a man of distinction in Marshfield. Charles born 1685, Nathaniel 1690, William 1691. From Capt. Isaac, we have been told, descended the late brave master of the Boston frigate, Capt. George – whose sons – George was a lawyer in Scituate, and deceased 1811, Amos was unfortunately killed by his cousin, Luther Little of Marshfield, in 1815, in a fit of insanity. They were shooting pigeons together at "Belle house neck," in Scituate. Amos was Town Clerk at the time of his death. Edward, the only surviving son of Capt. George, resides on the paternal farm, near Little's bridge.

One of the most distinguished descendants of this family was Solomon Lombard, born at Barnstable, 1701, graduated at Harvard College 1722, settled in the ministry at Gorham, Maine: he entertained more liberal sentiments than were tolerated by his brethren in his vicinity, which induced him to retire. He was afterward Judge of the Court in Cumberland County: a very active patriot in the Revolution, and drafted most of the publick papers of the time, relating to the Revolution, in that County. E. H. Lombard, Esq. of Hallowell, is his grandson.

Barnard Lombard had probably a brother Thomas at Barnstable, freeman 1641, whose sons were Jedidiah born 1640, Benjamin 1642, and Caleb. *Jedidiah* had three sons, of one birth, 1671, Joseph, Benjamin and Jeremiah. We notice in the Colony records, "Richard Berry, Jedidiah Lombard, Benjamin Lombard, and James Maker, fined for smoking tobacco at the end of Yarmouth Meeting-house on the Lord's day." Faithful tradition informs us, that the early settlers were greatly addicted to smoking, and that they would often disturb divine service by the klicking of flints and steel, to light their pipes, and the clouds of smoke in the Church. Hence that law of the Colony, passed 1669: "It is enacted that any person or persons that shall be found smoking of tobacco on the Lord's day, going to or coming from the meetings, within two miles of the Meeting-house, shall pay 12 pence for every such default, for the Colonie's use, to be increased," &c.

Richard Lombard was in Scituate 1640. He returned to Tenterden, England, (see Elder N. Tilden's will).

JOHN LOWELL.

appears in Scituate 1658, when he was married to Elizabeth, daughter of Richard Sylvester, and is called in the records, John Lowell of Boston. His children baptized in the second Church in Scituate, were John born 1660, Joseph 1662, Patience 1663, Elizabeth 1664. He brought another child to baptism in Scituate, viz. Phebe 1667, when he is called John Lowell of Rehoboth. He had a second wife 1666, Naomi, the sister of his former wife, by whom he had children, Margaret born 1667, Samuel 1669.

He seems to have been in Rehoboth 1670, as we observe in the Colony records, 1670, "John Lowell, jr. (with consent of John Lowell, sen. of Rehoboth) made choice of Joseph Sylvester of Scituate, to be his guardian." John, sen. died 1694, in Boston, and Naomi his widow administered. The name in the Probate records is *Lowle.*

The late Judge John Lowell, (father of Hon. John and Rev. Dr. Charles of Boston), was the son of John, whose father was Ebenezer, whose father was probably the John Lowell, jr. named in the above extract from the Colony records, or of Joseph. John died in Bristol, England, 1701, and his brother Joseph of Boston administered on his estate. An Ebenezer Lowell, or Lowle, died 1711, and his widow Elizabeth administered.

JOHN MAGOON (early McGoun).

was a freeholder 1666. He lived in "the Two mile." He had also a considerable tract of land on the west side of North river, near Hugh's cross, and Cornet's pond. His children, John born 1668, Elias 1673, Isaac 1675. This family have descendants in Marshfield and Pembroke.

JOHN MANSEL.

married Leah Simons 1744. His sons John born 1745, Joseph 1750, William 1754, Peleg 1757, and several daughters. John married Sarah Price 1766. This family removed to Maine.

SETH MAYO.

married   His children, Lydia, John, Jane, and William, born from 1751 to 1759.

RICHARD MAN (planter).

was a youth in Elder Brewster's family, and came to Plymouth in the Mayflower, 1620. He was one of the Conihassett partners in Scituate, 1646. His farm was at Man hill, (a well known place to this day), south of great Musquashcut pond and north of John Hoar's farm. There is no record of his marriage here. His children, Nathaniel born 1646, Thomas 1650, Richard 1652, Josiah 1654.

Nathaniel lived in Scituate, but left no family. In 1680, he made over his estate to his brothers Richard and Thomas, and took a bond for support. This was on account of infirm health. (Scit. Rec. Vol. 6.) See Appendix II.

Josiah deceased early or removed.

Thomas had children, Josiah born 1676, Thomas 1681, Sarah 1684, Mary 1688, Elizabeth 1692, Joseph 1694, Benjamin 1697.* Thomas had lands at Rehoboth, and probably deceased there. He was in the Rehoboth battle, with Capt. Pierce, 1676, and was severely wounded.

Richard had children, John born 1684, Rebecca 1686, Hannah 1689, Nathaniel 1693, Richard 1694, Elizabeth 1696, Abigail 1698.

John Man, a descendant of this family, lives in the neighborhood of Man hill. Rebecca, widow of Richard, sen. married John Cowen, 1656.

JOHN MANSON.

of Scituate harbour, married Meriam Curtis 1755. His son Capt. John, and grandson Capt. John, jr. are living and have families.

GERSHOM MARBLE.

from Boston, married Waitstill Ingle, in Scituate, 1697, and had children, John born 1700, Ephraim 1702, David 1704, Nathaniel 1706. This family removed early. David was in Scituate 1748; when his son Nathaniel was born.

HENRY MASON.

had lands in Scituate 1650: he soon removed.

WILLIAM MELLUS.

from Dorchester, married Jael Chittenden 1711, and Sarah Balch 1716. His children, Abigail born 1712, William 1718,

---

* Benjamin (son of Thomas) was the first of the family who settled in that part of Scituate which is now Hanover. He married Martha Curtis 1724. Benjamin, his son, married Gill – Bailey – and Dunbar. His sons were the late Capt. Joshua and others, perhaps – and the sons of Capt. Joshua (whose wife was Mary Cushing of Hingham) are Benjamin, Esq. and others.

John 1721, Abigail 1725. The widow of William, sen. (Sarah) married Dea. Samuel Stodder 1749. Abigail married Isaac Lincoln 1738. This family resided in the north parish. John removed early. William had children in Scituate, viz. Sarah Hart 1741, and others.

HENRY MERRITT.

was one of the earliest settlers of Scituate, though not a freeman until 1638. There is a deed in the Colony records, dated 1628, from Henry Merritt to Nathaniel Tilden, conveying planting lands on the third cliff, (see p. 8.) He was doubtless amongst the first settlers as early as 1626. His house lot in 1633, was at the corner where Greenfield lane and "the drift way" united: we believe it is now known as Merritt's corner. He had large shares in the New Harbour marshes. He was also one of the Conihassett partners. He had a son Henry, who deceased (without a family, probably) before 1673, Henry, sen. deceased 1653, and John administered.

John, the only son that left posterity here, succeeded to his father's residence. His sons were John, Henry and Jonathan, but we find no record of their births. Their father died in middle life.

Jonathan, the youngest son, had lands assigned him, and was living in 1699: but we find no trace of a family.

John, jr. left children, John born 1687, Thomas 1688, Elizabeth 1690, Mary 1692, Ichabod 1695, Hannah 1696, Henry 1699, Abigail 1700, (wife of Edward Jenkins 1728), Jonathan 1702, David 1703, Ebenezer 1705, Ezekiel 1709. - Most of these left families.

John married Hannah Peaks 1727, but left no children, probably.

Thomas married Abigail Woodworth 1711, and had children, Agatha 1711, Abigail 1714, Amy 1716, Mary 1718, Thomas 1721.

Ichabod left a son Joseph, born 1729, who probably removed.

Jonathan married Mehitabel Daman 1727, and had a son Simeon, born 1728. This family removed to Hebron, Conn. before 1736.

David married Hannah Barrell 1736, and had children, Lydia 1737, David 1740, John 1743, Hannah 1748.

Ezekiel married Rachel Vinal 1758, and left no family on record.

Thomas (son of Thomas) married Jane Nichols 1749, and had children, Elizabeth born 1750, Jane 1752, Thomas 1754, Jos. 1756, Mary 1760, Charles 1761, Jane 1764, Abigail 1766.

Henry (son of John, sen.) married Elizabeth Weyborn 1686: his children were Jonathan born 1687, Henry 1689, James 1691, Deborah 1694, Leah 1697, (wife of Benjamin Briggs 1719), Rachel 1699, (wife of Eleazer Peaks 1718), Isaac 1702. Of these, Jonathan married Elizabeth Whiton 1710, and Elizabeth, the widow of Rev. Nehemiah Hobart of Cohasset, 1740: his children, Deborah born 1711, (wife of Joseph Nash 1730), Nehemiah 1712, (died early), Jonathan 1715, Elizabeth 1719, Obadiah 1723.

Henry, jr. married Hannah Cowen 1712, and had children, Hannah born 1713, Mary 1717, Penelope 1719. Deborah 1720, Sarah 1724, Martha 1726, Henry 1728, Ruth 1730.

James (son of Henry) married Ruth Wade 1716, and had children, James born 1717, Elisha 1722, Seth 1724.

Isaac (son of Henry) married Jerusha Hayden of Braintree, 1724, and had children, Henry born 1725, Jerusha 1727, Rachel 1729, Isaac 1731, Delight 1734. This family removed to Charlton about 1736, where other sons were born, Job, Samuel, and Benjamin.

Jonathan (son of Jonathan) married Sarah Wade 1741, and left sons, Nehemiah, Joshua (who died young) and Daniel, (now living).

Obadiah (son of Jona.) married Deborah Litchfield, and left children, Hannah 1747, Lucy 1750, Jonathan 1754, Charles 1756, Malachi 1757, Noah 1759, Luke 1760, Gamaliel 1761, Deborah 1763, Malachi 1765, Ensign 1768, Israel 1770.

James (son of James) married Elizabeth Cole 1739, and had children, Ruth born 1740, James 1745, Mary 1749, Amos 1755, Elizabeth 1757, Melzar 1759, Asa 1761.

Elisha (son of James) married Priscilla Holbrook 1741. Children, Priscilla born 1744, Elisha 1746, (died young), Henry 1748, (who removed to Kennebunk), and Capt. Consider, who died 1831, leaving sons Elisha, Benjamin, Consider, Henry and Francis.

Seth (son of James) married Mercy Stodder of Hingham, and left sons, the late Dea. Seth, Major Paul, Barnabas (died early), and Caleb. These have families in Scituate.

Noah (son of Obadiah) married Elizabeth Bryant 1786. His son Obadiah deceased at the South: and his son Noah, a gentleman of enterprise, resides at New Orleans. Noah, sen. deceased June 1, 1831.

FAMILY SKETCHES.

CAPT. GEORGE MORTON.

a descendant of Secretary Nathaniel Morton of Plymouth, was at Scituate harbour, and married Sarah, daughter of Timothy White, 1746. His children, George born 1747, Sarah 1753, John 1756, Eli 1758, Rebecca 1761. George deceased 1825, without children.

JOHN MITCHEL.

from Marshfield, married Lydia Hatch in Scituate, 1738, (of the Two miles). His children, John born 1739, William 1741, Job 1743. His descendants are in Marshfield.

GEORGE MOORE.

was in the family of Edward Doten, (or Dotey), of Plymouth, 1630. In 1637, he had a grant of land in Plymouth, west of Derby's pond. In 1633 to 1638, he kept the ferry at Jones's river, (Kingston), and had there a grant of thirty acres. In 1643, he bore arms in Scituate. In 1642, he had a large tract of land south-west of Stockbridge's mill pond. George Moore's swamp and brook and bridge are well-known land marks, even now. His house was on the road from the mill above named to George Moore's brook, on the north-east side, and near that brook. In 1664, it appears on the Town records that "George Moore having fell into a distracted condition, Major James Cudworth and Cornet Stetson obtained leave of the honored Corte to sell his lands and appropriate the proceeds to his support." George Moore died suddenly, 1677. Jury's verdict, "That George Moore came to his death by a fainting fit, or a sudden stoppinge of his breath." Rhodolphus Ellmes, foreman.

EBENEZER MOTT.

probably from Braintree, settled in the Conihassett, at Hatchet rock. He married Grace Vinal 1700. Children, Ebenezer born 1700, Grace 1702, John 1707, Mary 1712, Elizabeth 1716, Nathaniel 1720.

Of these sons, *John* left a family. Stephen, his son, and Stephen, jr. are now living. Lieut. Atwood Mott, a worthy man, (the father of the wives of Nehemiah Merritt, Nathaniel Vinal and Laban Rose), was also son of Ebenezer, jr. He married Hannah Hood 1758. Hannah (widow of Laban Rose) was wife of Gamaliel Merritt, 1782.

JOHN NEIL (from Ireland).

was in Scituate in 1730, or earlier. He established a pottery of considerable extent – first at the south side of Wild cat hill, and afterward on the north side of Studley hill, near the residence of late Charles Tolman. He had children, John, (baptized 1730), Jane 1732, Martha 1734, George 1738. This family removed to Maine.

JOSEPH NEAL.

came from Provincetown about 1700. His house was near the head of the cart way that leads to Hobart's landing: he purchased of Dea. James Torrey's heirs. The house of Joseph, sen. was probably on the west side of the road, opposite to the "Neal field," so called. His children were Joseph, John, Anne, Thomas, Seth, Lydia, Job, Abigail, born from 1705 to 1721.

Job only left a family on record here. He lived on the south of the Church hill. Children, John born 1744, Job 1746, Joseph, 1748, Sarah 1751, Job 1753, Lydia 1755, Abigail 1759, Lucy 1761. His wife was Sarah Barker.

JAMES NEWELL.

an African slave of Mary White, 1690. Mary White had a farm in the Conihassett, one mile west of Merritt's brook, and she had the singular fancy to marry her slave. Tradition speaks of him as a respectable man. Their children, Joshua, James, Hezekiah, and four daughters, born from 1691 to 1706. James, jr. married Abigail Nichols 1739, and left sons James, Levi, Joshua and Daniel, born from 1740 to 1752. They have descendants in Scituate.

JOSEPH NASH.

whom we suppose to have been a son of James Nash, an early settler in Weymouth, had a house and lands in Scituate, at Greenfield lane, 1670, which he purchased of Walter Hatch. He removed to Boston before 1678. His son Joseph was born in 1678, in Boston, and on coming of age settled in Scituate, at Stoney cove brook, (afterward the residence of Dr. Isaac Otis, and of his son, Dr. James Otis).

He married Hannah Curtis 1700, and his children were Joseph, jr. born 1701, John 1703, Hannah 1705, James 1708. Elizabeth 1709, David 1712, Mary 1713, (died early), Ephraim 1715, Mercy 1718, Simeon 1720, Elisha 1722, Mary 1724.

Joseph, jr. married Deborah Merritt 1730, and had children baptized, Deborah 1733, Delight 1734, Deborah 1737, Joseph 3d. 1739, Mary 1740.

John married Hannah Buck 1728, and had children, Priscilla born 1729, John, jr. 1731, Joseph, 4th. 1732, Noah 1734, Zaccheus 1736, Seth 1738, Thomas 1740, (who married Eunice, daughter of George Stetson, 1766).

James married Sarah Litchfield 1737. Children, Sarah born 1743, Mary 1746, James, jr. 1748, Elizabeth 1751, John 1755, Ruth 1758.

David married Penelope Merritt 1740, had a daughter Miriam born 1746.

Simeon married Lydia Church, 1740, and died in the French war, at Ticonderoga, 1759. His son Thomas is living in Scituate, and Samuel married Jerusha Briggs 1783, and removed to Worcester.

Joseph 3d. married Lucy Peaks 1767. Children, Lucy born 1770, Solon 1772, Tilon 1774, Nancy 1777.

Joseph, 4th. married Thankful Hammond 1755; he had a son James, who had William and others.

Noah married Elizabeth Cudworth 1756. His son is Mr. John Nash, near the south Meeting-house, whose children are Deborah C., John King, Esq. post master, Nathaniel Cushing of Boston, Henry, Eliza and Israel.

James, jr. married Hopestill Agry and Ruth Merritt. Children, Ruth, James, William Agry, Joshua, Sarah, Deborah, and David, born from 1777 to 1794.

Solon married Sarah Bailey 1793, his sons are Joseph, and Solon; the latter is a merchant in Boston.

N. B. – James of Weymouth was representative from 1655, several years. He had a son Jacob, who was representative 1689 and 90, and a son James, whose posterity is in Weymouth.

JOHN NICHOLSON.

married Elizabeth Mott 1750. His son John born 1752, removed to Boston: he had a sister Lydia born 1653.

THOMAS NICHOLS (shipwright).

had lands near Hobart's landing, on the south-west, 1645. He had a daughter Rebecca, who married Samuel House, jr. 1664: a son Israel, and also Ephraim, in Hingham, from whom those of Cohasset descended.

Thomas succeeded to his father's lands in Scituate, and married Sarah, the daughter of John Whiston, 1663. His children, Sarah born 1668, Rebecca 1670, Joseph 1673, Susanna 1676, Mary 1679, Bathsheba 1681, Israel 1683, Patience 1685, Elizabeth 1690. Of these sons, Israel probably removed.

Joseph married Bathsheba Pincin 1696, and lived near George Moore's bridge. His sons, were Joseph, Thomas, Noah, (who died, all three in the French war), and Israel, Amos, Caleb and Job, from 1696 to 1716. Of these last, Israel resided at the paternal spot, near Hobart's landing. His sons were Caleb, Noah, Israel, Samuel and Thomas, (which last three died in the Revolutionary war), born from 1737 to 1755.

Caleb left a family: his son Caleb was killed by a fall from his house, south-east of White-oak plain, 1828, and whose three sons, Caleb, Henry and Reuben, were unfortunately shipwrecked and lost at Cape Cod, with Capt. Seth Gardiner, in the Cyrus, August 1830.

Noah (also son of Israel), left a family, Nabby, Betsey, (wife of Charles Jones), Cynthia, and Lucy, (wife of Christopher Cushing, Esq, 1818, and of Judge Wood of Middleboro, 1827).

JOHN NORTHY.

came from Marblehead, 1675, when he married Sarah, the daughter of Henry Ewell. He purchased lands of Thomas Ingham, north Walnut tree hill, and his house in 1680, was where the house of Joseph Northy, his descendant, now stands: Joseph is descended from the primitive John, through James born 1687, James born 1719, and Capt. Joseph Horn 1744.

James, born 1687, had also a son Eliphalet, who settled east of Valley swamp, and whose sons Robert and Abraham are living in Scituate, and Eliphalet at Concord, N.H., who married Abigail Stodder of Scituate, 1785.

THOMAS OLDHAM.

was a householder in Scituate 1650. His house was probably near King's landing. He married Mary, daughter of Rev. Mr. Witherell, 1656. His children, Mary, Thomas, Sarah, Hannah, Grace, Isaac, Ruth, Elizabeth, Lydia, born from 1658 to 1679. He died 1711. Thomas, his son, administrator.

Thomas, jr. married Mercy, daughter of Robert Sprout, 1683, and removed to the Two mile. His descendants are in Pembroke. Mercy, his daughter, married Andrew Newcome of Eastham, 1708, and Desire married Samuel Tilden 1717. He had a son Joshua (1684) and Mary, twins.

EMERSON ORCUTT.

from Abington, settled in Scituate, and married Ann Mansel, 1736. His children, Emerson, Elijah, Hannah, Seth. Seth married Sarah Collamore: she is now living.*

ROBERT OSGOOD.

was in Scituate 1690, and resided in the Conihassett. He married Sarah, daughter of Anthony Dodson. He left one son on record, David born 1700.

JOHN OTIS (early written Oates).

was born in Barnstable, Devonshire, England, 1620. He came to Hingham, with his father's family, 1635, when John, sen. had a house lot assigned him in the first division of lands in that town. The family residence was at Otis hill, south west of the harbour. John, sen. lost his wife Margaret, June 1653. He then removed to Weymouth, and married again, but the name of his second wife does not appear. Hobart's journal records his death "at Weymouth, May 31, 1657," aged seventy-six. His will is dated at Weymouth, the day previous to his

---

* There was William Orcut in Scituate, probably grandfather Emerson, whose children were John 1669, Martha 1671, Joseph 1672, Mary and Hannah 1674, Thomas 1675, Benjamin 1679, Elizabeth 1682, and Deborah 1683.

death, and gives legacies "To daughter Margaret Burton, (she was wife of Thomas B.* of Hingham), to daughter Hannah, (wife of Thomas Gile), and to her two children, Mary and Thomas. To daughters Ann and Alice (Otis), to wife 40S, son John executor." He had also a son Richard, who went early to New, Hampshire, was captured by the Indians, and carried to Canada: but who lived to return to New Hampshire, and it is said has posterity living. His will is in Boston Probate records, made before he left Weymouth.

John, whose posterity is very numerous, married Mary, daughter of Nicholas Jacob of Hingham, 1653. In 1661, he settled in Scituate, on the south of Colman's hills. In 1678, he went to Barnstable, and took up "the Otis farm," near Hinckley Lane. He left at Barnstable his eldest son John, and returned and deceased in Scituate 1683. His monument is in, "the old burying ground in Meeting-house lane": it is broken and defaced, but legible at this time. His children were John born 1657, a daughter 1660, (not named, but mentioned in Hobart's journal), Stephen 1661, James 1663, (died in Phipps's Canada expedition, 1690), Joseph 1665, Job 1667. The eldest daughter was Mary, he had also Hannah and Elizabeth. In his will, dated at Scituate, 1683, he gives "To eldest daughter Mary, (wife of John Gowin), and daughters Hannah and Elizabeth 50£ each. Houses and lands at Hingham and Barnstable, to John, Stephen, James and Job. To Joseph house and lands in Scituate, after his mother's decease."

As many of this family are acquainted with the, genealogy subsequent to the first two generations, we here only remark, that John, (third generation), in Barnstable, was the ancestor of the distinguished lawyers and patriots of the name of Otis in Barnstable and Boston, to whose fame, no commendation of ours can add. Capt. Stephen was the father of Dr. Isaac, the first regular bred physician who settled in Scituate, and to whom the Town "Voted a settlement of 100£ to encourage him to remain in the Town," in 1719. He is remembered by some of our aged people as a gentleman of uncommon accomplishments of person and of mind. His sons, Dr. Isaac settled in Bridgewater, and Dr. James in Scituate, who was the father of Dr. Cushing Otis of Scituate.†

---

* He signed the petition of Hingham people, with Dr. Child, (see Vassall).

† Dr. James Otis married Lucy Cushing of Falmouth, Cape Elizabeth, 1762. Children, Lucy, (wife of Thomas Barker Briggs), James, of Lyme,

Joseph, Esq. (son of John, 2d.) went to New London with his family, and has numerous descendants in Vermont, Connecticut, New York and the western States.

Job settled in Scituate, and has many descendants.

We add, that Capt. Stephen Otis was also the ancestor of Ensign Otis, at the Harbour, (see Thomas Ensign), and of Dr. Ephraim, of the west part of Scituate.

Capt. Stephen Otis's will, dated 1729, gives "To son Ensign the homestead, with all the upland and meadow on each side of the way, with the Tan house and Tan vats – to John, Hannah, Mary, Isaac, Stephen, Joseph, Joshua, out lands, &c."

WILLIAM PALMER, JR.

had lands in Scituate 1633. He came with his father, William of Plymouth, in the ship Fortune, 1621. William, jr, married Elizabeth Hodgkins of Plymouth 1633. He had a house between the road and Stedman's mill pond, (since Stockbridge's) 1645. This family has no descendants left in the Town. His son Thomas succeeded him – was living in 1680 – but left no family on record.

JOHN PALMER.

who settled in the south part of the Town, we believe to be the same who came with the first settlers of Hingham, 1635, and who was a freeman in Massachusetts 1638. He was freeman in Plymouth Colony 1657, and at the same time his two sons John and Elnathan. His house lot was near the junction of the roads, south-east of the Church hill, near the third Herring brook. "John Palmer's log bridge," so called, was built by him, 1660, over the third Herring brook, one fourth mile south of his house. Besides the sons above named, he had Josiah. Elnathan left no family here. He had a son Bezaleel, also, who left no family.

John, jr. had children, Elnathan born 1666, John 1667, (who married Mary Rose 1696), Hannah 1671, Elizabeth 1673, Bezaleel 1675, Experience 1679, Samuel 1683.

New Hampshire, Hannah, (late wife of Rev. Nehemiah Thomas), Hon. Cushing, of Scituate, Elizabeth, Abigail, (wife of late Capt. Seth Foster), and Thomas Esq. of New York, born from 1763 to 1776.

Josiah (son of John, sen.) had Josiah born 1685, Joshua 1687, Ruth, (wife of Jacob Bailey 1716).

Elnathan (son of John, jr.) married Mary, daughter of Thomas Clark, 1695. Children, Thomas born 1696, Sarah 1698, Ezekiel 1701, Deborah 1710.

Samuel (son of John, jr.) married Ann Clark 1709.

Bezaleel (son of John jr.) married Elizabeth, daughter of William Perry, 1705, (left Bezaleel, born 1706), who was killed by a fall in the ship-yard near the mouth of the second Herring brook, leaving children, Capt. Benjamin and others. The widow of Bezaleel, sen, married Benjamin Tolman.

WILLIAM PARKER.

was a freeman 1640. He had sixty acres of land north of Edward Foster's North river lot. His house stood in Parker lane, west of the small brook. In 1639, he married Mary, the daughter of Thomas Rawlins: and again 1651, Mary, the daughter of Humphry Turner. His children, Mary born 1639, William 1643, Patience 1648, Miles 1655, Joseph 1658, Nathaniel 1661. This family has spread wide in the country. Some descendants are in Boston.

Joseph remained in Scituate: his children, Alice, Mary, Joseph, Judith, Miles, from 1684 to 1702. His son Joseph was the last who lived on the paternal spot, save his only daughter Ruth, born 1711, who lived to a great age, and is remembered as the last of the family.

William, jr. had sons, (his wife Mary Clark 1693), Alexander, Joshua and Elisha, but they all removed.

Nathaniel died in Phipps's Canada expedition, 1690. His brother Miles was then living in Scituate.

William Parker died 1684. His will gives "To Joseph 10 acres near the land formerly John Bonpasse's, and 3 acres near where the Sweede's old house stood. To daughter Patience Randall – to grandchild Stephen Totman – wife Mary the homestead during her life, then to be divided between Miles, Nathaniel, William, Lydia, Mary, Judith."

THOMAS PARRIS.

From undoubted documents, (now in possession of Rev. Martin Parris of Marshfield), we learn that this gentleman was son of Thomas Parris, who came to Long Island, 1683, from London, from whence he removed to Newbury, 1685, and to Pembroke, Massachusetts, 1697; which latter was son of John Parris, a dissenting minister of Ugborough, near Plymouth, England; – whose father was Thomas, a merchant of London. The last named Thomas had a brother John, a merchant and planter of great wealth, who deceased in Barbadoes, 1660, who may have been the Mr. Parish mentioned in Winthrop's journal, Anno 1642. His original will is in possession of Rev, Martin Parris.

Thomas Parris, at the head of this article, (born May 8, 1701, at Pembroke), married Hannah Gannett of Scituate, 1724, daughter of Matthew Gannett. His son Thomas was born 1725. He had also other sons, born afterwards at Pembroke, Elkanah, Benjamin and Matthew. Thomas removed to Bridgewater, left a son Benjamin, who died without sons. Elkanah married Grace Mott of Scituate, 1761, and has a large family at Williamstown. Benjamin married Millescent Keith of Easton, 1753. Of his numerous family we name Samuel, born 1755, who married Sarah Pratt of Middleboro, is now Judge Parris of Hebron, Maine, and father of Albion Keith Parris, late Governor of Maine. Matthew (son of Benjamin) born 1757, married Mercy Thompson of Halifax, Mass. 1780, and was the father of Alexander Parris, Esq. of Boston, the distinguished architect.

Daniel (son of Benjamin) has a family in Halifax.

Martin, (son of Benjamin), a Congregational minister in Marshfield, married Julia Drew of Kingston, 1795. His son Samuel, of Brown University 1824, had commenced the practice of medicine in Attleboro, 1827, and deceased same year, greatly lamented.

Elkanah, above named, is called in our records in 1670, of Canaan, Connecticut.

WILLIAM PEAKS.

bore arms in Scituate 1643. He purchased lands of "goody Woodfield," widow of John. His house was at Hoop-pole neck, on the east of the "stepping stones" way, where his descendant Eleazer now lives. He married Judith, widow of Lawrence Litchfield, 1650, (she had been also wife of John Allen, sen.) Children, Israel born 1655, Eleazer 1657, William 1662.

Israel had a son Israel born 1687. William had three sons, Philip and Israel, (whose son was Eleazer, born 1736), and

William, (whose son was William, born 1719). William, sen. deceased 1686. His will, dated 1683, gives "to sons Israel and Eleazer lands at Hoop-pole neck – To son William lands at Showamet - to daughter-in-law Dependance Litchfield 30£, to two grandchildren, Experience and Remember Luce 5£ each – wife Judith, &c." William, jr. deceased 1717. His will gives "to wife Jean – sons Eleazer and Israel – to daughter Thankful Daman, and daughters Hannah, Judith, Sarah, Penelope, Susanna."

THOMAS PERRY (from Massachusetts).

was in Scituate before 1647. His farm was on the south part of Chamberlain plain; and perhaps his house where Gershom Ewell's now stands, He married Sarah, daughter of Isaac Stedman. There is no record of his children; but we find incidentally noticed, Thomas, William, Henry, Joseph and John.

Thomas married Susanna, daughter of John Whiston, 1671. He succeeded to Theophilus Witherell's residence by purchase, west of Dead swamp, (now Lot Litchfield's). His children, Thomas, James, John, David.

William married Elizabeth Lobdell, 1681, and settled east of the Church hill: his house stood in what is now Howland's field: he had twelve children, one of whom was Amos, who lived near Cornet's dam, where Samuel Tolman, sen. resides, and Elizabeth, his daughter, was the wife of Bezaleel Palmer, and secondly of Capt. Benjamin Tolman, and was the grandmother of the respectable family of Copeland. There are descendants in Hanover. William Perry also was owner of a half share in Conihassett, with William Holmes, in 1646. He left no family on record.

THOMAS PERKINS.

from Plympton, son of John, and grandson of Luke Perkins, is proprietor of the ancient place of William Holmes. He married Phebe, daughter of Col. James Curtis, 1828, and has a family.

JOHN PHILIPS.

an early settler in Duxbury, had several children, born probably in England. He married a second wife, as appears from the following extract from the Colony Records, viz. "a marriage contract between John Philips of Marshfield, and Faith Doten of Plymouth, 1667. *Imprimis,* that the children of both parties shall remain at the disposal of their owne natural parents. 2d. that the s^d Faith Doten is to enjoy all her house and land, goods and chattels, and to dispose of them at her own free will. 3d. that in case, by death, God shall remove the s^d John Philips before her, and she be left a widow, she shall have and enjoy one third part, or one part of three, of all his estate that he dieth possessed of, for her livelihood during her life – the other two thirds to return to the heirs of the s^d John Philips." He deceased 1677: Faith, his widow, administered; and property was assigned in division, to his daughters Desire Sherman, Elizabeth Rouse and Mary Doten.

He had a son John, jr. who married Grace Holloway 1654, and whose children, Hannah and Grace born 1654, Joseph 1656, Benjamin 1658, were baptized in Scituate second Church. We believe he had a son John, 3d. by a former wife, who married Ann Torrey 1677. The death of John, jr. was as follows:

Verdict.

"July 31, 1656,

"Wee finde that, this present day, John Philips, jr. came into his dwelling house, lately known or called Mr. Buckley's house, in good health, as good wife Williamson affirmeth, and satt upon a stoole by the chimney, and by an immediate hand of God, manifested in thunder and lightning, the s^d John came by his death," Colony Records.

His descendants are in Marshfield.

Benjamin married Sarah Thomas 1681, and had children, John born 1682, Joseph 1685, Benjamin 1687, Thomas 1691, Jeremiah 1697, Isaac 1702. Of these, John remained in Marshfield, married Patience Stevens 1710, and had sons, Nathaniel 1713, and others. Benjamin also had a son Benjamin, born 1719.

We believe Jeremiah Philips, who deceased in Marshfield, 1666, was a son of John, sen. We have seen no notices of a family. We think it also probable that Thomas Philips of Yarmouth, in 1657, and James of Taunton, 1658, were sons of John, sen.

JONAS PICKELS.

was in Scituate 1650. He had lands laid out north of George Moore's swamp. His house stood on the west side of the way, half a mile south of the present Town-house. He married Alice Hatch, (daughter of Elder William), 1657. His children, Mary born 1660, Nathan 1661, Lydia 1662, Jonas 1663.

Nathan succeeded his father. He married Miriam Turner 1687. Children, Mercy born 1688, Alice 1691, Nathan 1693, David 1695, Nathan 1699. Nathan succeeded his father: married Margaret Stetson 1731: and having no family, left his estate to the three sons of his sister, Mercy, wife of Dea. Joseph Cushing, viz. Judge Nathan Cushing, Pickels Cushing, and Hawkes Cushing, (which latter was the father of the late valuable and lamented Dea. Thomas Cushing and others).

EBENEZER PIERPONT.

from Roxbury, married Sarah, daughter of Judge John Cushing, 1750. His children, Nathaniel born 1751, Joseph 1754. Ebenezer Pierpont deceased 1755. His widow married again, Mr. Leonard, at Suffield, Connecticut, and removed with her sons, the elder of whom settled in Connecticut, and the younger at Roxbury. This family descended from John Pierpont, of Roxbury, by whose will, dated 1682, we perceive that he divided a large estate of lands, mills, malt house, guns and swords, &c. to sons John, James, Ebenezer, Joseph and Benjamin. John of Roxbury was son of James, one of the first settlers of Ipswich. He had another son, Robert, who also removed to Roxbury.

GEORGE PIDCOKE.

a householder before 1640, married Sarah Richards that year. There is no record of a family. He was living in 1670.

THOMAS PINCIN (or Pinson).

took the oath of fidelity in Scituate, 1638, and, had lands in 1636, "at the end of the hill, by the swamp, south of Satuit brook." This was opposite Buck's corner – late Anthony Waterman's. He married Jane, daughter of Richard Standlake, 1639. His children, Thomas born 1640, Hannah 1642, (wife of George Young 1661), John 1655, Joshua 1658. Waitstill 1650. Some of this family probably removed.

Thomas, jr. married Elizabeth White 1662, and Sarah Turner. Children, Thomas born 1662, Ebenezer 1668, and perhaps others. This family lived at Pincin hill.

Thomas, 3d. married Sarah White 1693, and no further race appears: it is probable he went to Bridgewater.

Ebenezer married Deborah — 1701. Children, Thankful 1702, Mary 1704, Thomas 1707, Ebenezer 1711, of the latter we can discover no traces here. This family lived in Parker Lane.

Thomas (last named) married Agatha Hammond 1735. Children, Thomas and Betsy born 1736, Mary 1738, Deborah 1741, Judith 1743, Simeon 1747.

Thomas married Ann Taylor 1755. Children, Elizabeth born 1756, William 1757, Benjamin 1760.

Simeon married Sarah Cole 1776. His sons Simeon, Perez and Elias are living in Scituate.

William married Elizabeth Beal of Hingham 1777.

John Pincin, who descended from some early branch of this family, was of Chesterfield 1788. He married widow Joanna Curtis of Scituate, Abner Pincin married Hannah Cowen 1770,

CAPT. MICHAEL PIERCE.

had been a resident at Hingham or Weymouth, before he came into Scituate. He purchased lands in the Conihassett, 1647. His house was on the Cohasset road, one mile from the present north Meeting house, at the well known place where Elijah Pierce now resides, of the sixth generation that has possessed it.

There is no record of Capt. Pierce's family here. Hobart's journal records, "Persis, daughter of Michael Pierce, baptized 1646," also "Michael Pierce's daughter born 1662, and Michael Pierce's wife died 1662." His first child may have been born at Hingham. Persis married Richard Garrett, 3d. 1695. Abigail married Samuel Holbrook 1682. He had a son Ephraim, who died early or removed.

Benjamin married Martha, daughter of James Adams, 1678, and succeeded to his father's residence. His children, Martha, Jerusha, Benjamin, Ebenezer, Persis, Caleb, Thomas, Adams, Jeremiah, Elisha, born from 1679 to 1699.

John (also son of Capt. Michael) settled north of the Conihassett burying ground. He married Patience, daughter of Anthony Dodson, 1683: his children, Michael, John, Jonathan, Ruth, Jael, David, Clothier, born from 1684 to 1698.

Hayward Pierce, Esq. late of Scituate, descended from Capt. Michael, through Benjamin, (who married Martha Adams), Benjamin, (who married Mary Cowen and Elizabeth Perry), Benjamin, who married Charity Howard and Jane Howard of Bridgewater, 1742 and 1750, daughters of Thomas. The sons of Hayward, Esq. are Hayward of New Orleans, Waldo and Bailey of Frankfort, (Maine), Elijah of Scituate, (on the paternal residence), Silas of Boston, – and his daughters, the wives of Mr. Lincoln of Cohasset, Mr. Nathaniel Cushing, and Mr. Walter Foster of Scituate. Benjamin and Jonathan, brothers of Hayward, Esq. removed to Chesterfield.

Capt. Michael has left evidence on record, in the Town, of his usefulness in publick affairs. But his memory is to be forever honored for the brave manner in which he fell in defence of his country. (See Military affairs).

He was in the Narragansett fight in December 1675, and escaped with his life, but to fall in a more terrible conflict in March following. His will is dated 1675; and the preamble is in these impressive words: "Being, by the appointment of God, going out to war against the Indians, I do ordain this my last will and Testament: and first I commit my ways to the Eternal God, &c." He then gives "to wife Ann [she was a second wife] the house which I last built, &c. To son Benjamin my present dwelling house – To son John all my lands in Hingham – to son Ephraim 5£ – to daughter Abigail Holbrook 5£ – to daughters Elizabeth, Deborah, Ann, Abiah, Ruth, Persis, 50£ each."

NEHEMIAH PORTER.

was in Scituate 1756. He was from Weymouth, probably. His residence was a half mile west of the south Meeting-house, now called "the Porter place." His sons were Nehemiah, Sylvanus and Benjamin. They all removed.

Capt. Edward J. Porter, sail maker, of Scituate harbour, is of another family, and came from Marshfield.

JONATHAN PRATT.

and his father, Samuel Pratt, were in Scituate 1676, and were probably of the Plymouth family. Samuel was one of the brave men who fell in the Rehoboth battle, 1676.

FAMILY SKETCHES.

Jonathan married Margaret Locke 1691. His sons Jonathan and Othniel, and five daughters, born previous to 1708.

The residence of this family was on the Plymouth road, now in Hanover, and one mile west of the Four Corners. Aaron Pratt of little Hingham, now Cohasset, was another son of Samuel.

ABRAHAM PREBLE.

was amongst the men of Kent, in Scituate 1636. He married Judith, the daughter of Elder Nathaniel Tilden. His son Nathaniel was born in Scituate, and baptized in Scituate second Church, 1648: soon after which he removed to Georgiana or York. Abraham Preble, Esq. a representative from York, 1719, was his grandson: and the gallant Commodore Preble was of the same family.

THOMAS PRINCE.

The first of this family who came to this country, settled at Nantasket in 1638. His name was John. He was the son of Rev. John Prince, rector of East Strafford, in Berkshire, Eng. born 1610. He had been three years at Oxford University, but he did not engage in the ministry. He was chosen the first ruling elder at Hull in 1644. He died at Hull, August 6, 1676, aged sixty-six. His children were John born 1638, Elizabeth 1640, Joseph 1642, Martha 1645, Job, 1647, Mary 1648, Samuel 1650, Sarah 1651, died early, Benjamin 1652, Isaac 1654, Deborah 1656, wife of William King, (of Salem probably), 1678, and Thomas 1658. Of these sons,

John remained in Hull, and deceased 1690.

Joseph married Elizabeth Morton of Plymouth, 1670.

Samuel, Esq. of Rochester and Middleboro, married a daughter of Gov. Thomas Hinckley, (a second wife), and by her was the father of Rev. Thomas Prince born 1687, graduated at Harvard College 1707, minister in Boston, and author of that most accurate work, Prince's Chronology. (Eliot's Biography).

Isaac married Mary, daughter of John Turner, sen. of Scituate, 1683.

Thomas married Ruth, daughter of John Turner, sen. of Scituate, 1685. We have placed his name at the head of this article, because he resided several years in Scituate, where his children were born, viz. Thomas born July 10, 1686, Benjamin, 1693, Job 1695.

It is conjectured that Gov. Thomas Prince of Plymouth Colony, was a relative of John of Hull.

THOMAS PRYOR.

came from London with Rev. John Lothrop, and was one of the Church in Scituate, 1634. He had lands on the east of Hickes's swamp, and probably his house was there. He deceased in 1639: he had a son John, in Duxbury or Plymouth. *Daniel* purchased Thomas Rose's house in the Two wide, 1664. There are no children on record. Thomas Pryor's will (1639) gives "to my son Samuel and Thomas in England 12d each – to Samuel 5£ if he come to this country. To son Joseph 5£. To daughters Elizabeth and Mary 6£ each; to John and Daniel the rest of the lands equally: To the Pastor (Mr. Lothrop) 10S."

RICHARD PROUTY.

was in Scituate 1670. His farm was north-east of Hoop-pole hill. His house was near the causeway over the swamp, called Prouty's dam, 1680. His first son was Edward, and had a house at Margaret's brook, on the west. His children were nine, (his wife Elizabeth Howe) sons James, John, Richard, Edward, Elisha, born from 1711 to 1732.

Isaac (son of Richard) married Elizabeth Merritt – sons David, John, Caleb, Adam, Job, James, Isaac, born from 1716 to 1732. Margaret Prouty, who gave the name to the brook, was an unmarried daughter of the elder Richard, and who lived to a great age, and though single, had a son Nehemiah born 1724.

Of the above sons of Edward, Jacob, David, John, Adam, James and Isaac, removed together to the town of Spencer, where they have respectable descendants. In Scituate and Hanover remain descendants of Caleb, and of William, another son of Richard, sen.

SAMUEL RAMSDELL.

was in that part of Scituate, afterward Hanover, 1711, when he married Martha Bowker of Scituate. He has descendants in Hanover, and in Weston,

JOHN RANCE.

was one of the purchasers of a scite for a Quaker Meetinghouse, 1678. (See notes on Society of Friends). We believe he removed to Barbadoes, and there deceased. His widow was in Scituate in 1697.

WILLIAM RANDALL.

came into Scituate before 1640. His farm was on the brook that falls into Till's or Dwelley's creek: His house was in the valley, twenty rods north of the brook on the west side of the way, where stands the mansion of Elisha Foster, sen. late deceased. There is no record of his marriage here: he probably married at Rhode Island, where we find some traces of him as early as 1636; or in Marshfield, where he seems to have been 1637. He was an enterprising and useful man in many respects; but unfortunately for himself, appears to have been litigious. There are several disputes on the Colony records, which he prosecuted with his neighbors about bounds of lands, and when the causes were decided against him, he seems not to have submitted very quietly. He was fined 1660, "for striking Edward Wanton," in one of these disputes: and in 1664, "for breaking the King's peace by poakeing Jeremiah Hatch with a ho-pole, was fined 3S. 4d." Colony Records. He, with his wife, were of the party that gained much strength from 1650 to 1670, which held it unlawful to pay religious teachers. His goods were occasionally taken by the constable. On one of these occasions, "1654 William Randall's wife fined for abusing the Constable, Walter Hatch." Colony Records. After these troubles, they both settled down to quiet members of Mr. Witherell's church. Their children were Sarah, born 1640, Joseph 1642, Hannah 1644, William 1647, John 1650, Elizabeth 1652, Job 1654, Benjamin 1656, Isaac 1658.

Joseph married Hannah Macomber 1673. He succeeded to his father's residence: his children Elizabeth and Ursula born 1673, Joseph 1675, Hannah 1677, Sarah 1680, Margaret 1683, Mercy 1684, Benjamin 1688.

Job, (shipwright, and a very respectable and useful man) settled one fourth mile south of the Herring brook hill, (now David Torrey's): his children, Mary born 1680, Job 1683, (who settled in the Two mile at Job's landing) James 1685, Nehemiah 1688, Lydia 1690, Samuel 1694. From this family the Randalls (Samuel &c.) in the west part of the Town are descended.

Isaac had a house a few rods east of his father's, (now Elisha Foster, jr.) he lived to the age of 102 – had two wives, Susanna Barstow 1684, and Deborah Buck 1692. His children, Isaac, Susanna, Jacob, Deborah, Robert, Ruth, Gideon, Rachel, Caleb, Elisha, Mary, Abigail, Grace, Peres, born from 1685 to 1716. These families had large tracts of land at Wild cat hill.

The first family residence was inherited by Benjamin, son of Joseph. He was father of Paul and Daniel, who removed to Harpswell, and of William and Ezra, who removed to Topsham, Maine, also of Capt. Benjamin, who built the house in which Seth Turner deceased 1830, one fourth mile south west of the south Meeting house.

THOMAS RAWLINS.

came from Weymouth before 1646, in which year he was one of the Conihassett partners in Scituate. He had left Weymouth with Richard Sylvester, (see Sylvester.) He purchased Anthony Annable's N. River lot 1642, and built his house where Deacon Thomas, and Deacon George King afterward resided, (now Col. Curtis's.) He had a son Joshua, (says Farmer) but he probably died early. *Thomas,* his son lived in Boston, had children, Caleb born 1645, Mary 1652, Samuel 1653: he married a second wife, widow Sarah Murdock of Roxbury, 1656. Mary, daughter of Thomas, sen. married William Parker of Scituate 1639, and left numerous descendants: and Joanna married Ephraim Kempton 1645.

Nathaniel succeeded to his father's residence 1650. He married Lydia, daughter of Richard Sylvester 1652, (she married Edward Wright 1664,) the children of Nathaniel, Elizabeth born 1653, Ruth 1655, Patience 1658, Nathaniel 1659, Elizabeth born 1661, (wife of James Torrey, jr. 1679.) Nathaniel, sen. died 1662. Thomas, sen. died in Boston, 1650, and gives in his will, "to wife Sarah, and to son Thomas a house in Boston, if he live there with his mother. To son Nathaniel, my farm in Scituate. To son in law William Parker of Scituate, &c." The descendants now write the name Rollin.

WILLIAM RICHARDS.

came into Scituate (probably from Plymouth) 1636. In 1639 he had a farm north of Cornet Stetson's, (divided by a ravine). Part of this farm was afterward that of Thomas Brooks, and now Ruggles. In 1650 he sold his farm to Gowin White for 75£ and removed to Weymouth. There is no record of a family here. In Weymouth, his son James was born 1658 and Benjamin 1660. His descendants are in Weymouth and elsewhere. There was an Edward Richards of Dedham 1639, from whom many have descended.

William died at Weymouth 1680: his Will gives "to wife Grace – to oldest son James, and sons Benjamin, John, William and Joseph."

JOHN ROGERS.

came into Scituate with Rev. Mr. Witherell 1644, and from hence we conjecture that he was a descendant of the Martyr of Smithfield, (see Witherell). Family tradition also asserts the same. He married Ann Churchman at Weymouth 1639 – where his daughter Lydia was born 1642. He died in Weymouth 1661. His farm in Scituate was a half mile south of Stockbridge's mill (now James Briggs's, alias Clerk Briggs's).

John his son, lived for a time at the place of Rawlins, (see Rawlins), and afterward succeeded his father. He married Rhoda, daughter of Elder Thomas King 1656. They were married by Gov. Endicott of Mass. there being no magistrate in Scituate authorized to solemnize marriages at that time. Rogers became a Quaker in 1660. His children were John, Abigail, (who married Timothy White 1678), Mary who married John Roues 1659, Elizabeth, who married Joseph White 1660, and Hannah, who married Samuel Pratt, (of Weymouth), 1660.

John 3d. had children, Alice, Daniel, Elizabeth, Thomas, Hannah, Joshua, Mary, Caleb, born from 1682 to 1718. This family is numerous in Marshfield. The primitive John at the head of this article had two other sons, Thomas and Samuel, who settled at the Rogers Brook in Marshfield. From Thomas descended the late Joseph, and Stephen his son, now living.

ISAAC ROBINSON.

was the son of the venerable John Robinson, the Puritan founder. He was freeman in Scituate 1636. His house lot was on the south east of Colman's hills, near the first Herring brook and opposite to "Schewsan's Neck." This house and land he sold to John Twisden 1639, and removed to Barnstable. He was a highly respectable man: an Assistant in the government: but having fallen under the displeasure of "the stern Thomas Prince, Gov." 1659, on account of his opposition to the laws against the Quakers, he was disfranchised: but he lived to be restored under Gov. Josiah Winslow 1673. His wife was Faunce, sister of Elder Faunce of Plymouth. He probably married after leaving Scituate. His son Isaac, who received a legacy in Mr. Hatherly's Will 1668, was unfortunately drowned at Barnstable 1668, (Verdict) "in going into a pond to fetch two geese, the pond beinge full of weedy grasse," (Col. Rec). Isaac, sen. lived 93 years. He had a brother John, who settled at Cape Ann, and whose son Abraham, the first born child in Mass. lived to the age of 102. (Farmer). John (with Francis Crooker) purchased lands in Scituate 1640, but did not remove hither.

DEA. THOMAS ROBINSON.

was in Scituate before 1643, at which date he purchased the house of Gen. Cudworth on the south of Colman's hills, which was sold to John Otis 1661. But Dea. Robinson's mansion was very near to the 2d. Society's first Meeting-house on the east side of the road. He married widow Mary Woodey at Boston 1652. (called of Scituate in the Record at Boston). His children, Thomas born 1652, Joseph 1656, Mary 1657, Mercy 1659. His sons removed. Dea. Thomas was unfortunately killed 1676. Verdict "killed by the fall of a tree." That he was brother of Isaac, we have not ascertained: It is more probable that he came through Dorchester, and was brother of William, and early settled there.

THOMAS ROSE.

was in the Two mile 1660. He had also a brother John in Marshfield, "who died 1676, gunning on the beach, (Verdict) perished by the severity of the weather." He had also a son

John, who was one of the slain in Rehoboth battle 1676. Thomas Rose married a 2d. wife, Alice, widow of Jonas Pickels 1666, and removed to Scituate proper, (see Pickels). At which time, we see on record a Covenant with the heirs of Jonas Pickels, "that if God give him children, he will give his estate equally to those children and to the children of Jonas Pickels." He had a son. Thomas,* who lived near him, fifty rods south west, on the same side of the way. He had a son Gideon born 1702, (who married Lydia Turner 1723), whose son Gideon lived near the north end of Jordan lane, where Laban, his son, deceased 1816. Thomas, sen. had a son Gideon, whose sons

Jabez left a son Jabez, born 1707.

Jeremiah married Elizabeth, daughter of Capt. Anthony Collamore, 1698: and deceased 1699, leaving one son Thomas, whose posterity are in Hanover. Elizabeth the widow, married Timothy Symmes.

ANSON ROBBINS, Esq.

Nathaniel Robbins, of Marshfield, married Hannah, the daughter of Samuel Witherell, and grand-daughter of Rev. William Witherell, and deceased in middle life, leaving 4 sons.

Joseph, of Hebron, Maine, who married the daughter of James Cushing, of Scituate.

Timothy, of Hanover, who married Mary Tilden 1770, and whose son Timothy married Hannah, the daughter of Jesse Wright of Scituate 1813.

Capt. Thomas, a ship master, who was drowned at Cohasset 1790. He married Sylvina Caswell, and left sons Walter of Machias, and Anson, Esq. of Scituate, a useful man in public business. The latter married Rachel, the daughter of Thomas Sylvester, and his children are George Anson, Walter, Matilda, Clarissa, Horace, Charles (died 1830, aged 14) and Rachel.

Luther, Esq. Postmaster of Greene in Maine.

There was a William Robbins of Hingham, who married Susanna, the daughter of George Lane 1665, and whose son Thomas was born 1665. William may have been the son of Richard Robbins, an early settler in Cambridge, for he removed from Hingham to Cambridge, and from thence to Boston, where he died 1693. Nathaniel of Marshfield may have been his grandson.

---

* Thomas of the 3d generation removed to Dighton.

JOHN ROWSE, or Rouse.

was the unfortunate man who was so severely dealt with for being a Quaker, (See our notes on the Society of Friends). He was resident in Marshfield, as early as 1640, and had lands at "Cares well creek." His sons John and George were born in Marshfield 1643 and 1648. There are descendants in Bristol and Norfolk counties.

CAPT. MOSES RICH.

mariner, from Barnstable County, settled near Buck's corner, in front of the old Parsonage. His first wife was Parker from the southward – his 2d wife, Thankful H. Jones, 1825. He has children, Moses and others.

JOHN RUGGLES.

a descendant from Thomas Ruggles of Roxbury, freeman 1632. John, son of Thomas, married – Craft 1639, and died 1658, leaving "house and land near Roxbury Meeting-house, on the hill," to wife and children. His son John was often a Representative from Roxbury, and first in 1658. John, his son, was born 1661: and John, his son, came to Scituate 1719. He purchased lands of John Barstow's heirs, midway between Herring brook hill, or the south Meeting-house and Jordan lane. His house was twenty rods south of the present road. He married Joanna, daughter of Thomas Brooks 1720: his children, Thomas 1721, Hannah 1723, Sarah 1731, John 1729, Grace 1725; of these Dea. John, a man remarkable for purity of character, lived to 1813. He inherited the farm of Thomas Brooks, his maternal uncle; (Thomas Brooks, having left no children) where Thomas Ruggles his son deceased 1830.

GEORGE RUSSELL.

previously in Hingham, purchased the house, land and saw-mill of Isaac Stedman (now Stockbridge's mill) 1646. The house stood ten rods south of the dam. He probably deceased in

FAMILY SKETCHES.

Hingham. George and Samuel his sons were in Scituate. George deceased 1675; he had been the ward of Capt. Cudworth 1668, whence we conclude that his father had deceased before the latter date. George, jr. left one son, who removed probably to Pembroke or Duxbury, as we notice "1683 George Russell of Namattakesett fined for not attending public worship," Colony Records.

Samuel (above named) was one of the victims of the Rehoboth battle 1676. The estate was then sold to David Jacob. (see Cornelius Briggs). George, sen. married a widow James of Hingham 1640, (Hobart's Journal) and had by this 2d. wife, Mary 1641, Elizabeth 1643, Martha 1645. He sold his half of the grist-mill to *Charles Stockbridge* 1665: the deed is signed by George Russell, and Jane, his wife.

JOHN SAFFIN, (Lawyer.)

The first notice that we have discovered of this distinguished man, is, that he was a Selectman in Scituate 1653, whence we conclude that he had been there something earlier. He had a farm on little Musquaschcut pond, adjoining that of John Hoar in 1654, and in 1660 he purchased Hoar's farm, and continued to possess these lands in 1673, when a share in the division of common lands was assigned "to John Safin's house and land." He married Martha, daughter of Capt. Thomas Willet of Plymouth. His children, John born 1662, Thomas 1664, Simon 1666, Josiah 1667, Joseph 1669. He removed to Boston before 1671, when he was a freeman there. He was Representative first 1684 – Speaker of the House 1686 – Counsellor after the Union of Plymouth and Massachusetts 1692. He removed to Bristol, (says Mr. Baylies) "about 1688." He was the first Judge of Probate for the County of Bristol from 1692 to 1701, when he was appointed Judge of the Superior Court, Mass. He died at Bristol July 29, 1710. He had married a 2d. wife before 1688, whose name was Lee, of Boston: (Baylies) and a 3d. wife at Bristol, Rebecca, daughter of Col. Nathaniel Byfield. The children above named were all born of his first wife Martha, the daughter of that distinguished Capt. Thomas Willet, who was Assistant in Plymouth Colony, from 1651 to 1664 – afterward the first Mayor of New York, after it was conquered from the Dutch, and who died at Barrington, R. I. 1674. (Farmer.)

DEA. RICHARD SEALIS.

was one of Mr. Lothrop's Church, who appears in Scituate 1634. He had a house in 1636, north of Thomas Ensign's (see Ensign) which he afterward gave to Eglin Hanford, his wife's daughter, by a former husband. In 1646, he had a house north of Satuit brook, (near the Methodist chapel as it now stands). He was one of the Conihassett partners 1646. His wife was Eglin the sister of Mr. Timothy Hatherly: she had been the wife of Edward Foster's father, and of a Mr. Hanford previously in England. He appears to have been an estimable man. He had two daughters, as appears by his Will, dated 1656. "To wife Eglin – to daughters Hannah and Hester, wives of John Winchester and Samuel Jackson." John Winchester was of Hingham, married 1634.

CAPT. PETER SEARS.

from Halifax, married Susanna Colman of Scituate 1777, and settled on the John Bryant place north of Hoop-pole hill Cedar swamp. He was an officer in the Revolutionary war, viz. Capt. in the corps of Mechanicks. He died 1820, aged 68. His widow died 1824, aged 73. His children were Peter, who died 1820, (leaving Peter and other children) – Sarah, the wife of Elijah Damon 1811, Mary, (the wife of Jacob Stockbridge), Lucy, the wife of Abiel Farrow, Dolly, the wife of Lot Litchfield, and sometime the wife of Joseph Stockbridge.

THOMAS SAVORY.

had settled in Scituate 1675: he was the son of Thomas of Sandwich. He had lands in the Two mile; but probably had no family: he was killed in the Rehoboth battle the following year.

ROBERT SHELLEY, freeman 1638.

had lands on the 3d, Cliff, near Gillson's windmill, in 1636. He went to Barnstable 1640. He has descendants in Raynham.

FAMILY SKETCHES.

JAMES NUTON SPARREL.

settled in Scituate, and married Ruth Vinall 1766. He was from Carolina, and a shipmaster. His children, Elizabeth born 1767, James 1770, Hannah 1772. Capt. James, his son, deceased 1826, leaving sons James N. of Scituate, William of Boston, (architect) John of Turner, Maine, and George P. of Boston.

BRYANT STEPHENSON.

had sons born in Scituate. Bryant P. born 1784, Reuben 1786, Benjamin 1788.

ROBERT STANFORD.

was in Scituate 1670 – but left no family here.

EDWARD SHOVE.

from Taunton, married Lydia Witherell, (grand daughter of Rev. William) 1704, his children, (twins) George and Mary born June 1705. This family soon removed. He was son of Rev. George Shove of Taunton, and born 1680. His mother was Hannah, daughter of Mr. Walley of Barnstable.

JAMES SKIFF.

from Sandwich, resided a short time in Scituate; he married Elizabeth Dwelley 1745, his son John, born the same year. His ancestor, James, was of Sandwich 1656, "appointed to exercise the militia," Colony Records.

THOMAS SERGEANT.

had children in Scituate, Elizabeth 1690, Thomas 1692, William 1696, Thaddeus 1700, Mary 1703. This family removed.

ISRAEL SMITH*

built the house of Mr. Matthew Tower, one mile north of the Church-hill, in 1646. He married Abigail Ford of Marshfield. His children, Joseph born 1747, Abigail 1750, Peleg 1752, Lucy 1754, Charles 1755, Alice 1757, Israel 1759. This family removed to Maine,

WILLIAM SOAN.

had lands at the head of Stockbridge's mill-pond, on Brushy hill brook 1663. He left no family on record save Mary, born 1668. His mother Elizabeth was 2d. wife of John Stockbridge.

THOMAS SOPER.

purchased lands of Samuel Curtis, (1690) one fourth mile west of Curtis hill. His house stood in the field, forty rods southeast of the intersection of the roads. His children, Elizabeth born 1695, Mary 1697, Abigail 1699, Joseph 1703, Thomas 1706, Sarah 1708, David 1709, John 1714. This family has descendants in Hanson, and perhaps in Weymouth.

John married Anna Woodworth 1743, Joseph married Lydia Stockbridge 1729, Thomas 3d. married Susanna Vinall 1773.

THOMAS SIMONS, (early Symonson.)

was the son of "Moyses Symonson" who came to Plymouth in the Ship Fortune 1621. Thomas was a householder in Scituate before 1647. His house was on the Green field, between that of Samuel Nash and John Turner, jr. He had sons Moses and Aaron.

Moses had children, (by his wife Patience —). Moses born 1666, John 1667, Sarah 1670, Aaron 1672, Job 1674, Patience 1676, (after her father's decease).

---

* Israel Smith was son of Joseph and Rachel Smith of Hanover, and born 1722. He had brothers Isaac, Peleg, Levi, Abiel and Joshua, born from 1720 to 1734. The wife of Joseph was the daughter of Isaac Randall.

Aaron married Mary Woodworth 1677. Children, Moses 1680, Rebecca 1679, Mary 1683, Elizabeth 1686, Ebenezer 1689, Lydia 1693. Both these families lived at the Green field.

Moses, (son of Moses) died in the Canada expedition 1690, (Probate Record). Job, (son of Moses) had lands south of "Old Pond," which he sold in part to Jonathan Pratt 1696.

Moses, (son of Aaron) married Rachel Cudworth 1711. His children, Moses born 1718, Aaron 1720, Rachel 1723, Leah 1725.

Ebenezer, son of Aaron, married Lydia Kent 1714. Children, Abigail 1715, Joshua 1717, Lydia 1719. Joshua had a son Elisha, whose sons are Judge William, Elisha, Benjamin and Franklin of Boston, and Ebenezer of Hanover.

Thomas, (at the head of this article,) had a brother Moses, who died in Duxbury 1689, and whose children were John, Aaron, Mary, the wife of Joseph Alden, Elizabeth, wife of Richard Dwelley, and Sarah, wife of James Nash (of Duxbury.)

ISAAC STEDMAN.

was in Scituate 1637. He sold his farm to George Russell 1650, (see Russell) and removed to Boston. He was often employed in public transactions of the Town while here: and in Boston, he seems to have been a merchant, by certain transactions of the Town of Scituate with him, after his removal. He died 1678. His will gives "to son Nathaniel my present house, and half the orchard down to the *Cold springe* – to son Thomas, half the orchard, and all the salt meadow: to my wife, I relinquish all her property, &c. – to daughters Elizabeth Haman and Sarah Perry, 40£ each."

BENJAMIN STUDLEY,

probably from Hingham, settled near Merritt's brook, a few rods south-east of the bridge, 1680. He married Mary, daughter of John Merritt 1683. His children, John born 1684, Benjamin 1687, James 1690, Jonathan 1693, David 1696, Mary 1699, Elizabeth 1701, Deborah 1703, Eliab 1706.

James married Sarah Farrow (of Hingham) 1717. Children, Sarah 1718, James 1720, Elizabeth 1725.

David married Susanna Vinton 1717. Children, Susanna 1718, David 1720, Amasa 1722, Daniel 1725.

David, jr. married Elizabeth Curtis 1744. His children, Mercy 1745, David 1748, William 1752, Elizabeth 1754, Amiel 1757, John 1760. William is now living, whose sons are William and Amiel.

There was also Benoni Studley in Scituate, of another family, whose children, John, Abigail, Joshua, Gideon, Sarah and Benoni, were born from 1702 to 1723: of this family is Lewis Studley, and several also of Hingham.

There was also a Joseph Studley, at Randall (now Studley) hill in 1700, from whom some families in Hanover may have descended.

ROBERT SPROAT, (or Sprout.)

was in "the Two mile" 1660, and his lands adjoined "the old Barker place," so called at that time, or "John Barker place." His children, Mercy born 1662, Elizabeth 1664, Mary 1666, Robert 1669, Anna 1671, James 1673, Ebenezer 1676, Hannah 1680.

Ebenezer, had two children born in Scituate, Thankful 1705, Abigail 1709, and then removed to Middleboro'.

James married Elizabeth Southworth of Middleboro 1712, and Rachel Dwelley 1727; he removed to Middleboro'. He had one son, Robert born in Scituate 1715: But from Col. Ebenezer above, most of the families of this name in Middleboro', Taunton, &c. we believe are descended. Also, Rev. Mr. Sproat, a distinguished preacher in Philadelphia, a few years since, was of this family.

Robert Sproat, sen. deceased at Middleboro 1712. His will gives "To daughter Mercy Oldham, and daughter Ann Richmond, each a lot in 'South purchase.' – To daughter Hannah Cane, and daughters Elizabeth and Mary Sprout, lots at Edy's pond – to James and Ebenezer the farm at Scituate, and undivided lands in Middleboro.' "

CORNET ROBERT STETSON.

received a grant of a considerable tract of land 1634, from the Colony Court, on the North River, which constituted his farm. His house was on a beautiful plain near the river. An unfailing and valuable spring, out of which eight generations of the family have been supplied, marks the spot. "Cornet's Rocks,"

FAMILY SKETCHES. 341

in the river east of his farm, are well known to those who navigate the river. He was possessed of considerable wealth, an enterprising and valuable man in the plantation, a deputy to Court, a Cornet of the first light horse corps raised in the Colony, a member of the Council of war, a Colony Commissioner for selling the patent line – in short, he lived long and left a good name at last. He died Feb. 1st, 1702, aged 90. His children were Joseph born 1639, Benjamin 1641, Thomas 1643, Samuel 1646, John 1648, Eunice 1650, Lois 1651, Robert 1653, Timothy 1657. These sons he was able to settle around him on his plantation. – *Joseph* left sons Joseph born 1667, Robert 1670, William 1673, Samuel 1679.

Benjamin had sons Benjamin 1666, Matthew 1668, (who died in the Canada Expedition 1690) James 1670, Samuel 1673.

Thomas had sons (by his wife Sarah Dodson) Thomas 1674, Gershom 1676, Joshua 1680, Caleb 1682, Elisha 1684, Elijah 1686, Ebenezer 1693.

Samuel had sons Samuel 1679, Jonah 1691, John 1694, Silas 1696, Seth 1698, Nathaniel 1700.

John had one son, Barnabas 1688.

Robert, who married Joanna Brooks 1670, left no family on record. Timothy probably left none.

Joseph, (son of Joseph) left sons, Nehemiah born 1696, Joseph 1698, Hezekiah 1703.

Robert, his brother, had sons Anthony 1693, Isaac 1696, William 1700, Gideon 1709, Robert 1710. (Anthony married Ann Smith 1717, and was the father of Isaac, who first settled south of George Moore's Pond, and of Charles and Ezra of Rochester, and of Elisha (born 1731), of Kingston and of Thomas of Barnstable). Isaac, above named, was father of David, Esq. of Charlestown.

Capt. Jonah Stetson (born 1691,) who married Mercy Turner 1720, was the father of Capt. Jonah, who married Elizabeth Hatch, 1751 – His son Micah is now living.

John (born 1694,) purchased the Wanton estate 1730, and was the father of Lydia, Mary and Eleanor, (Dr. Charles Stockbridge's widow). He was son of Samuel, the son of Thomas. He built the first tide mill at the Harbour. Stephen who married Experience Palmer* 1762, descended from the Cornet through Joseph, Robert, William and William. Stephen's sons (Stephen, Charles and William) are of the seventh genera-

---

* She died 1829, aged 97, a worthy woman.

tion, and the children of Charles are the eighth generation, who have inhabited the same spot of ground.

P. S. In 1660, and several years subsequent, "Cornet Stetson was Commissioner to act for the country in all matters relating to the trade at Kennebec." Also, 1665, for his services he had granted to him "200 acres south of Mr. Hatherly's grant, above Accord pond." Colony Record.

JOHN STOCKBRIDGE, (Wheelwright.)

took the oath of fidelity in Scituate 1638. He was one of the Conihassett partners 1646. He had a house near to John Hollet's, (perhaps a few rods south-west of Jesse Dunbar's). He had also a considerable tract of land, by purchase of Abraham Sutliffe, near Stockbridge's mill pond on the north and east. In 1656, he purchased half the mill privilege of George Russell, (with the saw mill, which Isaac Stedman had erected ten years before) and built a grist mill, in partnership with Russell. Nearly at the same time, (before 1660) he built the Stockbridge Mansion-house, a part of which is now standing, and is probably the oldest house in New-England, save one, viz. the Barker house at the Harbour. It was a garrison in Philip's war, and the portholes may be traced in the back part of the house, even now. He had married about the time of his arrival in the country, but the name of his first wife we have not learned. His children were Hannah, (wife of Serjeant Ticknor 1656.) Charles born before 1638. His 2d. wife was widow Elizabeth Soan, (mother of William), 1643, by whom he had Elizabeth 1644, (wife of Thomas Hiland, jr. 1661,) Sarah 1645, (wife of Joseph Woodworth 1669, – "a shop-keeper." Hester 1647. His 3d. wife was Mary, by whom he had Abigail 1655, and John 1657, (the last born in Boston).

The will of John Stockbridge is dated at Boston, 1657. His will gives "To eldest son Charles, my water-mill at Scituate, house, ground and orchard belonging to it, he paying to his sister Elizabeth 10£ at marriage, or at 21 years of age. To wife Mary, my house and land at Boston, also the house that Gilbert Brooks lives in at Scituate, with the land belonging to it; and these to youngest son John after her decease, he paying 10£ to his sister Mary; but in case he do not survive his mother, to be equally divided to all my children. To daughter Hester, the house that William Ticknor doth now live in at Scituate, with the ground and orchard, also my land at

Brushy hill and 4th Cliff. To daughter Hannah, wife of William Ticknor 40S. To daughter Sarah 10£ at marriage, or at 21 years of age. To wife Mary, all my household goods, and to eldest son Charles all my working tools."

Charles, the only son who survived, succeeded to the possession of the mills, and the Mansion-house near it. In 1665 he purchased George Russell's half of the mill. He also built, (by contract) the 2d. water-mill in the town of Plymouth 1676. In 1673, he was allowed by the Town, "30 acres of land on the 3d. Herring brook, on condition that 'he erect a Corn-mill on that brook, and keep and tend the mill fourteen years.'" The mill was built 1677, (now Jonah's mill, so called).

He married Abigail – . His children, were Abigail born at Charlestown 1660, (says our Record), John born 1662, at Boston, and died early, and at Scituate were born Charles 1663, Sarah 1665, (wife of Israel Turner,) Elizabeth 1670, (wife of David Turner,) Joseph born 1672, Benjamin 1677, Samuel 1679. Charles, sen. died 1683, intestate, his estate divided 1684, "to Charles, oldest son, (surviving) land at 3d. Herring brook, and half the corn-mill and three fourths of the saw-mill there: To Thomas, land also on 3d. Herring brook, half the corn-mill, and one fourth of the saw-mill: to Joseph, 50 acres of land in Duxbury, near Indian-head river, (now Pembroke – where late William Torrey, Esq. deceased,) also the reversion of a house of Hester Stockbridge in Scituate: to Abigail, wife of Henry Josselyn 18£. To Sarah and Elizabeth 17£ each. To widow Abigail, all the house, land, corn-mill and saw-mill on 1st Herring brook, until Samuel the youngest be of age, then Benjamin to have the above, except the parlour." (Probate Record).

Abigail, the widow, married Amos Turner, before 1700.

Charles left daughters, but no son that survived.

Thomas settled at the mill on the 3d. Herring brook: he left but one son, Thomas born 1702. His grandson Stephen deceased on the same place 1800.

Joseph married Margaret Turner, daughter of Joseph Turner, and removed to Duxbury, (now Pembroke) where his lands were situated. He lived to more than 100 years of age. His son Joseph married Ann Turner – and his son David married Deborah, daughter of Judge John Cushing, David, Esq. his son is now living in Hanover.

Benjamin married Mary Tilden 1701, and succeeded to the old Stockbridge Mansion and mills, by purchase, in part, of his brother Samuel. His son, Dr. Benjamin born 1704, was the 2d. regularly bred physician, who settled in Scituate. He was educated under Dr. Bulfinch, of Boston, and succeeded to the Stockbridge Mansion. There is undoubted testimony, that he was the great physician of his day. His account books exhibit sufficient evidence, that he was a consulting physician in difficult cases, in a circle, embracing the whole country from Falmouth to Worcester, and to Ipswich. He is remembered by a few aged people, as having held the reputation of the first physician of the time, and not the reputation of quackery, but that of an enlightened benefactor to mankind.* He is described as a gentleman of wit and taste, eminently pleasing in his own hospitable mansion, and the delight of literary society: and we may add, that he had made attainments in the science of music which were rare at that time. His wife was Ruth Otis, (daughter of Job). His only surviving son, Dr. Charles born 1734, succeeded him in his mansion and his profession. He was educated in medicine by his father, and attained to a high reputation. Like his father, he was pleasing in his manners, and accomplished in all literature, and tasteful arts. Dr. Charles born 1790, his only son, deceased early, after having commenced the practice of medicine.

Samuel, (son of Charles, sen.) married Lydia, daughter of William Barrell 1703, and settled at Mount Blue. His descendants are in that vicinity. James, his grandson, deceased 1819, leaving a family – his widow, Martha (Dunbar before married) deceased 1829, aged 91. The father of James was Samuel, who married Sarah Tilden 1737.

DANIEL STANDLAKE, (since Stanley.)

was a freeman in Scituate 1636. He settled amongst the men of Kent, on Kent street, the 3d. lot south side of "the drift way." There is no record of his children. His daughter Jane married Thomas Pincin 1639. He had one son Richard, whose house was on the west side of Walnut Tree hill, near that of Cornet John Buck. His children, Joanna born 1661, Lydia born 1664, (wife of Benjamin Sylvester) Mary 1665, Daniel 1669, Abigail 1671. This family removed soon after 1700. We observe in the Colony Record 1684, "Daniel Standlake (in the

---

* Dr. Benjamin educated many young gentlemen in Medicine, from Boston, and other towns, amongst whom we may name the distinguished Dr. Isaac Winslow of Marshfield, who married his daughter.

house of Richard) was killed by the discharge of a gun by Robert Trayes, a Negro – tried and acquitted – it appearing to be accidental."

Daniel, sen. deceased 1639. His will gives, "all my property to my wife, except my swine to my two children, they to have the females of the increase, and my wife to have the males toward maintenance of the children."

Richard Standlake deceased 1691. His will gives "to wife Lydia, all my estate to distribute to the children at her discretion. Codicil – my will is that my daughters Joanna, Lydia, Mary and Abigail share equally in the meadow lands."

There is no posterity of this family remaining here, save that of Jabez Stanley, the natural son of Jabez Rose and Abigail Stanley or Standlake born 1700. He married Deborah Turner 1731, Jabez, jr. married Mary Thrift 1765, had sons Jabez and Calvin, who probably removed.

DEA. SAMUEL STODDER.

from Hingham, settled on the west side of Brushy hill 1690. His children, Leah 1696, Rachel 1698, Seth 1700, (died 1712) Elizabeth 1702, Mary 1704, Sarah 1709. He married a 2d. wife, viz. widow Sarah Mellus 1749. He died 1762, aged 92.

BENJAMIN STODDER.

brother of the above, probably, married Mary, daughter of Israel Sylvester, sen. 1705, and lived in the west part of the Town. His children, Benjamin 1708, Mary 1711, Elisha 1715, Elijah 1719, Isaiah 1723. Some of these removed. Isaiah had a son Melzar born 1756, who left descendants.

Benjamin, jr. married Ruth Curtis 1737, and had children, Elijah born 1738, Seth 1741, Elizabeth (wife of Capt. William Brooks 1774). Elijah married Thankful Whitcomb 1766, and had children, Peres, Elijah, Thankful and Mary. He was often a Selectman. He removed to New Springfield, Vermont, where he recently deceased. Seth married Sprague, and deceased 1831, leaving sons Seth and Josiah, who live near Hingham line on the Mountain road.

HEZEKIAH STODDER.

another brother of Dea. Samuel, settled on Gillman plain 1711, and had children, Bathsheba 1711, Joshua 1713, Eunice 1715,

Hezekiah 1722. The latter succeeded his father, and had sons Laban, Hezekiah, Samuel, Obadiah, Deran and Bela, several of whom removed. Hezekiah 3d. has left sons in Abington and Scituate. His wife, Elizabeth Gardner.

The families of this name in this vicinity all descended from John Stodder of Hingham, who married Hannah, daughter of John Bryant of Scituate, 1665.

ABRAHAM SUTLIFFE.

sold lands in Scituate to Thomas Ingham 1640: also to John Stockbridge, "north-east of the Mill." He had a house north of Stockbridge's (as it was afterward built). He was living 1659 when "Abraham Sutliffe and Sarah his wife were ordered to make retraction for defaming John Sutton, in saying he was basely born." Colony Record.

He had one son Abraham, whose house in 1670 was at the foot of Curtis hill, north side of the road on the margin of the brook. He was succeeded by Samuel Curtis of York.

GEORGE SUTTON.

had lands laid out in 1638, on the 1st. Herring brook. His house was near John Daman's at the south-west end of Green field lane, where it unites with the Drift way. He married Sarah, the wife of Elder Nathaniel Tilden, 1641. Children, John 1642, Lydia 1646, Sarah 1648, (died early,) Sarah 1650, Elizabeth 1653.

John purchased Conihassett lands, south of Booth hill and near Bound brook. His house was near the Brook, a half mile south of that hill. He was an Ensign in Philip's war with Capt. Williams. He married Elizabeth, daughter of Samuel House, 1661. Children, Elizabeth 1662, John 1664, Mary 1666, Sarah 1668, Hannah 1670, Hester 1673, Benjamin 1675, Nathaniel 1677, Nathan 1679.

John married Ann Cole, and left sons John, jr. Seth and Nathaniel, born from 1705 to 1711. John, jr. had John, Andrew and Abner, who married Ann Hayden 1776: Reuben and Seth were sons of Abner.

Nathaniel had a son Ray born 1709. This family has become nearly extinct in this Town. Reuben deceased 1822, and his sons removed.

John, sen. deceased 1691, and names in his will – "wife Elizabeth, children, John, Nathaniel, Nathan, Elizabeth, Mary, Sarah, Hester."

There was a Simon Sutton, who bore arms in Scituate 1643: but soon disappears. John Sutton, who died at Rehoboth 1670, may have been his son. Ichabod Cook now occupies the farm that was John Sutton's in 1750.

CAPT. THOMAS SOUTHWORTH.

from Duxbury, son of Dea. James Southworth, and a descendant of Constant Southworth, an early settler of Duxbury, came into Scituate in 1800. He married Sarah, the daughter of Dea. Elisha James. He was a shipmaster, and an intelligent and exceedingly amiable man. He deceased at New Orleans, on a voyage in 1819. His mansion house stood near the gate that leads to the "Block house," and was unfortunately burnt in 1823 – and was replaced by the much smaller house which occupies the spot. His widow survives, and also his children, Capt. James, Lucy, Nathan, Thomas, Temperance and George.

THOMAS STAR.

son of "Comfort Star, who came from Ashford, Kent, Eng. in 1633, and settled in Cambridge," (Farmer,) was in Scituate 1644. His son Comfort was born 1644, and his daughter Elizabeth 1646. He removed to Yarmouth in 1648 or 9. He is styled Surgeon, and is noticed in Dr. Thatcher's Medical Biography as living at Yarmouth in 1670.

John Star of Bridgewater in 1645, may have been another son of Comfort Star of Cambridge. His descendants, Joseph, (with his sons Joseph and Robert) resided on the east margin of the Nippinicket pond, until 1800; at which time they removed to Maine.

Comfort Star, (another son of Comfort of Cambridge,) graduated at Harvard College 1647, and, (according to Farmer's register) was a minister at Carlisle, in Cumberland, Eng. – and afterward at Lewis, in Sussex, where he died 1711.

RICHARD SYLVESTER.

was in Weymouth 1633. We find that he gained an unfortunate notoriety, by espousing certain religious sentiments, too liberal for the age in which he lived. Mr. Robert Lenthal, his minister at Weymouth, advanced the sentiment, "That all baptized persons should be admitted to the Communion without further trial." (Magnalia I. 222.) This was a heresy to be noticed by Government, and he was ordered to retract in presence of the General Court; with which order he complied. Richard Sylvester, who held the same opinion, adhered to it, and in consequence was fined and disfranchised by the Government. This put him upon removing from the Colony, and he came to Scituate 1642. Thomas Rawlins, Thomas Clap, James Torrey and William Holbrook, came about the same time, and probably on account of holding the same sentiments. Sylvester settled in Marshfield, or rather in that part of Scituate called "the Two miles." He married the sister of Capt. William Torrey. His children were Lydia born 1633, John 1634, Peter 1637, Joseph 1638, Daniel 1642, Elizabeth 1643, Richard 1648, Naomi 1649, Israel 1651, Hester 1653, Benjamin 1656.

We observe an anecdote in Winthrop's Journal, respecting the unfortunate death of one of the above children. (Vol. 2, p. 77. See also Vol. I. 289.)

"Richard Sylvester having three small children, he and his wife going to the assembly upon the Lord's day, left them at home. The oldest was without doors looking to some cattle. The middlemost, being a son of about five years old, seeing his father's fowling piece stand in the chimney, took it and laid it upon a stool, as he had seen his father do, and pulled up the cock, the spring being weak, and put down the hammer, then went to the other end, and blowed in the mouth of the piece, as he had seen his father also do, and with that, stirring the piece, it went off and shot the child into the mouth and through his head. When the father came home, he found his child dead; the youngest child (being but three years old) showed him the whole manner of it." We find a fair record, that Peter born 1637, died 1642 – the date of the anecdote in Winthrop: and also, we find that the two elder sons John and Joseph survived and left families. Richard Sylvester deceased 1663, He names in his will, John, Joseph, Israel, Richard, Benjamin, Lydia, Dinah, Elizabeth, Naomi, Hester. The same year, "Richard Sylvester's widow, Naomi, allowed more than her husband's will." (Plymouth Colony Records.)

Lydia married Nathaniel Rawlins 1652, Elizabeth married John Lowell 1658. Naomi was John Lowell's 2d. wife 1666. Dinah probably did not marry, as also Hester.

FAMILY SKETCHES.

John left a family, Sarah 1671, John born 1672, Joseph 1674, Samuel 1676, Lydia 1679. Some of his posterity remain.

Capt. *Joseph* had a farm north of the Church hill, which, in part, he purchased of John Whiston 1664. His house stood where that of Mr. Samuel Waterman now stands. (See military affairs). He was Capt. under Col. Church, in the Eastern Expedition against the Indians, 1689. The next year he was Capt. (with 16 men from Scituate, many of whom never returned,) in Phips' Canada Expedition, and died in the service. His will was verbal;* and proved in the Court by three of his soldiers, viz. Benjamin Stetson, John and William Perry, giving "all my lands at Hugh's cross to son Joseph: the three younger sons to be provided for by their mother out of the remainder of my estate." Wife Mary, Executrix. His children were Joseph born 1664, Mary 1667, Anna 1669, Benjamin 1672, Amos 1676, David 1682. The descendants of this family are in Hanover. Joseph Sylvester, of Cumberland County, Maine, married Lucy Wade 1788. He lived at a place called Prout's Gore.†

Richard removed. He was in Milton 1678, when he married Hannah, the "daughter of old James Leonard of Taunton." See Records at Boston.

Israel had a house one fourth mile south-east of the south Meeting-house, on the margin of the 2d. Herring brook in 1670. That house was taken down by Elnathan Cushing 1829. His children were Israel born 1674, Silence 1677, Richard 1679, Lois 1680, Martha 1682, Mary 1683, Elisha 1685, Peter 1687, Zebulun 1689, Bathsheba 1692, Deborah 1696. Of the sons, Richard lived at the place of the late Elijah Turner, Esq. and had sons Nehemiah and Seth.

Peter married Mary Torrey 1712, had children, Peter 1713, Hannah 1717, Joshua 1717, Mary 1721, Levi 1723, Deborah 1726. In 1727 this family removed to Leicester, where there are descendants. Peter born 1713, had sons, Peter, Otho, Amos, Ezra, Elisha. Henry H. Sylvester, Esq. of Charlestown, N. H. we believe is the son of Peter last named.

Zebulun, (son of Israel) had a son Elisha, who succeeded to the residence at the Herring brook, (he was the father of

---

* Several Nuncupative Wills were allowed by the court after that Expedition.

† The Town of Turner, in Maine, was a grant to this family for services in the Canadian wars.

Thomas deceased, and Elisha living.) Zebulun had also a son Israel born 1717, and deceased at Snappet 1812, aged 95.

Benjamin, (youngest son of Richard, sen.) married Lydia, daughter of Richard Standlake 1684. Sons, Benjamin born 1685, Joseph 1688, probably his descendants are in Marshfield. Richard sold his Weymouth farm to John Holbrook 1650.

THOMAS TART.

was a Conihassett partner 1646. He was here 1640, when he is mentioned as a shop-keeper in the Colony Records. He built the first house on the ancient Ellmes farm, which he sold to Rhodolphus Ellmes 1659. In the deed, he is then called of Barbadoes. His daughter Elizabeth married Thomas Williams (we believe of Boston) 1638.

ISAAC TAYLOR.

from Massachusetts and probably from Concord, was in Scituate as early as 1686. He had several children baptized in the 2d. Church, viz. Isaac 1693, Mary 1696, (who was the wife of Mr. Nathaniel Brooks in 1723) Jonathan 1698, David 1700. The latter left a daughter on record, viz. Delight born 1732, Isaac, jr. married Ruth Green 1718. Children, Isaac born 1721, Ruth 1723, Isaac 1725.

WILLIAM TAYLOR.

was a brother of Isaac, and probably elder. His children on record were Lydia 1688, Elizabeth 1692, Mary 1696. This family has long since disappeared from our records. Benjamin Taylor married Anna Bates 1720, and John married Elizabeth Gilford 1730. Whose sons they were, it does not appear in our records.

WILLIAM THRIFT.

had several children born in Scituate, viz. Hannah 1732, Mary who married Jabez Stanley 1760, Hannah married John Gaynes of Boston 1759.

JOHN TWISDEN.

freeman 1639, purchased the farm of Isaac Robinson on the south-east of Colman's hills, the same year: which farm he

FAMILY SKETCHES. 351

sold to Thomas Robinson 1645, and removed to Georgiana or York. His daughter Elizabeth married Dea. Joseph Tilden 1649. Samuel Twisden, probably his son, had lands in Scituate 1670. He deceased here 1680, leaving no family on record.

SERGEANT WILLIAM TICKNER.

appears in Scituate 1656, in which year he married Hannah, the daughter of John Stockbridge, and succeeded to the mansion house of his father in law at the Harbour, (Mr. Stockbridge having removed to Boston about that time). Serj. Tickner was engaged in agriculture, navigation and mercantile pursuits. His "warehouse" is mentioned in our records in 1660. His farm was three fourths of a mile south-west from the harbour, now the well known place of Abijah Otis. He was often engaged in municipal affairs, as selectman, assessor, surveyor, &c. He was also in Philip's war in 1676, being a Serjeant in Gen. Cudworth's guard or "particular company."

We find the names of his children, by recurring to the baptisms in the 2d. Church in Scituate; and from the circumstance of his having belonged to that church, we know that he was of the moderate party of Puritans. (See Chap. on Ecclesiastical History.)

His son John was baptized May 1659, and William 1664. His wife Hannah deceased in 1665, and he married Deborah, the daughter of Thomas Hyland: she also deceased 1693, and her husband was then living. The latter wife left no children, that we have discovered, John, the eldest son, deceased in 1665.

Willam, jr. succeeded his father in business and usefulness in the town. He married Lydia, the daughter of Dea. Joseph Tilden, 1696. His children were Hannah, born 1697, John 1699, William 1700, Lydia 1702. He sold his farm, warehouse, &c. to Job Otis 1710, for 400£, and removed to Lebanon, Con. Of his children, we are able to give an account only of

John. He married Mary Bailey at Lebanon, Con. 1724, and deceased 1751, leaving children, Mary born 1725, John 1727, Lydia 1729, Isaac 1733, Elisha 1736, Hannah 1737, James 1740, (died 1812, without children) Irene 1747, David 1750, (died early) of these

Isaac deceased in Lebanon, Con. and if we mistake not, his son Isaac succeeded him, and deceased 1812, leaving children, David who died 1830, Asahel of Susquehannah County, Penn.

John, (of Clinton, Georgia) planter and merchant. Dr. Olney, a respectable physician, of Clinton, Georgia, William of Susquehannah, Penn. Mary, wife of Benjamin Woodworth of Columbia: and Clarissa, wife of Mr. Ormsby, of Clinton, Georgia. Most of these have families.

Col. Elisha (son of John and Mary Bailey), married Ruth Knowles of Truro, Mass. 1755, by whom he had children. Elisha born 1757, Ruth 1759, (died early) John 1761, (of Plainfield, N. H. and father of John, a merchant of Mobile, Erastus of Plainfield, and several daughters,) Paul Knowles 1761, (of Lebanon, N. H. and father of Isaac and Paul, and six daughters). Joshua 1765, (of Illinois) Ruth born 1767, (died early) Elias 1769, of N. H. (father of Olney, Joshua, Samuel, Elisha, William, Elias, Barton and three daughters).

Ruth, the wife of Col. Tickner,* deceased 1771, and he married Deborah Davis of Lebanon, Con. 1772, by whom he had Deborah 1773, (wife of Alfred Bingham, and mother of many children) James born 1776, (of Illinois, and father of Thomas, Hiram and others), Samuel born 1778, (of Lisle, N. Y, and father of Elisha, Lewis, David, Samuel, and daughters) Ruth born 1781, (wife of Daniel Richards of Illinois, and mother of 17 children) William born 1785, (of Lebanon, N. H. and father of William, of Boston, and others), Tryphena born 1787, (wife of Elisha Kimball of Lebanon, N. H. and mother of several children) David born 1791, deceased in Boston 1829, where he had been a broker, and leaving sons, William, Benjamin, George – and by a 2d wife, Baldwin.

Col. Tickner, the father of these fifteen children, removed from Connecticut, with several other families, in 1774, and settled in the plantation now called Lebanon, N. H. He had a command in the New Hampshire Troops, in the expedition against Crown point, &c. in the Revolutionary War. He died 1822. We give some further notice to one of Col. Tickner's sons, viz. *Elisha,* who graduated at Dartmouth College 1783. He was master of the Latin school connected with that College until 1786, when he removed to Boston, where he was Principal of a Grammar school until 1794, and afterward, a successful merchant. We believe that the primary schools of Boston owe something to Mr. Tickner, of their present happy arrangement: and we can add, that the establishment of the Savings Institution was an object in which he laboured with peculiar

---

* The name in Scituate records is uniformly written Tickner; the family now generally write Ticknor.

interest. He married in 1791, Mrs. Betsey, the widow of Dr. Benjamin Curtis; her maiden name was Billings of Sharon. She had several children, at the time of her second marriage, and after this marriage she had one son, viz.

George Ticknor born 1791. He graduated at Dartmouth 1807, and was educated for the Bar, under direction of Hon. William Sullivan. We trust we shall be pardoned for adding that he was in Europe from 1815 to 1819 at Gottingen, and on various travels, and during his absence, in 1817, was appointed *Smith Professor* of French and Spanish Literature, and Professor of Belles Lettres in Harvard University, on the duties of which office he entered in 1819. He married Anna, the daughter of late Samuel Eliot, Esq. of Boston 1821, and has children, Anna Eliot and George Haven.

ELDER NATHANIEL TILDEN.

came from Tenterden in Kent, with his family, before 1628. (See page 8.) He was chosen Ruling Elder of the first Church in Scituate 1634. His house lot was on Kent-street, the 3d. south of Greenfield lane. He had also lands at Long marsh: and lands also in 1640, on the east side of the North River, below Gravelly beach. We have not learned the name of his wife. His children were born in England, and were Dea. Joseph, Thomas, Mary, Sarah, Judith, Lydia, and Stephen, born, as nearly as we can conjecture, from 1615 to 1627. Of the daughters, Mary was the wife of Thomas Lapham, Sarah the wife of George Sutton, Judith the wife of Abraham Preble, and Lydia the wife of Richard Garret, all of Scituate.

Dea. Joseph succeeded to his father's residence in Kent street. He belonged to the 2d. Church, of which he was chosen Deacon 1655: and of course he belonged to the liberal or moderate class of Puritans. (See Chap. on Ecclesiastical History). He married Elizabeth, the daughter of John Twisden 1648. His children were Nathaniel born 1649, John 1652, Rebecca 1654, Joseph 1656, Stephen 1659, Samuel 1660, Elizabeth 1665, Lydia 1666, Benjamin 1668. Of the daughters, Rebecca married Lieut. James Briggs 1673, Elizabeth married Samuel Curtis, jr. 1690, Lydia married William Tickner, jr. 1696. Of his sons, Nathaniel married Mary Sharp 1673, and settled at the well known John Tilden Farm, a mile north-west of the Harbour. The house stood nearly where stands the house of John Man. His children were Nathaniel born 1678, (and whose daughter Ruth was born 1715) Elizabeth born 1681, Joseph born 1685, and by a 2d. wife, (Margaret Dodson) Mary born 1694, and Margaret 1696. John had lands contiguous to his brother Nathaniel's farm, but leaving no children, they were inherited by Joseph the son of Nathaniel. Joseph (last named) married Sarah, the daughter of Timothy White 1710, and had two sons, John born 1715, and Job 1725. The posterity of Job, probably are in Hanover. John married Sybil — 1744, and succeeded to his father's residence. His children were Thomas born 1743, Mary 1750, Sarah 1756. Thomas married Abigail Hatch 1766, succeeded to his father's residence, and had children, Abigail born 1767, Deborah 1770, Capt. John 1772, (who resides on the paternal farm) Amos 1774, of Scituate, near Merritt's brook, Thomas 1775, of Boston, Mary 1777, Lydia 1779, Patience 1781, Sybil 1783, (wife of Capt. G. W. Stetson) and Joseph 1785, of Boston.

Joseph (son of Dea. Joseph) was living in Marshfield 1693, and also Stephen, and we may add Samuel also, who settled on the North river, between Gravelly beach and Union bridge, whose son Samuel was born 1689, (by a first wife) his 2d. wife was Sarah Curtis 1694. The latter Samuel married Desire Oldham 1717, and his son Samuel was born 1718. The latter was the father of the venerable Dea. Samuel Tilden, now living, aged 94, and occupying land which his family has possessed since 1640. He is the patriarch of three numerous generations: his sons are Capt. Samuel, Capt. Jotham, Charles, Elisha, Dr. Calvin, Benjamin, Capt. Luther, Hatch, and Nathan.

Benjamin (the youngest son of Dea. Joseph) had a farm in Marshfield on the North river, a part of the lands above mentioned. He died unmarried in 1693, and left his lands to his "seven brothers and sisters," and not naming John, we conclude he had before deceased. Probate Records.

We return to Elder Tilden's sons.

Thomas was on the roll of those that bore arms in Scituate 1643 (with his brother Joseph) but we find no trace of a family. He may have returned to England.

Stephen (the youngest son of Elder Tilden) married Hannah, daughter of Thomas Little (of Plymouth and afterward of Marshfield) 1661. He resided principally in Marshfield. His children were Hannah born 1662, Stephen 1663, Abigail 1666, Mary 1668, Judith 1670, Joseph 1672, Mercy 1674, Ruth

1676, Isaac 1678, Ephraim 1680, Ebenezer 1681, David 1685. We have had little opportunity of tracing further the genealogy of this family; we can only add that David married Abigail Pitcher 1710, and had children, David born 1711, Abigail 1713, Hannah 1715, Elijah 1719, Mary 1722, Ezra 1724. Ebenezer had a family, Mary born 1715, Ebenezer 1717, and perhaps others. Joseph had a family in Marshfield, one of whom was Christopher, baptized in the first Church in Scituate 1712. The latter married Sarah Parrot of Boston, and there resided. He was the father of the late Maj. David Tilden of Boston (whose sons were David, Christopher, James and Nathaniel) and of the late Capt. Joseph Tilden, also of Boston (whose sons are Joseph, Bryant P. and William, — —) and of the accomplished wife of late Judge Nathan Cushing of Scituate.

Elder Nathaniel Tilden deceased in 1641. His Will gives "to wife Lydia, the income of my Stone house, with the lands, in Tenterden in Kent, Eng. in which Richard Lambeth now dwells, &c. &c. To son Joseph, a double portion, that is, as much as both Thomas and Stephen, (in lands, houses, &c. in Scituate and Marshfield). To Lydia and Stephen, my two youngest children, a maintenance till 21. To Judith, a cow. To Mary, wife of Thomas Lapham, 10S. To Sarah, wife of George Sutton, 10S." The inventory of his estate, in the Colony Records, shows that he belonged to the wealthiest class of early settlers. We remarked, in his inventory, "Ten stocks or swarms of bees, appraised at 10£" and it is the earliest notice we have met with, respecting the keeping of bees in the Colony.

Dea. Joseph Tilden died June 3d. 1670. His will gives "To wife Elizabeth 100£. To sons Nathaniel, John, Stephen, Samuel, Benjamin, lands already deeded to them. To daughter Elizabeth 10£. To sister Lydia Garrett 5£. To daughters Rebecca and Lydia, all my other goods in equal shares; also I acquit my brother Stephen of all dues."

Nathaniel Tilden (son of Dea. Joseph) deceased 1730. His will gives legacies "to wife Margaret - sons Nathaniel and Joseph – daughters, Mary Hyland and Margaret Foster – and the six children of daughter Elizabeth Hatch deceased."

There was a Thomas Tilden who came to Plymouth in the Ann, 1623. He may have been a brother of Elder Nathaniel, but could not have been his son. There was a Joseph Tilden also amongst "the Merchant Adventurers" in London 1626, who was probably another brother of the same family.

ROBERT THOMPSON.

was in Scituate 1712. His house was on the lane which leads north-west from Hobart's landing gate. Mr. Cushing Briggs now owns the place. He married Ann, daughter of John Barker, Esq. 1713. Children, Robert 1715, Barnabas 1717, Ann 1719, John 1720, Thomas 1721. This family soon removed.

JAMES TILL.

was in the family of Isaac Stedman 1639. He had a grant of Marsh land at Till's creek, which received its early name from that circumstance, (now Dwelley's creek, opposite Gravelly beach west-side of North river). He left no family here, and probably removed to Boston with Stedman.

THOMAS TOTMAN*

came from Plymouth 1660. He resided south side Church hill. His son was Stephen, whose children were Samuel born 1693, Stephen 1695, Mary 1696, Christian 1699. Of these, Stephen had a son Ebenezer born 1720, who left two sons, Thomas, who removed, and Stephen born 1756, a Revolutionary soldier; and who deceased 1830, leaving descendants in Scituate, Weymouth and Boston. Ebenezer married Grace, daughter of Hawkins Turner: she is said to be living now at Brookfield. She was born 1732.

CAPT. BENJAMIN TOLMAN.

came from Dorchester in 1709. He was the son of John Tolman, and grandson of Thomas Tolman, who came from England, and settled at Dorchester before 1640. He had also a son Thomas, whose posterity are in Dorchester and the vicinity. Capt. Benjamin of Scituate, married Elizabeth, the

---

* Mary, wife of Thomas Totman, died suddenly in 1666. Verdict of a Jury of 12 men, "That she did gather, dress and eat a root (which she judged the same she had eaten of before) of a poisonous nature, which we believe the sole cause of her death." Thomas Totman died suddenly 1678, Jury's verdict: "his own wilful abstractinge of himself from food."

widow of Bazaleel Palmer 1709. His residence was one fourth mile south-east of the Church hill. There he established a Tannery. His children were Benjamin born 1710, Samuel 1711, Elizabeth 1713, Joseph 1715, William 1716, Elisha 1718.

Samuel and Benjamin left no families. Elizabeth married Joseph Copeland.

Capt. Joseph married Mary, the daughter of "Lawyer: Thomas Turner" 1738. His children were Joseph and John, who survived, Samuel who died early, and daughters Hannah, Mary and Elizabeth, born from 1740 to 1755.

Joseph born 1750, and now living, married Bethia, daughter of Abiel Turner, 1771. Their children, Abigail 1772, wife of Capt. Samuel Lewis of Cincinnati, Roxana 1775, Arithusa 1777, wife of Mr. Nye of Falmouth: Hannah 1779, wife of Mr. Nye of Falmouth, Bethia 1785, Joseph Robinson of Scituate, born 1787, Mary 1793, wife of Samuel Hart, Naval Architect, Brookline N. Y.

John (son of Capt. Joseph) married Dolly, the daughter of Dr. Hall of Pembroke, 1784. He had sons who removed to Boston.

William (son of Capt. Benjamin) married Abigail Williamson 1740, and resided in Marshfield. His son Benjamin married Mercy Thomas 1764, and Benjamin, son of the latter, married Nancy Crooker 1784, and lived in Pembroke.

Elisha (son of Capt. Benjamin) married Miriam Turner 1741. His sons were Samuel (who married Rebecca Copeland 1784, and whose sons are Col. Samuel and Joseph) Charles who married Mary Sylvester 1774, (and whose sons were the late Elisha and Charles) Elisha born 1743, (died early) and Miriam 1740.

There was an Elkanah Tolman, from Dorchester probably, who resided a short time in Scituate: he had a son Ezra 1739.

We add that the primitive Thomas Tolman, who settled in Dorchester, lived to 1697, and in that year gives legacies in his will "to daughters Sarah Leadbetter, Rebecca Tucker, Ruth Ryall, Hannah Lyon, Mary Collins, and to sons Thomas 'my great chub axe,' &c. to John, meadow lands, &c."

BENJAMIN TOWER.

a descendant of Thomas, an early settler in Hingham, came hither from Weymouth 1716, and lived on the east margin of

Accord Pond. He married Bethia Woodworth 1718. Children, Deborah born 1718, Bethia 1720, James 1722, John 1724.

James married Margaret Day and Lucy Dunbar. He was a soldier at Fort William Henry in the French war. Matthew, his son, born Dec. 1st. 1755, (see Israel Smith) married Rusha Hatch of Marshfield 1781. He was a Revolutionary soldier, and deceased March 1831. His children, Rusha the wife of Samuel Eells of Hanover, Betsey the wife of Capt. Isaac Whittemore 1811, and of Ebenezer T. Fogg, Esq. 1820, and Benjamin Hatch Tower, Harvard Col. 1806, died 1808. Horace, an intelligent and enterprising young man, was lost at sea 1820, mate of a ship from Salem, George Hodges, Master.

John married Lydia Hollis of Weymouth 1746 – his son Jonathan Hollis died at Watertown, leaving sons, James and Jonathan Hollis.

SAMUEL TUELL.

a descendant of Daniel, of Boston, married Mehitabel James 1700, and left Thankful born 1701, Mehitabel 1703, and removed to Marshfield.

Benjamin Tuell, brother of the above, married Joanna Caswell of Hingham 1707. His son Caswell was born in Scituate 1716. This family removed early.

LIEUT. JAMES TORREY, Clothier, (see Mills).

was in Scituate before 1640. He purchased a house lot 1643, of John Stockbridge. His house stood 10 rods south of the gate that leads to Hobart's landing, (in the Neal field since called). The freemen also granted him a considerable tract of land south-west of his house lot. He was a man of great usefulness and respectability, as may be seen in other parts of this work.

He married Ann, the daughter of Elder William Hatch 1643. His children, James born 1644, William 1646, Joseph 1649, Damaris 1651, Jonathan 1654, Mary 1656, Josiah 1658, Sarah 1660, Joanna 1663, Bethia 1665 (a few days after her father's decease). Of these children,

Dea. James succeeded to his father's residence, and to his father's usefulness. He married Lydia Wills, (daughter of William, who lived on Wills' Island) 1666. She deceased early: and he married Elizabeth, daughter of Nathaniel Rawlins 1679, whose children were Ann 1680, James 1682, William 1683, Nathaniel 1686, David 1687, Elizabeth 1689, Samuel 1691, Rachel 1693, Joseph 1694, Stephen 1696, Lydia 1698: A. D. 1701, he married Eunice, widow of Jonas Deane, and had one daughter, Eunice born 1701.

Josiah had a considerable tract of land contiguous to Herring brook hill on the north. His house was in the valley one fourth mile north of the South Meeting-house, opposite to the present house of Mr. James N. Sparrell. He unfortunately lost his life, A. D. 1693. He was in the act of drying the Town's stock of powder on the roof of his house, when a spark from the chimney falling, his life was instantly lost, and his house laid in ruins. He married Isabel, widow of Samuel Witherell 1684: his children, Mary 1685, Josiah 1687, Ruth 1694, Caleb 1695, Jemima 1696, Keziah 1702, and the last four being children of a 2d. wife, Sarah Mendall, married 1692.

These two sons only of Lieut. James left families in Scituate. William (we believe) removed to Plymouth, from whom descended the late valuable Capt. William Torrey of Pembroke, a revolutionary officer, whose son Haviland is living in Hanover.

Of the sons of Dea. James Torrey, James married Sarah Collamore 1710, and lived in Marshfield. William lived a half mile north of Bumpus bridge, (near the house of late Walter Jacob). He married Margaret Buck 1706. Children, Margaret 1707, Abigail 1708, (wife of Samuel Howard of Bridgewater 1725). He married a 2d. time, Honour Rogers 1711, whose children were Honour 1712, William 1713, Hannah 1715, Samuel 1720, Mercy 1722, Eunice 1725.

David, son of Dea. James, married Hope Warren 1710, and had children, Stephen 1710, Rachel 1712.

Capt. Caleb, son of Josiah, succeeded to his father's residence, having built a house a few rods south on the margin of the hill. It was many years a tavern, and was taken down 1827. He married Mary Bryant 1731, Mary Clap 1735, and had children Ruth 1736, (wife of Robert Craig) Caleb 1738, (whose sons were Caleb deceased, and Daniel of Maine) Isaac 1740, died single 1812, Mary 1742, Deborah 1747, Hannah 1752, James 1755, (father of James of Maine, Rev. William of Canandaigua, and Charles deceased) George born 1758, (father of George, David, Isaac living, and Otis deceased, and

3 daughters). The descendants of Capt. Caleb are the only branch of the family remaining here. Lieut. James, of Scituate, was brother of Capt. William of Weymouth, so long a representative and "clerk of the deputies" in Mass. We observe in the Colony Records, that in 1665 Capt. William was the guardian of the four younger sons of Dea. James. Capt. William left sons, Rev. Samuel and William. Joseph (son of Joseph and grandson of Dea. James) removed to Leicester 1743.

HUMPHERY TURNER, (Tanner).

arrived, with his family, in Plymouth 1628. He had a house lot assigned him 1629, and he erected a house and resided there until 1633 probably; the latter being the date of the laying out of his house lot on Kent street, viz. the 4th. lot from the corner of Satuit brook. The farm, however, on which he resided, was east of Colman's hills, near the spot occupied by his descendant James Turner. The house was on the side of the road next the hill. He also had 80 acres granted by the freemen of Scituate, at the place now known as Union bridge on the west side of North river in 1636. This land remains in possession of his descendants. Humphery Turner erected a tannery as early as 1636. He was a useful and enterprising man in the new settlement, and often employed in public business. His wife was Lydia Gamer, who deceased before her husband. He died 1673, and left children named in his will, in the following order, "John, Joseph, young son John, Daniel, Nathaniel, Thomas, daughter Mary Parker – daughter Lydia Doughty – Grandchildren, Humphrey (son of Thomas) Mary Doughty – Jonathan, Joseph and Ezekiel (sons of John, sen.) and Abigail, daughter of Nathaniel." Executors Nathaniel and young son John. These all left families except Joseph.

John, sen. married Mary Brewster, daughter of Jonathan, eldest son of Elder Brewster. He settled 30 rods north-west of Union bridge, where he erected a tannery. His children were Jonathan born 1646, Joseph 1647, Joseph 1648, Ezekiel 1650, Lydia 1652, John 1654, Elisha 1657, Mary 1658, Benjamin 1660, Ruth 1663, Isaac 1665, Grace 1667, Amos 1671.

In 1683, "Twenty acres were laid out for John Turner, sen. east of Barstow's hill and adjoining the 3d. Herring brook."

Scituate Records, Vol. ii. p. 53. On this land lived his son Isaac, and two generations of his posterity.

"Young son *John,* (so named probably at request of a godfather) lived north-east of Hick's swamp, (near now Leonard Clap's). His wife was Ann James, 1649, (see William James). Children, David, (not married) Japhet, Israel, Jacob, Philip, Meriam, (wife of Nathan Pickels) Ann, (wife of Joseph Green of Weymouth) Sarah, (wife of Ichabod Holbrook).

Thomas lived near the Harbour (probably on the Kent street lot). He married Sarah, daughter of Thomas Hyland 1652. Children, Nathan, Elizabeth, Eunice, (wife of Thomas Buck, jr.) Mary, Humphrey, Thomas, Esq. Grace, (wife of Benjamin Stetson) Josiah, Charles, from 1652 to 1664.

Daniel removed to Barstow's (now North river) bridge. He married Hannah, daughter of William Randall 1665. Children, Lazarus, (who died in Phips' expedition to Canada 1690) Elihab, (no sons) Hannah, (wife of John Magoon alias M'Goun) Amasa, Mary, (wife of Mr. Fish) Abner, Elizabeth, (wife of Israel Holmes) Rachel, (wife of M'Alls).

Nathaniel lived on the paternal farm, east of Colman's hill. He married Mehitabel Rigby. Children, Nathaniel, Abigail, Samuel, Mehitabel, Lydia (wife of John James, 2d generation 1719).

We think not proper to pursue this genealogy, because there is extant a Genealogical table prepared by Hon. Charles Turner, jr. We rather proceed to name a few more of the ancient seats of this numerous family. At the west end of Parker lane lived Charles, (son of Thomas) who married Mercy Curtis (daughter of Samuel). He was succeeded by his son Charles who married Eunice James, (daughter of John) to whom succeeded his son, Hon. Charles, who married Mary Rand, (daughter of Rev. Mr. Rand of Kingston): he was 20 years minister of Duxbury, and afterward well known in political life, as member of the Convention that formed Massachusetts State Constitution, and of that which adopted the Federal Constitution, and also as a Senator in the State Legislature. He has been succeeded by Hon. Charles, jr. who married Hannah, (daughter of Col, John Jacob) sometime member of Congress, and now the Master of the Marine Hospital at Chelsea. His son, Theodore, now occupies the place, whose children are the 6th. generation that resided there.

One fourth mile south of the above, on the west side of the way, was the seat of Benjamin, another son of John, sen. He married Elizabeth Hawkins 1692, and was the father of Hawkins and Benjamin, which latter was the father of Capt. Elisha, an officer in the French war 1659 and 1660, in Col. Thomas's regiment.

Jonathan and Joseph (sons of John, sen.) resided near the place now occupied by Cushing Otis, Esq. opposite Union bridge lane; Joseph left no son. Jesse (the son of Jonathan) settled near the beautiful hills, one fourth mile north-west from Union bridge, on land granted to Humphrey his great grandfather 1636. His sons were Capt. Jonathan, a Revolutionary officer, who lived at the south side Mount Blue, Seth who deceased 1830, John now living, and Elisha deceased, whose widow, and only daughter Lydia (with her husband Samuel A. Esq. son of Hon. Charles, jr.) occupy the place of Jesse above described. Seven generations have owned that farm.

Philip, who first occupied the farm east of Hoop-pole hill, was the son of John, jr. (or young son John). His wife was Elizabeth, daughter of Joseph Nash, jr, His son Israel succeeded him, who married Deborah Lincoln, and was succeeded by Philip, his son, who married Juda Hatch and widow Sarah Vinal, which latter survives on the place, and is now the wife of Lazarus Bowker. Nathaniel, son of Philip, sen. named above, settled at the Four corners north of Studley hill, whose sons were Nathaniel, Elijah, Esq. and Job. Jacob, Esq. of Lyme, N. H. is grandson of Israel above, and son of Jacob.

John called "little John" lived at the Gravelly hill northwest a quarter mile from the south Meeting-house (see Dr. Barnes) his sons were Richard and Abiel. Richard was the father of Consider, a Revolutionary soldier, of whose skill at repartee many anecdotes are still told.* Abiel married Elizabeth Robinson, a lineal descendant of the celebrated Puritan John. His son Rowland survives, as also his daughters Bethia the wife of Mr. Joseph Tolman, and Martha of Elijah Clap; and Abiel (oldest son) at Livermore, Maine, born May 3d. 1741. Maj. Amos, son of John, sen. who married Sarah

---

* As a specimen of his facetiousness it is related, that when the army were throwing up the breast works at Roxbury, they struck upon the bones of an Indian burying ground: and Gen. Heath said as he passed by, "let those men lie, we have soldiers enough." "But, (said Turner) if your honor pleases, we want officers." In 1777 he was taken prisoner by Burgoyne, at Ticonderoga, and was kept in the camp until the surrender. We have been informed by a fellow soldier of his, that he used to afford infinite amusement to the officers, and that the Gen. once said to him, "I sha'nt exchange you, Turner; I shall carry you home; the king wants a fool." When Burgoyne marched out with his army and surrendered, Turner took occasion to pass near the Gen. and say, "we sha'nt exchange your Honor, the People *want* a fool."

Hiland, and Hannah, widow of John Clap, 1732, lived fifty rods north of Stockbridge's mill and Mansion. His son, Col. Amos, lived in Hanover, and left one son Amos, who removed to Medway.

Thomas (son of Thomas and grandson of Humphrey) was a lawyer of notoriety in 1690, and later. He resided near the Harbour, married Hannah, the daughter of Edward Jenkins 1693: from his son Ephraim, descended the family "whose schools of politeness (says a writer) have contributed so much to polish the manners of our Metropolis." David was the minister of Rehoboth. Thomas was the father of Col. George and Capt. Thomas late of Pembroke. He had daughters also, Hannah, (wife of Barnabas Barker) Relief, (wife of Gershom Ewell of Marshfield) Jemima, (wife of Capt. John Doggett) Lettice, (wife of Thomas Tilden) Sarah, (wife of Mr. Burr) Ruth, (wife of Mr. Titus) and Mary, (wife of Capt. Joseph Tolman).

The ancient Humphrey Turner farm has descended to Nathaniel, who married Mehitabel Rigby, to his son, Capt. Samuel, who married Desire Barker and widow Abigail Leavitt, daughter of Lieut. Thomas Gill of Hingham, to his son James, who married Mary Turner, to his son James, who married Deborah Lincoln, and to his sons Nathaniel and James; the grand children of Nathaniel being the 8th generation.

Scarcely another family has extended more widely than that of Humphrey Turner. A branch is in North Carolina, viz. Thomas, son of lawyer Thomas. But not all the people of this name in the country descended from Humphrey. There was Capt. Nathaniel of Massachusetts, who had a command in the Pequod war 1637, (see Savage's Winthrop.) Also Robert of Boston 1639, and Michael also, who left families. There was a Thomas Turner in Hingham 1637, whose son Thomas, was in Scituate 1680, and left sons, Thomas born 1682, William 1683, Joshua 1687, Caleb 1691, David 1693, Joseph 1696, Benjamin 1704. Some of their posterity, are in Pembroke, at the Brickkilns.

SAMUEL UTLEY.

was in Scituate 1648, when he married Hannah, daughter of Elder William Hatch. His daughter Lydia born 1653. The family soon disappears from our Records. It may be the same name as Uxley, early in Taunton.

GEORGE VAUGHAN.

was in Scituate 1656. In 1657, "Elizabeth, Joseph and Daniel, children of George and Elizabeth Vaughan were baptized," (2d. church). In 1658, John was baptized, and Mary 1660. This family was in Marshfield 1663, when "George Vaughan of Marshfield was fined for not attending public worship," (Colony Records). In 1669, "George Vaughan was licenced to keep an Ordinary at Middleboro." In 1676, "Joseph Ellis at Scituate with John Vaughan and Daniel Hicks, jr. going into the water of the harbour to swim, s^d Joseph Ellis was drowned. Jury's verdict, that the water in s^d harbour was the sole cause of his death."

George Vaughan died at Middleboro' 1694. His will gives "to son Daniel, to daughter Mary Washburn, to son Joseph, to daughter Elizabeth Howland, to daughter Mercy Due. Eldest son Joseph administrator." The wife of George Vaughan was Elizabeth Hincksman of Marshfield, married 1652.

WIDOW ANNA VINAL.

with three children, appeared in Scituate 1636. A record made by her son Stephen is extant, from which we quote "as I had the relation from my owne mother, I was born about the middle of Dec. 1630. We came into New England in the year 1636, and into the town of Scituate the same year."

Martha was the eldest of the three children; she was married to Israel Chittenden 1646. Stephen was born 1630, and John was two or three years younger.

Anna, this enterprising widow, erected a house in 1637, on the brook, (north of Stockbridge's mill pond, in later times). She seems to have possessed considerable property. Amongst the Conihassett partners in 1646, we notice Anna Vinal. She deceased in 1664: Stephen and John were administrators. Colony Records.

Stephen succeeded to his mother's residence. He married Mary, the daughter of Rev. Nicholas Baker 1661. Children, Mary 1662, Stephen 1664, (died early) John 1667, Adam 1670, (died early) Hannah 1671, Stephen, jr. 1675, Gideon 1678, Samuel 1681, Mary 1684.

John lived on the corner of Kent street and Meeting-house lane. He married Elizabeth, daughter of Rev. Nicholas

FAMILY SKETCHES.

Baker 1664. Children, John born 1665, Elizabeth 1667, Hannah 1669, Jacob 1670, Grace 1672, the wife of Ebenezer Mott 1700.

Stephen, jr. exchanged lands with John, jr. and took the residence on the corner of Kent street, where his descendants Capt. William and Charles now live. He married Mary Woodworth 1704. Children, Stephen 3d. 1705, Gideon 1706, Hannah 1711, Deborah 1714, David 1716, Issachar 1718.

John, jr. married Mary — Children, Jacob, jr. 1691, Elijah 1664, Elizabeth 1697, John 3d. 1699, Mary 1701, Ezekiel 1704, Hannah 1707, Sarah 1711.

Jacob married Mary Cudworth 1695. Children, Mary 1696, Israel 1698, Jacob 3d. 1700, Nicholas 1703, Job 1705, Jonathan 1707, Joanna 1711, Job 1713, Elizabeth 1715, Ignatius 1717, Seth 1719, and Joshua.

Jacob, jr. (son of John, jr.) married Elizabeth Simmons 1716. Children, Elizabeth 1717, Jacob 4th. 1719, Joseph 1721, Priscilla 1723, Mary 1725.

Stepken 3d. married Sarah Stodder 1729, and left no son on record.

John 3d. married Sarah Cudworth 1729, and left a son Benjamin, who married Sarah Merritt 1768.

Jacob 3d, son of Jacob, married Anna Ellmes 1730. Children, Nicholas 1731, Anna 1732, Jacob 5th. 1737, Clodius 1743, Mary 1748.

Jacob 4th. son of Jacob, jr. married Lydia Holbrook 1743. Children, Levi, Lot, and Jane, and perhaps others.

Joseph married Martha Jenkins 1745. Children, Joseph 1749, Asa 1753, Martha 1756, Capt. Nathaniel, (whose son is Dexter) and Capt. Ezra, who died at Matanzas, leaving children in Scituate.

Issachar, son of Stephen, jr. married Mary Chittenden 1741, Judith Bailey 1750. Children, David born 1742, (who lived in Maine, and whose sons David, Gideon, Otis and Job, live in Boston) Capt. William 1751, (whose sons Capt. William, Gideon, Abel and Charles live in Scituate) Mary 1755, Deborah 1758, Stephen 1760.

Israel, son of Jacob, sen. married Elizabeth Booth 1723, sons, Israel, Esq. and Jonathan.

Israel, Esq. married the daughter of Dea. Joseph Cushing, and left sons Israel, (whose daughter Sophia is wife of Capt. John Whitney of Quincy) Robert, Nathaniel, (whose sons are Capt. Howard, Nathaniel and Robert) Maj. William, well remembered for his enterprise in the fisheries at Scituate Harbour, and afterward for projecting the settlement at Quincy Point, &c. and Lemuel of Scituate Harbour, whose son is Cushing.

Ignatius married Mary Tilden 1743, and lived in Marshfield. Sons Stephen, Job and Ignatius.

Ezekiel, son of John, jr. married Mary Wade, and had children, Francis, Sedotia and Elizabeth. He removed to Maine.

Jonathan, son of Israel, sen. graduate Harvard College, was a preacher, but not settled. He married Chloe Pope 1765, Jonathan born 1765, is his son.

Seth, son of Jacob, married Hannah Tilden, and lived in Marshfield. Children, Seth born 1749, Joshua 1752, Hannah 1754.

Joshua married Ruth Randall 1756 – this was probably son of Jacob 3d.

MR. WILLIAM VASSALL.

The first notice given of this distinguished gentleman, in our early history, is, that he was amongst the Patentees of Massachusetts; Samuel, his brother, was another patentee, but he did not come to this country. Gov. Endicot was sent over by the Company to prosecute the plantation (Cradock acting as Governor in England) in 1628, Mr. William Vassall was one of Cradock's Assistants. In 1631, a complaint was "sent home" against the administration of Gov. Endicot, and William and Samuel Vassall were chosen referees on the part of the complainants, and Winthrop and Johnson on the part of the Company. Mr. Vassall had made a short visit to this country in 1630, probably with Gov. Winthrop, who arrived 12th. June 1630, but he returned the same summer, sailing about the end of July. The fact of his having been chosen a referee in the cause of the Browns, is taken by some of our historians for proof, that he was an Episcopalian. (See our chap. of Ecclesiastical History). Whether these transactions set him at variance with the settlers of Massachusetts, we know not: certain is it, however, that the stern Puritans of the day frowned upon him, either through envy of his talents or suspicion of his "leaning to the Bishops." Winthrop (Vol. ii. 262) characterizes him as "a man of busy and factious spirit." On his return to Boston in 1634, he proceeded immediately to Plymouth Colony, where puritanism had taken a milder form from the church of the tolerant Robinson.

Here he found a retreat much to his taste at Scituate, and

united himself harmoniously with Mr. Lothrop's church, in 1634-5, and enjoyed that peace until 1642, when President Chauncey came to be the Pastor. He soon entered into a controversy with Mr. Chauncey, on the subject of baptism, &c.; for an account of which, and for a true explanation of Mr. Vassall's religious sentiments, we refer the reader to our chapter on Ecclesiastical history.

In 1635, he had a considerable tract of land laid out to him, by order of Court, on a beautiful neck of land on the North river. He denominated his plantation "West Newland," his house which was erected 1635, "Belle house," the whole neck of land "Belle house neck," and a beautiful field of planting land on the north side of the neck, "Brook hall field."

His mansion is not spoken of by tradition as peculiarly magnificent, nor was it peculiarly substantial: it stood but about one century, having been taken down in 1742 by the second Judge John Cushing, and replaced by the mansion which is now standing. His plantation on the Neck was not large. Samuel Fuller and Resolved White owned the north end and Elder King the south, and the whole Neck not containing more than two hundred acres. In front of his Mansion was the "New harbour ferry," afterward Dogget's ferry, and now Little's bridge. Just below this ferry Mr. Vassall planted "an oyster bank" 1639, and had the privilege of it secured to him by law. What was the success of the project we have not learned, but it is not within the memory of any now living, that oysters were found in the river. He had other farms, and particularly, that which he purchased of Mr. Lothrop (see Lothrop) on the east of Colman's hills, when that Rev. gentleman removed to Barnstable 1639. This was afterward sold to Mr. Hatherly, and by the latter to President Chauncey, 1642.

While Mr. Vassall remained in Scituate, he was constantly employed in all public offices in the plantation: but he appears in no office in the Colonial Government, save as Counsellor of War. Whether this was owing to the suspicions that rested on him of "inclining to the Bishops," or to his own inclination, we may not fully ascertan. His brief experiment in affairs of government in Massachusetts, probably made him cautious. We learn from Winthrop (Vol. ii. 321) that Mr. Vassall went to England in 1646, to aid Dr. Child's petition for redress of wrongs and grievances in the Government: and that Edward Winslow being then an Agent for the United Colonies there, wrote a book against the petition, entitled, "New England's Salamander discovered," intending by this title a satire upon

Mr. Vassall, a man never at rest (as his enemy says) but when in the fire of contention." Winthrop adds, "finding no entertainment for his Petitions, he went to Barbadoes." Elliot observes, "when Jamaica was taken, he laid the foundation of the great estates which his posterity enjoyed until the Revolution," alluding doubtless to Maj. Vassall's family at Quincy, Boston and Cambridge, who were the descendants of Mr. William, and who, being loyalists, left the country in the Revolution, and abandoned such of their property as could not be carried away. Mr. Vassall's residence in the West Indies was "in the parish of St. Michael, in the Island of Barbadoes, where he deceased 1655," (Historical Soc. Pap. Vol. iv.) That he was one of the most wealthy of the settlers in Plymouth Colony, even before the acquirement of his West India estates, appears from many circumstances. He left Scituate for England 1646. We have very few means of preparing an account of his family. *Judith,* his daughter, married Resolved White 1640, (see White). *Frances* married James Adams 1646, (see Adams). Another married Nicholas Ware in Virginia, (says Mr. Baylies). Capt. John, the only son of which we have any knowledge, bore arms in Scituate 1643. In 1652, he was Lieutenant under Cudworth. In 1647, he was a freeholder and received assignments of common land in his own right. In 1661, he sold the "Belle house plantation" to John Cushing, and removed. While he remained in Scituate, he was a highly respectable citizen, and frequently associated with such men as Mr. Hoar and Mr. Saffin, as an "overseer," as the Selectmen were usually called.

We have so understood it (but without positive record) that Maj. Vassall of Quincy (above named) was his son; whose sons Lewis, John, and William, graduated at Harvard College 1728, 1732, and 1733.

That daughter of Mr. Vassall who married Nicholas Ware, had removed with her husband to Barbadoes before 1656, at which date, we observe in the Colony Records, that Frances, wife of James Adams, "sold to Nicholas Ware of Barbadoes, all her right to the estate of her late father, William Vassall, in the Island of Barbadoes."

We mentioned above, a controversy between Mr. Vassall and Mr. Winslow; and we will add here, that it does not appear that Mr. Vassall wrote anything on that occasion. The pamphlet of Edward Winslow was an answer to a pamphlet, entitled, "New England's Jonas cast up at London," by Maj. John Child, brother to Dr. Child who forwarded the petition.

The anecdote is briefly this. The people of Hingham having superseded Lieut. Eames, in the choice of Bozoun Allen, Capt. the Court refused to sanction the choice. Some warm expressions having fallen from the mouths of many of the people of Hingham on the subject, and a petition being presented which gave offence, the Court proceeded to fine and imprison many of the petitioners. This gave rise to an appeal to Parliament: and Dr. Child's petition was sent to England, under care of Dr. Child, William Vassall and Thomas Fowle. The substance of the prayer of the petition was "against the distinctions which are maintained here, both in civil and church estate," (see Hutchinson). They sailed from Boston in the ship Supply, 1646. It was known at Boston that the papers, containing the petition and the proceedings of the Massachusetts General Court, were about to be sent in that ship, and Mr. Cotton at the Thursday Lecture, preached from Cant. ii. 15. "Take us the foxes, the little foxes, that spoil the vines, &c." and in his Uses took occasion to say, that he advised the ship master, that if storms did arise, to search if they had not in any chest or trunk, any Jonas on board, which if you find, I do not advise you to throw the persons overboard, but the writings. Storms did arise: and some of the passengers remembering Mr. Cotton's Sermon, a woman from amongst them came from between decks, about midnight, to Mr. William Vassall, who lay in the great cabin, (but for the present was in the steerage door way looking abroad) and earnestly desired him, if there were any Jonas in the ship, it might be thrown overboard. He asked her why she came to him? and she said, because it was thought that he had some writings against the people of God. But he answered her that he had nothing except a petition to Parliament, that they might enjoy the liberty of English subjects, and that could be no Jonas. After this she went into the great cabin to Mr. Thomas Fowle, in a like distracted manner, who told her he had nothing but a copy of the petition, which himself and others had presented to the Court at Boston; but if she and others thought that to be the cause of the storm, she and they might do what they would with it. So she took and carried it between decks, to them from whom she came, and they agreed to throw it overboard: but they had many great storms after that. After their arrival at London, the report of an astonishing miracle was spread abroad, viz. the saving of the ship and passengers by throwing the petition to Parliament overboard: whereas "it was only a copy of the petition to their own Court at Boston; and the petition to Parliament was still in the ship, together with another copy of that which was thrown overboard, and were as well saved as their lives and other goods, and are here to be seen and made use of in convenient time." - *N. England's Jonas Cast up at London.*

It is worthy of remark, that most of the principles held by such men as Cudworth, Vassall, Hatherly, and Roger Williams, for which they suffered the persecutions of the early Colonial Governments, were such principles of civil and religious liberty as are now recognized to be the truest and best. The writers who gave an account of such men, were interested, and therefore not to be implicitly regarded, when they draw portraits of the men whom they wished to render odious. The way to test the true character of those persecuted men, and the false coloring of their interested historians, is, to compare their principles, with those principles which constitute that civil and religious liberty which we now hold so dear.

NICHOLAS WADE (His will is dated 1683.)

took the oath of fidelity 1638. His house and homestead were on the west side of *Brushy hill* and north-east side of the road where Shadrach Wade, his descendant of the sixth generation, now resides. In 1657, he was licensed to keep an ordinary or tavern. He married Elizabeth, daughter of Thomas Ensign, and his children were John, Thomas, Nathaniel, Elizabeth, Joseph, Hannah born 1656, Nicholas born 1660, Jacob 1661, of these children Jacob left no family here: he was living 1676, and received a legacy from his uncle John Ensign. Joseph fell with Capt. Pierce in the Rehoboth battle, 1676. Elizabeth married Marmaduke Stevens, and was divorced 1679. "Nicholas Wade, and his daughter Elizabeth, petitioned the Court for a divorcement from Stevens, he being a man of debased life, having another wife in Boston, and another in Barbadoes," (granted) Colony Records.

Thomas married Elizabeth, daughter of Thomas Curtis 1672. His children, Jacob born 1673, Joseph 1675, Sarah 1678, Thomas 1680, Hannah 1682, Ichabod 1685, Moses 1689, Deborah 1691, Rachel 1692. Some of these were born in Bridgewater.

Nicholas, jr. left a family, Mary born 1688, (wife of Ebenezer Woodworth 1712) Margaret born 190, Ruth 1692, (wife of James Merritt 1715) Nathaniel born 1694, died early) and Nicholas born 1696.

Joseph, (son of Thomas) married Ruth Gannet 1705. Children, Ruth 1706, Elizabeth 1708, Joseph 1710, Jacob 1712, Issachar 1714, Zebulon 1716, Sarah 1719, Simeon 1722. Some of the posterity of this family may be in Bridgewater. Zebulon married Mercy Norton of Edgartown 1744.

Issachar married Thankful Merritt 1750. Children, Hannah born 1751, Thankful 1752, John 1755, (who married Abigail Bates 1779) Issachar 1758, (married Mary Pierce 1783) Snell 1762, (married Charlotte Otis 1783) Nancy 1764, Elizabeth 1765, Lucy 1768. There were some branches of this family which we could not trace, for want of records.

Simeon Wade married Eunice Studly 1750, whose daughter Eunice married William Russell of Boston 1784.

Nathaniel, (son of Nicholas, jr,) married Hannah Vinall 1729. Children, Nathaniel born 1730, Levi 1732, Shadrach 1734, David 1738, Abednego 1750, Stephen 1755.

Nicholas (son of Nicholas, jr.) married widow Bathsheba Nicholas 1723, and lived, we believe, in Bridgewater.

Jacob, (son of Joseph) married Rachel Turner 1734. His son Jacob removed to Portland, and Sarah his daughter married William Hayden 1766.

Nathaniel, (son of Nathaniel) married Patience Hatch 1759. Children, Patience born 1760, Nathaniel 1762, Hannah 1766, Deborah 1771.

Stephen, (son of Nathaniel) married Mercy Pierce 1781, and had children, Abednego born 1782, Shadrach 1784, (who occupies the original farm) Mabel 1787, Betsey 1789, Hannah 1791.

NOTE. Jonathan Wade of Malden (freeman 1634) is said to have been a brother of Nicholas of Scituate; his posterity remains in Essex county.

EDWARD WANTON.

was in Boston before 1658: tradition says he came from London; and further, that his mother came with him; but of his father we have neither record nor tradition. He appears in Scituate as a resident in 1661, and had lands 1660. Before he left Boston, he became a convert to the faith of the Quakers, the narrative of which is as follows. The severity of the Massachusetts Government towards this new sect, having been carried to the extent of executing three of them in 1659, 1660 and 1661. Edward Wanton was an officer of the guard, on one or more of these occasions. He became deeply sensible of the cruelty, injustice and impolicy of these measures: he was greatly moved by the firmness with which they submitted to death, and won entirely by their addresses before their execution. He returned to his house, saying, "Alas, Mother! we have been murdering the Lord's people," and taking off his sword, put it by, with a solemn vow never to wear it again. From this time he conversed, on every opportunity with the Friends, and soon resolved to become a public teacher of their faith. In Scituate 1661, he purchased a farm of 80 acres, of William Parker, at the well known ship-yard, a little below Dwelley's creek. He had also extensive lands on Cordwood hill: and also south-west of Hooppole hill, which latter were sold to Nathaniel Brooks 1723. The house of Edward Wanton stood near the bank of the river, on the land that is now improved as a ship-yard, and on the spot occupied by the smaller Work-house. Here he conducted the business of ship building with great success: and we may add, that he held a distinguished place amongst the enterprising settlers of the Town. Of his success as a religious teacher we have spoken elsewhere, (see Ecclesiastical History). He remained firm and active to an advanced age. His last visit to Newport as a representative from the quarterly to the yearly meeting was in 1716, when he was fourscore and five years old, and he deceased soon after his return, Oct. 16th, 1716, and was buried on his own plantation, a few rods north-east of his house, where several of his family and of the family of Rogers have since been buried. The farm bears the name of this venerable man, though it has passed into the possession of another family nearly a century since. His name will go down to posterity so long as a history of the Town shall be known. His memory is held in respect, by tradition, from generation to generation. It may gratify some antiquarian, when we record, that a widow Mary Howland, a descendant, on the Island of Canonicut, has preserved some curious articles of the household furniture of Edward Wanton, which he brought with him from England.

He was probably married before he left England. In Boston were born to him Edward 1658, Margaret 1660, neither of which children lived to mature years: and their mother also deceased 1660-1. After his removal to Scituate, one of the Ministers, of his sect visited him, having recently come from England, and took an opportunity to recommend to him a woman of his acquaintance in England for a second wife: Proposals were accordingly sent in writing, and she came in compliance therewith. Her name was Elizabeth —. They were married 1663, and had children, Joseph born 1664, George 1666, Elizabeth 1668, William 1670, John 1672,

Sarah and Margaret 1674, Hannah 1677, Michael 1679, Stephen 1682, Philip 1686.

The will of Edward Wanton, dated 1716, gives

"To daughter Elizabeth Scot a mulatto boy called Daniel, if he be found, he being now run away,

To sons Joseph, William and John, all my lands at Pennsylvania, with all my money in the hands of Edward Shipin.

To grandson William, (son of William) one third of the sloop that Tobias Oakman goeth master of.

To son Philip, (lands, &c.) To daughter Hannah Barker 5£* To grand-daughter Mary Wanton (daughter of Stephen) 450£, when nineteen years of age, and the like sum to her sister Lydia. To grandson John (son of John) lands, &c. To Nathaniel Chamberlain of Pembroke, all my wearing apparel, and to Chamberlain's two daughters, Abigail and Joanna, 5£ each. Item 5£ to repair our meeting-house near Ichabod Ewell's. To son Michael, all the residue of my estate. Michael Executor."

Joseph removed to Tiverton 1688, and conducted the business of shipbuilding at "the narrows or gut." He married Sarah, daughter of Gideon Freeborn Nov. 9, 1689. He and his wife were both public speakers of the Society of Friends, and tradition speaks of their benevolence and charities. He deceased March 3d. 1754, at the age of 90. He had several children, of whom we will name Mary, the wife of Thomas Richardson, many years Treasurer and Receiver General of Rhode Island. Her daughter, Sarah Richardson, was wife of Thomas Robinson of Newport, and remembered for great accomplishments of person and mind. Gideon, the son of Joseph, was distinguished for his talents and influence. He was Governor of Rhode Island, 1747 and 1748. He married Mary Codman of Newport 1718, and left children: but the name in this line is now extinct, the last having recently deceased at Richmond, Virginia.

William, (son of Edward) began his distinguished course by stepping out of the rules of his religious sect, and performing some distinguished military exploits; and in the narrative of these exploits the name of his brother John must be associated with that of William. In 1694, when William was at the age of 24, and John at 22, a pirate ship having committed several robberies in the Bay, in which the family property had suffered losses, these two young men headed.

---

* Wife of James Barker, of the place called Drinkwater, in Scituate.

a party of volunteers, and captured the pirates, and carried them into Newport, where they were executed. Again in 1697, just before the peace of Ryswic, during the troubles with Count Frontenac, Governor of Canada, a French armed ship had taken several prizes in the Bay: and again William and John Wanton fitted out each a vessel from Boston, well manned with high spirited volunteers, and admirably accomplished their design. It is said that William ran under the stern of the French ship and wedged her rudder, while John and his party boarded. Whether this method of embarrassing the Frenchman were practicable or not, we do not know: we only state that this is a part of the fireside narrative, that has been handed down. It is also said, that the venerable Edward endeavoured to dissuade his sons from this enterprize as unlawful, according to the rules of their church; but on finding their determination fixed, he thus addressed them. "It would be a grief to my spirit to hear that ye had fallen in a military enterprize, but if ye will go, remember that it would be a greater grief to hear that ye were cowards."

The fame of this exploit reached England, and when the two Wantons went to England in 1702, they were invited to Court, and Queen Anne granted an addition to their family coat of arms, and presented each with two pieces of plate, with proper devices, viz. a silver punch bowl and salver. These pieces of plate are said to have been stolen from their houses at Newport, during the raging of the mobs in the political contest of Hopkins and Ward, with the exception of one piece, which is now said to be extant in Newport.

We now proceed with William. He left Scituate 1704, and settled in Newport. He had previously married Ruth, the daughter of Dea. John Bryant, sen. To this match, there had been several objections: the Quakers disapproved of his marrying out of the Society, and the Congregationalists of his marrying into theirs, and moreover the woman was very young; however, the sanguine temper of Wanton was not to be foiled, and he is said to have addressed the young woman in the presence of her family in the following words: "Ruth, let us break away from this unreasonable bondage. I will give up my religion, and thou shalt give up thine, and we will go the church of England, and go to *the D—l together.*" They fulfilled this resolution, so far as going to church and marrying, and adhering to the church of England during life. In 1732 he was elected Governor, and again 1733, and died near the close of that year. The house which he built and in which

FAMILY SKETCHES.

he deceased, is now occupied as a boarding house in Thames street, Newport. He left several children, among whom we will name Joseph, who succeeded to his father's mansion. He graduated at Harvard College 1751: he adhered to the church of England as his father had done. He is now remembered by some aged people, and described as a gentleman of the most fair proportions and majestic personal appearance. He was chosen Governor 1769, and re-elected for six successive years. He deceased 1782, and was buried in the Clifton burying ground. Joseph, his son, is the only survivor of the name in this branch of the family: he is an Episcopal clergyman in or near Liverpool, England.*

John, whose memoirs we have connected, in part, with those of William, was truly a remarkable man. After the death of his brother William, when strong political parties began to agitate the Colony, he was persuaded by his friends to permit himself to be voted for as Governor, with the expectation that he might unite the factions through the influence of his fame for personal bravery, and his credit as the most wealthy citizen of the Colony, for he had been eminently successful in trade. He had indeed renounced his military fame, and embraced the faith of the Quakers as early as 1712, and travelled much as a religious teacher. It was however thought to be a conjuncture, when it became his duty to heal the divisions of the times; and success attended the plan. He was chosen first in 1734, and re-elected for seven successive years. He died in office, May 5th, 1740, and was laid in the Coddington burying ground, where a marble monument was erected.

In one of the years of his administration, there were certain conflicting Indian claims to be settled within the Colony of Connecticut, and the cause was referred to the three Governors of Massachusetts, Connecticut and Rhode Island. At this trial, a question was agitated whether the Sachems should be permitted to speak in their own cause: Counsel contended that they should not, and two of the Board inclining to that opinion, Governor Wanton remarked, that as they had already agreed to admit the testimony of some of the na-

---

* Gov. Joseph married Mary, daughter of John Winthrop of New London. His daughter Ann married Winthrop Saltonstall of New London, son of Gen. Gurdon Saltonstall, Mary married Capt. Coddington of Newport, Elizabeth married Thomas Wickman of Newport (and one single daughter of this lady is now living,) Ruth married William Browne, Governor of Bermuda. Catharine married Mr. Stoddard and Mr. Detileur.

Information from James Bowdoin, Esq.

tives, it would be but proper, that their chiefs should be allowed to speak. "I have (says he) been accounted a man of courage in my day, but I think I shall turn coward and flee, if you bring in a body without a head." This sally carried the point; the Sachems were allowed to speak, and the Governor was often heard to express his admiration of the powers of oratory in those children of the forest.

He is described as of middling stature, thin features and fair complexion – remarkable for his gentle attentions to children, many of whom would gather round him to catch his smile in the street, or collect at his door, as he sat in his portico. He resided in a house which he purchased, opposite to that of his brother William. His wife was Mary Stafford of Tiverton. James, his son, inhabited his mansion, whose son George is the only survivor of the name in Newport.

John (son of Gov. John) married into the ancient and respectable family of Redwood. His son Jonas Langford Wanton, deceased at Cranston 1827, aged 88, and left no children.

Michael (son of the primitive Edward) settled on the paternal estate in Scituate. His marriage is on the Town Records, "to Mary New of Scituate 1704," but she was born in Newport. His 2d. wife was Abigail Kean of Pembroke 1716. He succeeded his father as the religious teacher of the Society of Friends, and was a successful propagator of the sect. He was a cotemporary with Rev, Nathaniel Eells of the South Parish in Scituate, and they are said to have lived in more harmony with each other than could be expected from the circumstances, Wanton being fired with the zeal of a new sect, and Eells entertaining contempt for an uneducated ministry. He is said to have been a man of so much meekness and gentleness, that all contention with the Congregationalists was laid aside; a circumstance which, if it did not contribute to promote his sect, at least disarmed opposition and persecution. He was cotemporary with Thomas Turner, a lawyer of facetious memory, whose sarcasms were often aimed at Wanton, and always received with such undisturbed good humor, that at length they became sincerely attached to each other, though of different temper and different sects. On one occasion, Wanton had been successful in a fishing excursion, and loaded his boat with fine hallibut, and calling, on his return, at the tavern at White's ferry, and finding an assemblage of gentlemen attending a trial by reference, he caused an entertainment to be prepared of his fish, and invited the whole company to dine. This was done in consequence of a sarcasm of lawyer Turner, who had thus addressed him, "Friend Wanton; you are like the Apostle Peter. In the first place he was a fisherman, and so are you – he was a preacher, and so are you – he denied his Lord, and so do you." It was agreed by the company that Wanton had the advantage on this occasion, He deceased in Scituate and was buried on the paternal farm. His children were Ruth born 1705, Mary 1707, Stephen 1709, and by his 2d. wife, Lusanna 1717, Hannah 1721, Michael 1724. Stephen inherited the family estate, which he sold to John Stetson 1740, and removed to Newport. He married Mary, daughter of Samuel Clark, of Canonicut 1736. His daughter Hannah is the mother of Stephen Gould of Newport, Cabinet Keeper of the Historical Society of Rhode Island.* Stephen Wanton deceased 1769, aged 56. Mary, daughter of Michael, married Daniel Coggeshall of Portsmouth, Rhode Island 1726, and Ruth married Freeborn of R. I.

Stephen (son of the primitive Edward) lived and died in Newport, leaving no children.

Philip, the youngest son, lived in Newport, and united the business of merchant and apothecary. He married Hannah, daughter of Thomas Rodman 1711. He died 1735, and was laid in the Clifton burying ground.

His son Philip succeeded to his father's mansion and business. He married Elizabeth, daughter of John Casey 1749, and Sarah Lawton 1761. Philip, his son, removed to Alexandria, on the Potomac 1790, where he resides with his family: he has several sons, by whom the name, which has become extinct in several branches, may be preserved.

Elizabeth, (daughter of the primitive Edward) was a member of the 2d. Congregational Church in Scituate 1711. She is called Elizabeth Scot, in her father's will 1716.

THOMAS WARDIN.

was in Scituate 1690. His wife was Elizabeth Sergeant. His children, Thomas born 1690, Elizabeth 1692, Frances 1695, Samuel 1698. The family probably removed to Boston.

CAPT. ANTHONY WATERMAN, (son of Thomas).

came from Marshfield 1760, and settled on the farm that was Capt. Joseph Sylvester's (see Sylvester). Here he erected a

---

* The author acknowledges the important assistance of this gentleman, in collecting the Notes upon this family.

Tannery, and conducted the business successfully. He married Deborah, daughter of Joseph Foster, of Plymouth. His children, Nathaniel born 1761, Anthony 1763, Thomas 1765, Foster 1768, James 1770, Samuel 1772, Jotham 1774, Deborah 1779.

Nathaniel left a family in Marshfield, and deceased 1820. His residence was east of the brook at Rogers hill, where he established a Tannery, and in which he is succeeded by his sons, Anthony and James.

Anthony (son of Capt. Anthony) resided at Buck's corner, near the Harbour. His son James, conducts the Tannery in the south part of the Town, at the ancient Tolman and Copeland place.

Thomas (son of Capt. Anthony) married Sarah, daughter of Maj. Nathaniel Winslow, and deceased early, leaving one son, viz. Capt. Thomas Waterman, who resides east of the brook, at the ancient Copeland place, named above. The widow of Thomas, sen. married Ebenezer Copeland, and now survives, a widow, having three daughters, Sarah, widow of Rev. Nathaniel Wales of Maine, Elizabeth, wife of Capt. Joshua D. Turner of Hingham, and Huldah, wife of James Waterman of Scituate.

Foster, Esq. (son of Capt. Anthony) has been a lawyer in Maine, and now resides in Scituate, single. He graduated at Harvard College, 1789, and was sometime Tutor at that College. *James* died early.

Samuel resides at the paternal place, where he conducts a Tannery. He married Sarah, daughter of Hawkes Cushing. His children, Sarah, (wife of William Winslow) Charlotte Cushing, Frances, Samuel, Lemuel Cushing.

Jotham (son of Capt. Anthony) graduated at Harvard College 1799. He was some time Minister of Barnstable. He married Bennet, and has a family, *Deborah* (daughter of Capt. Anthony) died early.

Nathaniel Waterman, Esq. who married Mercy, daughter of Joseph Otis, was brother of Capt. Anthony. He resided at Scituate Harbour. He was distinguished for his firmness and zeal in the Revolutionary War, having been on the Town's Committee of Correspondence in those times. He left one son Nathaniel, who resides in Maine. The wife of Thomas Hobart, Esq. of Hanson, is also his daughter. Also the wife of Anthony Waterman, jr. and the wife of Lemuel Vinal. This family descended from Robert Waterman of Plymouth, who married Elizabeth Bourn 1638, and who was afterward of Marshfield. He had a brother Thomas Waterman of Roxbury, who died 1670, leaving an only son, Thomas, who was in Hingham 1679, and whose son Robert was born 1680, as we see in Hobart's Journal. Robert, sen. of Plymouth died 1665, and Josiah Winslow and Anthony Snow were appointed guardians to his two youngest sons, Joseph and Robert, (Colony Records.) He had also sons, John born 1642, Thomas 1644, and perhaps others.

THOMAS WEBB, (from Boston).

married Mary, daughter of Dea. Samuel Stodder 1725, and succeeded to the residence of his father in law, on the west of Brushy hill. He had a son Thomas (his wife Margaret Woodworth 1747,) who succeeded him, and whose sons were Thomas born 1750, Barnabas born 1753, and Paul 1758. Barnabas occupies the paternal place. Thomas, sen. had also a son Samuel, whose sons were, Samuel born 1754, Otis 1760, and Lemuel born 1764: the latter has sons, Capt. Seth (son in law of Jesse Dunbar, Esq.) and Lemuel.

JOHN WARREN, (from Plymouth).

married Naomi Bates 1713. His children, James born 1714, and Hope 1716, (the wife of Capt. Caleb Torrey) John 1719, Nathaniel 1721, and others.

ISAAC WELLES.

took the oath of fidelity in Scituate 1638, and removed to Barnstable 1639. Joseph, probably his son, married Grace Dipple, in Scituate, 1666, and Joseph, probably a grandson, married Abigail Smith, in Scituate, 1705.

JAMES WERMAL.

took the oath of fidelity in Scituate 1638, and removed to Duxbury soon after. His son Josiah was in Duxbury 1670, and John (probably son or grandson) died in Bridgewater 1711, and his estate was settled by his widow, Mary.

OBADIAH WHEATON.

had children born in Scituate, Alice 1684, Lydia 1704.

JOHN WHISTON.

was in Scituate 1636, in which year he received a grant of land, nearly opposite to "Meeting-house lane" on the west. He had various other grants; but there was his house lot. He was a Conihasset partner 1646. His wife was the sister of Edward Jenkins. There are but two births of his children on record, viz. Increase 1656, Bathsheba 1660. John was the second son, born as early as 1647, Joseph was eldest. He married the daughter of William Brooks. We notice in the Colony Records the following entry: "1665, Joseph Whiston is authorized to sell lands for the use of his brothers and sisters, with the help of his father in law, William Brooks, and his uncle Edward Jenkins." His father, of course, had deceased about this time.* Joseph probably removed to Boston, as we find few traces of him after this date. *Sarah* married Thomas Nichols 1663, and Susanna married Thomas Perry 1671.

John jr. was a freeman 1660. He left children, Mercy born 1678, Abigail 1680, Joseph 1683, John 1686, Susanna 1688, (see baptisms). His farm was west of the Church burying hill, and his house twenty rods south of Capt. Joseph Sylvester's. His son John had sons, Increase born 1713, Joseph 1716. It has been said that this family, near the latter date, removed to Connecticut. Gershom Stetson succeeded to the possession of the house, which has been taken down many years since.

JOHN WHITCOMB.

we suppose to have come from Dorchester, in Dorset, England, from the circumstance that it was a common name in that vicinity, and that he came with the early settlers of Dorchester, N. England, who were most, of them, from Dorsetshire. He was in Dorchester as early as 1633, was a member of the Church 1638. In 1640 he appears in Scituate, when he

---

* John, sen. died intestate 1664. Joseph, (eldest son) received the homestead, allowing the income to his mother Susanna for six years. Joseph died in Boston 1666, and having no children, left most of his estate to his brother John, then aged 18, under guardianship of Edward Jenkins. Colony Records.

possessed a farm of 108 acres, near the mouth of the North river, on the Marshfield side. This he sold to Thomas Hickes 1649. In 1646, he became one of the Conihasset partners in Scituate. In 1654, he removed to Lancaster, and he may have purchased lands there a year or two earlier. His last sale of lands in Scituate was in 1654, when he conveyed a half share in the Conihasset lands to John Williams, jr. the other half he gave to his son Robert. He died at Lancaster, Sept. 24, 1662. He wrote his name in 1646, Whetcumbe.

There is no record of the birth of his children: most of them must have been born in England. From incidental records we find that they were Katharine, John, Robert, James and Job. Katharine married Rhodolphus Ellmes of Scituate, in 1644, and has a numerous posterity.

John removed to Lancaster, with his father, in 1654, and has posterity in that vicinity. Col. Asa Whitcomb of Sterling, a Revolutionary officer, was a descendant.

Robert remained at Scituate. He was the first of the family that settled in "the beaches" or beach woods, where several generations of his posterity have resided. He married Mary, the daughter of Gen. James Cudworth 1660. There is no record of his children; but we observe in Gen. Cudworth's will, that legacies are given "to grand children Israel, Robert, James, and Mary Whitcombe." There was another daughter, born probably after Gen. Cudworth's decease, viz. Elizabeth, wife of Daniel Lincoln of Hingham 1710.

Israel succeeded to the residence of his father Robert, sen. and left children, Israel born 1700, Mary 1703, Hannah 1706, Elizabeth 1709, John 1711, Noah 1714. Of these, Israel removed to Cohasset, where he left sons, Israel, Job, Joseph and Lot.

Israel, jr. left sons Jacob, of Springfield, Ver. Zadock of North Yarmouth, Samuel of Boston (whose son Samuel is a clerk in the Custom House) and Ezekiel died early.

Mary, daughter of Israel, sen. was wife of Aaron Pratt, and Hannah, wife of Jonathan Pratt, of Cohasset, brothers of Chief Justice Benjamin Pratt of New York. John (son of Israel, sen.) married Sarah Tower of Hingham 1734, succeeded to his father's residence in "the beaches," and left children, John born 1735, Elizabeth 1737, (wife of — Lincoln) Reuben 1740, who died single, Sarah 1744, (wife of Daniel Litchfield) Thankful 1746, wife of Elijah Stodder, Mary 1752, wife of John Ellmes, and Simeon 1762, who left no family. Of these, John, jr. married Hannah Nash 1758, and left children, John 1759,

William 1763, Charles 1766, Samuel 1769, Joseph, Noah, Mercy and Hannah. These are all living in Scituate.

Noah, youngest son of Israel, sen. married Mary Franklin 1742: his daughter Mary born 1744, Thankful 1746: he then removed to Randolph, where he had sons born, from whom many respectable families have descended.

James, son of Robert, sen. married Mary Parker 1694, and had children, James born 1695, died early, Nathaniel and James twins, "the one born August 19th. 1697, and the other August 21st." Mary and Joanna, twins, born 1699. We can give no further account of this family.

Robert, jr. had three daughters born in Scituate, Content 1695, Melea 1699, and Elizabeth 1700.

James, (youngest son of John, sen.) we suppose to have been the James Whitcomb who settled in Boston as early as 1665, and who is so respectfully mentioned in Mrs. Rowlandson's Narrative. He owned lands where the Tremont House now stands. The name of his wife was Rebecca, and he had sons, James born 1662, Peter 1664, and others.

RESOLVED WHITE.

son of William White, came to Plymouth in the Mayflower, with the first company of Pilgrims 1620. He had lands laid out in Scituate 1638, at the place afterward sold to Lieut. Isaac Buck, a half mile south of the Harbour, (see Buck). In 1640 he had a grant, by order of the Colony Court of 100 acres, upland and marsh, on Belle house neck, adjoining Mr. Vassall's farm on the south-east. He had also other lands adjoining by deed of gift from Mr. Vassall 1646. In 1662 he sold his house to Isaac Buck, and removed to Marshfield. He seems to have had two houses, the one near Buck's corner, and the other at Belle house neck. In Marshfield he settled near his brother Peregrine on the south river. He married Judith the eldest daughter of Mr. William Vassall, 1640. His children were, William born 1642, John 1644, Samuel 1646, Resolved 1648, Anna 1649, Elizabeth 1652, Josiah 1654, Susannah 1656. None of these children settled in Scituate: their posterity is found in Bristol County as well as Plymouth. Some of them may have removed to Barbadoes.

GOWIN WHITE, (Planter).

was one of the Conihasset partners in 1646. In 1650 he purchased a considerable farm of William Richards, who removed to Weymouth: it was on the south of Till's or Dwelley's creek, and now the Ruggles farm. There is no record of the family of Gowin White, but we find Joseph and Timothy to be his sons and heirs: also Sarah, who may have been his daughter, married John Bailey 1672.

Joseph married Mary, daughter of John Rogers 1660. She died 1677. Also his wife Susanna died 1698, and he married Elizabeth Vinal 1699. He had several children, viz. Sarah, who married Thomas Young 1688, Mary born 1671, Joseph born 1674, (who married Oseeth Turner 1696. Joseph, jr. died 1715, and Joseph, sen. 1711.

Timothy, (son of Gowin) married Abigail, daughter of John Rogers 1678, he settled on his father's Conihasset farm, a half mile west of the Harbour and near his brother Joseph. His children were, Timothy born 1679, Abigail 1682, Sarah 1685, (wife of Joseph Tilden 1710), Elizabeth 1688, (wife of James Cudworth 1712.)

Timothy, jr. married Rebecca Simons 1707, and succeeded to the paternal farm. His children, Timothy born 1708, Elizabeth 1710, Abigail 1712, Mary 1714, Rebecca 1717, Desire 1719.

Timothy (3d. generation) married Sarah Clap 1732, and succeeded his father in his residence. He had one son Timothy.

Timothy (4th. generation) married Catharine Ellmes 1763, and Temperance Bryant. He deceased 1825, and has left several sons, of whom Timothy, we believe, occupies the paternal farm, which has been cultivated by six generations.

We will add that Gowin White resided on this place in 1646. He married Elizabeth Ward of Plymouth 1638.

JOHN WEYBORN, (or Wiborn).

and Thomas Weyborn, sons of Thomas Weyborn, some time of Plymouth and afterward of Boston, were in Scituate 1660. Thomas was freeman that year. In 1680 he was in Boston, when we observe he entered "a protest against the unlawful chartering of a barque for a West India voyage by Samuel Clap, Thomas King and Theophilus Witherell of Scituate, in which barque Weyborn was partner." Colony Records. He married Abigail Elliot of Boston 1657.

John became possessed of a half share of Conihasset land in the right of Richard Sealis, probably by purchase. He had children, Abigail born 1658, Thomas 1663, Joseph 1664, (these born in Boston) and John 1670, born in Scituate.

John, jr. married Esther Ripple of Boston 1694. His children, born in Scituate, Elizabeth 1694, John 1696. In 1697 he was in Norwich, Connecticut; when he signs a deed of gift in company with Thomas Jenkins, who seems to be his brother in law, of the house and land which he had left in Scituate, to Joanna Colman; this house and land was sold by Joanna Colman, widow, to Experience Daman 1700. There was a considerable removal from Scituate to Norwich about this time. There is a land mark in Norwich called the Scituate line, to this day, which doubtless marked the purchase of Wiborn, Isaac Woodworth, the Colmans, and others from Scituate.

Thomas Weyborn, sen, died in Boston 1656. His will gives "To sons Thomas and James, &c. to wife Elizabeth one half the windmill in Boston, and 40S. per annum. To son John 40£ at 21, to daughter Elizabeth Merritt 5£, to daughter Mary 20£ at 16, and to board at expence of Thomas and James Executors."

WILLIAM WILLS.

was a freeman in Scituate in 1639. This name has been mistaken for Willis. In 1639 he purchased "Tongue Island" and adjacent marsh, of John Cooper, who removed to Barnstable. On this island, Wills erected his house. It is a marsh island, or island in the marsh, below Little's bridge, and now bears the name of Wills's Island. He deceased in 1688, at the age of 90. His will dated 1683, gives "to son Samuel all my estate, he to maintain his mother Lucy during life." Lucy, the widow, deceased 1697.

There was but two children of William Wills of whom we have found any traces. Samuel born 1640, (Colony Records) and Lydia, baptized 1645: she became the wife of Dea. James Torrey 1666.

Samuel left no son that we have discovered. His daughter Lydia born 1676, married William Clift of Marshfield 1691. The name of Wills Clift is now extant in that town.

In 1670 there was a Rowland Wills in Scituate, and mentioned in the Colony Records, as "brought into the Colony by John Williams, many years since." The Court ordered him "to send for his wife: if she come he may still abide; otherwise he must leave the Colony."

There was also a Thomas Wills, freeman, in Mass. 1636.

JOHN WILLIAMS.

came, we believe, with Mr. Hatherly from London 1632, and took up a farm on the north side of Scituate Harbour, very early. In 1646 he was one of the Conihasset partners, when his farm was included in Mr. Hatherly's 400 acres, which he accepted as his quarter of the purchase. The house which was erected by John Williams as early as 1634, has been built upon since, and if tradition be true, there is one part of the original building preserved. The massive beams, the wooden walls, interlined with brick, and the port holes, witness that it was a garrison house, as we know from records that it was. It is the oldest house in Scituate, if this be the original house. The Stockbridge house was built 20 years later. We think there are few if any older houses in New England than these.

The wife of John Williams was Ann. His children were John, Ann, Edward and Mary. Mary married Anthony Dodson of Scituate 1651 (see Dodson). Ann, the oldest of the family, married John Barker of Duxbury 1632. Edward was a householder in 1647. His house was on Kent street, at the corner where the cart way turns toward the 3d. Cliff. He deceased 1671, leaving no family; John his brother administered.

Capt. *John* was a householder in 1647, and bore arms 1643. He succeeded his father in his residence. He was a man of energy and activity, both in civil affairs and in war. He was commander of a company in Philip's war, and constantly on duty from March to the Autumn in 1676. He commanded the right wing of the ambuscade at the time when Philip fell. He lived to a good old age, and deceased in Scituate 1694, leaving no family, and making his sister's son, Williams Barker, his principal legatee. We know not that he was married. There was a John Williams, who was divorced from Elizabeth, daughter of Barnabas Lothrop of Barnstable, and afterward divorced from a wife Sarah. These divorces took place in 1666 and 1673, but this person being called in the Colony Records John Williams of Barnstable, we presume it was not our Capt. John. The will of Capt. Williams is dated at Scituate 1691. He died June 22, 1694, and gives

"To Nephew Williams Barker, son of John Barker, of Marshfield, the 200 acre farm formerly purchased of Mr. Hatherly, also legacies to nephews John Barker of Marshfield, and Abraham Blush of Boston. To my friend, Samuel Fuller of Rehoboth. To nephew Jonathan Dodson of Scituate. To my ancient servant (tenant) John Bailey, the farm on which he lives at the Neck in Scituate. To sister Mary Dodson, and to her daughters, Margaret Dodson, Mary Booth, Patience Pierce, Bethia Dodson and Eunice Dodson. To brother in law John Barker. Item, to my two boys, George and Thomas, whom I obtained, "with my sword and my bow," on condition that they take my name of Williams, lands at Showamett. (Note – these were Indians without doubt). To my servant Thomas Bailey – to my servant Wills, (Rowland Wills). To Daniel Hickes, (and to fourteen others named) each 5£ (or upwards)."

We believe few men had such estates to divide at that period. The farm on which he lived is perhaps the most productive of any in the Old Colony. We notice in the Town Records Anno 1679, that Capt. John Williams entered with the Town Clerk, the marks and brands of forty horse kind of his own: they were entered, according to custom, in order to reclaim them if they should stray, (Vol. 5.)

CAPT. WILLIAM WILLSON.

married Hannah Bourn of Marshfield 1741. His children were William born 1742, (died early) Hannah born 1741, Abigail 1747; the latter is now living and single. Hannah was the wife of George Cole of Swansey 1765, afterward the wife of Ebenezer Rogers of Marshfield, and again the wife of Caleb Torrey of Scituate. She deceased 1825. Capt. Willson's place of residence, was at Willson hill, now called, lately the residence of Henry Sheafe, Esq. of Boston, and now of Thomas Perkins, a native of Plympton. The writer of this history feels it but just to acknowledge some obligation to Abigail, above named, for traditions relating to the genealogies of Scituate families.

JOHN WINTER.

was in Scituate 1638. He had lands near Stoney brook cove and the stoney brook. His house was where John Briggs lived many years subsequently, and where Charles Ford now lives. In 1651, "John Winter was found dead, and Walter Baker was arrested on suspicion of murdering him," (cleared) Colony

Records. His widow married James Turner, probably of Hingham. John jr. was living 1663, when he had grants of land on the north of his house lot. Obadiah, another son probably, had grants in 1673. Catharine, a daughter of John, sen. was an unfortunate woman and received assistance from the Town several years subsequent to 1653.

CHRISTOPHER WINTER.

was probably a brother of John, sen. He was of Plymouth 1639, when he was "fined 10S. for publishing himself in marriage with Jane Cooper (daughter of John, probably) contrary to order and custom of this government," Colony Records.

He had lands in Scituate in 1657, and in 1660 he is called of Jones' river, now Kingston. His daughter Martha married John Hewett 1668, of Marshfield, and Mary married John Reed the same year.

WILLIAM WILCOME.

had land in Scituate 1673. He was one of the heroes who fell with Capt. Pierce 1676. He left no family on record.

PHILIP WILLCUT.

married Deborah Gannet 1711. His son Jesse married Lois Studley 1750. There may be descendants in Cohasset.

GEORGE WILLARD.

took the oath of fidelity in Scituate 1638. Few traces of him appear in our Records. He was here 1641, when "George Willard of Scituate was bound over for defamation, viz. for saying that they were fools and gulls for paying the rate (probably the rate for religious uses) that the churches here and in the Bay, held forth a devilish practice in that they did not baptize infants, and for contumeliously asking the Assistants why they did not take the oath of supremacy," (released). He appears first in Mass. Colony, and probably came to Scituate to shelter himself under the liberal influence of Mr. Vassall, as he settled near him. In 1644 he found himself accommodated (as to his notions of baptism) in Scituate, South Parish. His children, Deborah and Daniel, were baptized by Mr. Witherell 1645. Soon after he disappears: probably he went to Georgiana with Prebble and Twisden, who were of the liberal class of Puritans, if not Episcopalians.

OLIVER WINSLOW.

settled in Scituate about 1730; and we exhibit his connexion with the distinguished families of Winslow, in the following imperfect notes.

There were five brothers who came early to this country, viz. Edward and Gilbert, in the Mayflower 1620, John in the Fortune 1621, and Kenelm and Josiah before 1633. The residence of this family had been in Worcestershire, Eng.

Edward, the eldest, was born 1594, and was married before he left England. His wife, Elizabeth, deceased at Plymouth in the first fatal winter after their arrival, March 24, 1621, and he married Susanna, (widow of William White,) who had lost her husband nearly at the same time. This first marriage in the Colony, was solemnized in May 1622. Edward Winslow was an Assistant in the Col. Government several years, Governor in 1633-36 and 1644, and a Commissioner of the United Colonies 1655, in which year he died. His residence was at Marshfield, at his seat called Caresrull. His son Edward came with him from England. He had a daughter Susanna and probably others. His son Josiah was born at Marshfield 1629. He was also many years an Assistant in the Government, an intrepid commander in Philip's war, and Governor (the first who was born in the country) from 1673 to his death. His wife was Penelope Pelham, daughter of Herbert Pelham. She died 1703 aged 73: and Governor Josiah Winslow died Dec. 18, 1680, and was buried Dec. 23, (Marshfield Records.)

Some of his children, we have discovered to have been brought to Scituate 2d. church for baptism, viz. Elizabeth 1664, Edward 1667, died early, Isaac 1676.

The latter was a Counsellor after the union of Plymouth and Massachusetts Colonies. He died 1738, aged 62. His son Gen. John, was the enterprising officer so well known in our Colonial annals as Capt. in the expedition against Cuba 1740, Colonel at the extraordinary capture of Louisburg 1744, and afterward as Maj. General in the British service. His son, Dr.

FAMILY SKETCHES. 389

Isaac, a gentleman of distinguished accomplishments, succeeded to the family residence: His only son John, Esq. Counsellor at law, deceased at Natchez 1822. We believe, he has a son surviving.

Gilbert, who came with his brother Edward in 1620, settled, as we are informed, at Portsmouth.

John (another brother) was a merchant in Boston, after having resided a few years at Plymouth. He married Mary Chilton, the adventurous maiden, who disputed with John Alden the honour of having leaped first upon the Plymouth rock. We have few notes of the genealogy of his family. He had a son John, whose son John was born 1665. Isaac, Esq. now of Boston, is a descendant.

John, sen. deceased 1673, naming in his Will, "My wife, my son John, William Payne, son of my daughter, Sarah Middlecot, Parnell Winslow, daughter of my son Isaac, Susan, daughter of my daughter Latham, son Benjamin, son Edward, Edward Gray's children, by my daughter Mary Gray, my son Joseph Winslow's two children, my grandchild Mary Harris, my kinsman, Josiah Winslow, Governor of New Plymouth 20£ in goods, my brother Josiah's son 20£ in goods, my kinswoman, Eleanor Baker, daughter of my brother Kenelm Winslow 5£." We have seen in the Boston Records 1660, "Myles Standish married to Sarah Winslow," she was probably another daughter of Kenelm.

Kenelm was in Plymouth before 1633. He married Helen, the daughter of John Adams of Plymouth 1634, He had lands in Yarmouth in 1640: and he deceased at Salem, and was buried Sept. 13, 1672, (Marshfield Records). He had sons Kenelm and Nathaniel, and perhaps others.

Kenelm, jr. was resident in Yarmouth 1668, from whence he brought to the 2d. church in Scituate for baptism, Kenelm 1668, Josiah 1670, Thomas 1672. It is well known that many of the ministers in the Colony were opposed to infant sprinkling at that time. (See our Chapter on Ecclesiastical History.)

Nathaniel resided in Marshfield, married Faith Miller 1664, and had children, Faith 1665, Nathaniel 1667, James 1669, Eleanor, the wife of John James 1667, Gilbert 1673, Kenelm 1675, Josiah 1683. Of these, Kenelm had a son Nathaniel born 1709. Gilbert married Mary Snow, and had sons Issachar, Barnabas, Gilbert, Anthony born from 1699 to 1707.

Nathaniel, jr. resided in Marshfield; he married Lydia Snow (sister of his brother's wife, and daughter of Anthony Snow)

1692. His children were Lydia 1693, Thankful 1695, Snow 1698, Oliver 1702, (at the head of this article) Deborah 1708, Patience 1710, Nathaniel 1712, and by a 2d wife, Deborah Bryant of Scituate, married 1716, Ruth born 1718. Of these, Oliver married Agatha, daughter of John Bryant 3d. of Scituate, and succeeded to the residence of John Bryant, near the Cornet's old mill dam, on the 3d. Herring brook. He had a son Oliver, who was killed in the French war in 1758, at the age of 20, a son John, who removed to Nobleboro', Maine, and Maj. Nathaniel, a man who inherited the bold spirit of his distinguished ancestors. He was a firm patriot in 1776, entered the army, rose to the rank of Major, and acquitted himself with honor in the southern expeditions. He succeeded to his father's residence. He married Sarah, the daughter of Mr. Isaac Hatch of Pembroke 1766. His children, Nathaniel born 1767, and died 1830, leaving a family, Sarah born 1769, wife of Thomas Waterman, and now the widow of Ebenezer Copeland; Walter 1772, died early, Josiah 1774, died early, Anna 1776, wife of Dea. William Putnam Ripley of Plymouth 1810, Judith born 1780, the widow of Elisha Tolman: Lydia 1786, wife of Dr. Anthony Collamore of Pembroke, William born 1788, who succeeded to the paternal residence.

Oliver Winslow, a Revolutionary soldier, now living, was the son of Oliver, sen. by a 2d. wife, Bethia Pryor of Hanover, married 1749. He has a son Oliver. There was a son Joseph (of Oliver, sen. born 1753, and died early.)

Josiah, the youngest brother of Gov. Edward, was born in England 1605, resided in Scituate in 1637, when he was chosen an extra Assistant, "to consider and advise how the beaver trade may be upholden," Colony Records. He was afterward of Marshfield. He left a family; but we have met few notes worthy of insertion. His daughter Elizabeth was born 1637, Jonathan 1638, Mary 1640, Rebecca 1642, Susanna 1644. Jonathan had a son John born 1664.

There was a Samuel Winslow of Rochester, (probably son of Josiah, but of this we are not certain): He had sons Samuel and Richard baptized in Scituate 2d. church 1679. Samuel married Bathsheba Holbrook of Scituate 1700. Nathaniel Winslow (called of Freetown) married Elizabeth Holbrook of Scituate 1701. He may have been another son of Samuel.

FAMILY SKETCHES.

JOHN WOODFIELD.

was one of the Conihasset partners in 1646, and seems to have taken up lands, (probably without license as had others) before that time. His house lot was near Thomas Ensign's on the north. William James was his successor (probably by purchase) in Conihasset lands. In 1649 he sold marsh land and upland near "Lombard's rock," at the Great neck, in 1649, to John Williams, sen. Capt. Stephen Otis succeeded to a part of his Conihasset lands, by purchase of James. John Woodfield was one of "the agitators" in a Conference held between the two churches in Scituate, for the purpose of attempting a reconciliation in 1649. He deceased in 1669, giving in his will, his "whole estate to wife Hester." Hester, the widow, left a legacy in 1672, to Henry Ewell's daughter, (see Ewell.)

WALTER WOODWORTH.

was freeman in Scituate 1640, and settled amongst the men of Kent, 3d. lot on Kent street, south side of Meeting-house lane in 1635. He had other lands in 1635, viz. on the first Herring brook 30 rods below Stockbridge's mill: and on the northwest side of Walnut tree hill. He left no record of the births of his children; from incidental records we find Benjamin, Walter, Thomas, Joseph, Mary, wife of Aaron Simons 1677, Martha, the wife of Lieut. Zachary Daman 1679, Mehetabel, who was unfortunate in regard to her health, (see witchcraft.)

Benjamin was a soldier in Philip's war, and lost his life. Lands were assigned for his services, to Charles Stockbridge, for the use of Benjamin Woodworth's family 1676. He had daughters, Elizabeth, Deborah and Abigail, (wife of John Jackson of Plymouth 1695) and a son *Robert,* who settled in the west part of the Town, east of Symon's hill, where Dimmick Bowker now resides. His children were Ruth, born 1685, James 1689, Benjamin 1690, Elizabeth 1692, Joanna 1694, Robert 1697, Mary 1699, Deborah 1701, Ann 1704, Lydia 1706, James 1709. Of these, Benjamin married Mary Right 1712. Children, Benjamin 1713, and by a 2d. wife, Ann Torrey, Benjamin 1717, Joseph 1720, Anna 1723. *Robert,* jr. married Deborah Sylvester 1719. *James,* the youngest son of Robert, sen. married Sarah Soper 1731. Children, James 1731, Lydia 1734, (died single 1815) Sarah 1736, Bethia

1737, Joseph 1744, Sarah 1746, (the wife of Shearjashub Bourn) Mary 1742. James (son of James) married Mary Vinal 1749, and had sons Samuel 1750, James 1752, William 1754, Elisha 1756, Benjamin 1758.

Walter (son of Walter, sen.) left children, Mary born 1658, Mehetabel 1662, Ebenezer 1664.

Thomas (son of Walter, sen.) married Deborah Daman 1666, and had children, Deborah 1667, Hezekiah 1671, Katharine 1673. Thomas had lands in Little Compton 1674, but he did not remove. He kept "a trader's shop" 60 rods south of Stockbridge's mill. Hezekiah, his son, married Hannah Clap 1697, and removed, probably to Little Compton: and his son Ezekiel, of Lebanon, Connecticut, married Lydia Simons of Scituate 1723.

Joseph (son of Walter, sen.) married Sarah, daughter of Charles Stockbridge 1669. Children, Joseph 1670, Mary 1673, Benjamin 1676, Sarah 1678, Elizabeth 1680, Eunice 1682, Abigail 1685, (wife of Thomas Merritt 1711) Ruth 1688, (wife of Benjamin Sylvester, jr. 1718.) This family had lands also in Little Compton, and some of them may have removed thither.

Samuel Woodworth the well known Editor and Poet at New York, was son of Benjamin, whom we have named above as son of James and Mary Vinal. Benjamin has lately deceased, at the ancient Northy place, a half mile south of Stockbridge's mill. He had married the widow of Capt. Northy for a 2d. wife.

PETER WORTHLIKE.

a rare name, was in Scituate before 1670, and had a house and land, near to Granger's and Whiston's lots south of Meeting-house lane. He had daughters Hannah and Alice 1676, Mary 1678, Sarah 1682. He sold his estate to Timothy White 1683. He was an unfortunate man, affected with a disease of the eyes, of what nature, does not appear. In 1679 he was "fined by the Court for tavern haunting," perhaps, as the facetious Butler observes, he

> "Drank wine by quarts to mend his sight."

But if so, the experiment was not successful, for in March 1684, "The Town made choice of Capt. John Williams and Lieut. Isaac Buck, to be their agents, to bargain with the Doctor, in reference to the curing of Peter Worthlike's sight, the Town to defray the charge thereof."

THOMAS WRIGHT, or Right.

probably a grandson of William Wright, (who came to Plymouth in the Fortune 1621,) was in Scituate in the south part of the Town 1682. His children were Elizabeth born 1683, Jane 1685, John 1688, Martha 1690, (wife of John Ford 1713) Mary 1691, (wife of Benjamin Woodworth 1712.) Thomas Wright deceased 1691, and his widow, Elizabeth, married John Sanders, and left one son Edward Sanders, who went to Duxbury.

John, the only son of Thomas Wright, married Lydia Taylor 1709, and had children, Mary 1713, and John 1716, which latter had a son John born 1745, who married Mary Woodworth 1769, and whose children were James born 1769, John 1772, Mary 1780. James married Lucy, daughter of Abijah Brown, had daughters Mercy, Eleanor and Mary, and died early. His widow married Thomas Ruggles 1813.

There was an Edward Wright, who married Lydia the widow of Nathaniel Rawlins 1664, and whose children were Mercy born 1666, Hannah 1668, Grace 1669, David 1670, Edward 1671, Joseph 1673. This family removed early.

Jesse Wright, a descendant probably of Thomas, and son of John 2d. lived in Scituate, and left sons Thomas, of Scituate, James of South Boston, and Hannah, the wife of Timothy Robbins of Hanover.

GEORGE YOUNG.

came into Scituate from Plymouth (probably) in 1660. He had a brother John of Plymouth born 1647, son of John.

George married Hannah, the daughter of Thomas Pincin, sen. 1661, and settled east of Colman's hills on the margin of New Harbour marshes, where his descendants have lived until a late date. His children were Thomas, born 1663, Hannah 1666, Margery 1669, Elizabeth 1671, Patience 1673.

Thomas, married Sarah White, (a grand daughter of Perigrine) 1688. His children, George born 1689, Joseph 1692, (died early) Sarah 1695, Thomas 1698, (died early) Thomas 1700, Joseph 1701, Ebenezer 1703, Joshua 1704, Isaac 1706.

George, jr. married Margaret Frank 1716, and Mary Stockbridge 1722. His children, Isaac 1722, James 1724, Mary 1725, Deborah 1727, Reuben 1729, Job 1731, Priscilla 1732,

Lusanna 1734, Lillis 1736, Sylvanus 1739, Lucy 1741, Jane 1742.

Thomas, (son of Thomas) married Mary House 1750, and Jael Whiting 1756, and widow Hannah Barker 1760. His children, Sarah born September 2d. 1757, now living single, Thomas born 1758, who removed to Ashford.

Joseph (son of Thomas) married Lydia, daughter of William Barrel, jr. 1728. His children, Ruth born 1729, Ezekiel 1731, Sarah 1733.

Joshua (son of Thomas) married Elizabeth Cudworth 1732, and had children, Hannah born 1732, Joshua 1742, and perhaps others. He had a 2d. wife, Lydia Barnard of Boston 1751.

Ezekiel (son of Joseph) married Lusanna White 1755. His children, Joseph 1755, Lydia 1758, Gideon 1761, Christopher 1764, Stephen 1769, Ebenezer 1772, Joanna 1776, William 1779.

Joshua (son of Joshua) married Celia Little of Marshfield 1772, and had children, Elicia Baker 1772, Elizabeth Cudworth 1775, Celia 1777, Betsey 1780, Emily 1795, Peabody 1798.

Joseph (son of Ezekiel) married Desire Nash 1779, and had children, Ezekiel born 1779, Joseph 1786, Benjamin 1787.

Gideon (son of Ezekiel) married Lydia — of Carolina, and Betsey Man of Scituate 1795. His children, Lydia born 1791, Gideon W. Esq. Post Master of Scituate harbour, and others.

Job (son of George, jr.) was of Hanover, and the father of John Young, of Turner, Maine.

James (son of George, jr,) married Mehetabel Hatch 1753, and was the father of Mehetabel the wife of late Samuel Curtis of Scituate, at the North River.

There was a Robert Young of Hanover, who married Margaret Murfy 1732-33.* This family may be in Bridgewater. A Thomas Young married Hannah Barker, of Scituate 1760: and Joseph Young of Truro, married Anna Oldham of "the Two Mile" 1718.

---

* See Appendix VI, on DOUBLE DATING.

APPENDIX.

I.

See Page 192.

Upon the much to be lamented DEATH of the thrice three times Honoured JOSIAH WINSLOW, Esq. late GOVERNOUR, of New Plymouth and CARLO charus, beloved of his Prince."

>Within this Sacred Urn doth lie,
>The Quintesence of the Colonie;
>New England's Phoenix, Plymouth's glory,
>Meet subject for a compleat story:
>To whom at helm, we yield the praise
>Of blissful times of peacefull dayes;
>The Halcyon which controul'd our seas
>Of civil storms and broiles appease.
>Would you have me, him to descrie,
>Angels must limn him out, not I;
>A Sophoclean quill comes short,
>His worth and merits to report:
>Where Wisdom, Valour, Eloquence,
>Were center'd in great Eminence:
>Faith, Justice, Patience, every grace
>In this frayl clay tent had their place.
>For kind behaviour lov'd by all
>That knew him, eke both great and small;
>Grave, Prudent, Sober and Discreet;
>His whole deportment comlie sweet.
>Sound in the faith, a life untaint,
>So liv'd, so dy'd this noble Saint –
>Me thinks it cuts me to the heart,
>Of such rare gemms to be desert.
>He was a walking Christian bright,
>Whose life and conversation right,
>Adorn'd Christ's Gospel: some men talk
>Like Angels – yet like divells walk.
>He was not of a Cynick strain,
>But cheerful Patriot, dy'd in grain:

---

* Gov. Winslow deceased Dec. 18, 1680, aged 51.

To strangers and to neighbours all,
He was a Turtle without gall.
Compassion lodg'd within his breast;
To poore ope' were heart hand and chest,
Hard heartedness and cruelty
Seemed like vile Nero in his eye.
By th' acre he did not survey,
Nor by the pound did any weigh;
According to desert and merit,
They should his smile or frown inherit.
Religion e'er to keep he strove,
(False worship loves the darkest grove)
And civil Justice to dispense
According unto evidence.
On these two pillars founded are,
The firmest States for Peace or War:
Christ was his all, him might he gain,
Far wealthier he than either Spain.
But why do I burn Tapers in the Sun,
Or midst great Cannons, let fly my pot-gun:
His worth transcends the weakness of my quill,
As lofty mounts o'ertop the pismire hill.

The goodliest Cedar which this land e'er bore
Is hewn flat down and level'd with the shore:
Under whose shade and boughs we shelter'd were.
'Gainst storms of outrage, wrongs, oppression, feare.
Blessed with good Government, thrice happy we
Had we had eyes our happiness to see.
The sweetest Rose that e'er in Plymouth grew
Frost nips – dried up – like to the morning dew,
Yet leaving a sweet scent, mongst great and small,
Perfum'd his name from Carswell* to White-Hall;
Whereby great CHARLES enamored of his worth,
Lets the warm glances of his love shine forth
Upon New Plymouth: grac'd with Royal favour,
Let us be Loyal-bound, t'our good behaviour.
Strong were my feares, lest this strange blazing stream,†
Would be prognostick of some tragick theme;
Yet what it doth portend I cannot tell,
But here I come to ring the funeral Knell
Of a choice Worthy, and the people call
To come and solemnize the FUNERAL,
Of him, who late was foremost for his worth
Close lock't in Prison, cannot now step forth.

How many dangers hath this gentleman,
In's life escaped, both by Sea and Land!
Fort-fights,‡ Sholes, Quicksands, Quag-mires, Boggs and
    Sloughs,
Enough to plunge an hundred strong team'd Ploughs:

---

* Carswell or Carsrull was the name of Gov. Winslow's seat in Marshfield, so called from a Castle of his ancestors in England.
† The Comet which, our venerable Author seems half inclined to believe, was sent to foretell Gov. Winslow's death, was the great Comet of 1680, whose train extended more than 60 degrees, that is, across more than one third of the hemisphere. It makes its revolution in 575 years.
‡ "The Naraganset Fort fight" is meant.

APPENDIX.

Yet he brake through; but now we see him have
Mir'd and stuck fast in a dry upland grave.
The Pitcher that went oft whole to the well,
Comes home at last, crack'd like a broken shell.
Our Court of Justice sits in Widdowhood:
The Judge arrested – Baile will do no good.
Judges are stayes of States; when such stayes fall,
It bodes the weak'ning of the Judgment Hall. Isaiah iii. 2.

Somewhat above thrice compleat seven years since,
Plymouth hath lost blest Bradford, Winslow, Prince,
Three skillful Pilots, through this Wilderness,
To conduct Pilgrims; all three called t'undress
Upon the top of Pisgah; while we here Deu. xxxiv. 4, 5, 6.
Left Pilot-less, do without Compass steer.

Thrice honored Rulers, Elders, People all,
Come and lament this stately Cedar's fall,
Cut down at's height, full noontide, blest with shine
Of Royal favour, and (no doubt) Divine;
Freighted with tunns of honor. Every man,
At's best estate is altogether vain. Psalm xxxix. 5.

Ye birds of Musick, Lark, Thrush, Turtle, Quaile,
Ye pretty humming birds, and Nightingale,
Your doleful notes sigh over this sad hearse,
Sighs more suit Fun'ralls than a golden verse.
You that have skill in verse, let every Line
You here present, first pickled be in brine.
Had but the Muses heard thou hence wert gone,
T'attend thy hearse, they had left Helicon.
Thrice Royal CHARLES, were he in person here,
Into thy Urn, would drop a sacred tear.
Had I an hundred eyes like Argus, I
Would weep them all purblind, or pump them dry.
I'd rather drink the tears of my old, eyen
For sweet JOSIAH, than quaff muskadine.
Old eyes can shed few tears; but my old heart
More ready is to break, than eyes to smart.
Slight grief have tears, in troops that ready stand
To sally forth and but expect command:
But deep ingulphing sorrow strikes men dumb,
As frosty Winters do their joints benumb.

Curae leves loquuntur; urgentes stupent. Seneca. Trag.

Methinks I see Cape Cod, Manamoit high land,
Our Scituate Cliffs, and the Gurnet weeping stand,
All clad in mourning sable; brinish streames
Venting, to float a gallant Ship to th' Thames.
All creatures crowd to fetch so deep a groan,
Able to break an heart of hardest stone,
And all because their dear JOSIAH's gone.

POSTCRIPT.

I wish that He, who thee succeedeth next,
May, like to thee, keep close unto the Text,
Sacred and Civil; He shall have my vote,
While I am worth a Tester or Gray Groat.

          Moestus posuit
         WILLIAM WITHERELL
                 OCTOGENARIUS.

398   APPENDIX.

For the preceding curious relick of antiquity, we are indebted to the politeness of Rev. Zephaniah Willis: a copy has been preserved by the respectable family of Seaver in Kingston; which family was connected with that of the Winslows. In order to judge of its merits, it is fair to compare it with the common verses of 1680; and it is but justice to consider that the Author was 80 years of age. There is another Elegy by the same Author, written two years previous, and preserved by the family of Moody in Newbury. "On the piously affected Matron, Mrs. Sarah Cushing, the mother of twelve living children, and one dead child." It is in a similar strain. The lady was Mrs. Sarah, the wife of John Cushing, Esq. the first of the name in Scituate. She was the daughter of Mr. Nicholas Jacob, an early settler in Hingham. She died, according to our Records, March 9th. 1678.

By favour also of Rev. Z. Willis of Kingston we are able to insert the following Elegy by Rev. N. Pitcher. (See page 184)

"Upon the sudden and surprising departure of Mrs. Hannah Robinson, Ætatis 41, late Consort of the Rev. Mr. John Robinson, who with her daughter Mrs. Mary Robinson, Ætatis 16, perished in the Mighty Deeps, Sept. 22, 1722.

> Inspire my Muse! Ye lofty Beams of Light,
> In trembling airs perfume the sable Night;
> Tread soft, while we relate the Tragedy,
> Perform'd by Him who dwells and rules on High.
> Let thundering billows in due concert meet,
> And raging winds and waves each other greet,
> And all th' obsequious Elements combine,
> To pay Devotion to the Will Divine,
> Of Him, whose Infinite and matchless sway,
> The proudest of Created Powers obey.
> Behold the ghastly visage of each face,
> Besmear'd with Griefs, deep mourning in each place;
> Not one without a tear upon the Hearse
> Of the bright subjects of my Fainting verse.
>
>   REV. SIR,
> Can Heart conceive, or Tongue express your grief?
> Can any hand but Heaven's give relief?
> Who wounds and heals, who kills and keeps alive?
> And when depress'd, makes Grace to live and thrive.
> Behold bright Sovereignty in clear Displays
> Turning your Halcion into Gloomy days;
> Your Nuptial Knot, the fatal Stroke unty'd,
> By Heaven's Decree, on the Atlantick wide;
> The Noisy Waters, on the Seas that move,
> Which cannot quench the streams of Boundless love
> Translated yours unto the Joys above,

APPENDIX.

Transported far beyond all Fears and Harms,
Guarded by Angels to their Saviour's Arms.
You could not close your Vertuous Lady's Eye;
You must not see your dearest Consort dye,
Nor her expiring, gasping agonies,
Nor listen to her fervent Farewell cries,
Bright Hannah's prayers for you are swiftly gone
On Eagle's Wings, up to the Sapphire Throne,
And you are left to grieve and pray alone.
One of the Gowned Tribe and Family,
Of bright descent and Worthy Pedigree;
A charming daughter in our Israel,
In vertuous acts and Deeds seem to excell:
As Mother, Mistress, Neighbor, Wife, most rare;
Should I exceed, to say beyond compare?
Call her the Phœnix, but you cannot lye,
Whether it be in Prose or Poetry.
For Meekness, Piety, and Patience;
Rare Modesty, Unwearied Diligence;
For Gracious Temper, Prudent Conduct too,
How few of the fair Sex could her out do?
Beloved of all while living, and now dead,
The female Hadadrimmon's* lost their head.
Her precious Daughter bears her company,
Taking her flight up to the Joys on High
To dwell and feast with her eternally.
God's Will is done, 'Tis duty to resign
Yourself and all unto the Will Divine:
You often pray'd "God let thy Will be done!"
Still do so, now your dearest Ones are gone.
If your Great Sovereign takes but his own due,
You are obliged to Him, not He to you.

May God Almighty Sanctify this frown,
To the bereaved Family and Town:
May the tender brood, under your mateless wing,
When Clouds are passed over, chirp and sing.
May you Sir, fill the Consecrated Place,
With purest doctrines and displays of Grace,
Till you have run and finished your Race,
That when your dust shall unto dust go down,
You may receive the Bright and Massy Crown,
And with your dearest Ones enhappy'd be,
In light above, Throughout eternity.

N. P.

The above will probably be thought to display much less learning and force of thought, than the foregoing Elegy of the Octogenarian Witherell: which has the advantage in the mock sublime, and which approximates nearest to the burlesque, we leave to the reader to judge.

---

* Compare 2 Kings xxiii. 29. Lam. v. 16, and Zech. xii. 11.

APPENDIX.

THE Ministers of Duxbury have been Rev. Ralph Partridge, who arrived at Boston from England, Nov. 17, 1636, in company with the Rev. Nathaniel Rogers, having suffered extremely from stress of weather and shortness of provisions. (Winthrop Vol. 1. 205.) He settled soon after at Duxbury, where he deceased 1658. One of his daughters married the celebrated Thomas Thacher noticed in this work. (See Chauncy.) The successor of Mr. P. was Rev. John Holmes, probably the son of John of Plymouth. He was a student at Cambridge, but took no degree. His ministry was short, he having deceased Dec. 24, 1675. He left descendants, of whom, we are told, is the Hon. Abraham Holmes of Rochester. To Mr. Holmes succeeded Rev. Ichabod Wiswall. He was probably the son of Thomas Wiswall, of Dorchester. He also (Farmer) was a student at Harvard College, but took no degree. He wrote a Poem on the great Comet in 1680, which was sent, by Rev. Zephaniah Willis, to the Historical Society many years since. He died July 10, 1700, leaving one son Ichabod, who deceased in Boston 1767, aged 84. To Mr. Wiswall succeeded Rev. John Robinson, Har. College 1695, and a native (Mr. Willis thinks) of Dorchester. He married Hannah, the daughter of Mr. Wiswall his predecessor. The Elegy of Mr. Pitcher above, relates to the unfortunate loss of Mrs. Robinson and her daughter, on their passage from Duxbury to Boston, by the upsetting of the Coaster off Nantaskett, in a sudden tempest. A young gentleman of Duxbury, Mr. Fish, a member of Harvard College, also perished. The remains of the daughter were soon found and interred at Duxbury: those of the mother were found by the Natives at Race Point, Cape Cod, six weeks afterward. Her person was identified by papers preserved in her stays, and by a gold necklace, which was concealed by the swelling of her neck, which necklace is preserved by her descendants: a gold ring, which she wore on her finger was lost, plundered by the Natives probably, who had cut off the swollen finger in order to obtain the ring. She was buried at the Cape; a monument marks her grave, with an inscription by her husband, closing with this quotation from the Psalms "Thus He bringeth them to their desired Haven." Tradition speaks of Mr. Robinson as a man of extraordinary powers of mind and accomplishments of eloquence. He left the ministry before 1740, and removed to Lebanon, Con. the residence of the first Gov. Trumbull, who had married one of Mr. Robinson's daughters. Two sons, John and Ichabod Robinson, lived in Connecticut, and two other daughters – and the fifth (Hannah,) married Nathaniel Thomas, Esq. of Plymouth, whose only daughter Hannah was the wife of Col. John Thomas of Kingston, and the mother of the present Col. John Thomas, and of the wife of Rev. Mr. Willis. The next minister of Duxbury was the Rev. Samuel Veazie, Har. College 1736, (a descendant, we believe, of Robert, an early settler in Braintree.) To him succeeded the Rev. Charles Turner, of Scituate, Har. College 1752. He married the daughter of Rev. Mr. Rand of Kingston; he retired after 20 year's service, and was well known in public life, as Senator of Mass. He died at Turner, in Maine, about 1813. Rev. Zedekiah Sanger, D. D. was his successor, Har. College 1771, who afterward was Minister of South Bridgewater, where he died about 1818. To him succeeded Rev. John Allyn, D. D. of Barnstable; Har. Col. 1785. He retired in, 1826, and was succeeded by Rev. Benjamin Kent, Har, Col. 1820, a native of Charlestown.

APPENDIX.

II.

See Page 128.

While our work was in the press, we were fortunate enough to recover the original return of the losses of Scituate, in the eventful year of 1676, made by a Committee of the Town to the Governor, and alluded to page 128. This was found amongst the Winslow Papers, and very obligingly furnished to us by the Hon. John Davis.

"To the Honered Governor Josiah Winslow at his house in Marshfield; This deliver with speed.

HONERED SIR,

We whose names are hereunto subscribed, Received your order Bearing date the 16th of January, 1676, wherein you design us to send you a list of the names of all such persons, Inhabitants or strangers, of what perswation soever, with what losses they have sustained in their persons or estates, and are in distresse, which accordingly we have here done, according to our ability.   ISAAC BUCK, sen. ⎫
   Scituate the 26th.   JEREMIAH HATCH, ⎬ Selectmen.
   of January 1676.   JOHN CUSHING, ⎭

Joseph Sylvester – house and barn burnt, worth 100 00 00
Edward Wright – house and barn burnt, estimated. . . . . .
Nicholas Albeson – his house burnt 30 00 00
John Curtis, sen. – house and barn burn 40 00 00
John Bompas – house and barn burnt 35 00 00
Serj. Abram Sutliffe – house and barn burnt ., ... 50 00 00
Widow Blackmore – house and barn burnt 40 00 00
John Buck – house and barn burnt 40 00 00
James Torrey – house and barn burnt 45 00 00
Widow Torrey – house and barn burnt 40 00 00
Henry Ewell – house and barn burnt. 10 00 00
Thomas Woodworth – dwelling house burnt . . . .
William Wills – one ox, one horse, killed as they stud yoke . . 80 00 00
   Job Randall, his arme broken with a shott, which disabled him from work for a time.
   Joseph Thorne, shot through the arme, lame for a time.
   Theophilus Witherly, wholly disabled, and so like to be.
   William Perry, disabled by a wound diverse months.
   John Barker, was disabled by a shott diverse months.
   Jonathan Jackson, disabled by a shott some time.
   Timothy White has received damage in his hed by a shott.
       These widows lost their husbands by the enemy.
          Widow Pierce.
          Widow Russell.
          Widow Savory.
          Widow Willcome. (Not Whitcomb as in page 128.)
          Widow Pratt.
          Widow Blackmore.
   Anthony Dodson lost his son, who was under his government.
   Richard Standlake's family suffers much by the loss of his son Jeremiah Barstow.*

---

      * He was then in activity amongst the Indians.

Jonathan Turner lost his 'Prentice with Capt. Pierce.
Walter Briggs lost his Irishman at the swamp, which was his estate.

Strangers from Shipscot River

Mr. Dyer left all behind him, who sowed 16 bushells of wheat, planted a bushell and a half of Indian Corne, sowed 9 bushells of peas, left 56 hed of cattell, 30 swine, and household goods, and tackling for plow and carte.

John White, and John Lee his son in law, sowed 10 bushells of wheat, planted 2 bushells of Indian corne, 5 bushells of peas, 17 hed of cattell, 16 swine, one horse.

Philip Randall sowed 9 bushells of peas, 5 or 6 of wheat, 16 hed of cattell, 6 swine.

Widow Cole, 2 oxen – cowes, 2 heifers, sowed 6 bushells of wheat, planted 3 bushells of Indian corne."

We have seen amongst the Winslow papers, in possession of Hon. John Davis, several curious documents relative to Serjeant Johnson's claims at Scituate (see page 297) and particularly a letter from Gov. Josiah Winslow, (dated March 14, 1673-4) addressed to Gen. Cudworth, which probably contributes much to the ending of the controversy.

III.

See Page 198.

REV. NATHANIEL EELLS.

In our notice of Mr. Eells, we remarked that he was a firm opposer of Mr. Whitefield. We now add, that he subscribed the *Declaration* in favour of the religious revivals of those times, presented to the public by an assembly of ministers, convened at Boston, July 7th. 1743; but we observe in that curious document, that Mr. Eells and several others made an exception, by testifying at the same time, against itinerating, and invading the parishes of regularly settled ministers.

See "Historical Collections relating to remarkable periods of the success of the gospel, &c. By John Gillies of Glasgow."

In 1745, Mr. Bells had witnessed so many and so wild disorders in the churches that he thought it his duty to lay his sentiments respecting them before the public. There is extant a printed letter, addressed to his church and society. It may be seen amongst the Tracts in the Boston Atheneum. Vol. marked C. 4. 4.

It is ably written, and assigns reasons for not admitting Whitefield into his pulpit. Amongst his reasons are, that Mr. Whitefield had forfeited the Episcopal ordination which he had received, and was suspended from the ministry for his irregularity, and had received no other ordination. That his itinerancy tended to disorganization and confusion, inasmuch as he avoided such places as were destitute of teachers, and forced himself into those places where there were able and faithful ministers; that he lavished abuses upon the ministers of the gospel, encouraged diaorders and divisions, and availed himself of the assistance of disorganizers, "commending Mr. Tenant's Nottingham Sermon, in which Mr. Tenant outstripped Rabshakeh, in raillery against the clergy of this generation."

Appended to the letter, is a review, by Mr. Eells, of "a pamphlet put out by a number of ministers met at Taunton, March 12th, 1744, wherein they have published three reasons for countenancing and encouraging Mr. Whitefield." Their reasons are First, "because the doctrines which he preaches are agreeable to the standard of truth." Secondly, "because of his remarkable success." *Thirdly,* "because of his exemplary piety." To the first, Mr. Eels answers, by quoting some of Mr. Whitefield's doctrines, e.g. "that God loveth sinners as sinners, &c." and shrewdly questions whether they be agreeable to the standard of truth. To the second he replies in such language as the following, "It is to be observed with lamentation, that the success of his ministry (if it may be called success) hath been to raise in the minds of many a spirit of censoriousness and uncharitableness, of bitterness, anger, wrath, malice, envy, revenge, in many, as is evident to every observing eye, by the carriage of his admirers toward many of the brethren, with whom, before he came amongst us, they lived in peace and good agreement. Such success he hath had, to the grief of many godly persons." To the third reason he replies, "Is it exemplary piety for a man to break his ordination vows? Is it exemplary piety for a man that had the pastoral care of any church, to turn a vagrant preacher, and ramble about the world? Is it exemplary piety in him to disturb the peace of the churches of Christ in one place and another? Is it exemplary piety in him, to grieve the spirit of holy ministers and holy brethren, and provoke them to pray that God would rebuke him?"

Those readers who are acquainted with the history of Mr. Whitefeld, his success as a preacher, and the opposition that withstood him, need not be informed that Mr. Eells was amongst the moderate and cool opposers of that singular man. It would be easy to quote pamphlets written in 1745, and a few years later, which expose great excesses and irregularities, not to say immoralities, in Whitefield and his satellites. But this was not our object in noticing the pamphlet of Mr. Eells, but rather to illustrate the character and sentiments of the writer. Whitefield was a man of extraordinary powers of elocution, he won the multitudes, and became intoxicated with success. But as to real learning and solid moral worth, he was immensely below the Barnard's, Chauncey, Mayhew, Gay, Clap, and a host of others whom he dared to revile.

IV.

See Page 190.

Rev. NEHEMIAH THOMAS.

While our work was in the press, we were called to lament the decease of this worthy man. He died August 10, 1831. He had proceeded to the sea beach, in a remarkably sultry afternoon, (in company with his sister in law, Miss Elizabeth Otis,) for the benefit of fresher air. He had, perhaps rather imprudently, thrown off his shoes and stockings, and waded in the cool sea water. On his returning to his chaise, at the east end of the 3d. Cliff, and attempting to ascend the step, he fell and instantaneously expired, of an apoplexy. He was born Feb. 3d, 1765. He was a descendant of Nathaniel Thomas, an early settler in Plymouth Colony. His father was Nathaniel Thomas, Esq. of Marshfield, a worthy gentleman, who gave to his son, the advantages of a religious education, and also the best means of a liberal education that the country could furnish. He received his first degree at Harvard College in 1789. His Theological studies were pursued under the direction of Rev. Dr. Shaw of Marshfield.* He entered on the ministry in 1792. He preached for a short term to the New South Congregational Church and Society in Boston, in the summer of 1792; and in the autumn of the same year, was ordained in the first Church and Society in Scituate.

As to the faithfulness and ability, with which he has served that people, there is an impartial witness in the facts, that he attached a numerous society to his personal friendship, and to his ministry for thirty-nine years. His ministry, though not remarkably long, was yet the longest that has been exercised in that Society.

Mr. Thomas was distinguished for an open-heartedness and a guileless simplicity: for much freedom in expressing his own sentiments, and yet without that bluntness of manner which gives offence, and for much candor in accepting the same freedom from others; for readiness to give advice or reproof, and for meekness in receiving it: for willingness to lead, or willingness to be led, if thereby the true path might be found. In faith and affection, in character and practice, he belonged to the class of liberal or Unitarian Christians. He was not given to controversy: he never aimed at the notoriety of attacking the faith of others, while he practised no arts to conceal his own. Desirous of keeping the even tenor of his own way, without molesting or being molested, he beautifully exemplified those traits of courtesy and gentleness which adorn the Christian character, and that charity which is greater than knowledge, or zeal, or eloquence, or even miraculous faith.

With a constitution far from robust, he had been for years struggling against infirmities, and labouring on in his calling, often with despondent feelings, which nothing but a humble trust in Divine Providence could support. It is sixteen years, since the loss of a promising and beloved son, gave a sensible shock to his health. It is nearly four years, since a paralytic affection added an irrecoverable stroke, and though he had risen so far as to resume his labours, after a few months, yet from time to time, he had received strong intimations that the final attack of a mortal malady was threatening him. The loss of his admirable consort in March last, was another stroke which he was doomed to suffer, and there was still another, simultaneous, the hopeless bereavement of reason, of his daughter, Lucy Otis, at the time of her mother's decease. There was a train of calamities, thus following this worthy man, that has rarely been equalled. His burial was attended by a very numerous concourse, August 12th. A funeral procession accompanied his remains from his late mansion to the Meeting-house, where prayers were offered by Rev. Dr. Kendall of Plymouth, and a Sermon preached by the pastor of the 2d. Church, from Jeremiah xlv. 3, "The Lord had added grief to my sorrows." His remains were then deposited, for the present, in the tomb of the Stockbridge family.

---

* Not at the University, as remarked in page 190.

V.

In page 257, we remarked the unanimity with which the Senate confirmed the nomination of Chief Justice Cushing. We here think proper to add, that nothing but a confidence in his ability, and in his unshaken integrity, could have united contending parties on that occasion. It was well known to which party of the day, Judge Cushing belonged. We have evidence enough, that his sentiments were never disguised. We have before us at this time, a Charge delivered by him to the "Grand Jury of the District of Virginia," Sept. 23d. 1798, in which he eloquently portrays the horrors of the French Revolution, and admonishes against being deceived by French wiles, and taken in the "plot against the rights of nations and of mankind, and against all religion and virtue, order and decency." In the same charge he ably defends the Sedition Law, on the ground of its being a melioration of the law of England, by "allowing the party accused, to prove the truth of his assertions." And in defence of the Alien Law he is equally bold and decisive. He had a felicity of manner, and an unblemished dignity of character, which enabled him to be open and decisive, without kindling the rage of opposition.

See Page 359.

In our account of the family of Torrey, we mentioned a tradition that Josiah Torrey unfortunately lost his life by an explosion of gunpowder. We made this statement from tradition: but having discovered an important error, we add the following extract from the Church Records of Roxbury. "July 5, 1665, there happened a very sad accident at Scituate. Lieut. Torrey, having received order from the Gov. of Plymouth (by reason of the king's letter, that informs us that the Hollanders are coming against us) to look to the powder and ammunition of the towne; he went into the house of Goodman Ticknor, where the magazine of the town was, which was but two barrels of powder and opened them: and while the said Lieut. was drying some of the powder abroad upon boards, by some accident, he knows not what, the powder was fired, both that in the house and that abroad, the house blown up and broken in pieces, and the woman of the house, Goodwife Ticknor, miserably burnt on her body (for it seems that she was at that instant, stepping up on the barrel that was in the house, to reach something) and a little child was sadly burnt, and buried in the rubbish and timber: but the woman and child lived several hours after, (about ten or eleven.) Also the Lieut. was sadly burnt in his breast, face, hands and armes, yet he lived till the next day, and then died."

The unfortunate gentleman was the father of Josiah, and Town Clerk at the time of his decease. The wife of Serjeant Ticknor, who perished by this accident, was Hannah, the daughter of Mr. John Stockbridge, and the child was her eldest son John, then about six years of age. The decease of these three persons is entered on our records, viz. "Hannah, wife of William Ticknor, and John her son, July 5th, 1665, and Lieut. James Torrey, July 6th," but no account is given of the manner of their death.

We are indebted for the above extract from the Records of Roxbury, to Mr. Joshua Coffin.

We learn also, from the same persevering gentleman, that Mr. William Vassall (see page 366) is noticed in the Records of Roxbury, that Anna his wife was a member of the church there, and that his children, Judith, Frances. John, Margaret and Mary also appear on the records. We account for this very easily by recollecting Mr. Vassall's controversy with Mr. Chauncy, the minister at Scituate. These children were doubtless carried thither for baptism.

VI.

DOUBLE DATING. (Referred to in page 394.)

The first instance which we notice in our Records is that of the birth of "Joseph son of Henry Chittenden March 8, 1656-7. After the Calendar was corrected by Pope Gregory XIII. in 1582, though the correction was immediately adopted by all the Catholic countries, it was not adopted by England until 1752. This was the New Style, and the year being made to commence on the 1st. of January, instead of the 25th. of March, gave occasion to the double dates, which were practised here and in England, for a century previous to 1752. Most of the Nations having adopted the New Style, it was thought proper by the English, to pay some regard to it by double dating. It could be used only between January 1st. and March 25th. Thus, in the example above quoted, "March 8, 1656-7," it would be 56 in the Old Style, because the year according to that Style did not close until March 25, but in the New Style, it would be 57, because according to that Style, the year had already commenced on the 1st. of January. The double dating ceased after 1752. The correction of the Calendar however consisted in a more important alteration than that above named. It was found that the Julian year (adopted by Julius Caesar) consisting of 365 days 6 hours, and every fourth year of 366 days, was a fraction too long, and carried the Spring months gradually into the Summer: the error had already amounted to 11 days. In order therefore to bring the Vernal Equinox on the 21st. of March, the Pope ordered to strike out 11 days from Sept. 1582, calling the 3d. day the 14th. And in order to provide that the Equinox should continue to fall on the 21st. of March, the year was made to consist of 365 days, with an intercalary day in February every fourth or leap year, omitting this additional day 3 times in 400 years. It was omitted in 1800.

INDEX.

Aborigines	143	Counsellors	106
Agriculture	28	Churches reconciled	88
Alewive fishery	24	Colman's hills	8
Almshouse	113	Cushing, William, L.L.D	256, 405
American war	133	Cudworth, Gen. James	245
St Andrew's church	45	Deputies to Court	99
Andros, Sir Edmund	98	Deed of the Church	175
" his orders and arrest	105	Dunster, President	179
Animals	149	Dawes, Rev. Ebenezer	189
Allowed inhabitants	155	Dorby, Rev. Jonathan	201
Ancient landmarks	158	Division of lands	10
Assistants, list of	198	Double dating	406
Assinippi	43	Eastern Expedition	130
Baptist society	57	Earthquake	150
Baptism by immersion yielded	89, 173	Ecclesiastical history	59
Baptism of grandchildren	91	Education	92
Baker, Rev. Nicholas	181	Elders, Ruling	90
Barnes, Dr.	203	Elliot, letters to	76
Barstow, George	219	Electors, qualification of	106
Bees, first noticed	355	Elders, at Weymouth	196
Bells, church	33	Eells, Rev. Nathaniel	197, 402
Bird, Thomas, first settler	221	Ewell's, house burnt	126, 401
Blinman, at Marshfield	81	Friends, Society of	47
Bourn, Rev. Shearjashub	186	Ferries	15
Boundaries	1	Fisheries'	23
Bridges and ferries	15	" at Cape Cod	93
Brooks	21	French war	131
Briggs' harbour	23	Freemen, list of	153
Burying ground	115	Family sketches	164
Canal proposed	23	Gillman, Edward	4
Canada Expedition	130	Graduates	96
Census	157	Garrisons	125
Charter of William and Mary	106	Government	97, 104
Chauncey's letters	62	Gay, Dr. (Note)	202
" leaves Scituate	87	Grosvenor, Rev. E	187
" President	172	Green's harbour, channel	275
Colony line	3	Hanover incorporated	2
Conihasset grantees	4	Harbour	22
" partners	6	Hatherly, Timothy	280
" bounds	5	Haunted House	153
Clap, President	235	Hingham line	4
Cliffs	150	House lots, first	8
Committee of safety	137	Herring brooks	21
Commons	115	Hospital	112
Charities	112	Hinckley	284
Clerks, Town	112	Hoar, John	286

INDEX.

Indians	125 to 146
Ingham's wife accused	152
Judson, Rev. Mr.	57
Kent, men of	8
Laws against Quakers	49
Law for religious taxes	33
" against smoking tobacco	308
Lawyers, list of	97
Landings	115
Lawson, Rev. Deodate	195
Lothrop, Rev. John	167
Losses of Scituate	128, 401
Light house	22
Little's bridge	16
Mackerel fishery	24 to 26
Manufactures	29
Meeting houses	32, 37, 41, 115
Methodist Society	58
Marshfield line	4
Ministers of Hanover (Note)	2
Mills	16
Military affairs	117
Mariners, &c.	151
Mineralogy	149
Mortality, bills of	117
Municipal laws	110
Ministers of Duxbury	400
Mighill, Rev. Thomas	194
Name (Note)	1
Navigation	27
New harbour	22
North River	19
Narragansett war	126
Newman's letter to Cotton	122
Natural History	148
Norton, Humphrey	51
New Style	406
Officers of Revolutionary war	139
Ordination, Congregational	90, 178
Opinions in early times	91
Old Tenor	112
Old Style	406
Oyster bank	24
Parishes	30
Parsonages	33, 42
Pastor, distinct, from teacher	89
Phipps', Sir William, warrant	106
Physicians	114
Publick grounds	115
Philip's war	121
Pierce's defeat	122
Pequod war	117
Ponds	147
Post offices, &c.	163
Pitcher, Rev. N.	184
His elegy	398
Quakers, persecution of	48
Roads laid out	12
" in Conihasset	14
Records of churches	91
Rayner, Minister of Plymouth	78
Representatives	106
Revolutionary war	133
Rehoboth battle	122
Rhode Island's campaign	136
Revolu. soldiers and pensioner	130
Saxton, Rev. G	166
Senators	106
Schools	94
Ship building	27
Shore line	6
Settlement	7
Swamps, division of	12
Small pox	112
Soldiers, wounded	121
Showamett sold	128
Soldiers of French war	131
Stage roads and coaches	163
Surveys	147
Surface	147
The Two Miles	6
Temperance Society	113
Thacher, Rev. Thomas	176
Thomas, Rev. N.	190, 404
Torrey, James, death of	405
Topography	146
Tories, suspected	137
Training fields	115
Trinitarian Society	58
Union bridge	16
Union of colonies	117
Vassall, William	10, 366
" goes to England.	84, 369
" his religious opinions	89
Vessels, burnt at harbour	141
Vaccination	113
Witherell's ordination	82
" his life	190
" his elegy	395
War, Pequod	117
" Narragansett	120
" Philip's	128, 401
" French	131
" of Revolution	133
" of 1812	141
Witchcraft	3, 151
Wampatuck's deed	144
Whitefield	402